International News in the 21st Cen

International News in the 21st Century

Edited by Chris Paterson and Annabelle Sreberny

UNIVERSITY
OF LUTON

press

John Libbey
JL
LONDON · PARIS · ROME · SYDNEY

British Library Cataloguing in Publication Data
A catalogue record for this book is available from the British Library

ISBN: 1 86020 596 8

Published by John Libbey Publishing for University of Luton Press

John Libbey Publishing
Box 276
Eastleigh
Hants SO50 5YS
UK

e-mail: john.libbey@libertysurf.fr
website (incorporating ulp titles) www.johnlibbey.com

Cover Design by Gary Gravatt
Typeset in Van Dijck MT and Helvetica
Printed in Malaysia by Vivar Printing Sdn Bhd, 48000 Rawang, Selangor

Contents

Contents

Acknowledgements

This volume presents a collection of insights from journalists, scholars and in a few cases journalist-scholars who represent the leading organisations in global news and the cutting edge in international journalism research, theory and reform. We are grateful to all of the authors who have contributed but we owe a special debt to the professional journalists who accepted our invitation to pen a chapter. They are not paid to write in academic volumes and get little – or no – time and credit from their employers for doing so. They courageously write here in an unfamiliar style ('what do you mean, citation?'), and for an unfamiliar and often highly critical audience.

Many of the papers were initially presented at an international conference on global journalism in Leicester in March, 2000. That event was part of a collaboration between Sreberny and Paterson to continue a long and rich trajectory of news research at the Centre for Mass Communication Research (CMCR), of the University of Leicester that has made a substantial contribution over the decades to the study of news and its impacts. We owe an intellectual debt to that tradition.

The conference offered ample proof of the interest in international news and its future, and evidenced the passions, and insights, that emerge when journalists join with media critics and social scientists to discuss that future. Therein lay the genesis of this volume, but in subsequent years, new authors joined the project while others departed, and world events – not least of them the one known universally as 9/11 – intervened.

Our own circumstances also changed: Paterson took up a post at the University of San Francisco and Sreberny has moved to SOAS in London.

We are indebted to colleagues at the University of San Francisco and the University of Leicester for their support, and to Geoffrey Nowell-Smith of University of Luton Press for his belief in this project and his patience during the sometimes chaotic trans-Atlantic journey to completion. Magdelena Bober, now at LSE, was the principal administrator of the Leicester news conference and without her organisational skills that conference and this book might not have been possible. Jaideep Mukherjee, a PhD student at CMCR, produced the edited interview with the BBC's Chris Westcott in Chapter Four. University of

1

San Francisco student Victoria Leon Guerrero joined us in the final months of the project as an editorial and research assistant, and undertook much of the detailed copyediting and formatting. If these stellar students represent the future of international journalism and research, we can all breath more easily.

Finally, Paterson thanks, for endless patience and support – and dedicates his efforts to – Andrea and baby Oliver. Sreberny thanks Edward for being there.

CHRIS PATERSON AND ANNABELLE SREBERNY, JUNE 2004

Introduction
Shouting from the Rooftops: Reflections on International News in the 21st Century

Annabelle Sreberny and Chris Paterson

The significance and centrality of the news media in bringing global events into our living rooms has never been more evident. September 11, 2001 proved that, as a global real-time audience of millions watched in shock and impotent horror, sometimes from thousands of miles away, as a second jumbo jet was steered deliberately into the second tower of the World Trade Centre in the core of US television country, New York. The global audience often knew better than the people trapped in each tower what was going on, understanding that this was a terrorist attack before many in the building.

The Internet was frozen, unable to withstand the unprecedented numbers of connections, people trying to understand, trying to make contact, trying to say goodbye. Later, still photos, video footage and recorded mobile phone messages added to the mix of mediated representations of that day. People talked about becoming news junkies, desperately wanting to know more and to understand how such an event could be possible within the heart of America. Subsequently, the news diet differing from one national media environment to another, there were analyses of terrorism, expositions of Osama bin Laden and Al Qa'ida, analyses of growing political opposition inside Pakistan and attempts to explain the Taliban within the complex history and politics of Afghanistan. Later, still there was Afghan war coverage, and reconstruction coverage, and debates about the prison cages built in Guantanamo Bay.

Most recently, the US and British attack on Iraq in March 2003 brought other novelties in international news coverage, including split-screen techniques that echoed the US television series '24' and constructed a peculiar kind of 'war immediacy' so that some audiences could see American B-52 bombers being loaded with identifiable munitions at English airfields and live pictures of the traffic in Baghdad at the same time. Perhaps never have the non-combatants in a war been so vicariously close to the action. While many journalists were 'embedded' ('in-bed-with,' critics charged) amongst US and UK coalition forces, many remained non-embedded and filed reports from inside Baghdad and elsewhere. They did so in considerable danger, made graphically evident in the deaths of over twenty journalists during a conflict that included the bombing and shelling of numerous media installations. Yet the contradiction is that while there seems to be more information than ever before, evidence suggests that we know less and less and the difficulties of understanding and interpretation continue to haunt us. Like scores of television critics before him, Danny Schechter (Chapter 13) lamented, 'The more you watch, the less you know' (1998).

Neither journalists nor scholars could have imagined how interest in international journalism would mushroom after the events of September 11, 2001. The channels that carry international news and the people that report the stories seem ever more important to democracy, a vital part of civil society, providing links with people and events far away, in a manner that brings us into contact, albeit of a very particular kind. In the past years we have seen the practitioners of international journalism both lionised and castigated, held up as the cause of global conflict and as the possible solution. International news media are ever more controversial, criticised as inadequate, as biased, as over dramatizing events, as not providing enough history and context, as filled only with bad news, as bombarding us with images and facts, but no interpretation (or worse – 'factoids', in the tradition of US national quasi-tabloid *USA Today*). Everyone has an opinion on global journalism; and after 2001, no one doubts its importance and influence.

Yet much recent research on international news comes to the same, increasingly monotonous yet necessary, conclusion – that international news coverage is inadequate. For example, a two-year study by the International Council on Human Rights Policy in the UK examined how international media report human rights issues. While the media make more reference to human rights than ever before, the topic is seen by Northern, and international, media as a 'foreign' matter that concerns developing countries, rarely applying human rights principles to their own societies. Many aspects of human rights are underreported, with a strong focus on political and civil rights while economic, social and cultural rights tend to be ignored. The danger is that coverage is inadequate, superficial and subject to bias and that 'audiences that rely on the media to inform them are not always in a position to understand or judge properly the actions and policies of governments and other authorities' (ICHRP, 2002).

In Britain, Philip Harding (2003) writing about the dilemmas of news impartiality when addressing international audiences, notes that 'international broadcasting is about broadcasting to different countries, to different societies, to different cultures ... where the social, political and cultural differences between those societies will be far greater than any of the internal differences within them.' As an illustration of this range of difference, Harding notes that international broadcasting brings 'news of the Middle East to both Israelis and Palestinians and reports on Kashmir to India and Pakistan,' and argues that the news media 'have to be credible and comprehensible in Khartoum and Kalamazoo ... Mali has little in common with Malibu' (p. 66).

But news is also about bringing the rest of the world in. Television remains the primary medium through which the British public is informed about the developing world; three polls, in 1989, 1993 and 1997, suggest that remains true for 82-84 per cent of the public (Stone, 2000). Similarly, the Roper Organisation in the US, and other surveys, find that year after year Americans prefer and trust television news the most (Witt, 2002). The documentary tradition has almost no toehold in the United States, but even in the UK, where there has never been a disconnect between 'factual' and 'entertainment', there has been a marked decline in the amount of non-news current affairs programming filmed outside the British Isles – down fifty per cent in the decade 1989-99. The focus of documentary programming has shifted also, so that in 1998-1999, 'almost 60 per cent of programming on developing countries concerned travel (20 per cent) and wildlife (38 per cent)' (Stone, 2000:3), replacing the programs on human rights, development, the environment, religion, culture and the arts that were the main focus at the start of the 1990s. The public service ethos has not prevented the shift away from strong international documentary strands toward lifestyle and reality-based program and a menu of food, gardening and houses (Nason and Redding, 2002).

A concern about 'dumbing down' of television output is gaining momentum as evidence grows of a narrowing agenda of safe and formulaic programming which pushes out the harder political and foreign stories. News agencies, providing the source material for most international reporting, contributed to the trend with a significant increase in their sport, entertainment, and especially fashion, coverage since the mid-1990s (Paterson, 2003). Coverage of the catwalks of Paris and Milan, for example, costs TV news agencies little, and plays well in the male-dominated television newsrooms of the world. An internal survey of clients by APTN in 2000 found broadcasters more commonly demanding fluff of this sort, not news.

An intense dynamic is at work in the United States, with a 'shrinking of foreign news' on television (Utley, 1997). The events of 2001 led to soul searching amongst US broadcasters and a brief increase in international reporting (Parks, 2002), but broadcasters were in no position to return to the international coverage of two to three decades past, when the serious cutbacks began (Carter, 1992; Sanit, 1992). The attitude of the time was expressed by Thornton Bradshaw, Chairman of RCA (then owner of NBC), justifying cuts to international journalism by claiming, 'There's no reason that all three networks need to have people sitting around in Zimbabwe' (in fact, they never had) (quoted in Frank, 1991, 411).

In a country where less than 20 per cent of the population holds a passport and interest in international affairs is low, audiences reveal a marked lack of interest in foreign news (Pew Center, 2002). International editors point to such research to justify further cuts in global coverage, conveniently ignoring that Pew's survey found the public concerned that they lacked the background knowledge necessary to follow global events. In a study of public perceptions of coverage of the 1991 Gulf War, Taylor (1992) found CNN viewers critical of 'immediacy,' preferring reports to be given only when the facts are clear. Ironically, contextual detail is the first victim of news 'bean-counters' as stories are shortened, research 'in-country' more limited, and dependency on superficial news agency coverage increased. In the competitive market logic of commercial media, there is nothing to challenge this circular process of increasing ignorance. The cycle may be fuelled further by the tendency of news agencies (which, as we note below, tend to set the world's news agenda) to determine their coverage priorities based on the interests of their wealthiest, American, clients (Paterson, 1998; Schiff, 1996).

This brings us to the title of this introductory essay. Criticism of international reporting has shifted from 'pack journalism' and 'parachute journalism' (though these are no less problems) to 'rooftop journalism' We refer to the tendency of twenty-four hour global broadcasters to narrate major conflicts from the rooftops of luxury hotels, their celebrity journalists safely distanced from the violence and too often parroting words fed into their ear from London, Tokyo, or Atlanta. (We do however acknowledge that rooftops and international hotels have recently become targets in conflict, and note the many journalists killed or injured in such conflicts) Such 5-star rooftops offer ample space for a gaggle of satellite dishes, and a well stocked bar is always close at hand (a fixture of global journalism that never changes). But with increasing frequency, these journalists spend their days removed from the places and events they need to understand, shouting out a story dictated by home-bound editors and executives who live in fear of offending powerful sources, advertisers, and allies. They rarely stop to listen to either the subjects of their reporting or their increasingly bewildered and disenchanted audience.

A Long History of Debate

Debate about the amount, the focus, and the adequacy of international news coverage is not new but rather one of the longest-standing political and academic debates with international communications. In the mid 1970s, the nations of the then Third World voiced a number of concerns about the imbalance in international news flows. This led to calls for a New World Information and Communication Order (NWICO) and a redefinition of news as part of a broader redistribution of information resources (see for example Masmoudi, 1979). The NWICO debate occupied the United Nations Educational, Scientific, and

Cultural Organisation (UNESCO) and the Non- Aligned Movement for over a decade before a compromise resolution was reached on the role of the media. Still the United States, Britain and Singapore withdrew from UNESCO in 1984-5, and other world events moved the issue out of the international spotlight. Britain subsequently rejoined in 1997; more recently, media globaliser and self-proclaimed internationalist Ted Turner embarrassed the US government into consideration of mending its rifts with the United Nations by offering one billion dollars to pay US debts to the UN. In 2003, President Bush floated the idea of the US rejoining UNESCO, which formally took place on 1 October. The issues also seemed to recede as the 'emerging democracies' of Central and Eastern Europe joined the 'developing nations' of the old Third World in a rush to embrace the glittering new communication technologies of the West and the best and worst of Western-style journalism.

In the 1970s the arguments about international news centered on a few key concerns. One was about concentration in the global structure of news-gathering and dissemination, which more or less followed the global flow of economic and political power. Then, international news flows were dominated by the 'big four' Western news agencies (AP, AFP, Agence France Press and UPI – with TASS holding sway in the socialist world) who, through the numbers of international subscribers to their wire services, amount of news material distributed daily, and number of journalists based around the world, were able to set a substantial part of the international news agenda (Boyd-Barrett, 1980; Fenby, 1986; Friedland, 1992, Hess, 1996). Yet by the late 1990s a shift from text to image provision and an even greater concentration left only two companies, Reuters and APTN, providing video footage for most of the world's news channels (Paterson, 1998). Similarly, there is almost as much control now over international news text – in newsprint and cyberspace – by Reuters, Associated Press, and Agence France-Presse.

This structure reproduced news visibility and invisibility as gatekeeping decisions based on a more or less uniform set of news values were invoked by key gatekeepers throughout the global news system. There was a quantitative imbalance in news flow, with the Third World receiving far more materials about the First World than vice-versa. There was also far more attention paid to continual coverage of the global centers of the industrial world which contrasts with the intermittent images of the South in some form of crisis, whether Haiti, Bangladesh or Zimbabwe, whether political, economic or natural disaster. The qualitative differences were clear also. The closer to recognised centres of political and symbolic power, the more key individuals figured in news coverage – the whole world was bemused by Clinton and Lewinsky and mourned the death of Princess Di. Away from the centres of power sheer numbers matter, and violence, disruption and tragedy, especially when they are captured in dramatic pictures, are the key news ingredients.

When this structuring of international news becomes integrated into local news channels, it produces a common structure: a media map that is ethnocentric and narrow. In every country's media on any given day can be found a small set of common stories that are reported with virtually identical pictures or words. These may include one or two disruptive events – the war in Bosnia or Congo, an earthquake in Japan or forest fire in California – one or two predictable political or economic events from power centres – the presidential election in the United States, the latest directives from EU headquarters in Brussels, the exchange rate of the Euro and Yen – and one or two human interest events that included the bizarre, amusing and courageous – record multiple births, lovemaking between pandas, the lone yachtsman who forfeits victory to save a competitor. Local selection criteria also emphasise the significance of neighbouring countries and those with whom 'our' country (whichever it is) has close economic, political, and cultural ties. News is mostly politics and economics, and newsmakers are mostly government officials (Wu, 2003; Sreberny-Mohammadi, 1995; Hjarvard, 1995; Malik, 1992).

The UNESCO international news study, commissioned in the heat of the debate in 1978 and published in 1985 (Sreberny-Mohammadi et al, 1985) may have changed few minds but may have had some influence on the nature of the debate about the shortcomings of international news. The interest in foreign news research continued, and the project did seem to provide a framework for other studies; major communication research journals and conference programs of major academic research organisations continue to report studies of foreign news and international news flow, many owing some intellectual debt to the UNESCO study.

By 1989 a considerable body of research literature meant that the general parameters of the international geography of newsgathering were well-researched. Flow studies had shown a remarkably similar pattern of global news coverage which seemed to have solidified into a pattern structured on Cold War rivalries and tensions (Galtung & Vincent, 1992). In most major news channels across the regions of the world, the pattern of international news coverage presented the continual news-makers of the USA and Western Europe, the 'hot spots' of Third World crisis and a comparatively invisible world of state socialism, reported on within the Soviet bloc but not much outside. The South did not learn much about other regions of the South; African news channels ignored Latin America, and reciprocally, Latin American news channels ignored Africa, unless some major traumatic event occurred in either region (Sreberny, 1985). It made reasonable sense to claim that the world of the news was 'known' (Wallis & Baran, 1990).

The Altered Geo-Political Frame and Problems of Interpretation

Since 1989, major geo-political changes, technological developments and economic shifts have all played a role in reshaping the environment of international news-gathering. The global political context has altered significantly. The end of the Cold War, the fall of the Berlin Wall, and the splintering of the Soviet Union shattered the interpretive paradigm that had dominated international news-gathering and that had allowed an easy framing of and assignment of value to international news stories: pro- or anti-West, friend or foe, significant or insignificant. Instantly, the conceptual coherence of a 'Third World' was rendered a numerical misnomer, and was further challenged by the rapid economic development and democratisation of several countries, particularly in South-East Asia.

The shattering of the old interpretative paradigm revealed new, hitherto hidden, problematics. Slowly, awareness grew about pockets of endemic poverty in the North as well as the South. The continuing difficulty of economic development in Africa, constrained by World Bank and IMF-imposed conditions including structural adjustment programs, was evident in the crises in Somalia, Ethiopia and Rwanda, while the lethal spread of HIV/Aids is taking not only private but public toll in South Africa, Malawi, and elsewhere in Africa and on other continents too. As famously described by Benjamin Barber (1995), a reawakening of religio-political identities became evident in many places, creating new-old global affinities of religious culture. Islamist politics have made Algeria, Egypt, Turkey, Afghanistan, Pakistan all suddenly news-worthy. In the post-war context, there is consternation about the real possibilities of democracy in Iraq, given the contentions between Sunni and Shi'ites, Kurds and Arabs, and the viability of US-orchestrated political groups.

An highly globalised world consisting of a single global hegemon but with a number of other key economic centres, shifting peripheries and changeable loyalties, volatile border disputes, ethnic antagonisms, new forms of terrorism and of political solidarity constitutes a much harder environment to interpret adequately and frame simply for news viewers and readers. Novel political conditions pose challenges for political leaders, and real interpretative challenges for news reporters and editors which are not always adequately met. Indeed, in a context of such flux and crisis, questions about what the international news agenda is, and should be, have become urgent ones again (Van den Heuvel, 1993).

The Real Impacts of Technological Change on News Coverage

It is not only the political environment that has changed significantly. Developments in communications technologies, one of the fastest changing technology sectors, have had impacts on the mode of production, the mode of delivery, and the mode of reception of international news. In terms of the mode of production, technological developments essentially mean that more pictures and more stories can be produced and distributed faster than ever. Some changes in practice are clearly based around new technologies. The use of satellite telephones became widespread in the coverage of the Second Gulf War in 1991, although the 'live feed' element coupled with the control instruments of the news pool and Pentagon vetting of journalists precipitated very real concerns about the accuracy and diversity of coverage (Kellner, 1992; Bennett & Paletz, 1994). CNN's frequently live coverage meant the war was dubbed the first 'real-time war' (Flournoy and Stewart, 1997) and its rolling 24-hour coverage established a practice now emulated by scores of other news providers, one of the key new ingredients in the global news environment.

Dissatisfaction with CNN's American perspective also triggered the development of new channels, especially in the Middle East, designed to present news from a different perspective. The most notable of these is Al-Jazeera, whose coverage of Afghanistan and access to the Taliban and al-Qa'ida sources in late 2001 started to erode the global news hegemony of western news providers. Ironically, American networks were dependent on Al-Jazeera images and access to sources even as they publicly expressed contempt for the network.

In the 2003 war on Iraq, a mix of 'embedded' and non-embedded reporters, using night-vision cameras, satellite video phones, digital video-streaming and improved laptop video-editing, brought the war (albeit a sanitised, entertaining version) 'live' (or at least, quickly) to huge international television audiences. In Chapter 3, Baker describes the impact of these technologies for television news agencies. Audiences could watch, in real time, pictures of air-raids on Baghdad, troop movements through the Iraqi desert, night-time skirmishes in various locales, the wounded being patched up in poorly-provisioned Iraqi hospitals. But the ability to provide 24-hour live imagery and 'turbo news' doesn't necessarily make for better coverage or better understanding; the war on Iraq saw countless rumours elevated to the status of fact that were later rescinded (Miller and White, 2003).

The possibility of editing image and sound in the field using laptop edit consoles adds to the field reporter's workload, but reduces satellite costs for broadcasters (who can now transmit a one-minute finished story to London instead of fifteen minutes of raw footage). Some suggest that these technologies potentially give the location-based journalist a more significant role in determining not only the news agenda but the orientation of the news story (MacGregor, 1994). However, so far there has been little research to investigate such a claim. Whether speed improves journalism or not, politicians and diplomats are often reduced to watching television to know what is going on, an awkward reversal of knowledge that challenges the older set of relations between the foreign-policy making apparatus and the news production apparatus (Bennett & Paletz, 1994). The so-called 'CNN effect' is a widely used but ill-defined concept implying that media drive foreign policy through their coverage. While hotly debated, as Gilboa (2002) describes, little useful theory nor evidence of genuine effect has emerged.

The other technologically-driven change that has altered the international news environment is the colossal expansion of the Internet and its emergence as a powerful new mode of news delivery. As Allan explains in Chapter 16, the 2003 Iraq war is already being called the 'first internet war' for the unparalleled amount of news and information available on the Net. A website allows the traditional news channels to elaborate and develop stories, link to other resources, garner more authors, and is thus a significant additional space of news and commentary (www.nytimes.com, www.guardian.co.uk) and broadcasters (www.bbc.co.uk, www.cnn.com). These are also spaces of possible interactivity, with invitations to audiences to send in questions, comments, and interact with journalists and experts in on-line discussions. This helps to build new channel brand loyalty at a time when the profusion of channels allows for considerable fluidity and channel-hopping for alternative news providers. But while major media often promote the interactivity of their websites, there is some evidence that the 'new' journalism differs little from the 'old' journalism, in that journalists have little time nor inclination to interact with their audience (Burton, 1999).

The web provides a space where new producers interested in encouraging other voices can provide news. But this is not without its difficulties. Although only the major sites draw large audiences (BBC On-line, 1999; Paterson, 2003) more and more forms of electronic journalism constantly come on line. Major sites continue to experience steady growth, although few claim profitability. This is largely due to acquisition of smaller internet sites by the few largest ones, and by the massive subsidisation of internet ventures by the major conglomerates. McChesney (2000) argues these are willing to each lose $200-300 million yearly in order to dominate the Internet.

It is important to note that the track record of genuinely new media in the arena of international news is discouraging. The history of communications technology reveals a seemingly inevitable cycle of innovative content provision based on emerging technology being crushed, sidelined, or co-opted by the dominant institutions stuck in the dominant technological paradigms. Only when the wealthiest media institutions themselves adopt the new delivery technology does it become popular; but by then, any 'newness' of form has been extinguished. Winston (1995) refers to the tendency as 'the law of suppressing radical potential', observing that 'the breaks ensure that a technology's introduction does not disrupt the corporate or social status quo.'

From the onset of the new millennium, online news media have struggled. Beyond the high profile conversion of popular Internet based news services, like Salon, to commercial-laden, and/or subscription-only services (Hazen, 2003), are numerous cases of lower-profile new media failures. As with one of the first Internet news operations, and one of the latest to fail, Nando Times, Salon found out the only way to do quality journalism on a global scale is to raise millions of dollars from the venture capital sector to create infrastructure and pay top journalists (ibid). Venture capital, however, demands high returns in short, predetermined periods, but quality journalism cannot generate significant profit, and is often, and unpredictably, entirely unprofitable. When Salon's investors grew impatient for substantial return on the $80 million they had invested, Salon had a loyal enough and large enough readership to survive commercialisation (so far). Smaller and more specialised – and innovative – news services have not.

One of these was an innovative potential third television news agency, TVNewsWeb. It collapsed in 2001 after briefly posing a serious challenge to the two dominant players, Reuters and APTN. It seemed that even the forces of technological convergence, with which this upstart sought to bypass the traditional agencies, remain unable to dislodge the duopoly which has been controlling the international distribution of television news pictures since 1957 (when the precursor of Reuters Television, the British Commonwealth International Newsfilm Agency, was formed to provide a non-American alterative to the original precursor of APTN, United Press Movietone Television).

TVNewsWeb was created by Pete Henderson, a former BBC and freelance television news cameraman and founder of news services company Newsforce. In 1999 TVNewsWeb became an online broker for news video from around the world. Subscribers could purchase a story online and bring it into their newsrooms at broadcast quality (initially, through a satellite based system). In eighteen months of operation as a news agency, TV News Web came to be viewed as a genuine challenger by Reuters Television and Associated Press Television, especially after signing a deal with the BBC to distribute BBC stories. But the slow development of Internet video technology worked against them as they tried to implement a reliable and secure Internet distribution mechanism. According to Henderson, the venture capital firms which had provided their backing, 'didn't have the legs to run with us to see it through to success.' In 2001, editor Paterson spoke with Henderson in a London newsroom empty of computers, journalists, and activity, as the TV News Web founders suspended their business and searched for new backers. None have stepped forward.

The failed challenge to the leading providers of wholesale television news was mirrored in textual news. A former Reuters correspondent, Paul Eadle, and other partners, founded OutThereNews in 1996 to fill a perceived demand in cyberspace for high quality international reporting direct from independent journalists at the scene (Eadle, 2000; www.OutThereNews.com). At its height, the firm boasted of a network of 41 correspondents in 32 countries. In 2001, while OutThereNews was bringing unique inside coverage of Afghanistan to a global audience, financial backers pulled the plug and Eadle was forced to cease operations and lay off his London staff.

A third challenge to the dominance of global news agencies is posed by the start-up Globalvision News Network. They bring stories from journalists from a variety of local media around the world directly to subscribers who hunger for alterative and expert perspectives. But Globalvision (described by founder Danny Schechter in Chapter 13) continues to struggle financially, and briefly suspended operations at sister website MediaChannel in 2003. These firms created what Henderson (2001) termed 'electronic shop windows of content', as a means of bypassing the tri-opoly suppliers of news (APTN, Reuters, AFP), but at least two promised investors (who have little interest in news) more than they could deliver. At this stage it appears unlikely that either technological convergence or innovative journalism will dislodge news agency dominance in multimedia international news provision.

The Internet also provides a space for critical commentary on mainstream news coverage (eg www.opendemocracy.co.uk, www.tff.org, www.mediachannel.org). It houses media monitoring groups who specifically track certain kinds of coverage (FAIR.org) and it supports the work of indymedia networks which are active in many countries, posting alternative versions of stories and alternative stories they deem newsworthy (Alternet.org, Indymedia.org) The Internet also houses countless webloggers, writing diaries, think-pieces, stories, essays posted for an unknown – and unknowable – global audience. The British newspaper, the *Guardian*, started publishing the weblog of Salaam Pax from Baghdad during the Iraq War, and he now writes a column about post-war conditions there. Some traditional news providers feel threatened. For example, following the global spread via the Internet of a rumour that images of Palestinians celebrating the events of September 11th were falsified, APTN's Nigel Baker (who writes in Chapter 3) worried that the Internet was being used to discredit news coverage by leading news organisations (Keighron, 2001).

And with services like GlobalVision the Net provides a space where an active audience, if so inclined, can check one news report against another, making the biases and perspectives of new-gathering potentially more evident and accessible than ever before. This transparency of coverage is yet another nail in the coffin of the notion of objectivity. But the difficulty of the massive information-onslaught for the active audience is how to sort fact from fantasy, paranoia from grounded interpretation, and how to assemble an informed view from so much sheer information and so many competing interpretations. But this also begs the question of the inactive (majority) audience, loyal to mainstream journalism. Do the Internet's multiplicity of voices matter when few seek them out?

The Shifting Configuration of Corporate Players

In the early 1990s, the senior editor at Reuters Television (the former Visnews) told Paterson that the explanation of news coverage is obvious (academics, in his view, were on a constant search for irrelevant phantom explanations of journalism). His answer lay in the technology – and little else. If a television news agency or major broadcaster could not get video equipment to the scene of an event to record and transmit pictures quickly and cheaply, the event is not a story. Sad examples abound, as when a million refugees from the 1994 Rwanda genocide faced starvation at the Zaire border because news agencies – over budget from other events and lacking resources in the vicinity – chose not to make their plight a story until (days later and because of some Eurovision coverage) their clients demanded pictures (Paterson, 1997).

As Calcutt notes in Chapter 9, 'moral sense comes second to aesthetic sensibility'. At the wholesale level of news, efficient delivery of powerful imagery to clients is always the priority. Disturbing though it is, that Reuters thesis is broadly accepted among international news gatherers, and has particular merit in explaining under-coverage of Africa and other less accessible parts of the globe. Conversely, APTN's Nigel Baker observes in Chapter 3 that cheaper digital satellite gear now leaves the electronic media with few excuses for ignoring remote stories.

But the technocentric explanation has always conveniently and, perhaps necessarily, permitted avoidance of less comfortable explanations of editorial policy. There are many, as chronicled by news production studies dating back to Schlesinger (1978/1987), Halloran (1970), and Epstein (1974), but the least favourite of journalists and editors is the question of ownership. As of this writing, three corporations (Reuters, AP, AFP) dominate international wholesale news delivery and supply most source material for international stories on television and the Internet, while six operate the majority of major websites, commercial broadcasting/cablecasting, and newspapers worldwide (News Corporation, Bertelsmann, Vivendi, AOL-Time Warner, Disney, and Viacom). With the further deregulation of US broadcasting in 2003, concentration of ownership shows no signs of slowing. But intense grassroots resistance to media deregulation in the US has led some in the US Congress to speak of reversing the trend.

Intriguingly, few outside of academy, industry, and activist circles know about media concentration, for the mainstream media doesn't cover it, and the profusion of channels yields a convenient illusion of diversity. News technology is a double-edged sword. More news, faster news, prettier news – but is it better news? As Thussu (Chapter 2), Schechter (Chapter 13) and Allan (Chapter 16) acknowledge, more news options via digital satellite, Internet, and even mobile telephone, do little to change the traditional news landscape when the same few corporations dominate news provision and the same standard storylines and biases persist.

CNN is by now well-established as a major global news player, although its reach is predominantly to national English-speaking elites and the global business and educational traveller installed in plush international hotel rooms (Flournoy and Stewart, 1997; Volkmer, 1999). It established the much copied format of 24 hour rolling news. BBC Worldwide, established as a commercial operation independent of the main public service structure of the domestic BBC, has actively developed international distribution channels. These have not been unproblematic, with a falling-out with the Saudis leading it to being bumped from the Orbit network which broadcasts in to the Middle East and, as a gift to sensitive Chinese officials by Rupert Murdoch in exchange for access to the Chinese media market, the suspension of BBC news broadcasts from the STAR satellites. BBC World is the corporation's 24-hour rolling news channel, and has recently penetrated the US market.

Global and regional news agencies are crucial due to the potentially substantial agenda-setting influence on other media, but now even more crucial since they so effectively bypass or control the intermediary processors of news in cyberspace enabling them to directly reach – for the first time – a large portion of the mass news audience (and potentially cultivate a new audience uninterested in traditional media). News agencies have historically sought to minimise their public exposure, for their success had previously rested largely with their ability to make news audiences believe that their local media outlet – not an international agency – has brought them the news of the world. But now agencies depend on the popular appeal of their brand names for audience loyalty in cyberspace, and so market their names aggressively.

In the 1990s, Reuters became one of the top five global media corporations with its own, diverse, modes of international news diffusion, including direct video feeds and on-line access to news texts. It mixes specialist, business newsfeeds with broad-based international news provision, having acquired Visnews in 1992 and in the winter of 1995, signing an agreement to provide news for Murdoch's Sky. But by 2002, Reuters was in serious difficulty with job losses and share price falls (see Boyd-Barrett and Rantanen in Chapter 1), oddly proving that a century and a half of control of global news flow, near monopoly control over global financial trading, and their respected brand name are no guarantee of profitability.

There is good reason to fear corporate domination of global news, but there is little agreement on how serious the problem is. Paterson (2003) finds that websites that most people in the world go to for their news do little original reporting. Major news organisations simply provided nearly verbatim foreign news reports from Associated Press and Reuters 43 per cent of the time. Their dependence on the news agencies is heavy the rest of the time, but at least on some stories there is evidence that other sources were consulted. The major internet portals like Yahoo and AOL provide unaltered Reuters and Associated Press material at least 85 per cent of the time. Heavy dependence on the limited news diet of the major agencies results in limiting and homogenising public discourse on agency covered topics, but also limits the range of topics available for public consideration. CNN correspondent Ralph Begleiter suggested the problem with Internet news is that 'you can find what you want to know on it, but you miss the seeding of stories on subjects about which you may not know anything' (Hoge, 1997).

Southern international newsgathering agencies have attempted to provide something of a 'contra-flow' to the major western agency news flow (Boyd-Barrett and Thussu, 1992). IPS has survived in Rome but appears to be pressured in the new political environment under Berlusconi, and may need to search for a new base of operations. Gemini, which focused on news of the developing world, has collapsed and while at least two services, Women's Feature Service and DepthNews, provide international news and features with a specifically gendered perspective, their scope is limited (Anand, 1994;

Sreberny-Mohammadi,1994). Former Gemini editor Daya Thussu explores the alternative further in Chapter 2. Major public exchanges of news in the developing world, the Pan-African News Agency (PANA), and the Caribbean News Agency (CANA), also dissolved in the last half decade and have been reborn in smaller, mostly commercial, guises.

The Rise of Non-English International News Channels

By far the most significant recent development in the international news business has been the rapid rise of powerful non-English language players. The proliferation of niche language rolling news provision includes the Japanese Global News (Clausen, 2003), the Spanish ECO News, Chinese CCTV and Brazil's Globo News. Sonwalkar provides an critical analysis of Indian news media development in Chapter 6, and John Jirik describes the exportation of Chinese television news in Chapter 7.

The rise of CNN as a 'global' news provider during the 1991 Gulf War caused considerable consternation amongst Arab states, and much of the very rapid development by the Gulf States of satellite provision, telecommunications networks and varied forms of broadcast message delivery were precipitated by that crisis, both in an endeavor to provide the world with 'local' news and to develop an Arab perspective on the news. The most significant new player, already mentioned, is Al-Jazeera, the Arabic news channel hosted in Qatar and staffed by many journalists who started on the BBC Arabic Service. It added English-language transmission and an English-language website, both of which were the source of much controversy during the Iraq war. Also in the spring of 2003, as war against Iraq looked ever more likely, other Arabic channels were consolidated or were being rolled out. Al-Arabiyya, a 24 hour television news channel, was launched in February 2003 with a $300 million budget from Kuwaiti and Lebanese financers, and 500 staff, as part of the Saudi-owned MBC organisation but based in Dubai.

Some of the most dramatic pictures in the 2003 Iraq conflict, such as the aerial bombardment of Baghdad, have been relayed by government-run Abu Dhabi Television, based in the United Arab Emirates. Both Al-Jazeera and Abu Dhabi TV had an impressive network of correspondents across Iraq and the region as well as embedded journalists with coalition troops. Al-Jazeera had four correspondents in Baghdad, two in Basra, one in Mosul and one in northern Iraq, and its top news reporter Tayseer Alouni also covered the Afghanistan war. Another challenge to Western portrayals of Middle Eastern news comes from Al-Manar, the impressively well-produced news station of the Lebanese Hizbollah movement. The dogged refusal of Al-Manar's presenters to conform to journalistic norms – men are usually unshaven and without ties, and the women wear Islamic headscarves – would probably surprise Western viewers. More shocking to Western eyes is the unflinching emphasis of all these channels on the gory consequences of war, including the lingering close-up shots of corpses uniformly excised from British and US television.

The other significant tier of organisational actors, the regional news exchanges like Eurovision News Exchange, Asiavision, Arabvision, distribute to their member broadcasting organisations non-regional news feeds from the news agencies and major regional stories covered by their members (Hjarvard, 1994). In the main, the regional news exchanges include public service or government broadcasters, consider television news not a commodity but a public good, with cost-sharing of facilities supporting their non-profit exchange mechanisms (Hjarvard, 1994). There has always been strong competition across the three levels of players – the wholesalers, the transnational satellite channels and the regional news exchanges – that constitute the international news environment, with the latter facing particularly heavy pressure in the new deregulated, market-driven media environment. But the jockeying for new modes of distribution, the cost-sharing agreements and exchanges all mean that a neat distinction between these three 'tiers' has blurred long ago.

News Research

While political economic analyses of the changing global news landscape remains vital, we also suggest that we need better studies of how international news is made. The paradigm of news production research which has yielded our most influential theoretical understandings of news developed, and indeed matured, between 1950 (marked by White, 1964) and 1980 (marked by Fishman, 1980); after which time the news production process became a substantially less popular topic of analysis in mass communication research. Since then there have been remarkably few widely published research studies of news production which are both substantive and influential. Our understandings of news are, therefore, based upon very dated research. While the nature of news and the nature of news producing have changed in massive ways from two decades ago and beyond – globalisation, ownership, and technology are prime examples – news research has failed to keep pace. The notion that journalists objectively mirror the key events of the day is still widely accepted within the industry itself, however, evidencing the limited practical influence of the seminal early analyses of news.

Ironically, this lack of analysis of television news production at the global level comes at a time when news production, like the rest of mass media, has become internationalised – the result of transnational ownership of news organizations and increased production and delivery of television news worldwide – collectively regarded as the globalisation of news (ie, Boyd-Barrett, 1998). It is ironic that the largest globalised news companies have received the least scrutiny from scholars. Some influential news services like the BBC and CNN do receive a great deal of scholarly interest, but their is no evidence of either one collaborating with an extensive ethnographic study of news production in the past decade or more, even while many useful ethnographic studies of domestic production have been conducted (Cottle, 1999; Rodriguez, 1996; Helland, 1995; Dillinger, 1995). Perhaps even more significantly, insights into the culture and decision-making process within their parent media conglomerates is rarer still.

The Ethics of News Production and of Consumption

Some of the media actors described here offer new and competing frames of reference that challenge the dominant West-centric set of practices. This is increasingly evident in the realm of ethics, with controversies early on in the Iraq war about the appropriate images through which to show casualties and prisoners of war. British media practice has desisted from very graphic images of dead bodies, certainly when it involves allied forces, preferring to get bad news to families before the story breaks on television. With the variety of news producers now in the field, such niceties of broadcasting practice are severely challenged. Al-Jazeera made much of showing the horror of violence, with longer and closer shots of bleeding bodies and dead ones. The different visual practices raise the question of whether far greater weight has been accorded to pictures of western, white, bodies than to pictures of starving children, women refugees and male prisoners of war from non-western countries. The assumptions of 'our' (read British or Western audiences) distance from most sites and sights of suffering has actually produced a problematic ethics which, in its desire to be respectful to some, actually further objectifies others. It is uncomfortable when 'we' become the object of the gaze of others, but that is one of the consequences of the internationalisation of news production that is currently occurring.

Rolling news and immediacy have also not left much time for the sanitisation of imagery, and some of the real trauma and horror of war is reaching the audience. Silverstone (2002) has written of media literacy as a political project that involves the critical skills of analysis and appreciation of the social dynamics and social centrality of media as framing the cultures of the everyday. Media literacy above all requires an understanding of the non-transparency of media and of the moral implications of that non-transparency. It could be argued that the multiplicity of channels and the ability to read, hear and see news produced from within different political cultures and frames of meaning actually helps to revitalise the news and render its construction more obvious.

And how does the coverage of such traumatic events effect the journalists involved? How are they able to, and what does it mean that they do, maintain 'objectivity' in the face of unspeakable horror and suffering, or would they write a more 'truthful' story if a greater space for emotionality were allowed? The coverage by some of the non-embedded journalists trying to be truthful to what they were seeing and hearing, like the *Independent*'s Robert Fisk, rang with greater authenticity that the pontifications of politicians far from the front lines. Calcutt (Chapter 9), Stevenson (Chapter 12), Lynch (Chapter 14), and Brayne (Chapter 15) all explore the possibilities of a 'journalism of attachment' and new ethical codes in international reporting.

Global News in an Age of Conflict and Crisis

Following the attacks on Washington and New York in September 2001, and through the wars in Afghanistan and Iraq, the news media have increasingly found themselves at the centre of political and military conflicts and in controversies over their own roles as the leading international journalists face more pressure every month to toe the official company and often government line. International news coverage by US media turned especially ugly. With few exceptions, pretenses of objectivity or attempts to provide geo-political context were abandoned with the march to battle. Collaboration with government officials in the telling of the war story has been extensive, but perhaps not more so than when the American networks refused to show more than the briefest clips of the second videotaped speech by Osama bin Laden, on request of the White House, denying Americans an opportunity to learn more about the man their country was working so hard to eliminate.

In the first months of the war on Afghanistan (since pre-empted in television schedules by the even bigger war on Iraq), censorship within US media outlets was heavy-handed (examples are indexed at www.ncac.org). Senior executives at CNN, ABC and MSNBC went on record ordering their correspondents to stay in line with public opinion, and apologised to conservative critics for aspects of their news coverage (Rutenberg and Carter, 2001). ABC, NBC, CBS and CNN reporters in the field were under pressure to put a patriotic slant on their stories, not only from their editors at home, but from colleagues representing more blatantly patriotic conservative US media. Fox television reporter Geraldo Rivera, for example, told viewers in one of his stories from Afghanistan that he would personally kill bin Laden given the chance, and Fox's senior editor labelled the war 'a conflict between the United States and murdering barbarians' (Flanders, 2001; Rutenberg, 2001). To the concern of international press organisations, CNN plunged into the fray in Iraq when their "security guards" shot at Iraqi soldiers posted to a checkpoint, and a *New York Times* correspondent was reported to be directing a squad of US troops in the arrests and integrations of Iraqis. Reporters Without Borders worries that with the world's major news outlets playing the part of combatant, the few remaining governments that don't shoot journalists during conflicts may soon reverse that position (Azeez, 2003; Kurtz, 2003).

Gung-ho, one-sided reporting seemed to play well with US audiences, as Fox news ratings overtook those of CNN in the early months of the Afghanistan war (Rutenberg, 2001). But as Allan points out in Chapter 16, many in the American audience sought out critical coverage of the war from non-US media, with BBC and ITN broadcasts in the US (on cable and some public stations) showing marked increases in viewership, and American visitation of non-US news and alternative websites increasing (Flanders, 2001).

Television and print journalists have fallen victim to a more violent form of news management closer to the battlefield. As of this writing, twenty journalists are dead in Iraq, and several others have been killed in Afghanistan. If you consider how short the Iraq campaign was, Iraq will be notorious as the most dangerous war for journalists ever. But the significant and troubling difference from past conflicts is that now journalists have more to fear from their own side than from 'the enemy.' In an extreme example, in 2001 a bureau of Al-Jazeera, at the time working closely with CNN to provide the only US television coverage from Kabul, was destroyed by US missiles (BBC operations, some distance away, were bombed at the same time, and Radio Kabul had earlier been the target of US bombs). As with their destruction of Serbian television (and with it, as in Kabul, CNN's local coverage ability) in 1999, the Pentagon insisted they hit legitimate targets. A joint bureau operated by CNN and Al-Jazeera in Kandahar, Afghanistan, had been bombed by the US earlier. The targeting of journalists continued in Iraq, with the bombing of another Al-Jazeera bureau and killing of two international journalists by a US tank as they observed the conflict from their Baghdad hotel window (Fisk, 2003; CPJ, 2003).

At a time when major news services consider reporting on conflicts from the rooftops of luxury hotels hundreds of miles away, or 'embedded' reporting under the thumb of the combatants themselves, to be acceptable – even admirable – approaches to conflict journalism, there is little effort to hold combatants to account for their attacks on journalists. So the profession grows more dangerous than it has ever been, while news organisations and audiences display little interest in the work of the courageous journalists taking the greatest risks (like APTN's Miguel Gil, described by Baker in Chapter 3.)

In Conclusion

Our own project on International News in the 21st Century began in 1999 (when the title carried more cachet), as an effort to capitalise on the thirty-five year history of media research at the Centre for Mass Communications Research to spur a conversation between scholars and journalists about the prospects for the world's second oldest profession in the new millennium. Jim Halloran and Philip Elliott organised a conference at Leicester's CMCR in 1970 which similarly sought to bring media researchers together with media professionals. In a book reporting that conference, Elliot (1971) counselled:

> In itself, knowledge, far from being the means by which ... attacks (on media credibility) are furthered, is a means of setting the broadcaster free from ill-informed criticism, political prejudice, and opinions based on specific interests ... Trying to batten down the hatches will only make the suspicions grow a little bit larger ... both groups do share a common plank in their ideologies. This should serve as a basis for agreement between them. Both are in the business of trying to advance and communicate knowledge.

Our conference, in March 2000, gave voice to provocative predictions from a mix of international journalists and well known journalism and media scholars. Many expanded on and updated their work for this book, and many other authors have joined the discussion. This volume aims to address some of the continuities as well as the changes in news production and distribution by bringing together the varied perspectives of journalists and academicians, analysts from inside and outside the media. From the start this was meant to be a far ranging discussion – open to all approaches and perspectives. As editors, we have constrained it only through the wish to keep it international in nature – both in terms of authorship and the nature of the news examined – and to keep it forward looking. This collection of essays is less about contemporary practice than about the examination of trends as clues to the future.

We hope that this book will be of use to academics and their students, since we believe that the better informed audiences are, the better media choices and political choices they will make. The increasing interest in world events, albeit precipitated by tragic events, can be readily connected to renewed interest in the manufacture of international news and the ongoing debates about how we represent and understand other people, places and problems. As Schechter points out, the modern media educator faces an odd and daunting challenge: inspiring the next generation to build a better and more democratic media system when in fact, those students have never seen such a system. Concentrated corporate media is, for them, unremarkable, and a different kind of media unimaginable. As McLuhan remarked, 'we don't know who discovered water but we know it wasn't a fish. A pervasive medium is always beyond perception.' The insidious hegemony of global corporate media and global corporate news give most people neither genuine information options, nor the desire for them.

We also hope this effort to bring researchers together with journalists might help to usher in a more collaborative and conducive environment for research. Many of the key media institutions, including the US television networks and the BBC, are infamous amongst researchers for 'battening down the hatches' and making access and serious research almost impossible to undertake. Following their detailed, but often critical, studies of the BBC in the 1970s, Philip Schlesinger (1980) and the Glasgow Media Group's John Eldridge (2000) describe how they were ostracised by the BBC and how hostility to inquisitive researchers lingered for decades. Indeed, Paterson (1996) found suspicion and defensiveness among senior television news agency workers in London; but amongst their younger colleagues, an eagerness to be the subject of academic research.

In a context of such political complexity and moral ambiguity, perhaps there is a chance for a greater rapprochement and dialogue between professional journalists and academic researchers. Indeed, the changing work environments of both academe and the media means that more and more journalists are doing some teaching and/or research, and, on occasion, an academic becomes a journalist. Ideally, this volume will be a tool to help researchers focus their understandings of the new age of international journalism through discussion of key trends, and will provide perspectives to international journalists which are otherwise absent from the daily routines of 'making news'. Industry professionals might see greater value in increasing access for academic researchers; increasing their own exposure to academic research through increased dialogue; expanding their organisation's intake of research to include the external with the internal (the ever-popular industry consultant's reports); and finally and perhaps most crucially, to use increased dialogue with the academic community to demonstrate their public accountability and editorial independence.

Finally, we hope that this volume plays a part in encouraging greater dialogue between academics, media practitioners and media activists, as well as a more informed conversation within the audience-at-large about the nature of the international news environment that is increasingly shared but that still often works to divide us.

Bibliography

Anand, A. (1994, February) *Women's Press Service*, presentation to Women Empower Communication conference, Bangkok, Thailand.

Associated Press Television News (2000) Unpublished company report, prepared by Frank Magid Associates.

Azeez, Walé (2003, April 18) 'CNN armed guard not "dangerous precedent"' *Press Gazette*.

Barber, B. (1995) *Jihad vs. McWorld*. New York: Times Books.

BBC On-line (1999) Web is 'shrinking' BBC On-line available at http://news2.thls.bbc.co.uk/hi/english/sci/tech/newsid%5F428000/428999.stm

Bennett, W. and D. Paletz (eds) (1994) *Taken by Storm: The Media, Public Opinion and US Foreign Policy in the Gulf War*. Chicago: University of Chicago Press.

Boyd-Barrett, O. (1980) *The International News Agencies*. London: Constable.

Boyd-Barrett, O. (1998) 'Global News Agencies' in O.Boyd-Barrett and T.Rantanen (eds) *The Globalization of News*. London: Sage.

Boyd-Barrett, O. and D. K. Thussu (1992) *Contra-Flow in Global News*. London: John Libbey.

Boyd-Barrett, O. and Rantanen T. (eds) (1998) *The Globalization of News*. London: Sage.

Burden, P. (1999) *Interactivity and On-line News at the BBC*. Unpublished Masters dissertation, University of Leicester – CMCR.

Carter, B. (1992, June 10) 'Networks Cutting Back on Foreign Coverage', *New York Times*.

Chapman, G. (1987) 'Towards a geography of the tube:TV flows in Western Europe', *Intermedia*, 15 (1).

Clare, J. (1997) *News Production at APTV*. Unpublished Masters dissertation, University of Leicester – CMCR.

Clausen, L. (2003) *Global News Production*. Copenhagen: Copenhagen Business School Press.

CNN (2001, October 19) 'Roberston: Afghan civilians want word on what's next' http://www.cnn.com/2001/WORLD/asiapcf/ south/10/19/ret.rob ertson.otsc/index.html

Cohen, A., Levy, M., Roeh, I., Gurevitch, M. (1996) *Global Newsrooms, Local Audiences: A Study of the Eurovision News Exchange.* London: John Libbey.

Committee to Protect Journalists (CPJ) (2003) 'CPJ condemns journalists' deaths in Iraq'. http://www.cpj.org/news/2003/Iraq08apr03na.html

Cottle, S. (1999) 'From BBC Newsroom to BBC Newscentre: On Changing Technology and Journalist Practices', *Convergence: The Journal of Research into New Media Technologies* 5(3): 22-43.

Dillinger, Brent (1995) *Finnish Views of CNN Television News: A Critical Cross-Cultural Analysis of the American Commercial Discourse Style.* Doctoral Dissertation, University of Vaasa.

Eadle P. (2000) Transcript of remarks to the International News in the 21st Century Conference. Leicester: University of Leicester.

Eldridge, J. (2000) 'The Contribution of the Glasgow Media Group to the Study of Television and Print Journalism'. *Journalism Studies* 1(1).

Elliot, P. (1971) Chapter Nine in Halloran, J. and Gurevitch, M. (eds), *Broadcaster-Researcher Co-operation in Mass Communication Research.* Leicester: University of Leicester.

Epstein, E. (1974) *News From Nowhere.* New York: Vintage Books.

Evans, R. (1994, November), presentation at the First Satellite and Cable Television in the Middle East Conference, Dubai, United Arab Emirates.

Fenby, J. (1986) *The International News Services.* New York: Schocken.

Fishman, M. (1980) *Manufacturing the News.* Austin: University of Texas Press.

Fisk, R (2003, April 26) 'Did the US murder these journalists?' *Independent.*

Flanders, L. (2001, November 9) 'Media criticism in mono' WorkingForChange.com

Flournoy, D. (1992) *CNN World Report: Ted Turner's International News Coup.* London: John Libbey.

Flournoy, D. and Stewart, R. (1997) *CNN: Making News in the Global Market.* Luton: Luton University Press. Page: 28

Frank, R. (1991) *Out of Thin Air: The Brief Wonderful Life of Network News.* New York: Simon and Schuster.

Freedom Forum Media Studies Center Research Group (1993) *The Media and Foreign Policy in the Post-Cold War World.* New York Freedom Forum Media

Studies Center, Columbia University.

Friedland, L. (1992) *Covering the World: International Television News Agencies.* New York: Twentieth Century Fund.

Galtung, J. & Vincent, R. C. (1992) *Global Glasnost: Toward a New International Information/Communication Order?* Cresskill, NJ: Hampton Press, Inc.

Gilboa, E. (2002) 'Global Communication and Foreign Policy', *Journal of Communication* 52(4)

Gurevitch, M. (1991) 'The Globalization of Electronic Journalism', in Curran, J. and M. Gurevitch (eds), *Mass Media and Society.* London and New York: Edward Arnold.

Halliday, F. (1991) 'International Relations: Is there a New Agenda?', *Millennium*, 20 (1).

Halloran, J. D, Elliott P., Murdock G. (1970) *Demonstrations and Communication: A Case Study.* Harmondsworth: Penguin.

Hanson, C. (1997) 'The Dark Side of On-line Scoops', *Columbia Journalism Review* May/June.

Harding, P. (2002) 'Impartiality in international broadcasting', in Tambini, D. and J. Cowling (eds), *New News: Impartial Broadcasting in the Digital Age.* London: IPPR.

Hazen, D. (2003, January 23) 'Salon Goes for Broke' AlterNet.org,.

Helland, K. (1995) *Public Service and Commercial News* Doctoral Dissertation, University of Bergen.

Henderson, P. (2001) Interview with Chris Paterson, London.

Hess, S. (1996) *International News & Foreign Correspondents.* Washington DC: Brookings.

Hjarvard, S. (1994) 'The Global Spread of a European Model: Regional Television News Exchange'. Paper presented at IAMCR Conference, Seoul.

Hjarvard, S. (1995) *Internationale TV-nyheder. En historisk analyze af det europeiske system for udveksling af internationale TV-nyheder.* Copenhagen: Akademisk Forlag.

Hoge, J. (1997, November/December) 'Foreign News: Who Gives a Damn', *Columbia Journalism Review.*

Independent Television Commission (2000) *Television: The Public's View.* London: ITC.

International Council on Human Rights Policy (ICHRP) (2002) *Journalism, Media and the Challenge of Human Rights Reporting.* Geneva, Switzerland.

Keighron, P. (2001, November 16) 'War on the Web: Internet news comes of age', 'Broadband' supplement to *Broadcast.*

Kellner, D. (1992) *The Persian Gulf Television War*. Colorado: Westview Press.

Kurtz, H. (2003, June 25) 'Embedded Reporter's Role In Army Unit's Actions Questioned by Military', *Washington Post*.

Macdonald, A.(1994, October) 'BBC World Service Television', presentation at conference on Press Ownership in India, SOAS, London.

MacGregor, Brent (1994) Crisis reporting in the satellite age – the Gulf, Moscow, Bosnia. EFTSC conference, London.

Malik, R. (1992) 'The Global News Agenda', *Intermedia*, 20(1).

Marvanx, G. and G. Gerbner (1984) 'The Many Worlds of the World's Press', in Gerbner, G. and M. Siefert (eds), *World Communication: a Handbook*. New York: Longman.

Masmoudi, M. (1979) 'The New World Information Order' *Journal of Communication* 29/2, 172-198.

Massey, D. (1991, June) 'A Global Sense of Place', *Marxism Today*.

McChesney, R. (1999) *Rich Media, Poor Democracy*. Illinois: University of Illinois Press.

McChesney, R. (2000) 'The Titanic Sails On: Why the Internet won't sink the media giants' *Extra!* March/April.

Millar, S. and White, M. (2003, March 29) 'Facts, some fiction and the reporting of war', *Guardian*.

Nason, S. and D. Redding (2002) *Losing Reality: Factual International Programming on Uk Television*, 2000-2001. London: Third World and Environment Trust (3WE).

Parks, M. (2002) 'Foreign News: What's Next?', *Columbia Journalism Review*, January/February.

Paterson, C. (1994) 'More Channels, Fewer Perspectives :International Television News Provider Concentration', EFTSC Conference, London.

Paterson, C. (1996) *News Production at Worldwide Television News (WTN): An Analysis of Television News Agency Coverage of Developing Countries* Doctoral Dissertation, University of Texas.

Paterson, C. (1997) 'Global Television News Services' A. Sreberny-Mohammadi, D. Winseck, J. McKenna and O. Boyd-Barrett, *Media in Global Context* (eds.) London: Edward Arnold.

Paterson, C. (1998) 'Global Battlefields' in *The Globalization of News*. O. Boyd-Barrett, T. Rantanen (eds.), London: Sage.

Paterson, C. (2003) 'Prospects for a Democratic Information Society: The News Agency Stranglehold on Global Political Discourse' paper for the New Media,

Technology and Everyday Life in Europe Conference, London.

Pew Research Center For the People and the Press (2001, June 11) 'Internet News: More Log On, Tune Out'. Washington: Pew.

Pew Research Center for the People and the Press (2002, June 9) 'Public's News Habits Little Changed by September 11: Americans Lack Background to Follow International News'. Washington: Pew

Rodriguez, A. (1996) 'Made in the USA: The Production of the Noticiero Univision', *Critical Studies in Mass Communication*, 13(1), 59-82.

Rutenberg J. (2001, December 3) 'Fox Portrays a War of Good and Evil, and Many Applaud' *New York Times*.

Rutenberg J. and Carter, B. (2001, November 7) 'Network Coverage a Target Of Fire From Conservatives' *New York Times*.

Sanit, T. (1992) 'The New Unreality', *Columbia Journalism Review*, May/June.

Schechter, D., J. Brown and R. McChesney (1998) *The More You Watch*, *The Less You Know*. New York: Seven Stories Press.

Schiff, F. (1996) 'The Associated Press: Its Worldwide Bureaus and American Interests', *International Communication Bulletin*, 31(1-2): 7-13.

Schlesinger, P. (1980) 'Between Sociology and Journalism' in Christian, H. (ed.) *Sociology of the Press and Journalism* Keele, England: Univ. of Keele.

Schlesinger, P. (1987) *Putting 'Reality' Together: BBC News* 2nd Ed., London: Routledge.

Silverstone, R. (2002, Fall) 'Complicity and Collusion in the Mediation of Everyday Life', *New Literary History*.

Sonwalkar, P. (2001) 'India : Makings of Little Cultural/Media Imperialism?' *Gazette* 63 (6).

Sreberny-Mohammadi A., K. Nordenstreng, R. Stevenson (1984) 'The "World of the News" Study', *Journal of Communication*, 34(1): 120-142.

Sreberny-Mohammadi A., K. Nordenstreng, R., L. Stevenson and F. Ugboajah (1985) *Foreign News in the Media: International Reporting in 29 Countries. Reports and Papers on Mass Communication No. 93*. Paris: UNESCO.

Sreberny-Mohammadi A. (1991) 'The Global and the Local in International Communication', in Curran J. and M. Gurevitch (eds), *Mass Media and Society*. London and New York: Edward Arnold.

Sreberny-Mohammadi A. (1994) *Women, Media and Development in a Global Perspective*. Paris: UNESCO.

Sreberny-Mohammadi A. (1995) 'International news flows in the post-cold war world: Mapping the news and the news producers', *Electronic Journal of*

Communication, 5 (2&3).

Stevenson, R. L. and D. L. Shaw (eds) (1984) *Foreign News and the New World Information Order*. Ames, Iowa: Iowa State University Press.

Stone, J. (2000) *Losing Perspective: Global Affairs on British Terrestrial Television 1989-1999*. London: Third World and Environment Broadcasting Project.

Taylor, P. (1992) *War and the Media: Propaganda and Persuasion in the Gulf War* Manchester: Manchester University Press.

Tunstall, J. (1992) 'Europe as world news leader', *Journal of Communication*, 42(3).

United States Department of State (2002, September 12) 'United States Rejoins UNESCO' http://www.state.gov/p/io/rls/fs/2002/13482.htm.

Utley, G. (1997) 'The Shrinking of Foreign News', *Foreign Affairs*, 76(2).

van den Heuvel, J. (1993) 'For the media, a brave (and scary) new world', special issue on Global News after the Cold War, *Media Studies Journal*, Fall.

van Ginneken, J. (1998) *Understanding Global News: A Critical Introduction*. London: Sage.

Vincent R. and J. Galtung (1993) *Global Glasnost*. Cresskill, New Jersey: Hampton Press.

Volkmer, I (1999) *News in the Global Sphere: A Study of CNN and its Impact on Global Communication*. Luton: University of Luton Press.

Wallis, R. and S.J. Baran (1990) *The Known World of Broadcast News*. London: Routledge.

White, D. M. (1964) 'The gatekeeper: A case study in the selection of news' in L. A. Dexter & D. M. White (Eds.), *People, Society and Mass Communications*. New York: Free Press.

Winston, B. (1995) 'How are Media Born and Developed?' in Downing, J., et al, eds., *Questioning the Media: a Critical Introduction*. Thousand Oaks: Sage.

Witt, E. (2002, July/August) 'Necessary Embrace: The Public and News Media', *Public Perspective*.

Wu, H.D. (2003) 'Homogeneity around the World? Comparing the Systemic Determinants of International News Flow between Developed and Developing Countries', *Gazette* 65(1).

Part I: Structures

Chapter 1
News Agencies as News Sources: A Re-Evaluation
Oliver Boyd-Barrett and Terhi Rantanen

With his seminal study of news agencies in 1980, Oliver Boyd-Barrett put these influential – but previously indiscernible – institutions on the agenda of researchers and educators. Even at that time, the influence of news agencies was passionately debated in international fora. There was almost no public information about them, although their words and pictures have formed the bulk of national and international news for news media everywhere in the past 150 years. In their book, The Globalization of News, *Boyd-Barrett and Rantanen chronicled the turmoil and transition for agencies during the 1990s. As they describe here, the new century seems no less tumultuous – even as news agencies become increasingly recognised as fundamental agents of globalisation.*

Previous Research on News Agency Content: an Overview

Since Unesco's 1985 International News study (Sreberny-Mohammadi et al., 1985) there has been relatively little quantitative research on international news agency services. Consequently, we do not have many comprehensive studies that are comparable to earlier research analyses such as those of IPI, 1953; Schramm, 1960; Gerbner and Marvanyi, 1977; Boyd-Barrett, 1980; Weaver et al., 1985, particularly in the case of print news agencies (see Boyd-Barrett, 2000, for a more complete overview).

There are several reasons why large scale quantitative study of news agency content is less frequently encountered today. Compared to earlier studies, the volume of agency news has increased considerably and with it the magnitude and complexity of any analysis of total output. Compared to the 1985 data, the volume has increased from not more than 222 stories per day

(Weaver et al., 1985, 83) to millions of words per day (see Table 1). According to its own website (www.ap.org 2002) the Associated Press supplies 20 million words a day to its domestic members and foreign subscribers. Secondly, agency print news is increasingly accessed on-line and 'on-demand,' by both individual and institutional clients or readers, so that what constitutes an 'agency wire' (to use an older vocabulary) is no longer as clear as it once was. Agencies have greater scope for controlling the volume and range of news that is made available to individual clients. This volume includes both news that has come on-line within the current news-cycle as well as news stories from earlier periods. Thirdly, there has been a qualitative shift in media and communications studies, so that today there is less sympathetic interest in 'counting content' exercises that fail to address the semiotic complexity of processes by which texts are structured to make meaning and by which actual audiences make sense of texts. Thus the methods and theoretical premises of earlier news flow studies have come under more critical scrutiny. Fourthly, international news agencies have largely ceased to serve a political agenda as an object of study. From the mid-1970s to mid-1980s, when international news

Table 1: The Biggest News Agencies

Agency	Subscribers	Bureaux	Employees	Countries	Budget	Words per Day
AP	15000	236	3374	112	418M US$	20M
AFP	12500	95	2000	165	235M US$	1M
UPI	2000	57	300	75	24M US$	–
Reuters	54000	212	14600	158	5B US$	1M
DPA	2500	107	1886	75	136M US$	335000
Ansa	957	109	854	60	113M US$	300000
EFE	1235	77	1000	70	8,5M US$	500000

Source: Patrick White (1997) Le Village CNN. La crise de agences presse. Montreal: les Presses de l'université de Montreal.

agencies attracted unaccustomed attention, they did so because they were considered by many to be an exemplary case of the contribution of western media to processes of neo-imperialism. But the New World Information and Communication Order (NWICO) debate buckled under the impact of a largely successful neo-liberal counter-attack. Since that time the international news agencies have been less likely to be perceived as major players in the global media market. The development of international satellite television news services such as those of AOL Time Warner's CNN, BBC World or News Corp's BSkyB, though they may make generous use of wholesale news video provided by Reuters Television News or Associated Press Television (dominating the international television news wholesale market as they do the print market) and the Internet publicly eclipse the role of news agencies. The sales of multimedia corporations such as AOL Time Warner, Disney, or News Corporation far exceed even those of Reuters, the leading news agency in terms of profits (a relatively modest £3,885 million ($6.5 billion), in 2001 (aboutreuters.com, 2001). In October 2002, Reuters' shares fell more than 23 per cent to 160p ($2.70) after it cut revenue forecasts for the second half of 2002 and the first half of the next year (Burt, 2002).

A relatively outdated and not a comprehensive study on news agencies comes from the 1995 Foreign News Flow Study Project (Pietiläinen, 1998, 72). This study indicated that news agencies are still a significant, if not dominant, source of foreign news for media organisations. Their share among sources of foreign news is relatively modest in developed parts of the world such as the United States or Western Europe, where it is less than 30 per cent. But in other areas, news agencies deliver over 40 per cent of foreign news, and the percentage is much higher in the case of Africa where it reaches 75 per cent. (see Table 2). The data, however, are open to question. They show only the percentages of news sources that have actually been identified as news agencies in the text; therefore they are almost certainly an underestimate. We do not know the extent to which samples were weighted to include small

Table 2: The Most Important Source in Foreign News (only when the source was mentioned) in 1995

	Own Journalist	News Agencies in general	National News Agency	Reuters	AFP	AP	Other Source
USA (887)	50	14	0	8	0	9	18
Latin America (2256)	25	3	10	13	10	11	28
Western Europe (16967)	49	3	10	6	5	4	24
Eastern Europe (4828)	42	18	15	10	2	4	10
Far East (3528)	32	4	5	17	17	10	15
Africa (2333)	20	5	33	13	24	1	6
Asia (6608)	45	6	10	18	8	6	9

Source: Pietiläinen 1998, 72.

and middle-sized media, often the biggest users of news agencies. For example, most small and medium-sized newspapers in the United States depend primarily on Associated Press (Hess, 1996). Nor did the study take account of the importance of news agencies such as Reuters or Bloomberg as sources of financial news for financial markets, or the importance to television news broadcasters worldwide of the television news agencies, Reuters Television and Associated Press Television. Compared to the results of some earlier studies, however, the salience of news agencies as news sources may have diminished. Studies by Kayser (1953) and IPI (1953) showed that news agencies were then by far the major sources of foreign news for newspapers. In a 1985 study (Sreberny-Mohammadi et al., 1985, 50) news agencies delivered form 20 to 50 per cent of foreign news published by newspapers. Weaver et al. (1985) found news agencies' share of published foreign news to average 41 per cent rising to as much as 70 per cent in Asia. But this latter study, like that of Pietiläinen in 1995, was limited in as much as it focused only on agency sources that were actually identified as such in the news texts. Actual use is almost certainly much higher.

News agencies also serve important secondary functions. They alert leading retail news organisations to breaking news stories across the globe (notably in locations in which retail news media do not have local representation). They act as trusted sources of corroboration on which retail media may depend before going public with information for which there is otherwise only a single source (Boyd-Barrett, 1977). The 1995 data for media-rich continents, suggesting a fall-off in the use of agencies, may reflect an increase in the range of alternative news sources that are available, including both older 'supplemental' sources such as the New York Times News Service, and the emergence of international television broadcasters like CNN, and of on-line news providers such as MNBC. The Internet affords greater ease of access to the national news media of any country, and this may be sufficient for some smaller retail media. The Pietiläinen table does indicate that the three major international news agencies, Reuters, AFP and AP, still dominate the international news flow. It also reveals significant differences in the use of these agencies by retail media. It is Reuters that dominates as a source of foreign news across four continents, sometimes even exceeding the copy that is sourced to national news agencies in retail media.

Issues of news agency coverage were never simply to do with volume of use and other indicators of the quantitative significance of agencies as news sources. More fundamentally they had to do with issues of balance: balance between different countries and parts of the world, different sources and different topics. Inevitably, Western agency services were found to be very imbalanced, giving content preference to the region to which a given news wire was directed and then to the news of the United States and Western Europe; giving greatest weight to political, economic, and military news, news of international affairs and international sports. These imbalances were also reflected in agency deployment of resources and person-power. Official and elite news sources accounted for high proportions of all news provided.

Recent studies of television news agencies, including APTV (Paterson, 1998; Clare, 1998) suggest that these imbalances persist in the era of international television news agencies, only in a more intensive way. They show that these services demonstrate a strong emphasis on politics and conflict, on the First World, and a tendency for the emphasis on violence and conflict to be exacerbated in the case of Third World coverage. Clare's study of APTV found that only 8 per cent of APTV stories disseminated from London were contextualising features and backgrounders, 19 per cent were soft news features and 73 per cent were hard news. Europe accounted for 28.1 per cent of stories, the US for 22.9 per cent, Asia for 18.9 per cent, with other world regions trailing behind. International relations was the most common topic (29.1 per cent) followed by internal politics (25.6 per cent); these two categories together accounted for well over half of all stories. The next most important categories were culture and art (8.8 per cent) and internal law and order (7.7 per cent). Clare also identified an overwhelming reliance on government sources. Private citizens were second only to governments in his research, featuring as vox pop (brief comments from members of the public), giving opinions, or as demonstrators. Stories from elite nations outnumbered non-elite nations by more than two to one. Furthermore, items from non-elite areas such as Africa, parts of Asia, the poorer countries of the Balkans and the former Soviet Bloc nearly all concerned conflict, violence, and disasters. Only among the non-elite countries of Latin America was there a balance of hard and soft news and items other than conflict. He concluded:

> Elite nations are portrayed as having strong leaders constantly flying around the globe trying to broker peace deals and further the cause of international brotherhood. Their citizens, meanwhile, appear to be able to choose from a number of cultural pursuits, supported by stable business and innovative technology, while being allowed to make peaceful protests about important matters. Non-elite nations, in contrast, appear to be constantly embroiled in, or on the point of, violent conflict, either within or across their borders, while at risk from natural disasters. They have crisis-hit governments, untrustworthy leaders, volatile populations and when they do have elections, they do not meet the democratic standards of the west and are characterised by vote-rigging and violence (Clare, 1998, pp.62-63).

News Agencies in Crisis

In our recent work on news agency markets (Boyd-Barrett and Rantanen, 2000a, 2002; Boyd-Barrett, 2001) we have talked about the current crisis of news agencies, a crisis that is reflected in growing uncertainty among agencies, their sponsors and clients about the proper function of news agencies, the extent and nature of their influence, and what should and can be their role for the future. We have identified major challenges that face both international and national agencies and which influence their interrelationship. In summary, these are:

1 The reduction in the number of international press news agencies, with the diminution in the roles of United Press International and Telegrafnoye Agnetstvo Sovietskogo Snyuza (TASS), respectively, as global news agencies. (In 2000 UPI was sold to News World Communications, owner of *The Washington Times* and closely associated with the Reverend Sun Myong Moon) and the reduction in number of international television agencies to only two world leaders, Reuters Television and APTV, both closely associated with their print counterparts. This reduction is scarcely compensated for by the growth of financial and commodity news services (notably the appearance of Bloomberg and Bridge News; parts of Bridge were acquired by Reuters in 2001).

2 The supply of international news services is today much less susceptible to control within national markets where, previously, agreements between international and national news agencies gave many national agencies exclusive rights of access to the services of the international agencies in return for the exclusive feed of national agency news to the international agencies. The collapse of such arrangements is an outcome of political liberalisation (as in Central and Eastern Europe), and of economic liberalisation worldwide (which has made monopoly practices on domestic markets more difficult to sustain). It is also partly an outcome of technological innovation, including global satellite television and the Internet, which diversify sources of information (and increase the number of channels through which it is possible to access the same sources).

3 Processes of globalisation have undermined the very separation of 'national' and 'international' while regional entities (including EU, ASEAN, CIS, NAFTA, GCC, etc) and ethnic and linguistic categories of division (eg Chinese, Hindi, Hispanic, Islamic) have become more important. The shape and texture of the 'news net' (Tuchman, 1978) is undergoing transformation, and traditional structures of newsgathering may not have adjusted quickly enough.

4 Among many media-owned national news agencies relations between owners and managers are strained: managers typically want their news agencies to exploit new technologies to reach new markets, and to target clients directly rather than serving them exclusively through the channels of their retail 'owner-media' patrons. Owners, on the other hand, are tempted to intervene to prevent agencies from competing against them, and sometimes even to restrict the dissemination of news agency services to a broader range of media and non-media clients. Even among agencies that are not media-owned, media clients are concerned when they see agencies disseminate news or related services directly to online clients without channelling such services through 'retail' media.

5 In the case of State-owned agencies, relations between managers and State owners have deteriorated as governments reduce their financial support yet often continue to exert political influence or control over agency content, simultaneously undermining the financial basis of agency operation, and

making it difficult for such agencies to earn credibility as independent and impartial news sources on domestic and international news markets (Rantanen, 1998). Increasingly diverse attempts to reconcile State and market interests may be critical to the longer-term viability of State-owned agencies.

International News Agencies

Western agencies' financial circumstances have changed substantially, affecting, as we have seen, the rank order and status of the former 'Big Four' (the British Reuters, the French AFP, and AP and UPI of the United States), which now looks more like the 'Big Three.' After the collapse of Communism, the former TASS, official agency of the Soviet Union, lost its status as a 'Communist world agency' and under the new title of ITAR-TASS is now more of a national and regional agency. New players such as CNN and BBC World have penetrated the news agency field, in as much as they sell television news film to local broadcasters or make it available in exchange for local film; in addition they are *de facto* free news sources for any news organisations that care to monitor their direct broadcasts, especially for breaking news. The financial news market has experienced considerable activity since the 1990s, notably with the rise of Bloomberg and Bridge (both of which earn most of their revenues in the United States), but Reuters continues to be the market leader.

It is difficult to estimate the changing influence of different international agencies solely on the basis of the volume and usage of their services, as has been attempted previously (Weaver et al., 1985), since such quantitative studies are now less available. What we have is the data on size, wealth, clients and profits provided by the agencies themselves. As Table 1 demonstrates, Reuters is number one in almost all these respects. Compared to most national agencies (with the limited exceptions of the German DPA and the Spanish EFE) Reuters has a far greater international presence. Reuters also ranks significantly above other international agencies along many criteria, most notably revenue, profit, research and development. Several factors help explain Reuters' relative success (cutbacks in the 2001 recession notwithstanding). Reuters was a global company from its inception in 1851 and never operated as a 'national agency' in the same sense that the Press Association (UK) or ANA (Greece) are national agencies, with a commitment to local news provision for provincial media (often a financial drain). From some time after World War II Reuters distanced itself from its 'British-ness' (Boyd-Barrett and Rantanen, 2000b), whereas AP and AFP, which are the dominant national agencies of their respective countries, have less motivation, inspiration or ability to leave behind their national identities in international markets. In this sense, Reuters preceded many giant media companies that operate at a global level, from the 1960s beginning a more concerted attempt to customise news services for local consumption. By the late 1980s its staff was drawn from 160 nationalities. As early as 1977, Reuters was earning almost four times as much as AP or UPI in non-domestic revenue (Read, 1999, 477). Reuters has secured its financial base by becoming independent of media. An overwhelming majority (approximately

95 per cent in 2000) of its revenues derive from financial news for non-media clients - mostly stockbrokers, banks, money market and commodity dealers. In 2001 Reuterspace, a division of Reuters that encompasses traditional media sales, and which also incorporates a range of quite different activities such as the coordination of investments in new technology ventures, accounted for a modest $352 million or 7 per cent of total earnings.

Unlike other agencies, international and national, Reuters does not have to compete with its own clients on the domestic market when seeking out fresh sources of revenue. If it wished, it could ignore the traditional media market, since its revenues are secured elsewhere, but independent news provision helps underwrite its brand identity, and is valued by non-media clients. Reuters has been one of the leading agencies in adopting advanced information and communications technology. It adopted computerised distribution of information from the early 1970s, well in advance of the British national press; it has invested far more in research and development than any other agency. Reuters spent $414 million on research and development in the year 2000, and expected to spend $725 million on technology transformation (particularly the conversion to Internet delivery) in the period 2000-2004. It is now moving from a proprietary system toward an all-Internet model (Boyd-Barrett, 2001, Boyd-Barrett and Rantanen, 2002, and Lowry, 2001, for a full discussion of the implications of the Internet for news agencies).

However, this business model that seemed to work so successfully faced significant challenge early in the new millennium. Bloomberg increased its share of revenues from 19.9 per cent to 38 per cent of the $6.7 billion global market data sector between 1997 and 2001. During the same period, the combined share of Reuters and Bridge rose from 44 per cent to 46 per cent. Bloomberg expanded its client base of trading and investment terminals from 163,400 to 171,000 in 2002, while Reuters faced a decline from 315,000 to 300,000 terminals, possibly moving lower for 2003. This was the combined outcome of highly competitive pricing by Bloomberg and global recessionary factors that hit many of Reuters' traditional institutional clients. Reuters employed some 16,000 people worldwide (albeit in a climate of significant staffing cut-backs, 2001-2002), but still double Bloomberg's estimated 8000-strong payroll. While Reuters boasted more than 1000 products with different prices, Bloomberg sold one product at one price worldwide (Inside Market Data Reference, 2002; Grande, 2000).

AP has experienced an intensifying financial struggle, although it is difficult to know how seriously to assess this in view of the agency's not-for-profit status and the absence of public information (itself a worrying paradox in view of AP's almost complete dominance of the United States market). Although benefiting from the decline of UPI, AP has encountered growing competition from Reuters overseas, even from AFP (especially in Asia) and EFE (in Latin America), and has continued to encounter competition, at least on international markets, from newspaper syndicated services such as the *New York*

Times or *Los Angeles Times* (these are generally secondary subscriptions for US media taken out as additions to AP memberships or subscriptions), as well as from the news websites of major retail print and broadcast media. As the oldest co-operative agency in the world, establishing a model that inspired the organisation of numerous other agencies, AP now faces the same difficulties as they do in brokering the tension between owner and manager interests. By 1994, 94 per cent of the US newspapers were subscriber-members of the AP service, while only 11 per cent took UPI (White 1998, 51). Today, AP serves 5,000 radio and television stations and 1,700 newspapers in the United States. In addition, it has 8,500 newspaper, radio and television subscribers in 121 countries overseas. The AP is owned by its 1,550 US daily newspaper members. They elect a board of directors that directs the co-operative.

UPI has relinquished its aim to remain an international agency and provide a full-scale service. In 1999, the AP acquired United Press International's broadcast news customer contracts which serve more than 400 radio and television stations in the United States. Today, UPI Newswire provides 300 news stories per day. They mainly focus on the latest in science and technology, as well as business, national and international analysis. UPI Newsphotos produces about 150 photos a day (its international photo service was sold to Reuters in the 1980s).

UPI's quondam status as third member of the big league is now filled by the French AFP. AFP lags behind the AP (and of course Reuters) in every way except in the number of countries which it serves, due largely to its connections with what was once francophone Africa and the Middle East. AFP produces each day 400,000-600,000 words in text, 700 photos and 50 news graphics. AFP's worldwide network takes in 165 countries, of which 110 are home to bureaus, and 50 are covered by local correspondents. Although it continues to depend heavily on subscriptions from the French State (accounting for over 40 per cent of revenue and 46 per cent of clients) this is a reduction from over 60 per cent dependence on the State for revenue in the 1970s. The AFP faces the same problems as many national co-operative agencies: its media clients, also represented on its governing board, are reluctant to accept increases in the subscription fees that are necessary for continued investment in technology, new services and competitiveness. The French government has been reluctant to advance the cash thought necessary for complete technology transformation.

The one-time fifth member of the 'Big League' – although it never achieved a similar position to its Western counterparts (and often provided its service free of charge) – was the Soviet TASS. As mentioned earlier, since the collapse of Communism and the disintegration of the Soviet Union, TASS has become ITAR-TASS, the State-owned agency of the Russian Federation. It has been forced to reduce staff substantially. Currently, it has 74 bureaus and offices in Russia and in other CIS countries, and 65 bureaux in 62 foreign countries. Its authority as news source in Central and Eastern Europe has largely disappeared (Rantanen, 2002).

Hence there has been a significant change in the number and ranking of the international agencies. While Reuters has strengthened its position, being now very much in its own league, other agencies are struggling. The biggest national agencies such as the German Deutsche Presse-Agentur Gmbh (DPA), the Spanish Agencia EFE (EFE) and the Italian Agenzia Nazionale Stampa Associata (ANSA) continue to operate some international services, notably in South America and the developing world. For example, EFE claims that it sources 30 per cent of all the international news published in Central and South America. But these services are less comprehensive, their international services less well resourced than the services of the international agencies, and their revenues barely cover their costs, if at all.

National Agencies

By the year 2000, many national news agencies throughout the world experienced increasing difficulty. The industry as a whole might be said to have entered a period of significant crisis likely to transform the nature of wholesale news-gathering and distribution as it had operated for the previous 170 years. This was especially apparent in the developing world, in Central and Eastern Europe, and also in parts of the developed world. For example, some Scandinavian news agencies, operating in one of the richest media markets in the world, encountered serious financial problems, and the Swedish agency in 1999 even ceased to be a co-operative. Figures compiled by the Austrian Press Agency (APA) in 1999, on behalf of European Alliance of Press Agencies, for the first time compared key economic data of the news agencies of the EU countries (including Switzerland and Norway) and showed they enjoyed an exceptionally modest average annual revenue of €16.5 million ($19.4 million). These figures may not in all cases take account of 'daughter' companies entrusted with more entrepreneurial activity. (Note that later indications, monitored by Rantanen and Boyd-Barrett, 2002, suggest that European agencies generally had weathered the crisis better than had been expected). Those agencies that were significantly above the average tended to have sizable and wealthy markets and also, with the exception of the PA (UK), had significant international operations. The largest was AFP (France), more usually thought of as the third major international press agency, with a turnover of €195 million ($228 million). This was followed, some way behind, by DPA (Germany) at €99.8 million ($116.9 million), ANSA (Italy) at €91.6 million ($107.3 million), the PA (UK) at €87 million ($102 million), and EFE (Spain) at €70.6 million ($82.7 million). The smallest EAPA agency was ANA (Greece) at €6.6 million ($7.7 million). Average turnover per employee was €85,800 ($100,500).

Among agencies with highest turnover per employee, APA ranked number one with 127,660, followed by DPA at 108,640, NTB (Norway) at 103,500 and ANP (Netherlands) at 100,570. Turnover-yield (profit-turnover ratio) was low, with an average of 1 per cent, highs of 9 per cent (STT/FNB of Finland), 5 per cent (PA), 4 per cent (APA, ANA) and lows of 0 per cent (AFP, ANSA, EFE, NTB).

Before-tax profit averaged 0.15m Euro, with a high of 4.3m for the PA, followed by DPA (1.8m) and APA (0.97m). Lows of 0 per cent were recorded for AFP, ANSA, EFE, NTB. Average cash flow was 0.60m Euro, with highs for AFP (13.87m), the PA (9m) and DPA (7.55m), and lows of 0 per cent for ANSA, TT of Sweden, ANA. Cash flow-yield (cash flow-turnover ratio) averaged 4 per cent, with highs of 13 per cent for APA, 11 per cent for STT/FNB, 10 per cent for the PA and 9 per cent for DPA. Lows of 0 per cent were recorded for LUSA, ANSA, TT, ANA, EFE (Vyslozil, 1999).

Over-dependence on media markets is a key problem, especially for co-operative agencies. Tesselaar (1999) identified three major conflicts of interest between owner-clients and their agencies. These were: (1) the desire of owners for a closed circle of clients, in contrast with agencies' wish to stimulate an increase in client numbers; (2) the owners' preference to maintain ownership in the hands of traditional publishers, against the agencies' wish to extend ownership to all media; (3) the owners' interest in a 'business-to-business' operation as opposed to the managers' goal of a 'business-to-customer' orientation.

The situation in Central and Eastern Europe reveals the difficulties that the formerly state-owned and fully state-subsidised agencies face in a newly competitive environment in which the State is eager to maintain control but wants to reduce substantially the amount of subsidy. Co-ownership of a national agency is rare in the CEE; instead most agencies have remained in State ownership. Although there have been attempts to establish news agencies that are controlled by the Parliament (for example, in the Czech Republic, Hungary and Poland) instead of by the Government, many governments still want to maintain political influence over the agencies while reluctant to bail them financially. National agencies in Central and Eastern Europe have been forced to cut down their expenses, services and staff numbers (Rantanen, 1998). They are vulnerable, and in danger of becoming mere mouthpieces for their respective Governments simply because they cannot find other sources of revenues. International agencies have found it advantageous to sell directly to retail media and other clients in such national markets, where once they distributed indirectly through national agencies, often under compulsion from government. Now that the national news agencies' domestic monopoly is gone, there is less incentive for international agencies to use national agencies as intermediaries between themselves and retail media clients. National agencies become increasingly dependent on the more modest revenues which small and local media provide; yet these, in turn, increasingly belong to larger chains which may decide they have the resources to gather their own news of the capital city and other important news locations. Simultaneously, international news agencies, especially Reuters, have 'vacuumed' the financial news market to the extent that there is very little space for national agencies to expand. Most of them have chosen partnership with Reuters rather than competition.

News agencies in developing countries share some of the problems as their counterparts in CEE. For example, SHIHATA, the Tanzanian news agency, had practically ceased operations in 1996 (and was soon to close down completely). Reuters had interrupted its services because of unpaid fees; only one telephone was in operation, and there were none functioning in the regional bureaux; fax and telex lines were also cut (Kivikuru, 1998, 142). Many of their problems relate to a collapse in confidence in the desirability of State support for news agencies, a trend which has undermined agencies that had hitherto relied heavily on such support. Even intergovernmental or NGO support for such ventures has declined in the wake of the end of the Cold War. The combined forces of deregulation, commercialisation of media operations, and democratic forms of government have weakened enthusiasm for State protection of news agencies. As a result, national news agencies in developing countries face serious difficulties.

Conclusion

Since the 1985 International News study (Sreberny-Mohammadi et al, 1985), considerable changes have taken place both among international and national agencies and in their interrelationship. Together, international and national agencies had formed a nexus based largely on the exclusive exchange of news services, an arrangement that has structured the international news system since the 19th century. Current trends may have undermined the symbiotic relationship between national and international agencies, and in order to understand the nature of the transformations which are now occurring, it is important that research monitors both international and national agencies, as well as the rise of new global news media.

Although it is too early to gauge the consequences for news agencies of the crisis of September 11, 2001, it is not unreasonable to expect that the 'war on terrorism' will actually provoke processes of polarisation and fragmentation among mainstream news media of different countries and between mainstream and alternative news media within national markets. This might engender new markets for alternative news agencies, especially those that distribute by means of the Internet, thus exacerbating the competition experienced by established national news agencies in many parts of the world.

News agencies deserve scholarly attention not simply because they are agents of construction of what we have come to understand as the domains of the 'national' and of the 'international'– now somewhat limited concepts – but more practically, because there are grounds for considering that what agencies do and how they do it are important for the survival of a 'public sphere' of democratic dialogue, and also for global as well as for national and regional security. This is because agencies generally serve large numbers of clientele which differ in philosophy, technology, market ambition, wealth, geographical location and so on. In many countries it is they alone that have the resources and the motivation to sustain a nationwide, if not regional or global, structure of news-gathering, and it is often they alone that can best claim 'inclusiveness' in terms of national coverage, so that one may say of them that they are the informational backbone, or at least a significant contributor to such a backbone, which public debate takes for granted and on which it is based. Though not all agencies may perform this function brilliantly, the function emerges from an ideology of operation, mission or purpose, what you will, that has been historically moulded over 170 years, thus demonstrating a robust and perhaps surprising durability.

Agencies were the oldest electronic media, contributing to processes of globalisation from the mid-19th century. They started to transmit news from every corner of the globe with the speed of the telegraph, and thus they contributed to the compression of time and space that is the hallmark of globalisation. Today, we need to assess how news agencies contribute to and are affected by the current phase of globalisation, one in which the intense commodification of information is an outstanding feature. Forces of commercialisation and concentration have significantly corrupted the usefulness of many retail news media for the construction of a public sphere of knowledge and dialogue about global, regional and even national issues. Leading news agencies, whatever their faults, have been relatively protected up until now from the ferocity of these sources. It is very much in the public interest, in the interests of vital democratic debate, and of national and global security, that the informational spaces which news agencies have constructed should be preserved and indeed protected and nurtured.

However, news agencies themselves need to change and establish new business models (see Boyd-Barrett, 2001 for a more extended discussion). Some of them have successfully adapted to the era of the Internet, others find it a threat they find hard to cope with. The Internet, together with CNN and satellite channels, poses a real threat to the traditional role of news agencies as wholesalers that only reach their audience through other media. Agencies such as Reuters find the traditional division of the wholesale-retail dichotomy outdated, since they increasingly reach their customers directly and in their own languages (Reuters delivers its news in 23 languages), even if the principal sources of revenue continue to be for subscription services. Currently, 73 million people view Reuters news on the Internet every month. Although the figure is still low compared to the number reached by retail clients, it demonstrates an emerging trend (Rowley, 2001). Those who will be able to invest in technology will follow. Those who cannot will be fighting for their survival in the rapidly changing media global media environment.

References

Associated Press (2002), www.ap.org.

Boyd-Barrett, O. (2001) *Final Report of the Workshop on News Agencies in the Era of the Internet.* Paris: UNESCO.

Boyd-Barrett, O. (2000) 'Constructing the Global, Constructing the Local:

News Agencies Re-Present the World,' in Kavoori, A. and A.(eds), *The Global Dynamics of News: Studies in International News Coverage and News Agenda.* Connecticut: Ablex Publishing Corporation.

Boyd-Barrett, O. (1980) *The International News Agencies.* London: Constable.

Boyd-Barrett, O. (1977) 'The Collection of Foreign News in the National Press Organisation and Resources', in Boyd-Barrett, O., C. Seymour-Ure and J. Tunstall (eds), *Studies on the Press.* London: HMSO.

Boyd-Barrett, O. and T. Rantanen (2002) 'Global and National News Agencies: Opportunities and Threats in the Age of the Internet', in Briggs A. and P. Cobley (eds) *The Media: An Introduction, 2nd Edition.* London: Pearson Education.

Boyd-Barrett, O. and T. Rantanen (2000a) 'European National News Agencies: the End of an Era or a New Beginning?', *Journalism,* 1(1):86-105.

Boyd-Barrett, O. and T. Rantanen (2000b) 'News Agency Foreign Correspondents', in Tunstall, J. (ed.) *Media Occupations and Professions: A Reader.* Oxford: Oxford University Press.

Burt, T. (2002, October 17). 'Reuters sales warning spurs further cuts. Electronic information group warns of radical measures after drop in demand from financial services sector', *Financial Times.*

Clare, J. (1998) *Town Criers in the Global Village,* MA Thesis, University of Leicester: UK.

Gerbner, G. and G. Marvanyi (1992) 'The Many Worlds of the World's Press', *Journal of Communication* 27(1): 52-66.

Grande, C. (2000, October 17) 'With key customers in financial centres cutting costs, and rival Bloomberg stealing market share, chief executive Tom Glocer faces a deadline to deliver', *Financial Times.*

Hess, S. (1996) *International News and Foreign Correspondents.* Washington DC: Brookings Institution Press.

International Press Institute (1953) *The Flow of News.* Zurich: IPI.

Kayser, J. (1953) *One Week's News. Comparative Study of 17 Major Dailies for a Seven-Day Period.* Paris: Unesco.

Kivikuru, U. (1998) 'From State Socialism to Deregulation', in Boyd-Barrett, O. and T. Rantanen (eds) *The Globalization of News.* London: Sage.

Lowry, T. (2001, April 23) 'The Bloomberg Machine', *Business Week.*

Paterson, C. (1998) 'Global Battlefields', in Boyd-Barrett, O. and T. Rantanen (eds.) *The Globalization of News.* London: Sage.

Pietiläinen, J. (1998) 'Uutivirtojen maailma (The World of News Flows)', in Kivikuru, U. and J. Pietiläinen (eds.) *Uutisia yli rajojen. Ulkomaanuutisten maisena*

Suomessa (*News Across Borders. The Landscape of Foreign News in Finland*). Tampere: Helsingin yliopiston Lahden tutkimus- ja koulutuskeskus.

Rantanen, T (1998) 'From Communism to Capitalism', in Boyd-Barrett, O. and T. Rantanen (eds) *The Globalization of News*. London: Sage.

Rantanen, T. (2002) *The Global and the National. Media and Communications in Post-Communist Russia*. Boulder: Rowman & Littlefield.

Rantanen, T. and O. Boyd-Barrett (2002). 'State news agencies: Time for a re-evaluation', in Dorfler, E. and Pensold (eds) *The Various Faces of Reality*. Vienna: Innsbrucker Studienverlag.

Read, D. (1999) *The Power of News. The History of Reuters*. Oxford: Oxford University Press.

Reuters (2001) www.aboutreuters.com.

Rowley, R. (2001) 'New markets, new audiences', http://about.reuters.com/in vestormedia/home/anpresentations.asp.

Schramm, W. (1960) *One Day in the World's Press: Fourteen Great Newspapers on a Day of Crisis*, Stanford: Stanford University.

Sreberny-Mohammadi, A., et al. (1985) *Foreign News in the Media. International Reporting in 29 countries: Final Report of the 'Foreign Images' Study Undertaken for Unesco by the IAMCR*. Paris: Unesco.

Tesselaar, P. (1999) 'Private News Agencies and Ownership Conflicts', paper presented at the Annual Seminar of the European Alliance of Press Agencies: Athens.

Tuchman, G. (1978) *Making News: A Study in the Construction of Reality*. New York: Free Press.

Vyslozil, W. (1998) 'EU-News Agencies: comparative figures', paper presented at the Annual Seminar of the European Alliance of Press Agencies: Athens.

Weaver, D., et al (1985) 'The News of the World in Four Major Wire Services. A Study of Selected Services of the AP, UPI, Reuters, and AFP', in Sreberny-Mohammadi, A., et al. (eds) *Foreign News in the Media. International Reporting in 29 countries: Final Report of the 'Foreign Images' Study Undertaken for Unesco by the IAMCR*. Paris: Unesco.

White, P. (1998) *Le Village CNN: La Crise des Agences de Presse*. Montreal: Les Presses de l'Université de Montreal.

Interviews

Geert Linnebank, Editor-in-Chief, Reuters, 2001, July 20.

Chapter 2
Media Plenty and the Poverty of News

Daya Kishan Thussu

Journalist turned academic Daya Thussu draws from a long experience of working for major media of the global South. Here he details the disturbing disconnection between an ever expanding Northern media universe and the lack of useful information sources for (or about) the majority of human beings who live in the developing – mostly Southern hemisphere – world. The longstanding lacuna in coverage of the South by the dominant conglomerate-owned news services of the US and UK is all the more worthy of deliberation as the overall information gap between North and South grows and defies attempts at containment. As the South is increasingly presented to international news audiences as mysterious, threatening and manageable only by force, the poverty of news that Thussu illuminates becomes a more urgent threat to a peaceful world order than it has ever been.

This chapter aims to explore the apparent paradox between the proliferation of news and current affairs television channels and the decline in the quality and quantity of foreign news, especially about and from the developing world. Despite 24-hour television news and on-line journalism and a small but significant contra-flow in news from the South to the North, it is argued that issues concerning the world's poor are being increasingly marginalised as a softer, lifestyle variety of reporting appears to dominate global television news agendas. Recent studies in the United States and in Britain indicate a decline in foreign news: in the 1990s, the three major US networks more than halved their foreign coverage, and overseas current affairs programming on Britain's terrestrial television channels decreased substantially in the past decade (Utley, 1997; Barnett and Seymour, 1999; Stone, 2000).

In the market-driven broadcasting environment characterised by increasingly vicious battles for ratings, even the more liberal television networks have had to reorient their editorial priorities, with news about developing countries being one of the first casualties (unless it concerns 'humanitarian' interventions). The chapter examines the implications of this for television news in and about the developing world, at a time when news headlines increasingly cover Southern countries in relation to international terrorism, ethnic conflict, religious 'fundamentalism', immigration or the proliferation of weapons of mass destruction.

The Era of Media Plenty

It is a truism to suggest that we live in an era of media plenty. With digital broadcasting and on-line journalism, there are more news and information outlets available than ever before. The deregulation of broadcasting, coupled with the privatisation of satellite networks, has ensured that a range of dedicated news and current affairs channels are operating internationally, some catering to regional geo-linguistic demographic groups, others reaching a global audience. As well as the proliferation of news and current affairs television channels, the Internet has opened up new windows for international information.

It is television – the most global of the media and the one that transcends language and literacy barriers – that has experienced the greatest degree of change. That the image carries much more influence in shaping public opinion than words is well established. Even in media-saturated cultures such as the United States, television news is seen as 'authoritative' and therefore trustworthy. It has been argued that 'because of its wide reach and high credibility' television news has the potential to profoundly shape public opinion (Iyengar and Kinder, 1987: 1).

The global television news-scape changed in a fundamental manner with CNN's live 24-hour coverage of the US bombing of Iraq during the 1991 Gulf War, making it the world's first 'real-time' war (Flournoy and Stewart, 1997; Volkmer, 1999). There is little doubt that CNN, which calls itself 'the world's news leader,' established the importance of a global round-the-clock TV news network (Hachten, 1999). CNN claims to be the only network capable of covering international news instantly: with a network of 150 correspondents in 42 international bureaux and 23 satellites it is able to beam its programmes across the globe, reaching more than one billion people (CNN website). Though global news networks are not known for their financial successes – in many countries they are available on free-to-air platforms – they wield considerable international influence. Partly because the CNN channels are constantly monitored by news organisations worldwide, it has been suggested that the 'CNN-isation' of television news has become a model for expanding 'American news values around the world' (Papathanassopoulos, 1999: 22).

One reflection of this is the growth of CNN's imitators across the world. There are now a number of dedicated news channels available – though many primarily cater to the national or regional audiences, they are available outside their countries of origin. Most notable among them is BBC World, the BBC's 24-hour global news and information channel, until recently part of BBC

Worldwide, the commercial arm of the British Broadcasting Corporation. In 2003 it was available in 173 million homes, in 200 countries and territories worldwide. Another dedicated round-the-clock global news service is MSNBC, a joint venture between the software giant Microsoft and the National Broadcasting Company (NBC). In the US, the news and current affairs departments of the three established networks – ABC (American Broadcasting Corporation), NBC and CBS (Columbia Broadcasting System) – have had to adapt their operations to the 24-hour news cycle, while Fox Network, part of Australian-born US citizen Rupert Murdoch's media empire, has had great success with Fox News, a 24-hour channel blamed by many for the 'tabloidisation' of television news in the US.

Since 1997, the BBC has also operated News 24, an around-the-clock service available only on the digital platform for the UK audience, and Independent Television News has run an all-news ITV News channel since 2000 on the same platform to rival Murdoch's Sky News, available to subscribers in Britain and across Europe. Sky News, the first pan-European commercial news operation, was launched in 1989 and claims to have viewing figures of 80 million in 40 countries. Euronews, a consortium of European public sector broadcasters, is another example of a pan-European news operation, though its influence remains rather limited in terms of its impact on regional or even national news agendas. State broadcasters in both India and China – Doordarshan and China Central Television (CCTV) respectively – also have experimented with dedicated 24-hour news channels, though with limited success. CCTV9, the English-language international channel is available, since 2002, on the Sky platform.

Among the major private around-the-clock channels in operation in Asia are Murdoch's India-based Star News, which started as a bilingual news operation giving hourly news bulletins in English and Hindi (though since April 2003 providing news in Hindi only) and the Hindi-language Zee News, part of Zee network, India's largest multimedia corporation. In Latin America the major news operation is Brazil's Globo News, launched in 1996, and part of TV Globo conglomerate.

In the Arab world, the most significant new actor to emerge, quickly becoming known as the 'CNN of the Arab world' is the Qatar-based Al-Jazeera ('peninsula' in Arabic) television, which has redefined the parameters of broadcast journalism in a region where the airwaves have traditionally been used for what might be called 'dynastic propaganda'. Since its launch in 1996, Al-Jazeera has contributed significantly to democratising television news in the Arab world – taking it out of the closet of ruling dynasties to focus on lives and issues discussed in the bazaars and souks of the Arab world and often covering stories on topics such as human rights, gender-related issues and democracy, which have been traditionally seen as taboo subjects in many Arab societies.

Al-Jazeera acquired international recognition in the wake of the events of September 11, 2001 and their aftermath, being noticed outside its traditional geo-linguistic constituency as the only television network with a live satellite feed from Afghanistan during the US bombings in October-December 2001. International reporting of the US-led 'war against global terror' was considerably influenced by the way this pan-Arabic news network covered the story. This became the channel for an alternative discourse, broadcasting taped audio and video messages from Osama bin Laden and other Al-Qa'ida leaders. Al-Jazeera once again stole the limelight during the 2003 'Operation Iraqi Freedom' by providing a kind of discourse – showing the uglier side of military action, including death and destruction – that the Anglo-American networks were trying to avoid.

Whose News is it Anyway?

One does not have to be a media pundit to suggest that the West, led by the United States, dominates the world's entertainment and information networks. The major global players in most sectors of international media – news agencies, international newspapers and magazines, radio and television channels and programmes, music, book publishing, advertising and films – are mainly Western-based organisations (Boyd-Barrett, 1998; Tunstall and Machin, 1999; Thussu, 2000a). Western domination of the export market for world television programming alone is overwhelming. In 1999 the West accounted for 95 per cent of light entertainment programming; 91 per cent of TV dramas; 90 per cent of movies shown on television screens around the globe; 87 per cent of all films exported; 72 per cent of all children's programmes and 62 per cent of all factual programming. Even within the West, the American connection is well established, the United States alone accounting for 85 per cent of light entertainment exports; 81 per cent of television movies; 72 per cent of drama; 63 per cent of feature films; 60 per cent of children's programmes and 37 per cent of factual television programming (Balnaves *et al*, 2001).

In the area of factual television, the United States, though still the leader, does not have an overwhelming dominance. Britain, with its long tradition of public service broadcasting and leading position, and home to the world's main news agencies and newspapers, has 18 per cent of the global export share. Among non-Western countries, Japan remains a key player in factual television, with its national broadcaster, Nippon Hoso Kyokai (NHK), being a major producer and exporter of documentaries, often of historical, scientific, wildlife, travel and tourism variety rather than political ones.

There is evidence to suggest that Western control and its ability to set the agenda of international news has increased in the post-Cold War era. The globalisation of the US model of commercial television has rekindled debates about global information flows, which in the earlier context of the New World Information and Communication Order (NWICO) in the 1970s and 1980s, were mainly concerned with news agencies (Boyd-Barrett and Thussu, 1992).

As noted, though there are more producers of news images, the global news and information flow between African, Latin American and Asian media, is still mediated, to a large extent, through content provided by Anglo-American news organisations. More than 80 per cent of global news is distributed by just three news agencies – Associated Press (AP), Reuters and Agence France Presse (AFP). AP and Reuters, through their respective television news services – Associated Press Television News (APTN) and Reuters Television – are also providers of news footage to broadcasters worldwide. This can give them immense power to set the global news agenda (Boyd-Barrett and Rantanen, 1998; Tunstall and Machin, 1999; Thussu, 2000a).

Characterising television news as the news 'that matters,' Shanto Iyengar and Donald Kinder, writing in an American context, note: 'because they take part in the grand events of politics so rarely, ordinary Americans must depend upon information and analysis provided by mass media. This dependence gives the media an enormous capacity to shape public thinking' (Iyengar and Kinder, 1987: 2).

In the era of the round-the-clock global news, it is not just the American public whose thinking might be influenced by television imagery. Aware of the power of image diplomacy, the US government has successfully marketed a televised version of its post-Cold War foreign policy to international publics. Evidence of this can be found as much in the Bush (senior) administration's attempts to 'sell the war' during the 1990-91 Gulf crisis, as in the subsequent 'humanitarian interventions' – in Somalia (1992), Kosovo (1999), Afghanistan (2001) and Iraq (2003) – to name the most prominent examples.

The dominant news coverage can create a false debate: for example, the NATO 1999 bombing of Yugoslavia was presented on international television news as in fulfilment of humanitarian ideals of the West, while the fundamental change in the nature of NATO – from a defence alliance to an offensive peace-enforcing organisation, intervening in a region outside the remit of the North Atlantic alliance – was largely ignored (Thussu, 2000b). An emboldened NATO has since taken over the role of the global policeman – operating from Afghanistan to the Balkans and beyond.

The geo-political angle was largely missing from the television news coverage of the 2001 'war against terrorism' – and, some would say, the real story behind US military involvement in Afghanistan. Despite presenting their intervention as a humanitarian move to liberate the Afghan people (particularly women) from an oppressive regime, which it undoubtedly was, it is unlikely to have been a sufficient reason. That the US-based energy corporations are keen to build oil and gas pipelines from Turkmenistan through Afghanistan is well documented (Rashid, 2001). A recent report points out that 'Afghanistan's significance from an energy standpoint stems from its geographical position as a potential transit route for oil and natural gas exports from central Asia to the Arabian sea. This potential includes the possible construction of oil and natural gas export pipelines through Afghanistan' (Monbiot, 2001: 19). Similarly, one has to be extremely naïve politically to believe the official line – parroted on television screens 24/7 – that the 'regime change' in Baghdad was inspired by democratic ideals rather than the desire to take control of the world's second largest reserves of oil.

Apart from mainstream political news, the South also remains heavily dependent on US-led Western information sources, such as CNBC, Bloomberg CNN, for financial news, on crucial issues as foreign exchange trading and commodity prices. Unbiased information on such critical sectors of the economy – many developing economies continue to produce primary material for industrial nations – can be hard to get. They are also at a disadvantage by not having access to the latest financial data, essential in a globalised electronic economy.

With globalisation of economies and growing significance of electronic commerce, issues concerning financial security have acquired a new urgency. It is now being recognised that economic intelligence on international trade can be manipulated through faulty analysis or misinterpretation of commercial data. 'Much of the sea of information on which modern markets float is polluted with *misinformation*,' wrote one US observer (Rothkopf, 1999: 95). Obviously, the economies of the developing countries are those most vulnerable to such misinformation.

The Disappearing South

The growth in the number of media outlets has the potential for democratising newsflow, but in 'the murderously competitive environment,' as one commentator has noted, the 'deluge of new information' is 'in many ways an illusion' (Bird, 2000: 226). What appears to be happening instead is a homogenisation of news content. There seems to be an increasing tendency to cover visually arresting but 'soft' stories: the phrase 'lifestyle journalism' encompasses this trend. Even the more liberal media organisations seem to have reoriented their editorial priorities, with news from and about the global South being one of the first casualties. The British liberal daily, the *Guardian*, for example, no longer publishes its Third World Page and weekly Environment Guardian supplement – and has more pages for lifestyle features.

The fate of television series such as *Bandung File* and *South*, dedicated to covering the developing world and shown on Britain's Channel 4 television, is indicative of this trend. Such programmes attracted a small, though committed, viewership, hardly sustainable in a ratings-driven television system. In the US too, there has been a general decline in overseas reporting among main television channels (Utley, 1997). A recent Pew Center survey showed evidence that consumers of television news in the United States lack interest in foreign news partly because they have little background information about international affairs (Pew Center, 2002).

In Britain, with a long tradition of international programming, total output of factual programmes on developing countries dropped by almost 50 per cent between 1989 and 1999 (Stone, 2000). As a report for Britain's Campaign for Quality Television concluded: 'There is an overwhelming sense that the agenda is being progressively narrowed, and increasingly it is only the safe, formulaic and proven approaches that will get on screen.' 'In current affairs' the report said, 'this results in more crime and consumer stories at the expense of harder political and foreign stories' (Barnett and Seymour, 1999: 72).

It is not just a quantitative issue. The quality of reporting from the South seems also to have deteriorated. Coverage of the developing world has significantly changed, according to a report from the London-based Third World & Environment Broadcasting Project, a not-for-profit organisation. According to their research, in 1989 the largest category of factual programming about developing countries concerned human rights, development and environmental issues (30 per cent of the output); programmes about religion, culture and arts accounted for 20 per cent of output. Between 1989 and 1999, the project found that 'these categories have been replaced by Travel and Wildlife programming which do not offer complete portraits of the developing world' (Stone, 2000: 3).

In the past ten years, two of the key current affairs programmes on Britain's major terrestrial network, Independent Television – *This Week* and *World in Action* – have been axed and replaced by lifestyle documentaries. ITN announced it was cutting back its foreign coverage and instead would have more news on lifestyle and consumer issues (Wells, 2001). This decline has parallels with the proliferation of 'docusoaps' replacing serious factual programming and further eroding the level of public understanding of global affairs, especially those concerning the South.

The 'Unreported World'

One outcome of this shift in editorial priorities is manifested in the way many parts of the developing world are covered by television news. The absences from the foreign news agenda are staggering. A kind of news apartheid continues to afflict Africa, with more stories from that continent about wildlife than about the peoples inhabiting its 54 nations and their myriad problems.

One example of these absences is the almost total silence in the media about Coltan, the mineral that is used as a conductor resistant to heat and cold and valuable as a coat for electronic components in mobile phones and military aircraft. Coltan has been blamed for the continuing war in the Democratic Republic of Congo (DRC), home to 64 per cent of the world's Coltan reserves. The war, which when covered by television (itself a rarity), is often framed as an ethnic conflict, has claimed as many as three million lives in the past three years alone (Channel 4 TV, 2001). A report on Channel 4 Television's series, aptly called *Unreported World*, showed how this mineral, crucial for mobile telephony, was fuelling one of the world's bloodiest wars in one of the world's poorest countries (Channel 4 TV, 2001). Though admirable, the report tended to blame it on the greed of local miners and their business exploiters, without taking into account the chain that leads to the entire mobile telephony industry.

In covering other wars in Africa, for example, in Sierra Leone or in Angola – one of the world's longest-running conflicts dating back to 1970s – the focus seems to be on tribal rivalries and ethnic nationalism rather than on the underlying economic and political factors. The apparent inability or unwillingness of television news to provide a historical or political context to a conflict was in evidence during the coverage of the 1994 genocide in Rwanda, which claimed one million lives in a country of only seven million. Rwanda became a big television story only after it was framed as a humanitarian crisis, with an emphasis on Western support for refugees (Philo et al, 1999).

These 'absences' in international media content and resultant distorted views of the South can affect understanding of the developing world in the North and amongst the countries of the South since most newsflow continues to be from North to South and limited South-South news exchange takes place.

Poverty in the News

Studies in Britain and Ireland have shown the problems faced by television news in covering poverty (Golding and Middleton, 1982; Devereux, 1998). Critics have argued that because news is a commodity, there is a built-in discrimination against news events that cannot be 'sold,' resulting in a distorted presentation of events 'to make them more marketable.' Western journalists see 'aberrations' as 'news' which in turn 'obliges' them to 'sensationalise' (Somavia, 1976; Masmoudi, 1979).

The unquestioning acceptance of a Western definition of what constitutes news by the majority of journalists both in the North and the South affects the coverage of poverty directly and adversely. The other factor that has affected news values in the South is the growing commercialisation and privatisation of state-controlled media, which is increasingly being bought by media conglomerates. Although the original mandate of many broadcasting systems in the South stressed education and information, there is an increasing trend towards commercialisation. Market forces have entered the mass media in most of the South as a result of deregulation in broadcasting.

With the expansion of digital broadcasting and the resultant proliferation of television channels, more and more national all-news networks are appearing, contributing to growing competition for audiences and, crucially, advertising revenue, emanating mostly from transnational corporations on whose advertising support the media edifice is ultimately based. Given their dependence on advertising, the output of many television news networks may sometimes lack depth in their constant pressure to catch up with the speed and delivery of stories, and bow to the demand for infotainment. In this media landscape, as Robert McChesney has argued, 'consumerism, the market, class inequality and individualism tend to be taken as natural and often benevolent, whereas political activity, civic values, and anti-market activities tend to be marginalised or denounced' (McChesney, 1999:110).

This market-driven news agenda is in the process of globalisation as a result of deregulation and privatisation of broadcasting across the global South. Though the resultant availability of more media outlets has undermined the tight control of ruling elites on means of expression, the new news networks seem to be more interested in covering consumerist journalism than issues of social and economic justice. In much of sub-Saharan Africa and South Asia where low levels of literacy restrict the spread of the printed word, television could play a key role in popularising news about development issues. But the failure by policy makers to adopt a participatory approach to electronic media and unwillingness on the part of journalists to cover developmental stories continues to deny rural populations genuine access to the broadcast media, which remains largely urban-based and elitist with a heavy emphasis on entertainment. The public service ethos is being rapidly replaced by a journalistic culture aimed at satisfying the advertisers. In such an environment, the coverage of poverty on television, already distorted and extremely limited, may be further reduced.

Issues related to poverty do not fit into the traditional concepts of what constitutes television news. In reporting stories about the dispossessed the journalists get little in return except perhaps some moral satisfaction and professional pride. In contrast, if they cover celebrities and economic and political elites, they rub shoulders with the rich and famous and that proximity to power is what gives journalism much of its charm.

News about poverty may not produce 'sexy' copy. It deals with economic, social and political developments, which take time to unfold. Given the very short attention span of news journalists, it is an almost imperceptible process. But in the long term the outcome of such reporting could bring a change in the perception of the way in which news is defined, news agendas are set and information is disseminated.

While the application of commercial news values is detrimental to a rounded understanding of the issues in the news in the developed world, the impact is proportionately greater for the developing world. The result of this commodification process, according to this argument, is that most reporting of serious issues in the South is reduced to a simplistic version of often complex realities. With scant space to cover news from developing countries, these are often stereotyped into shorthand media clichés. While covering news of wars, disease, corruption and disasters in the South, international journalists are seldom encouraged by their editors to probe how the situation developed, how the event in question was related to its socio-economic and political environment, or to explore alternative viewpoints. As a result there is a steady underreporting of the cultural, economic and political progress being made by developing countries.

News values and training of journalists in the South are much influenced by the Western media. Indeed, Western news organisations have training programmes to teach Southern journalists how to improve their professional competence.

Often, they are trained to write more about the dominant sections of the society than about ordinary people. Few journalists, North or South, are trained in the economics and political sociology necessary for writing with insight about economic and social development.

Poor Alternatives to Market-led TV

What compounds the problem is the almost total absence of alternative media outlets emanating from the global South to put poverty back on the international news agenda. The South is not a homogenised set of countries, and their levels of economic, social and political development can vary considerably. Yet their diversity has an underlying unity. Most countries of the South were once part of European empires. Their evolution as independent nation states continues to be restricted by the fact that they have to develop in a global capitalistic setting which is controlled by a few countries in the North, a striking contrast from much of the North which developed by extensively exploiting the natural and human resources of its colonies in the South.

The concept of development news emerged as a response to the often bitter debates over the NWICO, which voiced Southern grievances about the perceived dominance of and 'one way flow of information' from North to South, which had contributed to the misrepresentation of the South in the global media. In addition, many analysts in the South believed that the media could be harnessed to promote social and political development in evolving a civil society and in nation-building within a democratic framework.

This was consistent with the dominant communications paradigm advanced by Western, mainly American, communications scholars, which urged that the mass media play a crucial role in society and by implication could be an agent in the development of the Third World. Communications research on what came to be known as 'development communication' identified with, among others, the works of Wilbur Schramm, was based on the belief that greater participation of mass media would help transform traditional societies. This pro-media bias was very influential and received support from many Third World governments and international organisations. Schramm saw the mass media as a 'bridge to a wider world' as the vehicle for transferring new ideas and models from the North to the South and within the Third World from urban to rural areas (Schramm, 1964).

The top-down approach to communications – a one-way flow of information from government or international development agencies via the mass media to Third World peasantry at the bottom – was seen as a panacea for the development of the newly independent countries. But such a linear and deterministic concept of 'development communication' operated mostly at a macro level and was predicated on a definition of development as following the model of Northern industrialisation and 'modernisation' measured primarily by the rate of economic growth. It failed to recognise that the creation of wealth on its own was insufficient: the improvement of life for the majority of the population depended on the equitable distribution of that wealth and its use for the public good. Moreover, the mass media were assumed to be a neutral force in the process of development, ignoring how the media are themselves a product of social, political, economic and cultural conditions.

In many developing countries economic and political power remains restricted to a tiny ruling elite, and the mass media play a key role in legitimising the political establishment. Since the media had, and continue to have, close proximity to the ruling elites they reflect that definition of development in the news.

In the age of the Internet, this modernisation thesis has become part of a neo-developmentalist agenda, promoted by the World Bank and the International Monetary Fund. Under the onslaught of neo-liberal ideology, so-called 'development journalism' has all but disappeared from news agendas. The central notion of alternative journalism – investigating the process behind a story rather than merely reporting the news event itself – has no place in a market-driven news environment which discriminates against news that cannot be 'sold', resulting in a distorted presentation of events to make them marketable. UNESCO-led initiatives to promote regional exchange mechanisms, established in the late-1970s, largely failed to make much difference to the global or even regional news agendas, which are shaped by geo-political or economic factors (Boyd-Barrett and Thussu, 1992).

Southern international news-exchange mechanisms, such as the Non-Aligned News Agencies Pool, designed to promote news among Non-Aligned countries, has dismally failed, primarily because it was accurately perceived as little more than a government-to-government exchange programme and thus lacks journalistic credibility, even within developing countries. Other alternative voices, such as the small but effective Gemini News Service, an international news agency based in London with an explicit development agenda, are now part of a non-governmental organisation, as is the Rome-based Inter Press Service (IPS), an international news agency. Both agencies have not been able to make themselves commercially viable and are therefore dependent on funds from Western aid agencies and UN organisations, acting more like a pressure group, putting Southern concerns on the UN agenda, rather than a professional news organisation.

The emergence of the Internet as an alternative medium has received much attention in recent writings. Organisations such as OneWorld Online, a site dedicated to providing alternative voices on issues of global importance particularly from a Southern perspective and launched in 1995, have made a mark. The Internet has been a major factor in the anti-globalisation movements, helping to scupper the World Trade Organisation's ministerial meeting in Seattle in 1999. One major success of such activism was to mobilise international support against the Multilateral Agreement on Investment (MAI). The MAI was being discussed within the OECD and if approved it would have given extraordinary powers to transnational corporations to move capital from one country to another (Kobrin, 1998).

However, it is important to emphasise that the Internet, though the fastest growing medium in human history, still remains out of reach for 90 per cent of the world's population. At the very minimum, one has to have access to a telephone line and a computer to be able to join the cyber world. According to a recent survey of the World Wide Web, more than 86 per cent of all Web pages were in English, although fewer than one in 10 people world wide speak the language. The almost mythical powers attributed to the Internet as a global alternative medium, given its role in promoting links among community groups, non-governmental organisations and political activists across continents, must be seen within the context of this global digital divide.

The Perils of Poverty

What gets left out is the fact that despite claims that free-market capitalism (read, globalisation) is a panacea for economic underdevelopment, poverty is actually growing in many parts of the world. The worst affected are countries in sub-Saharan Africa, crushed under a burden of mounting debt and facing a healthcare disaster in the form of the AIDS epidemic. Despite all moralising, Africa has been all but forgotten in the new global economic order – according to the United Nations Conference on Trade and Development (UNCTAD), Africa's share of the global $1.3 trillion foreign direct investment in 2000 remains below one per cent (UNCTAD, 2001a: 6).

Globalisation may have created prosperity for a few countries and the corporations based there, but market-based policies are also causing unprecedented misery in the South. The income gap between the richest fifth of the world's people and the poorest fifth, measured by average national income per head, has been gradually increasing. The 2001 *Human Development Report* of the United Nations Development Programme notes that 1.2 billion people are living on less that $1 a day and 2.8 billion on less than $2 a day (UNDP, 2001: 9). According to the International Labour Organisation, job losses in the public sector are having a devastating affect on employment, especially in the global South (ILO, 2001). Even UN officials are admitting that market-based economic policies are not working. Rubens Ricupero, Secretary General of UNCTAD, has called for 'a major reformulation of the reform agenda' (UNCTAD, 2001b: p. x).

Though they are crucially important, mainstream television news rarely covers such issues. The countries on the receiving end of neo-liberal 'reforms', increasingly termed 'failed states', whose sovereignty is in doubt (Krasner, 1999), were off the news agenda for most of the 1990s. Their problems are often dismissed in media reports as part of 'ethnic' conflicts. However, 'Third World threats,' especially emanating from Islamic fundamentalism, have acquired deadly urgency in the wake of the attacks on New York and Washington in September 2001.

The focus of global conflict is shifting towards the South – the events of September 11, 2001 and their aftermath have ensured that. The global South is the region from which 'threats' to the Western way of life are likely to emerge, from religious fundamentalism, to proliferation of weapons of mass destruction and international terrorism. Under such conditions, the world's major powers can justify military 'intervention' to defend their definitions of 'security' (Kagan, 1998). Already, the talk is of a new imperialism. To many the 'regime change' in Iraq is indicative of the new imperial order.

The media, and especially television, will have to resist the temptation to follow such an agenda. While Iraq dominated television screens around the world, millions of people in Africa were dying as a result of conflicts and hunger. The perils of poverty cannot be ignored, especially in the wake of the events of September 11, 2001. To adequately deal with the sharpening contradictions of free market capitalism, poverty of news will have to end and news will have to seriously tackle poverty by bringing it onto its agenda, harnessing the growing number of media outlets. After all, it concerns more than 80 per cent of the world's population, who continue to be largely excluded from the benefits of a globalised economy.

References

Balnaves, M., J. Donald and S. Hemelryk Donald (2001) *The Global Media Atlas*. London: British Film Institute.

Barnett, S. and E. Seymour (1999) *'A shrinking iceberg travelling south...' Changing Trends in British Television: A case study of drama and current affairs*. London: Campaign for Quality Television.

Bird, S. E. (2000) 'Audience Demands in a Murderous Market – Tabloidisation in US Television News,' in Sparks, C. and J. Tulloch (eds.) *Tabloid Tales: Global Debates over Media Standards*. Maryland: Lanham, Rowman & Littlefield.

Boyd-Barrett, O. (1998) 'Media Imperialism Reformulated', in Thussu, D. K. (ed) *Electronic Empires: Global Media and Local Resistance*. London: Arnold, and New York: Oxford University Press.

Boyd-Barrett, O. and T. Rantanen (eds.) (1998) *The Globalization of News*. London: Sage.

Boyd-Barrett, O. and D. K. Thussu (1992) *ContraFlow in Global News*. London: John Libbey, in association with UNESCO.

Channel 4 TV (2001, September 28) 'The real mobile phone war', *Unreported World*, Channel 4 Television.

CNN website (2003), http://www.cnn.com

Devereux, E. (1998) *Devils and Angels: Television Ideology and the Coverage of Poverty*. Luton: University of Luton Press.

Flournoy, D. and R. Stewart (1997) *CNN: Making News in the Global Market*. Luton: University of Luton Press.

Golding, P. and S. Middleton (1982) *Images of Welfare: Press and Public Attitudes to Poverty*. Oxford: Basil Blackwell.

Hachten, W. (1999) *The World News Prism: Changing Media of International Communication, Fifth Edition*. Ames: Iowa State University Press.

ILO (2001) *The World Employment Report 2001: Life at Work in the Information Economy*. Geneva: International Labour Organisation.

Iyengar, S. and D. Kinder (1987) *News That Matters: Television and American Opinion*. Chicago: University of Chicago Press.

Kagan, R. (1998, Summer) 'The Benevolent Empire', *Foreign Policy*.

Kobrin, S. (1998, Fall) 'The MAI and the Clash of Globalisations', *Foreign Policy*.

Krasner, S. (1999) *Sovereignty: Organized Hypocrisy*. Princeton: Princeton University Press.

Masmoudi, M. (1979) 'New International Information Order', *Journal of Communication*, 29: 172-195.

McChesney, R. (1999) *Rich Media, Poor Democracy: Communication Politics in Dubious Times*. Champaign, IL.: University of Illinois Press.

Monbiot, G. (2001, October 23) 'America's Pipe Dream', *Guardian*.

Papathanassopoulos, S. (1999) 'The Political Economy of International News Channels: More Supply Than Demand', *Intermedia*. 27 (1): 17-23.

Pew Center (2002) 'Public's News Habits Little Changed by September 11 – Americans Lack Background to Follow International News, Pew Research Center for the People and the Press. http://people-press.org/reports.

Philo, G., L. Hilsum, L. Beattie and R. Holliman (1999) 'The media and the Rwanda crisis: effects on audiences and public policy', in G. Philo (ed) *Message Received: Glasgow Media Group Research 1993-1998*. London: Longman.

Rashid, A. (2001) *Taliban: Islam, Oil and the New Great Game in Central Asia*. London: Yale University Press.

Rothkopf, D. (1999, Spring) 'The Disinformation Age', *Foreign Policy*.

Schramm, W. (1964) *Mass Media and National Development*. California: Stanford University Press.

Somavia, J. (1976) 'The Transnational Power Structure and International Information', Development *Dialogue*, 2: 15-28.

Stone, J. (2000) *Losing Perspective: Global Affairs on British Terrestrial Television 1989-1999* (Report of the Third World and Environment Broadcasting Project). London: International Broadcasting Trust.

Thussu, D. K. (2000a) *International Communication: Continuity and Change*. London: Arnold, and New York: Oxford University Press.

Thussu, D. K. (2000b) 'Legitimising "Humanitarian Intervention"? CNN, NATO and the Kosovo Crisis', *European Journal of Communication*, 15 (3): 345-361.

Tunstall, J. and D. Machin (1999) *The Anglo-American Media Connection*. Oxford: Oxford University Press.

UNCTAD (2001a) *World Investment Report 2001: Promoting Linkages*. Geneva: United Nations Conference on Trade and Development.

UNCTAD (2001b) *Trade and Development Report 2001*. Geneva: United Nations Conference on Trade and Development.

UNDP (2001) *Human Development Report 2001 Making New Technologies Work for Human Development*. Oxford and New York: Oxford University Press.

Utley, G. (1997) 'The shrinking of foreign news: from broadcast to narrowcast', *Foreign Affairs*, 76 (2): 2-10.

Volkmer, I. (1999) *News in the Global Sphere: A Study of CNN and its Impact on Global Communications*. Luton: University of Luton Press.

Wells, M. (2001, Novermber 22) 'ITN cuts jobs and shifts towards lifestyle news', *Guardian*.

Chapter 3
Invisible Giants, Quiet Revolution

Nigel Baker

Television news agencies supply the images, sounds and information for most international news stories for most broadcasters around the world. A decade ago, Visnews (the predecessor of Reuters Television) claimed over 1.5 billion people saw their pictures around the world every day (Tunstall, 1992). It is surprising, then, that the vast body of research on international journalism and globalisation tells us little about these organisations. Nigel Baker has led APTN from a small company lacking news coverage resources and clients (tentatively established by Associated Press in 1995 to test the waters in television) to its current leadership position. With more broadcasters using APTN footage to illustrate their newscasts than Visnews had a decade ago, and with more people around the world depending upon television, the influence of Baker's company on the way the world sees itself is awesome. This is the first time a senior journalist from a television news agency has provided a detailed, public, description of the workings and strategies of these 'invisible giants.' Research broadly supports Baker's insider view, but often reaches differing conclusions about the impact of the agencies and the reasons they do what they do (Paterson, 1998; Clare, 1997; Putnis, 1996; Cohen, et al, 1996; Hjarvard, 1996; Tunstall, 1992, and Boyd-Barrett and Rantenen in this volume).

Three people have transformed the way international television news has been collected and distributed in the last decade of the twentieth century and in the early years of the twenty-first. They are Saddam Hussein, Slobodan Milosevic and Osama bin Laden. Each has generated, or threatened, a prolonged conflict in difficult, inhospitable and sometimes unpredictable terrain. Each of those conflicts – the Persian Gulf crises, the civil war in Yugoslavia and the reaction to the attack on New York's World Trade Center – has prompted a financial spasm in the way TV broadcasters cover world affairs.

The prospect of providing sustained coverage from costly and logistically difficult locations, coupled with the cost of supplying more content on a wider number of platforms, meant broadcasters had to review the way they covered international news. Consequently, a great change during the 1990s was that broadcasters came to rely on the international TV news agencies more than ever before to be their eyes and ears – and prime provider of international coverage – in all corners of the world. The agencies became the key source of coverage of everything from the Paris fashion show to the renewed Intifada in the Palestinian territories. Among most broadcasters, however, 'the agencies', as TV foreign editors call them, have become synonymous with the journalism of the 'hell hole'. Baghdad, Sarajevo, Grozny, Pristina, Gaza and Kabul are the datelines where 'the agencies' are expected to be at their most reliant, most productive and most creative.

The broadcasters have searched their souls, as well as their news coverage budgets, after every major conflict since the 1991 Gulf War to find cheaper ways of covering the world. This gave the agencies an opportunity to perform better at a time when technology and deregulation of satellite provision also helped them to become the backbone of international coverage for the overwhelming majority of broadcasters.

This was a quiet revolution, as broadcasters generally see little merit in informing their viewers that they have not generated all their international coverage themselves. It could be argued that during this period the agencies became the invisible giants of television news. A key image of a gun battle or plane crash provided by one agency could be used by up to 400 national and international broadcasters, with the opportunity to be seen by hundreds of millions of people globally, far greater than the audience of any single broadcaster.

This chapter will attempt to give an insider's view of exactly who the TV agencies are and what they do. The author is currently director of content of Associated Press Television News (APTN) which, at time of writing in 2003, was the world's largest TV news agency by revenue and market share, according to the company's own marketing data. The insights offered here will hopefully debunk some of the myths about the decision-making processes which govern what TV news agencies cover, and describe the financial rationale which underpins their existence. That leads naturally to an explanation of how the agencies have harnessed digital technology to improve their service, and what that means for international TV news coverage in the future.

'Be First. Be Fast'

The world of the television news agency has traditionally been unrelentingly competitive. It becomes ever more so. At time of writing, there are only two international TV agencies: Associated Press Television News (APTN) and Reuters Television, owned by the world's two largest news agencies. They work in a world where there is the threat of the market allowing only one TV agency to survive, by constantly exerting price pressure. Broadcasters, generally, are remarkably unforgiving if a TV agency does not perform at a high level constantly. If a TV agency misses a key image in an event, the perception of its customers is, effectively, that it has missed the entire story. This contrasts markedly with the written word distributed by wire services. For example, the symbolic handshake image in Middle East peace negotiations would be the anticipated headline shot by broadcasters worldwide. Thus, it would be the iconic image that broadcasters expected TV news agencies to provide. However, from the author's experience in many TV, radio and print newsrooms over a 30-year period, there is not the same pressure on a wire service to deliver such a tightly defined version of a story in the printed word. Quite simply, if a TV news agency misses the memorable shot which encapsulates the entire story, there is no recovery and it has failed in the eyes of its customers, whatever other coverage it provides. If a wire service reporter misses the key quote, there is normally a method of recovery, possibly by catching a replay of the vital moment on TV news coverage. In the written word, omissions or underperformance are more easily corrected or disguised.

Against this background, a TV agency constantly has to second-guess the broadcasters' needs and react fast to a breaking story. APTN recently asked a foreign editor of a US TV network what his over-riding requirement was from an agency. His characteristically terse response was: 'Be first. Be fast.' Those four words summarise more than any other what makes TV agencies 'tick'. It is a world where the difference between success and failure in delivering the video to customers can be measured in minutes. If, for example, a key story of Australian interest is delivered to the Australian TV networks five minutes after their main evening newscasts, its value to them will be diminished immensely. In a time-sensitive business, they would prefer part of the story by their main deadline, rather than the whole story five minutes after it. The same is true for broadcasters in every major news market around the world.

This means that TV news agencies do not agonise unduly about covering a breaking news story. The broadcast clients might say they want time to think about whether they are interested in the story. By the time they decided they were, there would usually be no means of obtaining coverage if the agency had not taken a positive decision to react swiftly and cover the story immediately. In a sense, broadcasters who sign up to an agency not only regard it as a way of obtaining cost-effective international news coverage but also consider it an insurance policy. It gives them a pictorial guide to how world events are playing out. They may not always want to use the footage, but are comforted by the fact that an agency provides them with a way of knowing whether a story they read about on the wires, or in a newspaper, is visually compelling beyond its news value in the written word.

The content of TV news bulletins in most countries of the world is a trade-off between stories which are deemed important and those which are visually interesting. In a visual medium, editors of TV news broadcasts do this deliberately to attract and retain the attention of viewers. An extreme example would be a spectacular car chase by police in the United States, where dramatic footage has been filmed from a helicopter. This might be used on news bulletins in most TV channels in the world because of its eye-catching nature. However, on radio and in newspapers the story might well go unreported because it held no real news value other than its visual appeal.

Graphic, or iconic, images that neatly portray the essence of a story are the 'language' of international TV news agencies. The agencies provide video with 'international sound' – that is, only the ambient sound captured by the microphone and the words of interviewees. There is usually no reporter commentary. The use of agency material by broadcasters hangs on the visual strength of the images or the verbal power of the sound bite. A broadcaster filming a report for itself can add drama, interpretation or nuance with the correspondent's voiceover or piece-to-camera (referred to in the United States as a 'stand-up'). The agency footage, ideally, has to show events as they unfold so the story is self-evident to busy editors viewing the material without commentary and possibly monitoring other sources of news, in video and print, simultaneously.

So those in the forefront of deciding on which events are covered by the TV agencies broadly take into account the following factors when deciding which stories to cover:

- The demands of the day.

- The anticipated demands of the customers in all world markets.

- The televisual impact of a story.

- The budgetary resources of the agency.

- The skills of individual journalists.

The demands of the day. To most journalists, this element of the equation might seem blindingly obvious, but might not always be apparent to others. There are certain stories which the agencies know will be used the world over. An extreme example of this is the attack on the World Trade Center in 2001. There would be no hesitation by any international TV news organization in throwing colossal resources at such a story, on the simple assumption that it will generate immense interest throughout the world. Experience has taught the TV agencies that on a 'normal' day there are usually three to five international stories which will be of interest in most countries in the globe, usually highly visual stories which can be classed as breaking news. A major plane crash or earthquake would fall into this category. Similarly, dramatic pictures of a development on a 'running story', like the Israeli-Palestinian conflict, would come into this bracket. These stories would tend to provide the focus for the majority of the agencies' coverage and financial resource in a given day.

The anticipated demands of customers. Beyond doubt, TV news agencies are businesses, which exist to serve the needs of their customers. (This topic will be revisited while looking at the financial aspects of the agencies a little later in the chapter). To this extent, the agencies will tend to favour covering stories which reflect the needs and interests of their main subscribers. The countries that represent the biggest agency markets are the United States, Germany and Japan. The classic example of how this may determine coverage is if six tourists from any of those nations were, for example, taken hostage in the Philippines, the agencies would be highly pro-active in obtaining coverage of the story. The same is unlikely to be the case if the hostages were from Uruguay, Tajikistan or Nepal, as those countries do not represent significant markets. There is another tier of customers from medium-sized markets who also have significant influence on coverage because they represent highly competitive markets where broadcasters tend to change their agency allegiances frequently or whom agency journalists regard as industry opinion formers. Three leading examples of this are the United Kingdom, Australia and Taiwan. While the UK market is not in the top three it contains one of the world's biggest TV news broadcasters, the BBC, which has two strong competitors in Independent Television News (ITN) and Sky News. Peers in other markets respect the opinions and preferences of all three companies. Australian broadcasters tend to be highly vocal within the industry internationally and influence industry judgements in other English-language TV markets like Canada and New Zealand. Taiwan, meanwhile, is a highly fickle and competitive market. Again, the need to retain significant Taiwanese business might mean TV agencies would be more inclined to cover a foreign diplomatic tour by a Taiwanese leader than a Lithuanian leader.

The televisual impact of the story. Television is ultimately about strong visual images. They are the major 'currency' of international TV news agencies because there is no common language among their customers. A TV news agency is more likely to provide coverage of a dramatic forest fire than a localised diplomatic row between two nations for one simple reason: broadcasters all over the world are likely to use the action pictures. 'Talking heads' discussing a political row in foreign language are less likely to be used. This is, of course, a question of degree, where we are talking about stories that form the medium tier of coverage below the top three to five major stories of the day. A diplomatic row between the United States and China over what action to take, say, against North Korea might fall into the top category of story. Excerpts from statements by the appropriate government spokespersons in Beijing and Washington would be provided. Normally the selection of these excerpts would be made by the agency journalists, who would decide, on the basis of their professional experience, what they thought was new and newsworthy, or contributed to the development of an ongoing story. While broadcasters often use short sound bites of five seconds or so, an agency might provide several longer excerpts, of perhaps twenty seconds, from each speaker to allow broadcasters a choice of which perspective they wished to give on the story. There is a growing tendency to provide those excerpts in the native tongue of the speaker to try to appeal to the local market and to avoid the appearance of imposing an Anglo-American perspective on every story. This has been an allegation to which TV news agencies have allowed themselves to be open, as their main language of operation is English. This is partly because of their ownership and partly for financial convenience. Over the years, they have found it the most understood tongue and, thus, avoided the expense of translating their service into many languages. Usually, they provide a written translation of non-English sound bites so their content can be understood by the widest numbers of customers.

The budgetary resources of the agency. Harsh choices on which coverage to provide have to be made on a daily basis by both agencies, based on the availability of funds. It takes a high level of skill to balance the demands of known fixed events which require coverage, like international summits and elections, with unpredictable levels of breaking news. As TV agencies have, historically, been relatively fragile businesses, they cannot afford to spend endless funds. If there is a major call on their resource, like the US war on terror in Afghanistan or the NATO strike on Yugoslavia, agencies will cover these aggressively at the expense of other events in the world. The main customer base of the agencies will expect blanket coverage of the major event. This often has the effect of marginalising the reporting of regional events, for example, a conflict in Africa, which might at other times attract more coverage.

The skills of individual journalists. This factor has a more profound effect on the world's TV news coverage than anyone might realise. No professional news organisation will pressure a journalist to go into a conflict zone where it is difficult and dangerous to gather the news. Here, it is the determination and skills of individual journalists which ensure that crucial pictures of world events come to the attention of the viewer. Agencies can nurture the career of the courageous practitioner and create the framework in which they are able to operate, but finding an individual who can make a difference to the world's news coverage is rare.

One such example of this kind of practitioner was cameraman Miguel Gil, who achieved more in the five years he worked for APTV and its successor, APTN, than most TV journalists achieve in a lifetime. He abandoned a career as a corporate lawyer in his native Barcelona, took off on his motorbike and travelled to Sarajevo to cover the Bosnia conflict as a freelance journalist. After working for Spanish newspapers, he began work for APTV in Sarajevo in 1995. He showed an unusual aptitude for camera work and developed a rare desire to use television to tell the story, particularly of the innocent victims of war.

He covered conflicts from the Balkans to Baghdad, and from Rwanda to the former Soviet Union. He worked best alone and often endured extreme physical hardship to get the story. But his pictures – used by most of the world's broadcasters – were often capable of shaping, or changing, world opinion. In the build-up to Kosovo conflict, he spent a year undercover with the ethnic

Albanian resistance, the KLA, winning awards for his chronicling of their battles against the Serbs. When the NATO strike on Yugoslavia came in 1999, he persuaded the Serb authorities in Kosovo's capital, Pristina, to let him be the only western TV cameraman to remain when all others were ejected or felt it was too dangerous to stay. He captured unique images of ethnic Albanians being expelled from the city by train in scenes reminiscent of the Nazis transporting Jews from Germany. The pictures strengthened world opinion against the Serbs, although, ironically they had felt the images would demonstrate their liberality in letting ethnic Albanians leave the city.

After his marathon in Kosovo, he felt the besieged residents of Grozny, in Chechnya, had the story which most needed telling. In late 1999, their city was under prolonged, round-the-clock aerial bombardment by the Russians in their battle with Chechen separatists. No western journalist had been to the city for many months for fear of being kidnapped or killed by the Chechens. It took Miguel a month to arrange the contacts to escort him from neighbouring Dagestan. He walked overland by night, through snow, for several days, to reach the capital, Grozny, in December. His pictures gave a graphic account of the plight of thousands of people living in basements to avoid the shelling. In the words of Miguel: 'There wasn't a second of any minute, of any hour, of any day in Grozny when I didn't think I was going to die.'

His pictures demonstrated the intensity of the bombardment in what otherwise might have been a hidden war. Miguel survived that conflict only to be murdered in Sierra Leone the following year, along with Reuters correspondent Kurt Schork, when they were ambushed by anti-government guerrillas.

Miguel paid the ultimate price for his journalistic endeavours but he provided an outstanding example of how an agency cameraman can provide the world with unique insights into conflicts which no-one else is capable of doing, or prepared to do.

It also highlights the fact that on many occasions TV agencies are about the 'journalism of access'. The agencies have staff or 'stringers' in most countries who often gain access to a story, where a foreign correspondent cannot, because of their ethnic origin or contacts built up from being based in the country. The agencies tend to retain full-time staff where there is a major running story in, say, Jerusalem or Beijing. In many countries, however, they retain what they call stringers, which is a flexible way of employing people with local skills and knowledge. A stringer can be defined in many ways – from a person on a full-time contract renewable annually, to local journalists or camera operators given a guarantee of a certain number of days' work a year in return for first call on their services, to freelancers who are only paid if they are called on to cover a specific story.

The 'skills of individual journalists' might also embrace a tenacious or insightful desk editor at head office. A single editor's belief that a story needs telling, and a preparedness to devote journalists' time to getting it, can make the difference between the story appearing on the world agenda, or not. An agency is often the first, or only, way of the world knowing of a story. For example, when American troops entered Afghanistan after September 11, 2001, thousands of Afghanis in remote areas were caught between the retreating Taliban and American troops. A senior editor at APTN felt that those people might be cut off without food. Accordingly, the senior editor invested time and effort in sending a camera crew to a remote mountain area where, indeed, local tribes people were only keeping alive by eating grass. The story made headline news in the United States and was followed up by several broadcasters from around the world as an illustration of how innocent people were being caught up in the war.

Shaking Up the Market

No one has yet become rich running a television news agency. A snapshot of their financial profile sounds almost like that of an airline business – high investment for very modest returns – highly competitive with the potential to offer excitement on occasions.

The agency subscription market for international television news coverage to broadcasters is worth around US $250 million dollars a year worldwide. The money goes mainly to four players – APTN, Reuters, the European Broadcasting Union (EBU) and CNN, with curious inter-relationships between the four. CNN and the EBU are both customers, and commercial rivals, of APTN and Reuters. The agencies feel unable to decline the revenues that come from their relationships with CNN and the EBU but often feel it is a curious co-existence.

- APTN and Reuters sell material they have mainly generated themselves, each having around one hundred camera crews around the world and the ability to access material from many of the world's major broadcasters, particularly in the UK and United States. At time of writing, APTN had sole international distribution rights for material from ABC of America and Sky News of the UK. Reuters had access to material from NBC of America and ITN of the UK.

- The EBU runs a satellite news exchange primarily of material from European state broadcasters, but allows European commercial broadcasters, US and Japanese TV networks to become associate members and for APTN and Reuters to have access to exchanges. The EBU exchange relies heavily on the two agencies to contribute breaking news, particularly from outside Europe.

- CNN sells the output of its international service to other national broadcasters, effectively as an agency feed. Again, however, it relies heavily on the agencies for video of breaking news.

The economics of the TV agencies entered a period of extreme turbulence in 1994. The two agencies in existence then, Reuters Television and Worldwide

Television News (WTN) had been marginally profitable. Then came a third entrant to the market, when the Associated Press launched APTV in November 1994. The effect was to spark a prolonged battle for survival among the three agencies, denying any of them profitability and forcing a market rationalisation in 1998. At that time, Walt Disney, the ultimate owners of WTN, decided to dispose of it. It was purchased by the Associated Press that merged it with APTV to form APTN (Associated Press Television News). By 2003, APTN claimed the largest market share by both numbers of customers and revenue, with 350 broadcasters subscribing to its news service. Another 150 were buying its sports service, Sports News Television (SNTV), which was a joint venture with Trans World International, the world's leading manager of television sports rights.

APTN became profitable after its acquisition of WTN. While Reuters does not report the financial performance of its television wing separately, the company has been said to be have been troubled by the TV revenue figures.

By 2003, a new competitive landscape had emerged among the agencies where two leviathans, the Associated Press and Reuters, were battling for market leadership – with APTN claiming the largest market share by number of broadcasters and revenue. Both were deemed to provide a credible and reliable service. Prior to 1998, Reuters had been perceived for several years as the undisputed market leader, with WTN and APTV regarded as being lower-cost alternatives, but with less breadth of coverage.

However, two strong performers surviving in the market place caused many broadcasters who traditionally took all the agencies to ask the question: 'Could we survive with one agency?' This syndrome was exacerbated by the harsh economic conditions of the early part of the 21st century. Faced with cutting staff or the cost of external suppliers, many broadcasters looked seriously at reducing their spending on subscribing to agencies.

This threatened a period of price compression within the agency business. As neither parent company would feel comfortable without a video component in the multimedia age, the most obvious reaction to this pressure would be to exploit new technologies and working practices to reduce the cost of their operations, or broaden their markets.

The irony is that the same digital technologies which allow wider markets for video also reduce the barriers to entry for new competitors and potentially lead to a reduction in the sale price of video.

Historically, the agencies have sold their service to broadcasters on a three-year subscription basis. The annual rate has ranged from two million US dollars to twenty thousand dollars, depending on the size of the television station or network and the size of its audience. This subscription model is vital for agencies to be able to predict their revenues so they can maintain the extensive infrastructure needed to provide their service. However, the cost of their newsgathering has traditionally not been covered by the subscription revenue for their general news service. Consequently, agencies have only been self-sustaining if they have also sold incremental services like sport and entertainment news and earned additional commercial revenue from their technical infrastructure.

The current market of TV broadcasters is a relatively small one, which became adept during the 1990s at keeping the agencies as their journalistic guard dogs – fed just enough to provide a good service but hungry enough to battle each other for premier position. Broadcasters tend to discuss their agency relationships with each other and some seek to negotiate in groups or to confer about their tactics for handling the agencies. It was by this principle that they allowed a third agency to exist in the mid-1990s in order to shake up the market place. One Swiss TV executive told me: 'We allowed APTV to grow because we thought Reuters had become arrogant and WTN had become lazy. We wanted to stir up the market.'

The effect has been just that. Beyond doubt, the breadth and quality of service, and customer responsiveness, has improved dramatically. Each delivers material live, or in edited form, by a permanent satellite network worldwide. Before the competition of the three-agency market, Asia and Latin America typically only received pre-recorded coverage fed to them in two half-hour satellite 'windows' a day. The material was often from the previous day, which would now be unacceptable. However, all this serves to underline that agencies are a business. There is a confusion in the minds of many that agencies perform the role of a public service broadcaster with a mission to cover stories of note wherever they happen in the world. Like public service broadcasters they guard jealously their reputation for accuracy and impartiality, but there the similarity ends. Agencies exist as a business to serve the needs of their customers. It should, therefore, be of no surprise that the agenda of the agencies is often swayed in favour of those customers.

An illustration of the regional make-up of the customer base of the agencies can be given by looking at the where the subscription revenue for APTN's core news service came at the beginning of 2000. It excludes incremental services like sport and entertainment and, in the case of Middle Eastern broadcasters, some customised, unilateral coverage.

Table 3. Originof APTN Subscription Revenue, 2000

Europe	51.7%
Asia	20.4%
N. America	15.7%
Middle East *	8.0%
Latin America	4.2%

(*Includes Arabic-speaking North Africa.)

The revenue from central and southern Africa was so small as not to register. It is worth noting, however, that 8 per cent of the APTN coverage budget that year was spent providing stories from Africa. This hopefully will provide an explanation to those who wonder why Africa, particularly, is not covered more. The answer is simple. There is currently no revenue base there for the agencies, but coverage is provided of African stories of major world interest, or of interest to the main agency markets.

In 2001, the overall expenditure on news coverage by APTN rose by 20 per cent to accommodate a huge volume of coverage required from the United States and Afghanistan after the attack on the World Trade Center. However, the effect was also partly to reduce coverage from Africa, where spending on newsgathering was half that of the previous year.

The Connected World: Nowhere to Hide

It is important to understand the forces driving the agencies to understand where their futures lie. Their success – and survival – will depend primarily on their ability to provide more coverage, from more locations either live, or more frequently, than in the past. The key to that success will hang on technology for many years to come. Technology will drive the evolution of international coverage in the broadcast TV news industry, which nowadays often judges itself more by the speed of its delivery than by the strength of its journalism. An illustration of this was during the war in Iraq in 2003. APTN launched an incremental service, called APTN Direct, with two additional satellite channels dedicated to live events from the Middle East (principally Iraq) and live political reaction to unfolding events from the United States and Europe. Such was the interest in more live coverage that 40 broadcasters, from the United States to the Middle East to China, signed up to APTN Direct in the 10 days leading up to the start of the war. During the 26 days of war the service delivered 900 hours of live coverage. The key events, from the American bombing of Baghdad to the advance of US marines into the city to the symbolic fall of Saddam Hussein statues, were provided live – in stark contrast to the beginning of the 1991 Gulf War when initially only CNN was able to report live, using an audio circuit but with no pictures. After the 2003 conflict several broadcasters asked for the APTN Direct service to be made a permanent feature to cover all major stories, which at the time of writing was under consideration.

The growth of 24-hour news channels on television has been pivotal in driving the demand for live coverage or, at the very least, greater speed of delivery. In a survey of sixty-four broadcasters in thirty-six countries, carried out for APTN by the international broadcasting research company Frank N. Magid Associates in February 2000, 60 per cent said they had increased the amount of news they produced in the previous two years. This was widely attributed to the proliferation of news channels. Some 43 per cent of the broadcasters said they were planning more channels dedicated to news programming. The main increases were set to be in Asia and Europe, although the appearance of little increase in the US market was seen as reflecting the fact it was ahead of the rest of the world in having a high volume of news channels.

The ability to feed this burgeoning market hangs on another facet of the quiet revolution which has transformed the way agencies have provided news since the mid 1990s. There are four key aspects to this – all linked to digital technology. They are:

- An increase in digital satellite capacity coupled with telecom deregulation in many world markets.

- The ability to transmit video by satellite telephones.

- The ability to transmit video via the Internet or company wide area networks.

- The advent of videophones.

Increased digital satellite capacity and telecom deregulation. Digital technology and increased competition in the satellite market has served to vastly enhance the amount of satellite capacity agencies can buy on any given day, and thus increase the amount of video which can be delivered, particularly live. An analysis by APTN showed that in the three years between 1997 and 2000 it was possible to drive down the average cost of a ten-minute international satellite booking into its London headquarters by 70 per cent. This excluded permanent satellite connections into London from bureaux in the United States, Moscow and Israel. A classic example was the satellite route from Indonesia to London, where the cost of a 10-minute satellite booking was cut by 80 per cent because of aggressive negotiation with a new commercial provider in a market which had previously been highly regulated. The effect on the market was for more coverage to be delivered from Indonesia. Whereas the agencies would have previously delivered video once a day if a major story broke in Jakarta, it soon became the norm to feed material up to four or five times a day. Thus, falling satellite prices made countries more connected to the international television world.

Transmitting video by satellite telephones. This, arguably, was a momentous development, which meant that, suddenly, no part of the world was immune from same-day, or same-hour, television news coverage. In 1997, news agencies suddenly acquired the ability to compress video digitally and transmit it down a satellite telephone in file form.[1] Sending two minutes of video took, on average, around 40 minutes. The satellite telephone and store/forward compression unit needed to do this fitted into a suitcase. Previously, sending video from anywhere other than a fixed TV earth station would require up to two tons of equipment.

Before this development, decisions on whether to cover a story might well have been taken on the basis of how practical it was to provide timely coverage in a cost-effective way. The advent of feeding video by satellite telephone simplified the decision-making process. Suddenly TV news agencies and broadcasters could report within the hour from anywhere in the world provided they had the right equipment and a power supply.

An early example of this was demonstrated by APTV in the former Zaire in 1997 when forces loyal to rebel leader Laurent Kabila began their campaign to seize power. The Associated Press crew spent several weeks charting the advance of the rebel forces across the country. Previously, the cost of keeping a crew with the forces – and chartering a plane at regular intervals to fly their video hundreds of miles to an earth station in Kenya – would have been prohibitive. It would have cost tens of thousands of dollars in charters, if you could have found a pilot prepared to make the journey, and then nearly three thousand dollars for each satellite feed. The inevitable decision would have been to abandon the forces at an early stage and catch up with them weeks later in the capital Kinshasha. Instead, at the cost of a few hundred dollars a day, the world saw history in the making, with daily updates of the troops' advance. A Reuters crew who initially tried to follow them, without a store/forward device, abandoned their efforts when they realised their coverage was always going to be several days out of date compared with its competitors.

Transmitting video via the Internet or company-wide area networks. This is a technique in relative infancy in 2003, but which is increasingly being used by the agencies, and broadcasters, to move video in non-realtime from locations where there is an Internet connection. This is a cheap way of moving video if it is compressed into reasonable-sized files. However, the transmission time is difficult to predict if you are at the mercy of available bandwidth on the Internet. It can take several hours to transmit a two-minute, broadcast-quality report. Specialised compression equipment is required and there is a need to have access to an Internet connection, so it is not a method which is currently usable in the middle of Afghanistan or the African bush.

The advent of videophones. The American strike on Afghanistan in 2001, in the wake of the attack on the World Trade Center, was deemed by the TV news industry to be the 'war of the videophone.' This was a device which allowed live video of usable quality to be transmitted by satellite telephone.[2] It also made it possible for TV correspondents to report live from a location and also to hear the questions of an anchor interviewing them from the TV studio. The device was pioneered primarily by CNN and again offered the technical flexibility to provide live coverage from extremely remote locations.

Of course, the other side of this revolution in collecting news video is the creation of new digital markets for the distribution of it. These have been slower to materialise than expected. The availability of video clips on the Internet has been limited in attractiveness, primarily by restrictions of bandwidth and the slow take-up of broadband technologies. The advent of video clips on 3G telephones has suffered constant delays. The burst of the dot.com bubble and the collapse of share values in the telecom sector in 2000/1 both served to suppress investment in technologies to make video more readily available on new platforms. There is no definitive view of the size of these markets, regarding the appetite for news video, and no fixed timescale for development.

Attempts to broaden the market for news video by using the Internet generated negligible revenue before the time of writing of this chapter. The most high-profile attempt was the creation of TVNewsweb.com, which closed in 2001 after a two-year lifespan when it finally ran out of funds. It was a bold attempt to create an online marketplace where broadcasters could buy video from smaller, regional TV news agencies, other broadcasters and freelance journalists on an ad hoc basis. It did not, however, have the strength of content, or regular coverage, to make it an attractive alternative to the main news agencies.

APTN launched APTNvideo.net in late 2001 to sell video to non-broadcasters in multiple digital formats. The initial interest was from newspaper websites and portals, but the market was initially very small compared with the broadcast market. It demonstrated a different appetite for video online than for video on TV. The most sought-after items were memorable clips of video, which could be viewed repeatedly – such as the terrorist planes striking the World Trade Center. There was no early apparent appetite for a comprehensive daily diet of TV coverage online.

Conclusion

The twelve years between two wars in Iraq – from 1991 to 2003 – serve as appropriate points between which to measure the advances in TV agency coverage. The comprehensive coverage provided by both agencies in 2003 was in marked contrast to their performance in 1991, when they offered only very basic coverage on which broadcasters could not dependably base their reporting of the war.

In the 12-year span, agencies have improved their breadth, quality and speed of coverage. The intense competition in the mid-1990s, when three agencies were slugging it out for market share, had the effect of driving up quality and making agency coverage technically better and more journalistically robust. The importance of agencies to broadcasters grew because most were under pressure to cut back on their own international coverage in response to falling revenues, while at the same time needing to find more and more content for a growing number of channels.

The advance of digital technology and the widespread deregulation of tele-communications created an expectation among broadcasters that no part of the world was immune from same-day coverage. Indeed, agencies have helped shape that expectation, using speed of delivery as a competitive tool, and are nowadays often at the forefront of using the latest technology to do so.

The agencies' immediate challenge is to continue harnessing the digital revolution to keep ahead of the curve in providing cost-effective coverage for the embattled TV news market, facing pressures from shrinking audiences and an advertising slump in the early 21st century. The successful agency will be the one that most skilfully harnesses new technology to deliver more material live, at a competitive price. It is unlikely to leave many funds for innovative enterprise journalism – with agencies having to strike a balance between providing live 'coverage' as opposed to purely edited reports, which are more journalistically rounded. On current trends, the focus for the agencies will be to continue to supply the main stories of the day at even greater speed.

However, as financial pressures on broadcasters increase further, their dependence on agencies can only grow, as ultimately the amount of usable and relevant material they supply represents good value for money. On balance, the threat of a 'one agency' market is unlikely to become a reality in the near future as news broadcasters privately appreciate that the current competition creates a higher level of performance in news coverage and allows them negotiating power on price.

A unique – and increased – flow of live material is also the best opportunity the agencies have for capturing new markets. The kind of distinctive recorded video clip that is currently popular online is not a daily occurrence. New platforms – such as news websites and wireless mobile devices – are of interest to a younger demographic than traditional broadcasters. The new platforms get their highest numbers of hits during major, breaking news events where a speedy, or live, flow of material is crucial. The next step in the quite revolution is for agencies to become the main conduit of any major news event *live* for the world's media.

References

Clare, J. (1997) *News Production at APTV* Unpublished Masters dissertation, Leicester: University of Leicester, CMCR.

Cohen, A., M. Levy, I. Roeh and M. Gurevitch (1996) *Global Newsrooms, Local Audiences: A Study of the Eurovision News Exchange*. London: John Libbey.

Hjarvard, S. (1995) *Internationale TV-nyheder. En historisk analyze af det europeiske system for udveksling af internationale TV-nyheder*. Copenhagen: Akademisk Forlag.

Paterson, C. (1998) 'Global Battlefields', in Boyd-Barrett O. and T. Rantanen (eds), *The Globalization of News*. London: Sage.

Putnis, P. (1996) 'Producing Overseas News for Australian Television', *Australian Journal Of Communication*, 23(3).

Tunstall, J. (1992) 'Europe as World News Leader', *Journal of Communication*, 42(3).

Notes

1   Editors note: Greenpeace pioneered this technique as early as 1995, when they used ship to shore telephones to transmit video to the news agencies in London from their stand-off with the French navy in the south Pacific, as France attempted to conduct nuclear tests.
2   Editors note: Unlike the store/forward technology which preceded it, the new generation of satellite videophone depend on extreme compression of the digital video signal to enable transmission of a live image.

Chapter 4
New Media at the BBC World Service

Chris Westcott and Jaideep Mukherjee

Despite the often self-promoting hype around CNN (much of it fuelled by the long-standing fascination of mostly American academics with the Atlanta company), the BBC has long been the world's most influential broadcasting organisation. Its news coverage resources rival those of the major news agencies. Through numerous media, their news reaches a massive English and non-English speaking audience around the world. Here, a leading figure in the BBC's expansion into new media describes the transition from old media to new for the World Service, the traditional global outlet for the BBC. Chris Westcott was interviewed in London by Leicester University researcher Jaideep Mukherjee in Spring 2003. Westcott has since moved to head up the BBC's news monitoring division, a resource even news agencies do not have.

Q: Could you clarify the operational and management structures of BBC Online?

A: There are essentially two components to the BBC's online operation and this is based on the way the BBC is funded. The first component is a public service funded component and the second component is a commercially funded component. The commercially funded component is much, much smaller than the public service component and essentially it is the public service component that, I think, most people know and refer to when they talk about the BBC's online activities. The commercial aspect of the BBC's online operations is essentially about e-commerce and is not directly relevant to international news.

In the context of this project, I believe that it is within the public service component that all the material that is available on the website – on international news, international business, etc – can be explored.

We have a large public service funded operation – operating both in the UK and internationally. This used to be known as BBC Online and has been recently re-branded as BBCi. Within that umbrella organisation all the divisions that constitute the BBC contribute online content to the overall online operation. There are about sixteen individual divisions in the BBC of which the majority are output facing divisions. All the divisions contribute content to radio, TV and to the online operation as well. Some of these divisions are Children's BBC, BBC Radio, BBC Television, BBC World Service and BBC News.

The BBC World Service Online works across all the forty-three languages that the BBC World Service had traditionally broadcast in as a part of its radio operation, and in some cases the World Service shares responsibility with colleagues in other BBC directorates. Two such directorates that are closely associated with the English language part of the content are BBC News and BBC Sport. As a part of this, the World Service co-funds the creation of a certain amount of content that is available on the public service websites.

So there exist sets of vertical organisational lines that come down through the organisation, essentially divided by the operational divisions. Then there are sets of horizontal lines, where the individual divisional operations link up in a matrix formation across the organisation, to produce content between them. One of the divisions in the BBC is called the New Media Division and its job is to act as a provider of core new media activities like design, technical development and technical infrastructure, and it is through this unit that a large proportion of the public service sites originate.

Within the public service operation, there exist two streams of public service funding. The first of which, that everybody in the UK is familiar with, is the licence fee. The second stream, which comes directly to the World Service, is called grant-in-aid – coming through the Treasury from the Foreign Office. The grant-in-aid funding is in addition to the licence-fee-led public service funding. The BBC World Service is funded differently from the rest of the BBC, because its remit is specifically to provide content for outside the UK (ie not to provide content whose primary focus is inside the UK).

There is, on the face of it, a very large, complex and constantly evolving structure and what has been described above is the configuration as it exists presently. Also, the BBC's internal structures change quite often for operational reasons and the structure described is one that has been put into place within the last calendar year. That is as much to accommodate the changes that occur across the BBC on a regular basis as to account for the dramatic recent growth of online media, particularly in importance, over the last five or six years. In terms of the BBC, the online operations have gone through a major transformation – from being a small cottage industry to emerging as a large component of the BBC's overall strategy. So the way in which it operates inside the organisation has had to change significantly to reflect that.

Q: You mentioned that the World Service is now providing content in all the forty-three languages in which it broadcasts. Within this content, what is the proportion of news to other material and how is that determined?

A: Virtually all the material that the World Service provides for its radio and online output is what is referred to as *news* and *information* in its broadest sense. There is only one language, and that is the English language, in which the World Service provides content that exceeds that remit – beyond news and information – into what might be called an *entertainment* content, ie music, drama etc. In the forty-two other languages, the World Service's content is primarily news and information. One thing that the World Service has striven for, effectively in the last decade, is that the Service should work to a much more broader definition of *news* and *information* or *current-affairs* than news organisations have traditionally worked to. This is because it is thought to be important within the Service itself and also because audiences have fed back to say that this is what they want.

So, to cite a practical example of that, there has traditionally been a large concentration on international geo-politics as the staple of news organisations such as the BBC World Service. But surveys have shown that audiences want a broader agenda than that. The Service has reacted by customising content and audiences, in turn, have responded by increases in numbers that listen to radio broadcasts and visit the World Service's websites. Audiences demand an agenda that encompasses business, technology, science, health, environment, and – particularly because the Service operates internationally – they would like content that incorporates an element of English language teaching. That is because many people want to learn English as a second language or have English as a second language and would like to improve usage. So it really is *news* and *information* in their broadest senses which make up the news or news agenda for an organisation like the BBC World Service.

Q: You referred to branding and target audiences in an earlier answer. Are there any specific target audiences for these services that can be inferred from the way they have been branded?

A: This is a pertinent point, something that content creators in the Service constantly debate, analyse and refine. If I were to provide you with a glimpse into the history of the World Service, it will help clarify the context in which I will provide the answer.

For a large part of its existence – the BBC's World Service started in 1932, just over seventy years ago – the Service has broadcast international news on short-wave radio. This meant that the Service could cover large areas of the world with common content. The language that was used to broadcast globally was English and specific large areas of broadcasting territory could be covered with other key languages – for instance, Chinese (covering the whole of Mainland

China, including what is now Taiwan and Hong Kong) and Arabic (which covered the whole of the Middle East). The essential editorial policy was to create content that worked in these languages – covering broad continental sweeps, whether it be in the former Soviet Union, in the case of the Russian Service, or the Middle East, for the Arabic Service.

As the World Service entered the 1980s, and certainly throughout the 1990s, there was an inclusion of an increasing amount of content which is referred to as 're-broadcasting'. This, essentially, is working with syndicated partners, who take the BBC's content and re-broadcast it from their own radio stations. These are FM radio stations with a much smaller footprint, as an FM radio station typically reaches a 50-100 km radius from the transmitter. The World Service then started having content being delivered to much smaller, targeted, geographically specific audiences – particular niche audiences. That initiated changes in the way editorial content could be 'cut and diced' for much smaller, defined geographical areas.

The arrival of the Internet was almost like the discovery of a second short wave, in that it is a global medium. I do accept the fact that it is not truly global if, say, one lives in Myanmar, where it is illegal to own a modem, or one is located in parts of the world where there are no telephone lines and or one can never expect to afford a computer. The arrival of the Internet presented the World Service with a number of opportunities and a number of branding questions. The first one was language. In short-wave radio the only global language was English and because of the way the BBC had set up radio transmitters, English was broadcast over virtually all continents. But because of the way the Internet works, any language put on a site immediately becomes global and can be seen anywhere. One of the first languages the World Service worked with was Arabic and once an Arabic website was on line, irrespective of which geographical regions Arabic was most commonly used, anyone anywhere in the world with access to the Internet could start to see content from the site.

So the Service started to develop diaspora audiences and, as is known from the World Service's Arabic online operations, there exists significant interest in the content from North America and some parts of Europe where there are a large number of Arabic speakers. Another global language that would be an example is Spanish. In the Spanish Service the radio operations are targeted to South and Latin America, but Hispanic communities throughout the US are picking up the Spanish online output. So a converged operation like the BBC's immediately develops the ability to reach diaspora audiences in particular countries, as well as traditional audiences in specific geo-linguistic territories.

The challenge then is to combine the branding of these services with the editorial direction to ensure that the World Service is delivering the best content, ie most relevant to these audiences, and that becomes quite difficult. Because in some cases the content for traditional language audiences might not be optimised for diaspora audiences and so thought then has to be given to how the content can be changed, and along with it the branding. Branding has to work together with content, and in some cases the branding is the content. That raises questions about what the World Service calls itself on air and how it cross-promotes between radio and online. How much of 'themselves' do audiences see when they go on line and how does the content present itself most relevantly to audiences – these are the questions in an evolving area that content creators in the Service try to work their way through.

Q: How do you see these synergies or distinctions developing in the future?

A: It is important to remember that in some cases there are no synergies. For instance, if the diaspora audience want a different product from the traditional territory audience, then the World Service will have to think carefully about how to change the editorial mix, to offer audiences content that works across both sectors.

Where there are synergies, the focus is to get the content working for multiple audiences, as well as the content working across multiple platforms – both of which are equally important. Operations like the BBC World Service Online cannot succeed without doing both simultaneously. Content needs to work across a wide range of audiences, which means thought and planning need to go into how content is segmented, how it is signposted and produced for delivery – across an array of technical platforms.

We also have to see to it that the Service doesn't bankrupt itself in trying to produce content for each individual platform every time. So there exists a little *mantra* in the World Service, which basically runs along the lines of 'produce once, distribute many times'. What that means is getting as close as possible, within the limitations of editorial constraints, to producing content in a way that is essentially platform-neutral, so that it can be then packaged and delivered across short-wave radio, FM radio (in the future, digital radio) fixed Internet connections and mobile Internet. What no organisation can do, and the 'dot com' crash proved this in spectacular fashion for many start-up companies, is no matter how well funded they are they cannot generate individual content flows for individual delivery platforms using exclusive groups of content creators. It just can't be done, it's too difficult.

Q: So in terms of newsgathering, is it essentially a common pool, ie the common cadre of BBC journalists, that BBC Online and the BBC World Service dips into to meet its requirements?

A: In terms of the BBC's newsgathering, I think it is pretty unique. The way in which the BBC does its newsgathering defines one of its key competitive strengths, and hence one of the 'unique selling propositions' (USPs) in terms of the product delivered. The BBC possesses one of the world's, if not *the* world's, largest newsgathering operations and it prides itself in basing correspondents and reporters around the world, all the time. And this is not just by flying them in once there is a story and flying them out again. Clearly the BBC does deploy extra teams into particular hotspots, recent events in Afghanistan being a classic example. But the teams that went into Afghanistan could build upon the experience and knowledge of the fact that, until a few years ago (when the Taliban decreed that the BBC could no longer maintain a correspondent in Kabul), there was a BBC Afghanistan Correspondent and a bureau in Kabul. The BBC has maintained a bureau in Islamabad and in Tehran, and continues to maintain journalists around the world.

This newsgathering operation feeds most notably into the BBC's English language services, as the English language operations provide the core of the content that is consumed in the UK. But it also provides a large component of the content that is delivered internationally in radio, online and TV (BBC World) and also works as an engine room for content that is then used in other language operations. What the World Service has been able to do over the last decade is invest quite heavily in individual languages. So it doesn't just take material in English and translate it into other languages, it carries out original newsgathering and original journalism in all the forty-three languages that the World Service operates in.

So the BBC may well have an English language correspondent in, for instance, Islamabad but it will also have a journalist working for the Urdu Service, whose work might be supplemented by an analyst from the Urdu Service working from Delhi. So there is a richer, more nuanced flow of material into the organisation, which editors then have to ensure is mirrored back out into the richness of the overall product and delivered to audiences. I believe the BBC is doing that well, and indeed the growing audience figures support that contention. The BBC World Service is the world's largest international broadcaster, with a weekly audience of over 153 million people – which is larger than that of its two main competitors, the Voice of America and Deutsche Welle, combined. So the BBC World Service is by far the world's most successful international broadcaster and I believe that the reason for that, in part, is the fact that the Service is able to blend the benefits of this immense newsgathering and original journalism operations in all of the operating languages.

Q: You suggested that that the nature of the BBC's newsgathering operation adds to the richness of the news and information output of the World Service and BBC Online. Do the BBC's traditional media services also use this specialist, original journalism in regional languages?

A: Yes, BBC's traditional media services would, and there are some notable recent examples, particularly following the events of September 11 and the situation in Afghanistan. Having people who speak Farsi and Pashtu has been of immense value to the BBC in many ways across its newsgathering and news production operations. And indeed, very regularly, senior members of the Persian and Pashtu Services have been on the main BBC domestic news programmes in the UK – both on radio and on TV – enriching the content that the BBC is offering back to licence-fee payers in the UK.

The only journalists who were given accreditation to, and were allowed to report live, the inauguration of the 'handover' government in Afghanistan were from the Persian and Pashtu service of the BBC World Service. The only journalists who had major access to the participants at the UN-sponsored conference held prior to that in Bonn were from the same Services. It is because of the World Service's knowledge, its experience and relationships, that it has unfailing access to public figures that no other media organisation is able to match, and this remains a key USP for the BBC *per se*.

To give you another recent practical example, a woman journalist from the BBC's Pashtu Service interviewed Tony Blair and it made a lot of press coverage in the UK. The week after, the US Secretaries of Defense and State, Donald Rumsfeld and Colin Powell, requested to be interviewed by the same journalist. And that is because they knew that their voices would be heard on the BBC's Pashtu Service in Afghanistan, where over 70 per cent of the population listens to the Service. And that is the kind of reach and the kind of journalistic integrity that both audiences respect and public figures recognise.

Q: You mentioned earlier that the Internet was 'a new short-wave radio', and there are obvious benefits of convergence that the Service has taken advantage of. What specific impact has convergence had on the BBC World Service's news dissemination?

A: I think convergence has allowed the World Service to achieve three of its key strategic aims. Firstly, it has allowed the Service to deepen and enrich relationships with existing audiences by allowing it to offer material on line that enriches the radio-listening and TV-viewing experiences of audiences. The Internet not being a medium that is 'time limited', material can be put up there which people can come back to when they want. It is also an 'on-demand' medium, so if audiences miss material on radio or TV, they can come back and get it online. That has proved particularly successful for the BBC, because the World Service works in the global context and because most of the languages it broadcasts in are broadcast only for a few hours every day. The audio of virtually all the broadcasts is put on the website for audiences to come and listen to whatever they want, on demand. The audiences are able to use the website as people use the VCR to 'time-shift' their TV viewing. This has proved immensely valuable for people who speak a particular language but do not live in the particular area where the World Service broadcasts on short-wave or FM radio. If, for instance, one wanted to listen to the Arabic broadcasts from anywhere in the UK, ie where it isn't available on short-wave or FM, it can be done from the BBC World Service Online website.

The second area that convergence has benefited the World Service has been in building new audiences. There is evidence that significant proportions of people who use the World Service's websites do not listen to the BBC on radio or watch BBC channels on TV. The BBC is seen to be more relevant to these people's lives, because it is available on a medium that they use – in effect helping the BBC to build new audiences. But building these new audiences is not only about creating an audience of people who don't come across the BBC, but it is also extending the times of the day that they can use BBC Online. That is particularly important for the World Service in reaching the 'work audience', in other words, reaching audiences while they are at work.

If you think about the ways in which the Internet spreads out across the countries of the world, it tends to start within the work audience because people are wired first in their workplaces. Only after that, and depending on demographic and other factors like GDP and costs of phone lines, does it spread into homes. The kinds of people that the World Service aims to reach are the opinion-formers, movers and shakers – the categories of *cosmopolitans* and *aspirants* – and many of these people use BBC Online at their work, in their education, allowing the World Service to build new audiences.

The third way the World Service benefits is by initiating a process of thinking of people as being more than just audiences, but as participants in the processes of news and information. Traditionally in radio and TV, particularly in international radio and TV, it has always been immensely difficult to 'close the feedback loop' – ie to get relevant feedback from audiences. The World Service can do international phone-in programmes and people can write to us, but that often goes into an extended and delayed loop. It is not a very good experience for broadcasters or for the audience, both of whom want more information. This makes closing that feedback loop extremely difficult. But with the World Service going on line an immediate feedback loop exists, which is e-mail. So the BBC has not only developed new kinds of radio and TV programmes that take advantage of the closed feedback loop, which then enriches its radio and TV programming, the BBC is also trying to create unique on line experiences. For instance, facilitating an online forum, where audiences can email the correspondent in Kabul to ask questions and the website will run the question-and-answer session with the correspondent. So the online component has helped steer the World Service towards an immediate active relationship with audiences who were for so long in a passive receiving mode – where delivery platforms, that were editorially impossible before, have now been created and activated.

Q: In terms of allocation of resources and content of broadcasts, how much of the World Services output is divided between online and traditional media?

A: It is probably easier to explain in terms of 'resource input' than by a measure of output because the difficulty with measuring output across media is that whilst the output on radio or TV is calculated in hours, the measure for online output is determined in pages.

In terms of resource input, the World Service aims, during the present three-year planning period, to raise the level of investment in on-line operations to between eight to ten per cent of the total investment in the World Service. That figure may not appear to be very substantial, but the important point would be to consider the rate of increase. BBC Online really got going within the BBC about six or seven years ago and to get from zero to ten per cent investment within a large organisation like the BBC, with the nature of its public service commitment within the UK and incredible pulls on its resources, in such a short period of time is indeed remarkable.

Though only ten per cent of the BBC's resources can be attributed to the online operation, the new media, like other traditional media, can tap into the immense richness that the BBC has of content and content production skills – the journalism, the correspondents and the infrastructure that makes the whole thing work. An immense amount of investment is actually leveraged across the organisation – bearing in mind that the BBC's total annual income is to the tune of £2 billion. ($3.4 billion) And one of the things that the BBC has tried to do over the last few years is to work out how best to leverage that large investment in radio and TV across the new media operation. If the new media operation were to be a stand-alone organisation, the BBC would have to spend a lot more money than is currently done to achieve the same benefits – because there exists this immense organisation churning out content continually for radio and TV so far and so fast.

Q: You mentioned that the Internet was available – in theory at least – in every part of the world. But does the BBC's increasing emphasis on online operations and the technical sophistication of the sites not end up excluding some of the traditional audiences of the World Service?

A: This is something that the BBC agonises over a lot and picks up quite often in listener feedback programmes. People often write in and even, interestingly, send e-mails querying the constant emphasis on the fact that the BBC World Service has a website.

I think there are two answers to that. First, there are undoubtedly audiences for whom the chance of using anybody's website, let alone the BBC Online's, is vanishingly remote. There are large parts of the world where the thought of ever owning a computer, and indeed ever seeing one, is far out of most people's range of expectations. That is why the BBC is continuing to make extremely large investments – in some cases even switch resources into – in continuing to deliver content by short-wave, medium-wave and FM radio. The World Service is presently in the process of making a very large investment in a new short-wave transmitter station in the Gulf, which will serve audiences in South Asia, Southwest Asia and North Africa. Although the BBC is moving very aggressively into new media, it is not being done at the expense of existing audiences in areas of the world where they have no other source of information. These are audiences that are referred to as *information poor* audiences and for these audiences the World Service is the only, or one of the few, providers of information that they can have. The Pashtu speakers of Afghanistan are a good example of this. There has been no TV until recently, there have been no newspapers and there has been no independent radio; and the only way they could find out what was happening the world over was through the BBC Pashtu Service. The World Service has remained committed to that end and has recently switched more resources into that operation.

However the Service also caters to groups referred to as *cosmopolitan* and *aspirant* audiences.[1] In many parts of the world where these audiences are served, the audiences are seen to be working in quite technologically sophisticated environments – for instance, large tracts of Southeast Asia, parts of the African continent, South America and increasingly the Indian subcontinent. And it is quite sobering – to be living in Western Europe and working in an industry dominated by North America – to see just how fast these developments are taking place. For instance, although there exist parts of Africa where owning a PC still remains a dream, there are now more mobile phone connections in Africa than there are fixed landline phone connections.

Technologies do spread extremely quickly and in some cases they go into areas much more rapidly than they do in so-called developed western countries. In Africa for instance there are countries that are leapfrogging generations of technology, like the spread of mobile telephony in urban centres of Nigeria. With that, especially in the business community, come all the things that people need to do business with, like the Internet now being a business tool just as much that the phone is a business tool. So services like the BBC can piggyback on the fact that for once a broadcast or content delivery medium also becomes the same medium that people need for their businesses. This could not have been said for radio or TV. The industry is beginning to see a very rapid take-up of the World Service's on line content in many more countries across the world. Recent statistics from the World Service's websites reveal that on a single given afternoon there were visits from eighty-nine countries in a two-hour period of a what is called a 'normal' news day. Going down that list to identify the high-GDP, North American, Western European type countries, perhaps ten or fifteen countries could be listed. To get down to eighty-nine countries means the Service's online content is reaching countries and people, admittedly not in large numbers, who would have otherwise been thought to receive the BBC's content only on short-wave radio.

There is also evidence of that process accelerating rapidly. At the end of 2001, for the first time there were more people who do not know English at all or do not use English as a major language using the Internet than those who know or use English. That switch between English being the dominant language of the Internet to English no longer being the dominant language has occurred far faster than anybody had predicted. That is why I think that the World Service's presence on the net in forty-three languages will be one of the cornerstones of the World Service's future success, as there will be an increasing number of people coming on to the Internet who speak Spanish, Arabic, Russian, Hindi, Urdu, etc. So the BBC will continue to develop world-class sites in these languages, which will, hopefully, be coincident with these people 'arriving'. But we will also take *first-mover* advantage, which the World Service clearly did in the Arabic-speaking parts of the world when it pioneered an Arabic online operation in mid 1999 and the competition followed.

Q: In terms of television and online operations of the BBC's World Service, who does the BBC see as its competitors?

A: In new media, and in some respects this goes for TV as well, there are some large global competitors who are predominantly strong in English, but are now starting to develop strengths in other languages. Those key competitors have largely emerged from North America and these are CNN, MSNBC and Yahoo. They are the BBC's *global* competitors in the online medium. Then there are a whole trench of traditional media organisations which have gone online, who can become *regional* competitors; for instance, newspaper groups, TV and radio operating groups. Then below that are competitors at the *local*, linguistic level.

The Internet has often been called *the million-channel universe*. Effectively anybody and everybody can be a publisher on the Internet, but not everybody gets as much traffic to their homepage since not all Internet users are aware that they exist. The challenge for users is to find what audiences are looking for in this million-channel universe. So in effect, anybody can become a competitor to the BBC and it has to continually find ways of cutting through that crowd, using all the brand strengths that it has, and enable people to find and use the BBC's Online sites. The BBC's established syndication arrangements, which number over a thousand in radio, can be duplicated and we aim to establish similar syndication arrangements for online content, so that the sites can be found by users across a whole range of portals, platforms and services – in the same way that audiences might be able to do on radio or TV.

Q: How does the BBC look at emerging traditional and new media players like Al-Jazeera and tehelka.com who are creating an impact in localised, and often linguistically specific, markets?

A: I think that there are two types of competitors that the BBC faces online. First is the very strong local competitor and second, others who have moved to a different part of the value chain from where they traditionally operated. In the second area, I refer particularly to news agencies – which till the advent of the Internet have really only been lesser-known content providers to other better-known content providers. Earlier, if one looked hard enough, a Reuters or AP tag on a newspaper article or a photograph could be spotted. But with the spread of the Internet, a lot of agencies have sold directly into websites and you might spot an AP or Reuters news-feed on some portals. And interestingly, these news agencies now see the BBC as a competitor of theirs, as well as having relations with the BBC at other points in their value chains. So in one part of the BBC's value chain there exist contractual relations with these news agencies to supply the BBC with news and in another part of the value chain they are competitors to the BBC. The really interesting organisational dynamic to observe here is that a competitor in one part of the value chain can be a collaborator in another part of the organisation.

At the local level the BBC has seen the rise of some very strong individual portals or news operations and have also seen the waves of the dot com crash spread out beyond North America. Many organisations are now in a precarious financial position. And many organisations which have recently arrived in the media industry, particularly in to news as a subset of the media, have failed to appreciate just how difficult it is to run such operations well and to do it consistently, 365 days a year on a 24/7 basis. It is a very expensive business where experience and history counts for a lot.

So, in parts of North America, Latin America and parts of the Southeast Asian markets, the prominent emergence of some brands and the rapid disappearance of many of those brands all happened very quickly because they just could not make it pay and there isn't a commercial model to make it work. Where the BBC sees itself having an edge over any such organisation is that it brings to the table an immense organisational strength and depth, and an international perspective, making people come to the BBC for their news. They come to the BBC because they are aware that the BBC will set the world into context and not just provide them with news of the local sport, weather or traffic. What the BBC have done in radio, and are looking to do in online operations, is to partner with organisations where the content is complementary, and where the organisations can then work together and serve audiences better.

So to have a partnership with a news provider who is particularly strong in a specific territory but for a whole set of reasons, including those of cost, is unable to serve its audience with international news, the BBC could provide the international news component with the local partner providing the local component. It is a strategy that has served BBC radio well and is now being applied to the online operations. There are some successful examples of this operating in Eastern Europe – one in Poland, which has worked well in radio and is beginning to be adapted online – where the BBC might become an international news provider to a Polish news portal. What the BBC is looking to do with its developments in South Asian languages – Hindi and Urdu – is to have that same set of relationships with portals and news providers in South Asia.

There is one underlying difficulty that has so far prevented the BBC from replicating the Polish success story in other territories or as much as some of the potential partners might like the BBC to do. That is due to restrictions created by news legislation in Intellectual Property Rights (IPRs) and this continues to be a nightmare in any medium.

Q: Do you see the lead that traditional media have over new media in breaking news ever changing?

A: This is something that the BBC, unlike a lot of other news organisations and some of its key competitors, does not agonise much over and that is largely to do with the way the BBC is funded. Virtually all of the BBC's competitors, whether in online, radio or television, are driven by the bottom line, money. There has been an immense concern in traditional media organisations that audiences will be cannibalised by new media and that the profitability of the traditional media part of the organisation will diminish as a result. So, goes the argument, a breaking story would not be put on the newspaper's website before the newspaper hits the streets, as people might not buy the newspaper because they might have read the story online; or a story might not be put on a broadcaster's website before the main TV evening news bulletin goes on air, because the news bulletin might attract less viewers or sell less advertising. In some major North American news organisations like the *New York Times*, the *Washington Post*, ABC, CBS and NBC this tussle between new media teams and traditional media teams has been observed, over where the news goes out first – on the TV news bulletin, the newspaper or the news organisation's website.

The BBC has not faced this dilemma to that extent. Though I won't deny that there have been internal tussles between TV, radio and new media teams, but there hasn't been that same concern that there is going to be any damage to the bottom line, because there is no bottom line to damage. What there has been is a genuine concern about is that, if the BBC initiates one activity that diminishes audiences for another activity, the purpose is seen as self-defeating. If, instead, audiences can be moved from one medium to another, is that actually augmenting the size of the audience and enhancing the value of the content to the audience? When the BBC online operation was at its infancy and still finding its feet, it was very difficult to convince colleagues in radio and television that new media was going to do anything other than take radio and television's audiences away. This was despite the fact that all new media news professionals at that stage had all previously done either radio or television at some stage of their careers. However over a period of time everybody within the organisations realised that this dynamic, ie online taking radio and television's audiences away, was not going to be the case.

There are diminishing audiences anyway on mainstream news programmes on traditional media. The best TV audience ratings for news continue to remain flat and are not climbing, except for periods of extraordinary demand – for instance, following the events of September 11. Also the fact that people were leading increasingly complex and disparate lives was clearly evident. The notion of the family sitting down for so-called *appointment viewing* is gone. There are multiple media outlets in most people's homes – multiple TV sets, multiple radios and in some cases even multiple computers and mobile phones. It is therefore beholden on the BBC to produce news, information and other content on as many platforms as people want to receive it. And the BBC was getting substantial audiences online for news and information while continuing to get substantial audiences for the radio and television programmes. Not only is there no evidence to suggest that BBC Online has cannibalised radio or TV audiences, but on the other hand it is now being observed that, particularly in Online and with the advent of digital TV, these media can be brought together to achieve, one of those much overused words, *convergence*. With digital TV too, a clear *feedback loop* works, with audiences being offered alternative versions of available content, making their experience of the content far richer and even building a virtuous circle where the BBC could soon be moving audiences between different platforms, while providing different kinds of experiences on each platform. Audiences get a far greater value from the whole experience than they would have from the sum of the experiences of the individual parts.

The BBC does not have any hard and fast rules about which medium should break the story, since different media are viewed as providing different facets for every story and different media platforms are considered appropriate for different kinds of stories, meeting diverse audience needs. Where the BBC has been most successful is by using a policy of leading with whichever medium can turn out the material fastest. The BBC is unusual in that it has news services available 24-hours a day in radio, TV and online operations, so it is very rare that one medium has a clear lead over others, and also because the material comes in through a relatively common newsgathering process. Only very rarely, perhaps for legal or contractual reasons, would a breaking story be held back to go on a particular medium first.

What the BBC does, is that if there is prior knowledge that a major story is likely to be broken on a particular programme on radio or television, it ensures that associated web content is available and ready to go online. This requires a degree of forethought and planning and is not a race over who goes first.

Q: Do you see this trend continuing or changing in future?

A: I actually see it growing and for a number of reasons. The most important is that this sort of content is what the BBC Online's audiences want, since serving the audiences needs is a touchstone for success of any media organisation. There are also a number of practical internal organisational reasons, to do with efficiency and efficacy, where the BBC faces growing costs for providing content for an increasing number of platforms. And this is the only way an organisation like the BBC can work, since it will never have enough money to do it all individually.

Q: How have the events following on from September 11 and the 'war on terror' impacted on BBC Online's operations?

A: It has had an undoubted impact on news consumption, as it can be measured that it has gone up. Wherever it has been able to be quantified, there have never been so many people watching, listening or surfing for news, but whether that is a long-term trend is difficult to determine at the moment. Within the media community, there has been a lot of agonising on this issue and some very interesting debates on whether this marks a return to serious journalism. There was the feeling throughout the 1990s that there was a push towards dumbing down and infotainment in news content, particularly among North American news organisations, particularly where they dramatically cut back on their news staff. The question is whether this is a kind of temporary blip, and that is a difficult one to answer. For most news professionals in North American or Western European news organisations, it was by far the biggest story that they will ever do, but for people in other parts of the world, it does not rate and for very good reasons it is not a very big deal.

It has also had an impact on the rate at which the BBC was rolling out its news services. On the World Service radio, the BBC has had to dramatically increase the number of hours that were broadcast in a range of key languages (Arabic, Farsi, Pashtu and Urdu). The rate at which websites in these key languages are being rolled out has also been substantially accelerated.

As to key longer-term trends, what it goes to demonstrate is that, while organisations like the BBC World Service can plan lots of things, it is extremely difficult to reach an ideal or optimum level of readiness. This is because news organisations by definition tend to be *reactive*, in the sense they have to react to events. What it essentially comes back down to is having an organisational structure that is sufficiently flexible to respond as fast as possible to immense changes. Whoever on September 10, 2001 could have forecast any of the events that the world would witness and the responses that news organisations like the BBC, would have had to make? Luckily because of forethought, planning and the way many news organisations operate, the BBC and other organisations were able to respond in the way that they did. It was a major shock, but the BBC was able to respond, and the key lessons to learn would have come from what did go well and what did not go well, and to build an organisation that is sufficiently resilient to be able to deal with other major events as well. It is the core capabilities and the core competencies of an organisation like the BBC that gives it the ability to turn the material around and produce the output that makes sense for its audiences.

Q: What achievements of BBC Online over the years make you most proud?

A: The thing that I am really proud of is that the BBC is giving many more people in the world the chance to access what I believe is some of the highest quality content available anywhere in the world – and that extended range and ease of reach is what the Online operation has delivered for the BBC. The ability to not limit output by geography and to make it available anywhere, anytime and to anybody, given the limitations of technology, is an immense achievement. I am also proud of having been one of the people who started this medium, to see it successfully face and negotiate the questions that were asked of it – questions similar to the ones faced and negotiated by BBC Radio and TV when they commenced operations. Online's success has also been important to the BBC, as this was the first instance that the organisation was starting work in a new medium for over 50 years, since the time that TV operations commenced in 1945. And, it shows that the BBC can still do it and still respond to challenges thrown at it.

News events that have demonstrated the particular values of this medium followed the two earthquakes in Turkey and western India. These natural disasters showed how powerful this medium was when people started sending the Service e-mails asking about friends and relatives affected by the quakes. The Online Service ran a sort of a bulletin-board service, providing information for whoever needed it and all of this online and on the e-mail, at a time when phone lines did not work. BBC Online has, in the cases of Albania,

Serbia and Kosovo, provided lists of missing persons and their relatives on the websites, based on those supplied by the Red Cross.

Also, this medium provides a unique platform for those keen on enhancing their skills in and understanding of the English language. Online is a superb medium in which to teach people the English language, where one can teach or learn pronunciation, punctuation, spelling, grammar, and almost everything else in a uniquely interactive way.

The Online service has also won – across the BBC – an immense number of awards for online output and I am particularly proud of that peer recognition from others in the industry. The News site has won four consecutive BAFTA (British Academy of Film and Television Arts) awards for news and in July 2001 it won the *Webbie*, which is regarded as the Internet equivalent of the Oscars, for being the best website for radio operations in the world.

Notes

1   Cosmopolitan audiences – those in the upper quartiles of education and income; Aspirant audiences – people who are moving up the economic and educational ladder while in secondary and tertiary education (Westcott).

Chapter 5
The World's Windows to the World: An Overview of 44 Nations' International News Coverage
H. Denis Wu

This chapter situates international news, and the controversies surrounding it, historically and geographically. Interest in the flow of news between nations surfaced in the 1960s, as emerging nations (all possessing a vote in the General Assembly) looked to the United Nations to remedy long standing structural inequities which disadvantaged them relative to the wealthy, northern hemisphere, former colonial powers. The flow of news was one such issue, dominated as it was at that time by five giant news agencies (Reuters, Associated Press, Agence France Press, TASS, United Press International) and focusing on the news of a few elite, industrialized nations. With backing, IAMCR researchers conducted a massive study in the early 1980s documenting the flow of news among nations (UNESCO Newsflow Study: Sreberny-Mohammadi et al., 1985). Here, Wu describes a repeat effort in the mid-1990s (the most recent mapping of international news flow on record). He demonstrates that the major news production centers of the world – especially the US and UK – continue to make headlines in most places, but also that the media of many nations devote more of their attention to their immediate region than to the news that wire services deem most important. Denis Wu was a principal co-ordinator and statistician for the 1995 international news flow project while a doctoral student at the University of North Carolina.

Communication scholars (Gerbner & Marvanyi, 1977; Schramm, 1959) have long been intrigued by the striking differences in international news coverage across nations, regions and continents. Their inquiries usually start with the ideal assumption that news coverage should, theoretically, reflect the world as it is and cover events without bias. But, undoubtedly, different countries have many different, if not oppositional, windows in which they see the world, resulting in widely varied understandings and interpretations of identical events. Given all the empirical evidence and case studies accumulated in the past few decades, however, there has not yet been a project that systematically draws samples from every corner of the world and presents evidence showing to what extent the globe is portrayed differently in the news media of different countries.

Professors Annabelle Sreberny of the University of Leicester and Robert Stevenson of the University of North Carolina at Chapel Hill took on the challenge and initiated this ambitious multinational collaboration. They aimed to piece together the puzzle of international news during two selected weeks of 1995. The researchers sent out invitations to as many media researchers around the world as possible, hoping to collect data from as many countries as possible. Without outside funding and resources from any international organisation, the scope of this international news flow research project was unprecedented. With the contribution of experienced researchers from around the world and the standardised procedures of media sampling and coding, a certain degree of quality control was insured.

They studied forty-four countries, encompassing every part of the world.

European countries represent the highest number of participants (20); whereas Africa and the Middle East, given their numbers of nations, are somewhat underrepresented. Despite its imperfections, this project resulted in a great opportunity to systematically examine the portrayal of the world in each nation's media. Presented in this report is the highlight of each nation's news coverage in the first two weeks of September 1995.

Method. Experienced researchers in the forty-four participating countries received standardised sampling and coding instructions and conducted content analysis to record elements of all international news selected in the two-week sample period (September 3-9 and 17-23,1995).[1] Detailed information on news media sampling guides, coding instructions, specific codes and final media samples are available from the author. Only one coding item in the content analysis project was used in this study, 'the most important country mentioned in the news story',[2] which records the major, or the first, country covered. The reason the coding of 'dateline' was not used to represent the covered country is that dateline is not normally used in some countries' news media and that sometimes correspondents may not be able to report at the venue of the event. Each news story's major or the first mentioned country is tallied under every one of the 214 (guest) countries in the world.[3]

Prior to sketching the news landscape of each nation, some background information during the period when the sample was selected is useful for understanding and interpreting the results. A number of significant events took place during the two-week period that influenced the media agenda worldwide and the prevalence of specific countries included in the study. The list of these 'newsworthy' international events includes the United Nations Women's Conference held in Beijing, China; NATO's military actions and peace negotiation in Bosnia-Herzegovina; France's series of nuclear tests conducted in the South Pacific and the demonstrations and protests that followed; an explosion in BBC's studio in India; and another explosion at a Jewish school in Lyon, France. It is likely that the countries involved or the venues where these events occurred attracted more coverage in the press around the world at that time.

What follows are the results of the international news coverage study in the 44 surveyed countries:

Argentina. The country that got the highest number (250)[4] of news stories in Argentina's news media was the United States. Spain distantly followed the United States, garnering less than half of the coverage of the United States (94). The rest of the countries that received a reasonable number of news stories wee either European countries such as France (61)[4], the United Kingdom (57), Italy (36), or Argentina's Latin American neighbors: Brazil (50), Chile (37), Mexico (31), and Colombia (27). Four powerful countries in other parts of the world – Japan (29), Russia (26), Germany (25)and China (22) – also received significant coverage.

Armenia. Russia received the highest number of news stories (161) from this former Soviet Union republic in Asia Minor. The United States (70) only got about half the coverage of Russia. The other countries that were significantly covered included Armenia's close neighbours (except for France, which received 26 news stories) Georgia (30), Turkey (33), Azerbaijan (28) and Iran (15). Most countries in Africa, Asia-Pacific and Latin America were not covered in the Armenian media.

Australia. With its unique location in the southern hemisphere, does Australia represent a distinctive, 'down under' perspective on international news selection? Three countries received over one hundred news stories – the United States (305), the United Kingdom (154), and France (107) – with the United States leading the pack. Australia's increasing interest in and identification with the Asia-Pacific region was shown in its moderate amount of news coverage on China (71), Japan (58), India (33), New Zealand (32), Indonesia (29), Hong Kong (25) and Papua New Guinea (18). Three other remote countries in discrete regions – Bosnia (52), Russia (31) and South Africa (19) – also received significant coverage.

Austria. Surrounded by many countries in Central Europe, Austria's news media devoted a lot of space to her adjacent neighbours and other European countries. Her German neighbour received an unparalleled amount of space, a total of 231 news stories. The United States, the superpower across the Atlantic, also received impressive coverage with 200 stories in the Austrian press. Other prominent nations that received a fair amount of coverage included France (131), the United Kingdom (97), Bosnia (69) and Italy (66). Russia (52), Spain (39), Slovakia (30) and Switzerland (28) also enjoyed fair representation. Lastly, two influential countries in the Far East, China and Japan, were also covered with a substantial number of stories (36 and 27 respectively).

Belgium. France, Belgium's southern neighbour, which shares its language, received the largest number of news stories (183). Slightly behind France, the United States captured 141 stories in the Belgian press. The United Kingdom (88), Germany (85) and the Netherlands (84) seemed equally covered in the second rung. Bosnia (62) was abundantly covered, too. Other European nations, Italy (54), Russia (53) and Spain (46) also received a fair share of newshole. China (30) was the only non-European nation on the top-ten list. The rest of the nations that had more than 20 stories were Israel (24), Denmark (21), Japan (21) and Algeria (20).

Benin. Because only one newspaper was included in the study of Benin, the number of stories allotted to foreign countries is inevitably smaller compared to other countries in the sample. The nations that received significant coverage in Benin's newspaper, *La Nation,* seemed to fall into two groups: African countries – South Africa (14), Algeria (5), Côte d'Ivoire (5), Kenya (5), Nigeria (11) – and Western powerful countries such as France (10), the United States (11) and the United Kingdom (4).

Brazil. The United States captured the lion's share of Brazil's international news coverage (84). The next group of nations, Argentina (19), France (18), the United Kingdom (17), Bosnia (15), and Italy (12) were in the second rung of news prominence in Brazil. Other than China (9) and Japan (7), the next cluster of moderately covered nations were in either Europe or the Americas, including Colombia (5), Canada (4), Cuba (4), Mexico (4), Germany (4), Portugal (3) and Spain (3).

Bulgaria. Two countries dominated Bulgaria's international newshole – the United States (174) and Russia (112). The second-rank group of countries that received extensive coverage in the two weeks is all located in the Balkan Peninsula: Albania (23), Bosnia (40), Greece (32), Romania (12) and adjacent Turkey (15). The rest of the salient countries were mostly in Europe, such as Italy (26), France (63), Germany (51) and the United Kingdom (25). Lastly, Israel (23) and China (25) were also covered somewhat prominently in the Bulgarian press.

China. The United States (68) was placed in the central spotlight of the Chinese press. The nation's neighbor, Japan, only received 25 stories. Other salient nations in China's media were Bosnia (18), Russia (16), France (14) and the United Kingdom (11). Germany (9), Australia (6), Mexico (5), Italy (4) and South Africa (4) are also notable. A great number of nations across different continents received one or two stories, indicating an effort of the Chinese media to monitor various corners of the world.

Côte d'Ivoire. As in Benin, there was only one daily newspaper (*Le Jour*) coded in Côte d'Ivoire, which makes it harder to detect the trends in international coverage. Of the countries that received a relatively large number of news stories, most of them were in Africa – Algeria (3), Burundi (3), Egypt (4), Ghana (3), Liberia (5), Mali (4), Nigeria (4), South Africa (4), Zaire (4) and Zimbabwe (5). The United States, however, topped them all with 9 stories. France (4) and Israel (3) were rather salient in *Le Jour*, too.

Cuba. Based on the coding of Cuba's two broadcast media, its Western neighbour, Mexico, received the highest number of news stories (11), followed by France (9) and Argentina (8). The second tier of salient countries included two world powers: the United States (6) and China (5). Surprisingly, Cape Verde, a small island in the Atlantic, received three stories, the same amount of news, as did Ecuador and Iran. It seems harder, as in other countries whose media sample is limited, to identify any trend of international news coverage in Cuba.

Cyprus. Bosnia (15) and France (14), two of the nations where newsworthy events took place at the time, got the highest number of stories in the press of this Mediterranean island. Several countries in close proximity, including Israel (3), Macedonia (3), Russia (5) and Turkey (3), also received a fair amount of coverage. In addition, the United States (9), China (6) and the United Kingdom (5) were emphasised in Cyprus's media. One should note that the sample of Cyprus only included one week of news.

Estonia. Russia (79), Estonia's mighty neighbour and former ruler, was the most covered nation in this Baltic nation's media. The next tier of countries that occupied a significant part of the newshole of Estonian media included the United States (46), France (41) and Finland (31). Estonia's press devoted its attention rather evenly to other European countries. The following list of countries indicated the trend: Bosnia (19), Germany (18), Sweden (18), the United Kingdom (10), Latvia (9), Lithuania (9), Ukraine (8), Spain (9) and Croatia (7). Outside of Europe, China (16), Israel (18) and Japan (12) were also covered extensively.

Finland. With eight news media constituting the Finnish sample, countries that had extensive coverage are easily spotted from the statistical output. The United States beat all other nations with more than 300 news stories during the sample period. The runner up was Sweden, Finland's neighbour, which was featured in 213 news stories. The United Kingdom (178), Russia (170), France (150) and Bosnia (140) were the four other nations that received more than 100 stories. Other countries that received fair coverage were spread across Europe – Estonia (43), Norway (49), Germany (85) and Italy (38) – as well as selective spots of the world, such as China (53), Japan (45), Israel (34) and French Polynesia (26).

Gambia. As with other countries where only one newspaper was selected, it is somewhat tricky to identify the countries that were emphasised in Gambia. Based on the limited sample, Bosnia topped all countries with nine stories in

The Observer. Sierra Leone (8) and Liberia (4), both located in Western Africa, also received significant coverage. The rest of the list includes large countries such as China (4), France (4) and the United Kingdom (5). It is interesting to note that the United States, often on the top of the list of most covered countries, only received three stories.

Germany. At first glance, the nine news media that constitute the German sample covered world economic powers most extensively, including the United States (812), France (482), the United Kingdom (322) and Italy (234). Its neighbouring countries, Switzerland (156), Austria (140), and the Netherlands (100) and three populous countries Russia (285), China (124) and India (66), were also covered prominently. The other countries that received remarkable attention from the German media during the time included Israel (96), Bosnia (120) and Turkey (77) – the first two were constantly involved in conflicts; the third had a large number of immigrants living in Germany. Most countries mentioned so far received more than one hundred news stories in the sample period; on the other hand, Third World countries received scanty coverage – the majority of them either did not get covered at all or received fewer than ten news stories during the two weeks.

Greece. The conflict in Bosnia and former Yugoslavia (Serbia) drew the most attention in the Greek media over the two weeks. France (22) and the United States (20) also received significant coverage in Greece. Aside from France and Bosnia, other European countries that were moderately covered were Belgium (5), Italy (5), Russia (7), the United Kingdom (5) and Spain (4). Only one country outside of the Western world, China (8), was covered substantially.

Hungary. A first glance at the countries that got abundant coverage in Hungary's media shows that Europe was heavily covered. Particularly worth noting are Russia (142), Germany (120) and France (94). The other countries in Europe that also received significant coverage were Austria (40), Bosnia (49), Croatia (19), the Czech Republic (24), Italy (77), Poland (30), Romania (80), Slovakia (94), Spain (26), Switzerland (25), Turkey (23), Ukraine (27), the United Kingdom (74) and Yugoslavia (23). Nevertheless, the United States (232) was covered with the largest quantity of news items, and was distantly followed by runner-up, Germany (120). In other parts of the world, only three countries – Japan (26), China (29) and Israel (33) – received a fair number of stories.

India. The United States captured the first notch among the countries that were covered by India's news media (73). India's former colonial power, the United Kingdom, also received a significant number of news stories (35). The countries adjacent or close to India all got heavy coverage as well, including Afghanistan (8), Bangladesh (14), China (17), Nepal (19), Pakistan (43) and Sri Lanka (18). The rest of the countries featured in the Indian press were the traditional powers: France (13), Germany (13), Japan (15) and Russia (14).

Indonesia. The United States received the highest number of news stories (99) in the press of this vast Southeast Asian country. Countries in Asia-Pacific overall earned noticeably more news space than those in other regions. Among the prominent ones, China received 30 stories, followed by Japan (21), India (14), Malaysia (9), and the Philippines (11). Apart from these, other countries that were significantly covered were all European: France (36), the United Kingdom (30), Germany (15), Italy (10) and Russia (10). Interestingly, the Netherlands, Indonesia's former colonial power, received five stories.

Iran. The most striking characteristic of the Iranian media's map of the world was the emphasis on the Muslim/Middle East. The long list of the countries that were prominent included: Afghanistan (32), Algeria (18), Azerbaijan (22), Egypt (19), Georgia (16), Iraq (50), Israel (47), Pakistan (22), Saudi Arabia (14), Syria (18) and Turkey (21). Nevertheless, it was the United States (164) that topped all the countries covered in Iran's press even though the relationship between these two was hostile. Other countries that also attracted the Iranian media's attention were Bosnia (37), France (52), Germany (46), Italy (37), Russia (64), Spain (21) and the United Kingdom (86) in Europe; and China (55), India (25), Japan (43) and South Korea (21) in Asia.

Ireland. The United Kingdom (544) was covered more significantly than any nation in Ireland. The United States (236) received roughly half the amount of the coverage of the United Kingdom. The third nation on the list of prominent nations was France (102), followed by Bosnia (56), China (35), Germany (33) and Italy (33). European nations and venues of international events such as Bosnia and China seemed to be the main foreign news fodder of Ireland. Aside from the aforementioned nations, South Africa (24), India (23), Russia (20), Israel (18), Canada (17) and Spain (14) seemed well represented.

Israel. The United States received far more coverage than any other countries in Israeli news media (230). The second-tier group was composed of France (107) and the United Kingdom (98). The Israeli press generally divided the international news space into a cluster of powerful nations (in terms of economy or geographic size) and the Middle East. China (35), Germany (56), Italy (41), Japan (44), Russia (46) and Spain (25) belonged to the former group, while Egypt (19), Iran (38), Iraq (19), Jordan (16) and Syria (18) made up the latter group. The only outlier that cannot fit into either group is Bosnia (36), which received a substantial chunk of newshole, too.

Japan. Japan has a slightly different preference in foreign news compared to other developed countries reported thus far. The United States was spotlighted in the Japanese media with more than 600 news items in the sample period, distantly followed by France (283) and China (223). Japanese news media appeared to favour developed, powerful countries (in addition to the above countries, the United Kingdom (88), Germany (57) and Russia (77) were salient), and its neighbors in the Asia-Pacific (Korea, Taiwan, Hong Kong and Vietnam) were covered extensively. Japan also focused on the warfare in Bosnia (86) and the nuclear tests in French Polynesia (52) – the latter focus was probably part of the reason why France led among the European countries in the rank of news stories.

Kenya. The most evident trend discernible from the frequency output is that Kenya covered African countries more extensively, particularly those located in its region. The African countries that received significant coverage included South Africa (42), Uganda (24), Algeria (21), Sudan (15), Somalia (14), Tanzania (14), Egypt (14) and Nigeria (13). Surprisingly, China, perhaps due to its role as the host of the United Nations Women's Conference, received the largest amount of news coverage (64). Other countries that were prominent in Kenya's press were also well represented in other countries' counterparts, for instance Bosnia (14), France (20), India (19), the United Kingdom (29) and the United States (44).

Kuwait. As in Kenya's case, Kuwait's international news coverage reflects a strong regional flavour. Not only did the countries in the region generally receive substantial coverage but also one of them, Egypt, received the highest number of news stories (30) in Kuwait's media. What follows is the list of those prominent countries in the region: Saudi Arabia (28), Oman (15), Syria (12), Iraq (11), Iran (6), the United Arab Emirates (6) and Jordan (5). The world's major countries that received the largest amount of coverage, including the United Kingdom (7), the United States (6), Canada (6), China (7) and Russia (8), also had similar numbers of news stories in the Kuwaiti press. Surprisingly, France, a frequent nation on the most covered list, was not covered at all.

Lebanon. Three countries dominated the Lebanese news media during the period: the United States (138), France, (129) and Israel (114). The other countries that also received significant coverage can roughly be lumped into two groups: Middle Eastern countries and the world powers. The former group was composed of Algeria (31), Egypt (92), Iran (39), Iraq (49), Jordan (30), Saudi Arabia (20), Sudan (19), Syria (43) and Turkey (23). The latter group consisted of the United Kingdom (34), China (45), Germany (37), Italy (28), Japan (18) and Russia (54). Also on the list of salient countries was Bosnia (22).

Malaysia. The regional power, China (56), superseded the usual suspect – the United States (26) – to be the nation in the spotlight of Malaysian media. Malaysia's journalistic attention was also somewhat regional, focusing copiously on Hong Kong (6), India (4), Pakistan (4) and the Philippines (4), among others. Perhaps due to the limited media sample, the number of nations covered is not great, which merits caution when interpreting the results.

New Zealand. Will New Zealand monitor the world differently from countries in the northern hemisphere and resemble Australia's choices? According to the results, the United Kingdom (176), the United States (173) and Australia (147) – New Zealand's English-speaking relatives – dominated the international newshole of New Zealand's media. The second tier of media attention was given to the French nuclear tests off the New Zealand coast: France (70) and French Polynesia (52) therefore claimed a substantial share of the total newshole. The rest of the space was somewhat evenly allocated to the warfare in Bosnia (36) and to miscellaneous countries such as China (32), Japan (36), South Africa (28), Russia (23), Hong Kong (22) and Sri Lanka (22).

Interestingly, information flow between Australia and New Zealand was not balanced – New Zealand covered more about Australia than vice versa.

Nigeria. International news coverage in Nigeria can be summed up with a couple of points. First, two English-speaking countries – the United States (25) and the United Kingdom (27) – were almost equally emphasised in the news media. Secondly, other than these two highlighted nations, international news space in Nigeria was quite dispersed among other countries, with only slightly more emphasis given to the African continent. The following group of prominent nations reflected the worldview of Nigeria's press: Brazil (6), China (9), Israel (5), Japan (5), Liberia (7), South Africa (13) and Zimbabwe (9).

Norway. The French nuclear tests held in the South Pacific got the highest attention in the Norwegian press, which resulted in the abundant coverage of France (75) and French Polynesia (20). It is interesting to note that the news media in Norway devoted substantial space to a very limited number of countries. The highlighted countries in the Norwegian news media can be categorised into two groups: European countries – Bosnia (45), Germany (10), Italy (11), Russia (17), Sweden (23) and the United Kingdom (41) – and other big nations – China (30), India (8), and the United States (55).

Portugal. The United States (114), once again, topped all countries in the frequency of appearance in the Portuguese press. The second tier of prominent countries covered included the large European powers such as France (85), Spain (84), Italy (52), Germany (48), the United Kingdom (44) and Russia (31). It is fascinating to discover that three Latin-language European countries – France, Spain, and Italy – received more coverage than the Anglo-Saxon Britain and Germany. Another group of well-represented countries, including Angola (21), Mozambique (15) and Brazil (34) shared a common nexus as former Portuguese colonies. Other countries that were also highlighted were not uncommon in other host countries' media, including Bosnia (38), China (35), Israel (20), Japan (20) and South Africa (14).

Romania. The Romanian press devoted the largest space to covering the United States (77), which received even more than its mighty neighbour, Russia (50). France (47) also received a substantial share of news coverage, followed by the United Kingdom (36) and Italy (35). Three nations in Eastern Europe, Bosnia (25), Poland (18) and Hungary (17) and two other European nations, Spain (17) and Germany (15), were also covered with decent volume. Aside from these European nations, only Israel (14), Japan (12) and China (11) were able to make the cut to appear in the Romanian press.

Russia. The first impression one would get from the frequency output of the news coverage is that the Russian press covered more East European and Central Asian countries that were either part of the former Soviet Union or within its radius of influence. Of these nations, some received large numbers of news stories individually – Bosnia (38), Georgia (20), Lithuania (12), Ukraine (11) and Estonia (10). Nevertheless, the United States, Russia's traditional rival, got the most attention (42). Other than China (15) and Japan (18), the other countries that were emphasised in Russia's news media were all in Europe – France (33), the United Kingdom (20), Germany (15), Spain (10) and Sweden (10).

Senegal. The international newshole in Senegal's media was largely devoted to African countries: Algeria (12), Cote d'Ivoire (23), Kenya (5), Mali (9), Niger (5), Nigeria (11), South Africa (20), Sudan (8), Zaire (7) and Zimbabwe (7). Some of these above countries share the French colonial background. The most covered was France, with 24 news stories, which is only one more story than Côte d'Ivoire got. Surprisingly, only three other countries outside Africa – Bosnia (12), the United States (12) and the United Kingdom (8) – were salient in Senegal's press over the period.

South Africa. The United States and the United Kingdom were the two countries that jointly dominated South Africa's international news space during the time frame, both receiving more than 100 news stories. Distantly following were other prominent countries around the world: Australia (11), China (24), France (27), Germany (17), Italy (11), Japan (17) and Russia (18). Bosnia (18) and Israel (12), two conflict spots of the world, also received significant coverage. It is worth mentioning that overall the countries in Africa were more substantially covered than those in other continents, even though only two countries – Zimbabwe (11) and Kenya (14) – stood out from the list as being prominently covered.

Slovenia. Slovenia's media published or broadcast more than two hundred stories about the United States during the sample period. Its western neighbour, Italy (121), gained the second place among the more prominent countries. It is interesting that Slovenia's international news menu mainly concentrated on European countries. Almost all of the countries in Europe were covered in those two weeks. What follows is a list of salient European countries in the Slovenian press: Austria (34), Belgium (21), Bosnia (50), Croatia (51), France (78), Germany (81), Russia (84), Spain (28), the United Kingdom (64) and Yugoslavia (38). Outside Europe, however, only China (50), Israel (32), Japan (21), Canada (20), India (20) and Australia (13) appeared frequently in Slovenian media.

Spain. The United States (170) and France (138) dominated the international news in Spain's media. Bosnia (77), Italy (74), the United Kingdom (64) and Germany (64), belonged to the second tier of prominence in Spanish media. It is noticeable that Spain's international coverage was dispersed rather evenly, as indicated by the fact that countries highlighted here are located in every continent. For example, in Africa, Algeria (30), Morocco (14) and Guinea (17) were salient; in Latin America, both Colombia and Mexico received 17 stories, respectively; Israel (18), in the Middle East, received substantial coverage; in Asia-Pacific, China (48), Japan (23) and French Polynesia (17) all were covered with a substantial number of stories. In addition to the European countries already mentioned, Russia (43), Portugal (19), Yugoslavia (16) and the Vatican (15) were also conspicuous.

Thailand. Compared to the last few countries, Thailand's media provided a strikingly different news menu for its audience. The list of the salient countries in the Asia-Pacific that were well represented includes China (49), Japan (28), Vietnam (24), India (23), Australia (15), Cambodia (15), the Philippines (12), South Korea (12), Myanmar (12) and Pakistan (10). Nevertheless, the United States topped them all with more than one hundred news stories (115). The United Kingdom also occupied a large portion (77) of the available international newshole in Thailand's media. The rest of the countries that were also emphasised were all in Europe: France (32), Bosnia (20), Russia (20) and Spain (12).

Turkey. Once again, the United States (118) surpassed all other countries in international news coverage in Turkey. The runner-up of the coverage contest was Bosnia, which received 80 news stories. Economic powers in Europe, such as France (50), Germany (40), the United Kingdom (44) and Italy (22), as in other host countries, received substantial coverage in the Turkish media. What is unique here is that the countries surrounding Turkey all got fair amounts of coverage. For example, Russia and Iraq both had 33 news stories. Other countries in the nearby region, such as Azerbaijan (11), Greece (23), Iran (19), Israel (13) and Saudi Arabia (11) were well represented. China (33) and Japan (11) were the only two countries in the Far East that were salient in the Turkish press.

Ukraine. The first characteristic one would be struck with by the Ukrainian press is that the countries in Eastern Europe were covered significantly. Of these nations, Russia led with 58 stories. Bosnia (13) and Georgia (7), also in the same region, also received substantial coverage. The nation that occupied second place in Ukraine's press, however, was the United States (34). The rest of the countries that received substantial coverage belong to the group of world economic elites – France (8), Germany (7), Japan (7) and the United Kingdom (11).

United Kingdom. With 12 media included in the British sample, the difference between the countries that got heavy coverage and those that did not looms more significant. The country with the single largest part of the newshole is, unsurprisingly, the United States, which received a total of more than 800 stories during the two weeks. With less than half of the news stories that the United States received, France is the runner-up, perhaps thanks to the incidents that occurred in Lyon and French Polynesia. Next, Bosnia (201), Germany (117) and Russia (115), and to a lesser extent, Italy (73) and Spain (63), were the prominent European countries in the British press. Aside from the above countries, there seemed to exist a colonial link among the well-covered countries listed below: Australia (60), Hong Kong (28), India (81), Ireland (90), New Zealand (28), Pakistan (26) and South Africa (76). Last, three other usual suspects – China (62), Israel (49), and Japan (61) – were also covered heavily.

United States of America. The long-lasting conflict in Bosnia received more attention than any other countries in the US news media during the sample period. Next to Bosnia (101), the United Kingdom (72), France (57) and Japan (54) all got substantial media attention, followed by conventional powers like China (50) and Russia (35). Israel (41), a frequent conflict spot in the Middle East, also generated a great number of news stories in the US media. The third level of American media attention was paid to the country's neighbours, Canada (26) and Mexico (17), and to two countries further afield, Germany (18) and India (18). As in the other host countries, a large number of countries, especially in the Third World, did not receive any coverage in the American news media during the two-week time frame.

Venezuela. Regional countries were very much emphasised in Venezuela's news media. The United States, the superpower of the hemisphere, was the dominant news superpower with 155 news items. Those countries in Latin America that were also salient in the Venezuelan press included Colombia (57), Ecuador (28), Mexico (27), Argentina (20), Peru (12) and Cuba (10). The other group of prominent nations were all located in Europe – France (58), Bosnia (22), Spain (22), the United Kingdom (19), Italy (18), Russia (11) and Germany (10). Interestingly, China was the only country located outside of America and Europe that received significant coverage.

The World in the World's Media

Presented below are the aggregate results from the international news coverage of the 44 countries. The primary purpose is to draw a more comprehensive picture of the mediated world with which to extract a general pattern of international news flow. According to the numbers of news stories tallied for each country (see Table 1), the top ten most-covered are as follows: the United States (6699), France (3280), the United Kingdom (2833), Russia (1992), Bosnia (1696), China (1495), Germany (1391), Italy (1206), Japan (913) and Israel (771).

It is intriguing to note that seven out of the ten countries that received the largest amount of coverage are economic powers. Except for Canada, the G-8 countries were all copiously covered in the world's press. The United States, dominant in almost every country's newshole, snatched roughly sixteen per cent of the world's available space for foreign news. Also salient in the news world were China and Russia, both having formidable military and political clout. The substantial coverage of Bosnia and Israel seemed a product of the conflicts that were taking place in both countries at the time. Using a different measure, the average percentage of newshole each country received in the forty-four nations (see the second column of Table 1) also resulted in similar ranking, suggesting a consistent pattern of international news coverage.

The list of the most covered nations shows that countries with political and economic clout tend to be emphasised more in the press. Other than being a world power, the only alternative way to be cast in the world's spotlight is to have large-scale, disruptive incidents. And that, of course, is why Bosnia was so well covered at this time. The same justification can be applied, although probably to a lesser extent, to the cases of France and China, where major international events were taking place.

	number		average share
US	6699	US	15.57%
France	3280	France	7.84%
UK	2833	UK	6.92%
Russia	1992	Russia	5.18%
Bosnia	1696	China	4.92%
China	1495	Bosnia	4.78%
Germany	1391	Germany	3.18%
Italy	1206	Japan	2.46%
Japan	913	Italy	2.44%
Israel	771	Israel	1.91%

Table 1. The top ten countries covered in the media of 44 countries

These results also indicate that international news coverage is highly uneven, not only at the level of each individual country, but also at the level of the world as a whole. Even with the combined news sample, many countries in Africa and Latin America, such as Cameroon, Central African Republic, Reunion, Honduras and Guatemala, did not appear on the world media's radar screen, while a few others got abundant coverage worldwide. How each country's media selected news stories and presented the world merits further investigation and theoretical discussion.

Another potentially significant phenomenon derived from this forty-four country comparison is that news media in most countries seemed to devote more space to covering their respective regions than remote parts of the world. This trend of regional focus can be demonstrated vividly when one compares the international news coverage in any European country with that in any African nation. Although it is technically difficult to define a region and to empirically test the notion,[5] cross-national findings may indirectly provide evidence to support the trend found in earlier literature (see Sreberny-Mohammadi et al., 1985; Cooper, 1988; Nnaemeka and Richstad,1980).

This basic comparison can lead to a demonstration of the universality of news value or agenda selection from the specific cases of Bosnia and French Polynesia. These two geographic areas would not have been emphasised in the world's media if the incidents were not considered newsworthy by the gatekeepers around the world. On the other hand, one might contend that this phenomenon of similar 'news diet' could be due to the influence of international news agencies. Because of the limited 'news menu' provided by the major transnational news services, dependent media, particularly those in the South, would likely take the feeds. In the cases of Bosnia and French Polynesia, both factors are simultaneously at work. The potential impact of transnational news agencies on news coverage might be investigated further with a more advanced method.

This primitive examination of international news coverage may appear overwhelming since each country's news window to the world is vitally different. It could be the case that the underlying determinant of each nation's angle to see the world is as different as the variation of the coverage. Yet, it is imperative for researchers to seek and seize the most fundamental denominators that shape the mediated world we read, listen to, watch, and eventually treat as reality. Because the impact of this difference is too huge and broad, we simply cannot ignore this inquiry.

References

Cooper, A. M. (1988) *Televised News of the World in Five Countries: Regional Congruity and Isolation*, paper presented to the 38th annual conference of International Communication Association, New Orleans.

Gerbner, G. and G. Marvanyi (1977) 'The many worlds of the world's press', *Journal of Communication*, 27(1): 52-66.

Nnaemeka, T. and J. Richstad (1980) 'Structured relations and foreign news flow in the Pacific region', *Gazette*, 26: 235-258.

Schramm, W. (1959) *One Day in the Worlds' Press: Fourteen Great Newspapers on a Day of Crisis*. Stanford: Stanford University Press.

Sreberny-Mohammadi A., K. Nordenstreng, R., L. Stevenson and F. Ugboajah (1985) 'Foreign News in the Media: International Reporting in 29 Countries'. *Reports and Papers on Mass Communication* No. 93. Paris: UNESCO, 1985.

Notes

1   Cuba, Cyprus, Gambia, Greece, Indonesia, Nigeria, Norway, Thailand, and Venezuela only completed the first week of sample.

2   The project recorded three countries mentioned in each news story. However, the volume of coverage each country received using major country coded or all three countries coded was found almost identical (in terms of the variance among countries). Based on the thirty-eight-country sample, the Spearman correlation coefficient between the two measures of coverage reaches .972.

3   The list of the countries of the world came from International Monetary Fund (IMF) and International Telecommunication Union (ITU). Whenever a country is listed in either organisation, it is included and tallied. The countries included 29 developing countries (based on International Monetary Fund definitions): Argentina, Armenia, Benin, Brazil, Bulgaria, China, Côte d'Ivoire, Cuba, Cyprus, Estonia, Gambia, Hungary, India, Indonesia, Iran, Israel, Kenya, Kuwait, Lebanon, Malaysia, Nigeria, Romania, Russia, Senegal, Slovenia, Thailand, Turkey, Ukraine, Venezuela; and 15 developed countries: Australia, Austria, Belgium, Finland, Germany, Greece, Ireland, Japan, New Zealand, Norway, Portugal, South Africa, Spain, UK, USA.

4   The number in parentheses that follows each country's name is the number of news stories.

5   The notion of region could be composed of psychological elements and history of transnational interaction, rather than purely determined by geographic boundary or distance.

Part II: Alternatives

Chapter 6
News Imperialism: Contra View from the South
Prasun Sonwalkar

The rise of international news channels from countries of the South, carrying a variety of Southern perspectives, is probably the single biggest change in the global media landscape over the last decade. Such a development challenges the old paradigm of media imperialism and is broadly considered to be a good thing. Sonwalkar, a former editor of India's Zee News, maps out the rapid and massive rise in privately-owned 24-hour news channels in India as a response to economic liberalisation. However, he argues convincingly that these developments are not universally welcomed in the region, where India is increasingly seen to play the role of regional cultural hegemon, functioning as a 'little media imperialism'. He also makes the case that such channels, while subscribers to international news agency feeds, actually rely on Indian news agency material that indigenise even international news coverage.

Countries of the South, or what used to be called the Third World, have long been seen in communications research as abject and passive recipients of western cultural products. Cultural or media imperialism – of which news imperialism is an important sub-set – is always seen to emanate from the West. In such a model, everything, from culture to politics to news agendas of the South, is supposed to be dictated by the cultures or politics or news agendas of the West. The South is invariably viewed in terms of perpetual destitution. Even recent debates about 'dumbing down' of media content are devoted to the contents of television and tabloids in the West, as though such post-modern trends cannot arise in what are viewed as the 'pre-modern' mediascapes of the South.

This chapter presents a contra view of such linear perspectives by setting out the case of news in India and South Asia, a region categorised by virtually every economic indicator as one in the 'South'. The account is based partly on practitioner experience as a journalist over nearly two decades in Indian press and television industries. Framed within the debate about 'media imperialism', or Western hegemony of news production (through news agencies and other outlets), I set out the news-scape in India and South Asia from a political economy perspective, present empirical data about the development of news production and dare to suggest that globalisation of market practices and technology have the potential of remarkably revitalising local news agendas in ways that were unimaginable even a decade ago. In large multicultural settings such as India, for the first time, local cultures and politics are being presented and represented within the country and to the rest of the world in ways that not only enhance local democratisation, a sense of nationalism and regional cohesion, but also a greater awareness and integration with global cultures and global politics.

The thesis of West-rooted 'media imperialism' may well hold its ground in absolute economic terms due to wider reasons of international political economy (the strength of the dollar and the pound, for example), but at the beginning of the 21st century, there are clear indications that its assumptions cannot go unchallenged in certain sectors of international communications. I suggest that the situation in relation to television news in India and South Asia demonstrates a density and vibrancy that is rarely witnessed even in 'developed nations'. Here, international news channels and agencies play a marginal role in the marketplace of news. This is partly due to a local economy catering to a large and burgeoning middle class, the kaleidoscopic socio-cultural diversity of the region, the localisation of technologies and the enhanced global connectivity of peoples and cultures. A dense multi-lingual scenario in the region – millions speak each of the eighteen major languages – supports a large number of regional language channels, resulting in 'a Babel in the skies' (Joshi, 2000).

The exponential growth of 24-hour news channels in South Asia also says something about the high political awareness of a population that, ironically, has consistently recorded low levels of mass literacy. Television news, dominated by politics, feeds grassroots political awareness in a region that has long had a tradition of debates over local, national and international developments. As Sreenivasan Jain, a television journalist, observes, 'We are a news-hungry country, opinionated, alert, fond of showing off our grasp on current affairs. We are also a news-rich country, a country hypersensitive to news, generating every minute a flicker, a blip, or an upheaval waiting to be reported. It is, in other words, a country ripe for round-the-clock news culture' (2003). As a medium, television's ability to enhance and nurture a high level of awareness is ideally suited for a milieu marked by low levels of literacy. As Rajagopal notes, since the mid-1980s television has reshaped the context in which Indian politics is 'conceived, enacted and understood' (2001). As the following argument shows, news channels are drawing more and more citizens into an increasingly visual public sphere.

Furthermore, there are signs that Indian media content, including news, is seen elsewhere in South Asia as the Indian version of what Nye & Owens call 'soft power' (1996). Fears within the region about cultural aggression or invasion from India are reminiscent of the concerns that were raised during the UNESCO-sponsored debate over a New World Information and Communication Order in the 1970s. India's strengths in film are well known, but the proliferation of television since the mid-1980s has further enhanced India's cultural appeal in the region and created commercial opportunities to reach out to the 25-million strong South Asian diaspora across the globe. I have elsewhere suggested that at the regional level, Indian cultural industries have the makings of 'little cultural imperialism' (Sonwalkar, 2001; see also de la Garde, 1993).

Entertainment on Indian television consolidated itself soon after Zee TV began operations in 1992 with indigenously produced and culturally closer programming, and led the way for other channels such as Sony. Since 1996, the genre of news and current affairs has emerged as a major player in the region, attracting large ratings and advertising revenue as 24-hour news channels compete to cover a wide range of issues and events amidst the heat and dust of the Indian sub-continent. In literacy-deficient India, viewed from Anderson's perspective of privileging print capitalism in the discourse of nationalism (1991), television, rather than print, may have a greater role for citizens to constantly reinforce the idea of belonging to India.

In order to make my argument I start with a brief political economy of Indian news channels. I then examine the cross-border viewership of Indian channels and explore the low coverage of foreign events and the low use and localisation of foreign agency output on Indian news channels. Media is nothing if not dynamic. It is a site where the dictum of change being the only constant is played out on a daily basis across continents and time zones. This underlying truism, particularly when framed amidst the shifting quicksands of globalisation in the 21st century, not only validates the broad perspectives set out in the chapter but also highlights their discursive nature. Given their all-pervasive influence on human life, the need to constantly monitor media developments, and incorporate them in scholarship, is perhaps never greater than now.

A Political Economy of Indian News Channels

Doordarshan, India's state-owned television network, enjoyed a monopoly in the genre of news and current affairs until the early 1990s. CNN's coverage of the 1991 Gulf war created an appetite for television news. At around the same time, India liberalised its economy that helped open its skies to satellite television. Several indigenous and foreign media players emerged on the scene to provide general entertainment. Channels such as Zee and Sony provided more indigenised cultural entertainment and soon proved a commercial success while others such as Rupert Murdoch's Star Plus were forced to adapt to local programming. From 1996 onwards, 24-hour news channels entered the fray and tried to retain and enlist eyeballs by covering South Asia's vast menu of newsworthy events and issues relating to politics, terrorism (Kashmir, northeast India, the Tamil issue in Sri Lanka), economy, society, etc.

By 2004 at least seven major private 24-hour news channels were in operation with footprints in 40 countries across South Asia and beyond:

- Zee News (Hindi language); part of the Zee Television network

- Aaj Tak (Hindi); part of the India Today Group

- Headlines Today (English); part of the India Today Group

- NDTV India (Hindi); launched by the independent television production house, New Delhi Television Ltd (NDTV), which, until 31 March 2003, provided news content to Murdoch's Star News channel

- NDTV 24 X 7 (English); launched by NDTV

- Star News (Hindi); part of Murdoch's bouquet of channels in Asia (editorial content produced by a newly established editorial team after contract with NDTV was not renewed after 31 March 2003)

- Sahara Samay National (Hindi); part of the Sahara Media & Entertainment Network, a division of Sahara India, an Indian industrial house with interests in banking, aviation, real estate and media.

In addition to these, the Sun News channel caters to the large Tamil audience in South India as well as the Tamil diaspora, and had received government clearance to launch three other regional language news channels (Udaya News, Surya News and Teja News). Apart from the Sahara Samay National channel, the Sahara group was in the process of launching as many as thirty-one city-centric, free-to-air, digital satellite Hindi news channels in large Indian states: six in Uttar Pradesh and Uttaranchal in north India, four catering to local news in Delhi and the National Capital Region, six covering Bihar and Jharkhand in east India, five in Madhya Pradesh and Chhattisgarh in central India, five covering Gujarat and Maharashtra cities in west India and five catering to Rajasthan in north-west India. Several more channels were in the pipeline as media companies acknowledged the popularity of news on television, particularly in the Hindi/Hindustani language.

A key feature of the above list of news channels is that, except for Murdoch's Star News, they are not owned by any western media company. In the early 1990s, as Murdoch and other international media players eyed the lucrative Indian market – a 300 million-strong middle class estimated to grow to 445 million by 2006-7 – there was much concern about Indian culture being threatened by the invasion from the skies. The debate soon petered out, as viewers preferred programming that was culturally closer which forced international channels to localise content in terms of language and idiom. In 1996, Star News was the first 24-hour news channel on the scene. It enjoyed much credibility as the channel's news content was provided until March 2003 by NDTV, a respected Indian production house headed by Prannoy Roy, who had built a reputation on Indian television over a decade covering elections, budgets and foreign events. Star's contract with NDTV was part of its Indianisation drive, and allowed much editorial freedom; the channel soon became popular among the English and Hindi-speaking elites and middle class due to Roy's brand image and NDTV's sophisticated production values and high journalistic profile.

Other channels such as Zee News and Aaj Tak followed, and soon recorded high ratings. By 2003, news on Indian television had changed beyond recognition. As Wildermuth notes, 'Gone are not only the days of the public broadcaster's uncontested monopoly...but also the days when the threat of 'Murdochisation' of Indian [news on] television could be mobilised in an attempt to ward off the widespread criticism of the inefficient, amateurish and hegemonic character of [news and current affairs] produced by DD [Doordarshan]' (2001: 149). Amidst the intense competition, Doordarshan launched DD News, a 24-hour news channel, but its launch as well as closure in 2000-01 went virtually unnoticed. It was relaunched in 2004. The April 2003 ratings repeated earlier trends in which international news channels such as BBC World, CNN and CNBC consistently record low ratings in a marketplace dominated by Hindi-language channels such as Aaj Tak and Zee News, which accounted for more than seventy-five per cent of the viewership of news channels (Annuncio et al., 2003).

There is a strong reason for the suzerainty of Hindi or, more accurately, Hindustani-language news channels. Hindustani, comprising a delicious blend of Hindi and Urdu, is the language of parlance of a swathe of population across most of north, west and central India and Pakistan, and is widely understood in other parts of India, Nepal, Bangladesh and Bhutan. Hindustani is also the language of Bollywood; it 'is the *lingua franca* of an area the size of a continent, stretching over many nations from Peshawar to Chittagong, with a population of a billion people' (Ahmed, 1992: 290). Since Star's contract with NDTV ended, it broadcasts exclusively in Hindi with a newly established editorial team. As Sharma (2003) observes, 'All of a sudden, Hindi journalism has become hip and happening as journalists from the English media are defecting to the upcoming Hindi channels. That's where the viewership, better salaries and job opportunities will be'. The sheer numbers of viewers familiar with Hindi or Hindustani in South Asia attracts much advertising. Politically, this section of the population is also among the most aware since the Indian parliament is dominated by constituencies in the 'Hindi belt' of north and central India.

The news channels soon began covering events in South Asia extensively, and on several occasions live, drawing increasing numbers of viewers across the region. Some of the major events covered closely include the India-Pakistan clash in Kargil in Kashmir that almost led to another war (1999), Kashmiri militants hijacking an Indian Airlines aircraft from Kathmandu (December 1999-January 2000), the events of September 11 and their impact on the region (including Afghanistan and Pakistan), a terrorist attack on the Indian parliament building in New Delhi (December 2001), the massive earthquake and Hindu-Muslim clashes in Gujarat, general elections (three between 1996 and 1999), a summit meeting between Pakistan President Pervez Musharraf and Indian Prime Minister A B Vajpayee in Agra (2001), the general elections in 2004, etc.

Research shows that India's news consumption has nearly tripled since 2000 (Reuters, 2003). America's 'war on terrorism' after September 11 has proved to be 'manna from heaven for those in the news business' (Bindra, 2001). Viewership of news channels accounts for only three per cent of total television viewing in India, but news as a genre has grown by over 100 per cent: 'Between August 2001 and July 2002, the average television ratings for Aaj Tak jumped by 108 per cent, while the ratings of Star News and Zee News increased by seventy-six and twenty-nine per cent, respectively' (Bansal, 2002).

The burgeoning viewership of news channels has begun eating into the advertising revenues of general entertainment channels. According to industry estimates, revenues of the news channels are growing by twenty-four per cent, which could raise broadcasting revenue from $1 billion to $2.9 billion in 2007 (AP, 2003). Singh notes that 'all categories of advertisers are keen on investing in news channels because of the higher returns they offer compared to entertainment channels' (2003). The revenue of general entertainment channels dwindled from sixty-five per cent to fifty-three per cent of the total advertising budget between September 2001 and July 2002, while the revenue of news channels increased from eleven per cent to seventeen per cent (Bansal, 2002). As watching news increasingly becomes a 'national habit' (Chatterjee, 2003), Prannoy Roy's NDTV was able to tie up advertising worth $ 25 million before launching its two news channels in April 2003. Within the news channels universe, Hindi-language channels cater to a mass viewership base but with a low purchasing power, while English-language channels have a lower – but influential – viewership base and a high purchasing power.

The size of the Indian economy supports a large and growing media industry. India's privately owned television news channels stand out in the region (and within the South) where most governments are known to keep a tight control on the media. The channels are watched widely beyond its borders, partly because of the overlap of cultural and linguistic identities across the nation-states of South Asia and partly due to India's relatively open democratic politics and culture, as well as its more developed professional practices. As Pakistan's former information minister Javed Jabbar observes, 'The sheer size of the Indian economy in comparison to the Pakistan economy means that both through Zee TV as well as through advertisements for Indian products beamed on Star TV, BBC, MTV and Prime Sports, there is greater information flow from India into Pakistan rather than an equitable flow' (1994: 235).

The increasing number of news channels has resulted in wider networks of news bureaux across India and South Asia. Events that would be rarely seen on television until a few years ago are now routinely covered, often live. For the first time, several regions, peoples and events are being drawn into an increasingly visual public sphere. The latest newsgathering technologies and methods have been adopted. Prannoy Roy's team has exclusive access to nine helicopters; as he stated on NDTV's website, 'I know this is common for news channels all over the world, but for the first time in India we will have a fleet of helicopters exclusive to NDTV – to ensure we get you the news first, fastest and with the right perspective' (Roy, 2003).

As in the genre of entertainment, fragmentation and localisation are increasingly emerging as a theme in news as well. Apart from the move towards city-specific news channels, the Indian news universe is marked by a unique feature: the operation of localised community 'channels' by neighbourhood cable operators with large subscriber bases. These 'channels' are disseminated straight from the cable operator's control room to the subscriber's home (without needing satellite uplink), and not only provide films and other entertainment such as neighbourhood contests and draws, but also 'live' coverage of community events, public meetings during elections and so forth, and attract considerable local advertising. Since 1998, cable operators in cities with large middle class base such as Mumbai, Bhopal, Pune, Bangalore, Jaipur and Indore, have also started community news bulletins that have become increasingly popular. The bulletins are professionally produced, and include discussions in the cable operator's studio with prominent guests such as former prime ministers, local celebrities and politicians, etc. This sector of Indian television industry remains an under-researched area.

The positive developments are also accompanied by a downside. The vast menu of daily newsworthy events and issues in an unpredictable and unruly democracy in India, and elsewhere in South Asia, represents a challenge to the news channels. These are early days for Indian news channels but they have already come in for criticism for providing 'more of the same', 'dumbing down', focusing on politics, metropolitan and elite issues and blanking out the media-poor segments of the population. As social scientist Viswanathan observes, 'India must be the only country where at any given time thirty per cent of our population is trying to secede and we don't even know it nor do we care. And the real tragedy is that people still read papers and watch TV for the news' (Phatarpekar, 2002). Such criticism is remarkably similar to that levelled against the media in the West, particularly in relation to the media coverage of ethnic minorities or deprived regions in Britain and the United States.

Cross-Border Viewership of Indian Channels

India's television and news industry dominates South Asia, where other countries have different approaches towards their respective media systems. Its dominance of the region's airwaves, carrying Indian cultural world-views and political perspectives, is galling to others with different political and religious systems but who nonetheless are attracted by the commonality of culture. Viewers in Pakistan, Bangladesh, Sri Lanka and Nepal find entertainment originating from India – through Bollywood and television – irresistible but are uneasy about India's political positions that frame content on news channels. As Jabbar states, 'I am concerned about the influence of Indian satellite television on our people' (Baru, 2000).

Within the sub-continent, India is widely seen as an overbearing Big Brother: '(Many) Pakistanis and Bangladeshis see "Indian" as a rather imperialistic term' (Sardar, 2001). Elites in India's neighbouring countries not infrequently speak of cultural imperialism emanating from India. As Barraclough notes, "In Pakistan, discussions about satellite television are often couched in terms of the medium's role in furthering expansionist Indian or Western agendas ... [The] popularity of Zee news and current affairs is deeply disconcerting. A major part of the country's news and information sector is coming from programming which primarily caters for its neighbour and rival' (2001: 226, 228).

The tense relationship between India and Pakistan is often reflected in the use of military terminology in popular discourse, which also extends to the cultural realm. Ved notes that '[In Pakistan] cultural relations are termed as invasion from India. The latest example of this is the satellite TV channels, which are being dubbed as part of a new and sophisticated intrusion to capture the minds of the Pakistani youth' (2001). Baruah is more specific about the military terminology used: 'In Pakistan, a paranoid military Government is in a rush to create a "media deterrent" against Indian television channels, which are widely seen by the elite of the country. Zee TV and Sony have penetrated into upper middle class Pakistani homes as never before' (2000).

The cross border viewership of channels means that during times of political crisis, such as between India and Pakistan, respective governments routinely ban cable operators from carrying news telecasts emanating from the rival country to counter what is seen as official propaganda. This was evident during the 1999 Kargil crisis, dubbed India's first television war, and during the tensions in 2002 when the two nuclear neighbours nearly went to war (again). The bans, however, are rarely strictly implemented. The 2001 summit meeting between Musharraf and Vajpayee in Agra was also covered extensively, with NDTV's reportage on Star News being widely viewed and appreciated in Pakistan. As Pakistani columnist Ahmed notes:

> The Musharraf – Vajpayee summit may not have yielded sensational results but, during the visit, what the private TV channels of India achieved cannot be ignored. In particular, the coverage and discussion offered by Star TV was nothing short of a breakthrough. While the officials struggled with joint texts as expressions of minimal accommodation, TV advanced the bilateral debate at a much higher intellectual level. No Pakistani effort could have achieved this, given the fact that there are no private channels here (2001).

In the backdrop of uneasy political relations between India and Pakistan, news items on Indian channels that are perceived to be objective or politically convenient are often picked up and broadcast on Pakistan's state-owned PTV, along with the logos of Indian news channels. Commentators in the Pakistan press often make the point that unprofessional coverage of events often makes Pakistani viewers turn to Indian channels to get the latest about events involving Pakistan, such as the Kargil conflict. However, the media scenario in Pakistand has also openend up with the Pervez Musharraf government opening up the skies to private companies. New channels such as Geo TV, ARY Digital became increasingly popular even as cable operators in the country went on an unprecedented week-long strike in August 2003 to demand that the military government lift the ban on showing Indian channels. During the strike they also took the new Pakistani private channels off air.

The popularity of news on Zee TV in Pakistan has seen many of its politicians reach their constituents within that country through the (Indian) channel. Before the dismissal of the Benazir Bhutto government in 1996, former Prime Minister Nawaz Sharif, then in the opposition, often exhorted large audiences at his public meetings to watch Zee TV instead of PTV. Pakistani politicians who have figured in Zee's popular political chat shows such as *Ap Ki Adalat* (Your Court) include Bhutto, cricketer-turned-politician Imran Khan, Qazi Hussain and the London-based Altaf Hussain of the Muttahida Quami Movement (MQM, a movement which espouses the cause of Muslims who migrated to Pakistan from India in 1947).

Regular feedback from viewers in the region is yet another indicator of the influence and reach of Indian news channels. Many viewers, including politicians, based in Nepal, Pakistan, Bangladesh, the Middle East, Gulf states, and Mauritius contact newsrooms to comment on news stories on air or offer leads and suggestions for coverage of their domestic politics. I have personal experience of such interaction as Editor of the Zee News channel in 1999, particularly during the India-Pakistan clash at Kargil. A viewer from Lahore in Pakistan called up while a studio discussion was being telecast and complained about the low audio level of a particular discussant, and requested that the level be raised. He also added: 'Bahut mazaa aa raha hai' ('I am immensely enjoying the discussion'). A Dubai-based acquaintance of a Zee News correspondent called up to say that the correspondent's story from Kargil was seen on PTV there along with the Zee News logo. London-based representatives of the Muttahida Quami Movement would often call up the newsroom to request coverage of their cause since the channel is widely seen in Pakistan.

Such cross-border feedback is a regular feature in most television newsrooms, including regional language ones. As Umesh Upadhyay, senior television producer, notes:

> We have always got good response from viewers abroad, particularly from Indians in the Gulf countries, the Middle East and the neighbourhood. Earlier, the feedback was in the form of letters; now thanks to e-mail the feedback is greater. The feedback is for our

programmes shown on Zee TV and Doordarshan. For example, we recently had a story on a society in Chandigarh (Punjab) that manufacturers artificial limbs, for which we got several requests from Bahrain and several other countries asking for the society's contact details for potential help for the viewers or their relatives/friends or wanting to donate money.[1]

After NDTV stopped producing news content for Star News, its website was flooded with responses from across the globe, wanting to know when Prannoy Roy and his team would be back on air. Sharma, News Editor of five Eenadu TV channels in Telugu, Marathi, Kannada, Bengali and Urdu, observes:

> Our first news bulletins began in 1995, in Telugu, but it was not till 1997 that we started thinking about feedback. We used to get thousands of letters a day; most of them were related to non-news programming. After our Bangla, Kannada, Urdu and Marathi channels were launched during 1999-2000, we realised we were getting mail about news as well. We started filing this feedback into categories: news content, production values, anchoring, and the like. What started as a casual exercise in numerical backslapping is now a serious part of our news business. We have a separate section, called the feedback section, for all programmes on our channels. Over a dozen people handle this job. We now receive mail on the net too, from as far as the United States, Australia and New Zealand where we are visible. Most of it is complimentary but there is also criticism; for example, of how a particular event was treated or how certain points were missing from a story, etc. We have tried to incorporate valuable feedback into our news operations.[2]

Most Indian news channels have stringers or bureaux in neighbouring capitals such as Kathmandu, Dhaka, Islamabad and Colombo; Zee News has a bureau in London as well as stringership arrangements in Gulf countries with high Zee subscriber base. During ongoing events, phone-ins with prominent actors in the region are regularly aired. During my tenure in Zee News, several freelance television journalists from neighbouring countries would make contact to seek arrangements for coverage since the channel had large viewership in their areas.

Foreign Content on Indian News Channels

As noted earlier, the daily menu of news in South Asia is rich and extensive but, due to the sheer geographical and logistical dimensions, news channels are unable to do justice to all events and issues that they would like to cover. Given the wide range of newsworthy events within the region, international news is routinely accorded low priority in the news agenda, except during major events such as September 11, the Iraq war or the Challenger shuttle disaster (with Indian-born astronaut Kalpana Chawla on board).

During such events, when foreign footage is widely used, the need to have indigenously produced coverage from an Indian perspective is widely debated in media and political circles (Jain, 2003). Foreign news figures less in television bulletins partly because the viewership base, particularly those of Hindustani-language channels, is considered to be less interested in happenings outside India and the region. Off-beat foreign news items relating funny or unusual happenings have a better chance of being included towards the end of bulletins than news about, for example, Kosovo, East Timor, or O. J. Simpson: 'Indian viewers are not particularly interested in foreign news, and those few that are, would much rather see the coverage on the BBC or CNN' (Bhatia, 2000). The viewer has a choice of watching foreign news on BBC and CNN, and domestic or regional news on various Indian channels.

The usage of foreign video news agencies' output on Indian channels is also contrary to the contention that western news agencies dictate news agendas in developing countries.[3] Zee News, for example, subscribes to Reuters feeds, as do others, but very few items disseminated by the agency are used during times when there is no major international crisis (such as September 11). Some items perceived to be of interest to Indian viewers are used, though in a manner different from that suggested in the discourse of media imperialism. Usually only the facts in a foreign news copy are picked up, the rest is discarded; moreover, the very act of translating the contents of the story disseminated in English into Hindustani considerably localises the flavour and perspective. The footage is also rarely used in the same format and sequence as disseminated by the agency. It is routinely cannibalised, as it were; its sound is muted, and overlain with a Hindustani voice-over in a new sequence. For example, a reference by the US president to India at a forum in Washington would involve using the muted footage of the President speaking at the White House lectern while the Hindustani voice-over would convey the news of the day.

One of the reasons behind the low use of foreign video agency output is the background of journalists manning television newsrooms. Most have a print background and give priority to monitoring developments first on the tickers of the two Indian news agencies, the United News of India and the Press Trust of India, whose foreign copy often arrives faster than the video feeds of Reuters or other foreign video agencies (the two agencies have correspondents in major foreign capitals and also maintain news exchange agreements with international agencies). Given the intense competition between news channels, stories are put on air almost instantly, long before foreign video feeds arrive, by picking the news peg from agency copy, translating it and preparing a package using file footage. By the time the foreign video feed of the relevant news item arrives, the story has run on the channel for some time, and is considered ripe for replacement. The bulk of output provided by foreign video agencies, thus, invariably ends up in archives as file footage.

The production process is similar in language channels, as Sharma, news editor at Eenadu, observes:

> Apart from hourly updates, we have three half-hour prime bulletins in a day in which we try to include a 3-minute to 4.30-minute foreign

news segment. This is wholly from Reuters feed in the form of stories, round-ups and soft segment of 30-40 seconds as the last story. But when there are more advertisements, this segment gets the axe. We have separate desks to rewrite the scripts accompanying Reuters feed, for two reasons. One, our story format is different. Two, we have our own story perspective. The scripts are translated from English into Telugu, Kannada, Marathi, Bangla and Urdu. International visuals are used as file footage. We have an extensive library under a chief librarian who is assisted by 24-hour teams. Their main task is to select storage feed from news tapes, and catalogue them name/visual-wise. Archival footage is used in analytical stories, news documentaries, current affairs programmes, year-end round-ups, or any other programmes where you have to recollect past events.[4]

Apart from in-house resources for newsgathering (satellite links between studio and bureaux, camera & correspondent teams, etc.), Indian news channels use output provided by Asian News International (ANI), a large Indian video news agency that also provides footage and editorial content to foreign news channels and agencies. It has a wide network of camera & correspondent teams within India, South Asia and beyond. Indian channels also rely on ANI feeds for the many domestic and regional stories that they are unable to cover. The single largest source of external news footage for an Indian channel, apart from its own newsgathering set-up, is not a foreign video agency but ANI. A major proportion of sub-continental footage telecast on foreign news channels such as the BBC, CNN, CNBC, NHK, etc. is provided by ANI, which also provides complete daily news bulletins and current affairs programmes to various ethnic channels operating in Europe, the US and other countries where the South Asian diaspora is present.

Editorially, Indian news channels have largely inherited the hierarchy of the press, which has a much longer history and established conventions. Television news is a recent phenomenon, and many key newsroom positions are still manned by journalists with long experience in print. Thus politics, the mainstay of news content in the Indian press, also dominates prime time television news content. Jeffrey's observation for the Indian press is also valid for television: '[Indian] newspapers [use] Indian news agencies to report Indian weather, Indian cricket, Indian stock-market prices and Indian politics to remind us editorially every so often that we were Indians' (Jeffrey, 2000: 9).

Conclusion

India is a media-rich poor country with kaleidoscopic cultural diversity that supports a complex indigenous television industry. In 1991, when foreign media players began eyeing India, CNN's Ted Turner told his executives: 'We could all lose our buns out here' (Rusbridger, 1994). India's media industries demonstrate a vibrancy and growth that is rarely associated with countries of the South. The mushroom growth of news channels has enhanced the visual dimension of India's public sphere and improved the information opportunities among influential sections of the population. News channels' compulsion to retain and increase viewership is likely to enhance democratisation as the search for fresh news pastures draws newer issues, regions and peoples into India's newly-visual public sphere. However, this may take some time to unfold, given the fact that news channels are a recent phenomenon in India and the region.

At the wider level, the 'West-to-Rest' linearity implicit in the discourse of media imperialism clearly needs to be revised to incorporate regional hegemons such as India. Trajectories of international communication are increasingly asymmetric, reflecting a post-modern matrix of local and global influences, even in traditional South Asian societies. Globalisation ensures that Western technologies and professional values are reinvented, localised and customised in non-western settings. Sreberny points out that the earlier assumptions of blanket effects of western media products ignore the 'complex (re)negotiation of identity(ies) *vis-à-vis* the 'dominant' and 'foreign' cultures, shifting in focus depending on the specific locale of the actor' (2000: 109). As Indian news channels raise their ability to cover the diverse menu of newsworthy events in the region, the 'local' is likely to continue its domination of news agendas. The launch of several city-specific news channels across India may set the trend for similar ventures in other countries in the region.

References

Ahmed, Akbar S. (1992) 'Bombay Films: The Cinema as Metaphor for Indian Society and Politics', *Modern Asian Studies*, 26(2): 289-320.

Ahmed, Khaled (2001, July 27-August 2) 'Khaled Ahmed's Analysis', *The Friday Times*.

Anderson, B (1991) *Imagined Communities: Reflections on the Origin and Spread of Nationalism*. London: Verso.

Annuncio, C., G. Bhatia and C. Alvares (2003, May 26) 'Turbulence in the Air', *Outlook*.

Associated Press (2003, April 16) 'India's News Wave of 24-Hour Channels', *Associated Press*.

Bansal, S. (2002, October 23) 'The News Channel Boom', *Business Standard*.

Barraclough, S. (2001) 'Pakistani Television Politics in the 1990s: Responses to the Satellite Television Invasion', *Gazette*, 63 (2-3): 225-239.

Baru, S. (2000, June 30) 'The Infotainment Wars', *Business Standard*.

Baruah, A. (2000, February 20) 'Give Peace A Chance', *The Hindu*.

Bhatia, S. (2000, January 4) 'Wrong News Can Be Bad', *The Pioneer*.

Bindra, P.S. (2001, November 18) 'Profitable War: News Channels Show Rise in Viewership', *The Week*.

Chatterjee, S. (2003, January 5) 'Indian News Channels Vie to Grab a Larger

Slice of Ad Pie', *Indo-Asian News Service*.

de la Garde, R., W. Gilsdorf and I. Wechselmann (eds) (1993) *Small Nations, Big Neighbour*. London: J. Libbey.

Jabbar, J. (1994) 'The Media Factor in the Pakistan-India Relationship', *South Asian Survey*, 1 (2): 231-237.

Jain, S. (2003, April 27) 'Last Word: No Bore and Gush', *The Week*.

Jeffrey, R. (2000) *India's Newspaper Revolution*. London: Hurst & Co.

Joshi, N. (2000, June 12) 'A Babel in the Skies', *Outlook*.

Nye, J.S. and W.A. Owens (1996) 'America's Information Age', *Foreign Affairs*, 75 (2): 20-36.

Paterson, C. (2001) 'The Transference of Frames in Global Television', in Reese, S., O. Gandy and A. Grant (eds) *Framing Public Life: Perspectives on Media and Our Understanding of the Social World*. New Jersey: Erlbaum.

Phatarpekar, P. (2002, October 14) 'Degeneration X', *Outlook*.

Rajagopal, A. (2001) *Politics After Television: Hindu Nationalism and the Reshaping of the Public in India*. Cambridge: Cambridge University Press.

Reuters (2003, April 17) 'TV Channels Eye Pot of Gold', *Reuters*.

Roy, P. (2003) 'A Special Message from Prannoy Roy', www.ndtv.com.

Rusbridger, A. (1994, April 9) 'The Moghul Invasion', *Guardian*.

Sardar, Z. (2001, July 30) 'More Hackney Than Bollywood', *New Statesman*.

Sharma, A. (2003, February 22) 'Hindi in the News', *Business Standard*.

Singh, J. (2003, April 15) 'India's TV News Boom', BBC South Asia website, http://news.bbc.co.uk/1/hi/world/south_asia/2947087.stm.

Sonwalkar, P. (2001) 'India: Makings of Little Cultural Imperialism?', *Gazette*, 63 (6): 505-520.

Sreberny, A. (2000) 'The Global and the Local in International Communications', in Curran, J. and M. Gurevitch (eds), *Mass Media and Society*. London: Edward Arnold.

Ved, M. (2001, July 17) 'Why are we afraid of a failure?', *The Times of India*.

Wildermuth, N. (2001) 'Striving for Credibility: News and Current Affairs on Star TV India', in Hjarvad, S. (ed), *News in a Globalised Society*. Göteborg: NORDICOM.

Notes

1   Personal communication, 7 December 2001.
2   Interview with author, 2 December 2001.
3   Editors' note: Much of the basis for the contention is anecdotal, but Paterson found in a

1995 study that 'smaller broadcasters ... typically demonstrate complete dependence on agency (television) coverage,' providing at least limited recent support for the news agency dependency hypothesis which drove the New World Information Order debates of the 1970s.

4   Interview with author, 2 December 2001.

Chapter 7
China's News Media and the Case of CCTV-9
John Jirik

China is of increasing significance among non-Western global media players. In what is becoming the typical pattern, not only is it reaching out in Chinese to its transnational diasporic communities, but it is also attempting to address the global English-speaking audiences through new channels. Starting with an analysis of China Central Television's global English-language channel CCTV-9, Jirik provides a critical analysis of the multiple tensions that affect Chinese news provision. These include the continuing role of the Communist party even as the party line is increasingly blurred. There is also the growth of hybrid media forms of ownership and control, within which Chinese media conglomerates are emerging while foreign capital finds ways in. As in other parts of the South, such as the Middle East and Latin America, China's media finds itself between the state and the market facing pressures from within and without. The solutions it creates demand the attention of news media scholars.

This chapter looks at news media in China.[1] It takes as its starting point a fundamental assumption in Chinese news theory, and much analysis of Chinese media, that news is the mouthpiece of the Chinese Communist Party and government. I argue that this assumption, although warranted, obscures as much as it illuminates. While it illuminates the formal relationship between political institutions and media, the mouthpiece metaphor assumes a single voice, which ignores increasing pluralism within the Party and increasing diversity in media. To see as unity the practice of sorting out differences behind closed doors before issuing public statements neglects the very real differences that characterise debate within China's polity today. In particular, as analysts note, factionalism and fragmentation have been increasing since 1978, in line with decentralisation of power triggered by economic reform (Castells, 1998; Wu, 2000).

With the Party leading the charge towards a market economy, it is broadening its representative base beyond workers, farmers, soldiers, public servants and intellectuals to embrace 'any advanced element of other social strata', including businesspeople (Wang, 2002b). In line with changes that economic reform is bringing to the media sector, the relatively monolithic news system of the pre-reform era is fragmenting and reconfiguring. Moreover, news never just happens. It not only relays policy, but also reflects the professionalism of journalists, the sources on which they draw, and a range of political, economic, cultural and organisational frameworks that guide news making. As a result of all of these developments, news in China has a rather more heterogeneous character than the mouthpiece metaphor suggests.

My focus is the English language news carried by China's national broadcaster, China Central Television (CCTV). I carried out the research detailed below between early 1999 and the middle of 2000 as part of the team that makes the news. The English news is the centrepiece of CCTV's expanding English language service, including its global English language channel CCTV-9. With the launch of CCTV-9 in September 2000, shortly after I left Beijing, the editorial team at the English news tripled in size and personnel changes were made. However, although the discussion below is specific to the practices I was part of, the general tenor of the news team's work remains the same. I spent over a year working with the team, asking questions and recording my impressions. I spoke to a range of personnel from senior managers to junior reporters throughout my time in Beijing. The fragments of conversations I present here all took place between late 1999 and early 2000. Although I do not identify anybody, in line with the wishes of my interlocutors, I believe that the narrative I have constructed reflects the diversity of feelings and opinions I encountered at CCTV. One colleague, who read a draft of this chapter, called it accurate. Others may disagree.

I came to CCTV from Reuters where I had worked as a television news producer since 1992. My background facilitated transition to China's state broadcaster, and I soon found a niche in the newsroom. I was able to compare newsroom cultures, journalistic expectations, the contextual and institutional pressures on newsmakers, and the various ways in which journalists work to inform their publics in differing contexts. I refer to a number of stories that happened while I was in China, but also, in the context of this publication and by way of comparison, I refer to the 9/11 story, since it was simultaneously a local and global story in its impact and ramifications. The English news team watched and analyzed Western news for its editorial and production values as a constant part of the refashioning process underway in Chinese media. In its simplest form, my conclusion following this research was that journalistic practices at CCTV's English news were more similar than dissimilar to journalistic practices in the news environments with which I was more familiar.

Chinese and US Journalism in the Global News Environment

In discussing the mouthpiece metaphor, what is usually not stated is that it always infers another presumably quite different news system, the 'Western' press model in which journalists report 'just the facts' in a value-free and context independent environment. This model is taken for granted by its practitioners as the norm for journalism worldwide, while the mouthpiece model is automatically assigned an inferior place. However, US press coverage of 9/11 revealed the limitations of this assumption of universal best practice. While the coverage was professional in terms of relaying events as they unfolded, it was also, and understandably, very US-centric. Embedded in a sense of nation, and national ideals and belief systems, the mainstream US press reported 9/11 in no less an ethnocentric fashion than mainstream media in any country would in the case of an attack that was an affront to national sovereignty.

Journalists, by definition, no less in China than in the United States, report facts and tell stories about events as they see them. But the social, political, economic, cultural and institutional environments of news making always shape these stories, often in subtle and unnoticed ways, rarely as vividly and directly as the case was with 9/11. In particular, the role of US media on 20 September 2001 in relaying without comment President Bush's explanation to Congress of the attacks in terms of hatred for US freedoms, without investigating the validity of this claim, showed the degree to which US media can also be mouthpieces for power. As a result, US reporting of 9/11 and its aftermath ironically have given Chinese journalists one more reason to shrug off criticism of their mouthpiece role as considerable differences between the two media systems narrow in this particular respect.

The Political Economic Context of Chinese Journalism

In China, the Party oversees media work. But today analysts do not so much see a united Party as factions and formations within the Party structure, evolving and dissolving as the ebb and flow of power shapes and changes relationships (Castells, 1998; Ma, 2000). While the Party structure remains intact, and perhaps even is strengthening as it becomes more flexible in dealing with new problems brought on by embrace of the market, discipline is becoming an increasingly visible problem. Whereas some analysts see corruption, including in journalism, as symptomatic of a failing system, others see it as more the result of a system constantly adapting to new circumstances, with the attendant opportunities and problems this poses for Party members (Castells, 1998; Huang, 2000; Zhao, 1998).

Moves by the Party to increase its representative character include inviting businesspeople to join at the 16th National Party Congress in November 2002. This coincided with the elevation of a new generation of leaders with Hu Jintao replacing Jiang Zemin as head of the Communist Party. Ding Guangen, head of the Party's Publicity Department, which oversees media, stepped down to relief from the sector. However, no indications have yet emerged that his successor, Liu Yunshan, will move any faster on media liberalisation. The leadership change followed China's entry into the World Trade Organisation (WTO) in December 2001. WTO entry does not require China to open its media industry to foreign investment. However, in a sign that the government sees more competition as inevitable, in December 2001 it folded CCTV into the China Radio, Film and Television Group (CRFTG), a media conglomerate. CRFTG is the biggest, but only one of several such groups to emerge recently, to take on the transnationals as they increasingly make their way into China (O'Neill and Leung, 2001; *Straits Times* , 2002).

WTO entry was only the latest move by China to modernise and engage the world on its own terms, following initial experiments with market reform begun by Deng Xiaoping in 1978. Following adoption of Deng's 'four modernisations' of agriculture, industry, science and technology, and defence, while the state retained administrative fiat over media, fiscal responsibility was shifted to media managers. State subsidies to the sector were gradually reduced throughout the 1980s. Faced with the loss of state support, media increasingly turned to advertising, which since 1979 has grown from nothing to a multi-billion US dollar industry (AFX News Limited, 2002; Gao, 2002; Pan, 2000). Today, advertising, including programme sponsorship, is the most lucrative revenue source for Chinese media. With the growth of a revenue stream dependent on audiences and demographics, the relationship within and between media sectors has become increasingly competitive, even antagonistic, in the bid for market share (Gao, 2002; Li, 2001).

Although the details of the shift to a commercial model in media differ in different media sectors, the general picture has been the same in all sectors. In order to fulfil the dual function of Party and government mouthpieces and revenue earner, media were dispersed on two sides of an axis according to their specific relationship to power. On the one side, non-political media achieved relative editorial autonomy. On the other side, news remains subject to a series of checks and balances that aims at shoring up the Party line (Chan, 1995; He, 2000a; Huang, 2000; Zhao, 1996). But given media's profitability, even this schematic representation ignores the degree of horizontal and vertical integration within the sector as Party-affiliated umbrella institutions operate both news and commercial media sites, or operate news sites as increasingly commercial outlets. In addition, as China ponders increasing competition from foreign media, issues such as convergence and conglomeration only make the distinction between Party and non-Party line journalism increasingly difficult to maintain (Lee, 2000a; Ma, 2000; Wu, 2000). For journalists struggling to determine the limits to reporting, the Party 'line' has become the Party 'blur' (Jirik, 2001; Lee, 2001).

Developments in Different Media Sectors

The literature on developments in China's different media sectors is limited by the difficulty of describing and analyzing the media environment, given its size, diversity, contradictions, and the pace of change. Moreover, focus on success defined as success in the market has overshadowed analysis of the limitations to reform, although this trend is changing (Lee, 2001; Sun, 2001; Zhao, 1998). In what follows, I limit myself to the briefest overview of print, television and the Internet.[2]

An extremely rich literature deals with print journalism (as a starting point, see Jia, 2002; Lee, 2000b). Spectacular examples of market success identified include the *Beijing Youth News*, the *Chengdu Business News*, and *Southern Weekend* (Huang, 2000; Lee, 2000a; Zhao, 1996). The latter paper, one of the most popular in the country, is a constant source of controversy for the Party. However, as a publication of the Southern Daily Group, which is associated with the Guangdong provincial government, at times *Southern Weekend* has been protected from criticism by regional authorities (Lee, 2000a; Mitchell, 2001). Nevertheless, its ties to the Party also make it vulnerable. Editors have been alternately praised for its hard-hitting coverage, and damned (Forney, 2001). The topsy-turvy fate of *Southern Weekend* shows both the scope and limits for dissent within Party ranks, suggesting the limitations rather than strengths of the mouthpiece metaphor, as well as the difficulties journalists face in an environment when today's top story will only lead to recrimination tomorrow.

In television, China's dominant information medium (Redl and Simons, 2002), developments have been no less frenetic than in the press sector. In an industry now almost entirely reliant on advertising for revenue, the state broadcaster CCTV competes for audience attention not only with a plethora of provincial and municipal channels and other legal outlets, but also with illegally distributed satellite downlinks and pirate cable (Chan, 2000; Levander, 2001; Ma, 2000). However, the biggest threat to CCTV's near-stranglehold on television news in major markets may neither be domestic competition, nor global operations such as Britain's BBC World Service, US-centric CNN International, and Japan's NHK World TV, all relatively inaccessible for language and political reasons. Competition is also increasing from developments in culturally familiar hybrid media forms, which exhibit both Party and non-Party characteristics that blur the boundaries of ownership and control.

The best example of this new media form is Hong Kong-based Phoenix TV, which currently has a small and restricted but growing audience on the mainland for its news programming (Mooney, 2001; Redl and Simons, 2002). Phoenix is part owned by Rupert Murdoch's News Corporation. It is informally associated with the Party through its CEO, Liu Changle, a former military affairs correspondent for state radio, now a wealthy businessman, and its executive vice-director, Wang Jiyan, former deputy director of the Beijing

Broadcast Institute (BBI). At the time of the launch of its news channel in January 2001, Phoenix boasted a raft of former BBI students and CCTV employees. News Corp is a global media conglomerate, which owns the Fox Network in the United States, STAR TV in Asia, and holdings in Europe and elsewhere. A colleague at CCTV described Phoenix as a 'frontline Communist Party stronghold.' Phoenix's news programming toes the Party line on key issues like Taiwan, but reports openly on anything not forbidden. To the chagrin of CCTV, audiences widely praised Phoenix's round-the-clock coverage of 9/11, in contrast to CCTV's restrained reporting (Ding, 2001; Hui, 2001; Li, 2002; Mooney, 2001).

An increasing source of information for a small elite in China is the Internet. Although figures for online access vary, estimates in mid-2002 suggested between forty-six and fifty-seven million users (3.5 per cent to 4.4 per cent of China's 1.3 billion population). This put China either second behind the United States or third behind Japan in numbers of users (CNNIC, 2002; Greenspan, 2002). Information access, including news, rates well ahead of entertainment and e-commerce as the prime motive for going online (CNNIC, 2002; Shen, 2002). However, like developments elsewhere, utopian hopes for the medium face political and commercial constraints. The usual arguments for a public cyber-sphere in China have been put forward from a range of interests, not least from the transnational corporations that stand to gain most from accessing the Chinese telecommunications market following WTO entry, which opened up the sector to limited foreign participation. Not surprisingly, making readily available to Chinese netisens information that might foster civic discourse is not high on their agenda, although amongst people with access, a lively cyber-culture exists (Levander, 2001; Lynch, 2000; Zhao, 2001).

The government is caught between promoting the Internet for its efficiencies as a business and information tool while restricting its attractions as an alternative to official information (Shen, 2002). Regulations in 2002 held ISPs responsible for content. Major service providers, including big Chinese portals like Sina.com and Sohu.com, as well as Yahoo's Chinese portal, had all agreed to abide by voluntary policies acknowledging government guidelines (Bodeen, 2002). Although Beijing seems determined to police the Internet, the trajectory of online information access remains uncertain. Since its commercialisation in 1995, the number of China's Internet users has been doubling every six months (Amnesty, 2002). As a result, as the infrastructure and user numbers expand exponentially, the ability of authorities to track activity is likely to decrease, even if attempts to increase surveillance continue to intensify. Moreover, China's netizens for the most part are students, urban professionals and service workers, businesspeople, academics, and public servants. As the country's current and future political, economic and cultural elites, these demographics are key to the future of the Party and reform, and pose a difficult target for a severe crackdown. However, authorities are continuing to detain users they deem subversive (Amnesty, 2002; CNNIC, 2002; Cohn and Barker, 2001; Kahn, 2002; Shen, 2002).

For journalists in all media, the task of serving two masters – Party and market – has produced a range of dissonant behaviours from outright denial of the party market nexus to fatalistic acceptance of apparently opposing tendencies (He, 2000b). The Party is moving to defuse this dichotomy by extending its authority over the market, formally separating its regulatory and business functions, while commercialising many of its media operations (O'Neill and Leung, 2001; Zhao, 1998). Faced with reconciling contradictions, journalists adopt localised strategies that protect them from criticism and permit them to function in a personally satisfying manner (Pan, 2000). Although the Party has significantly eased editorial control of all but a few major media, the Party line remains an unbreachable but shifting horizon. However, analysts contest the likely direction of future trends. Some see a Party shifting its focus from media control to authoritarian supervision along the lines of developments in Taiwan before the island's unexpected democratisation (Lee, 2001). Others see a Party not so much in retreat as one undergoing a profound change of identity and gaining a new confidence in managing media contradictions rather than stifling discontent (Castells, 1998; Zhao, 1999). Either way, because the Party line is no longer clearly marked on many issues, uncertainty represents both a threat and a challenge.

CCTV-9 and Transnational Broadcasting

On 25 September 2000, CCTV launched its 24-hour global English channel, CCTV-9. A little over a year later, on 22 October 2001, CCTV signed a deal with AOL-Time Warner (ATW) to distribute the channel in the United States. Other deals quickly followed suit, including with two of Murdoch's vehicles, Phoenix TV and STAR TV. European distribution of CCTV-9 by Murdoch's BSkyB and Vivendi Universal was under discussion in July 2002 (Jacob, 2002; Leung, 2002). The deals are largely meaningless from a short-term economic point of view. In the United States, they give several cities one more cable channel to choose from. In exchange, Mandarin language channels were allowed into Cantonese-speaking Guangdong Province, without the usual restrictions put on foreign media, such as limiting access to select mainland institutions, foreign compounds, and three-star and above hotels (Redl and Simons, 2002). The significance of the deals lay in Beijing's decision to grant the transnationals limited access to China's huge domestic market, which has four hundred million television households, in exchange for overseas distribution of CCTV-9. Given the potential for profits in China, the transnationals will do nothing to provoke discomfort amongst China's political elites. ATW, for example, acquired its channel ready-made from Singapore-based producer Robert Chua, whose motto for it was 'no sex, no violence, no news.' At the time of writing, STAR TV's *Xing Kong Wei Shi* (Starry Sky Satellite TV) was slightly more risqué, featuring shows like *Woman in Control* (a male beauty contest show), *LIVE from Xing Kong Dance Club*, and late night talk in the vein of David Letterman. It also has no news (Jacob, 2002; Kempner, 2001; Landler, 2001; McDonald, 2001a).

The Party Line

The establishment of CCTV-9 is a strong indicator of the importance that Beijing places on making its voice more accessible globally than is possible with Mandarin language programming, which is supplied internationally through CCTV-4. The core of CCTV-9 is the news. It provides Chinese perspective on events and issues in China and abroad, and an alternative to news about China from video wholesalers Associated Press Television (APTN) and Reuters Video News (RVN), and video retailers such as CNN.

Zhou He (2000a) coined the term 'Party Publicity Inc.' to describe the current role of image managers that news media play in China. Quizzed about this, journalists with the English news accepted the label as accurate. However, as public relations practitioners their task was made exceedingly complex by the instability of the Party line. As a result, in terms of putting a Chinese spin on events and issues, instead of the pro-active role PR experts play in the West by placing items in the news, they tended to work in the reverse fashion, ensuring only that any item that ran did not breach reporting guidelines.

Keeping in mind that most successful Chinese journalists are Party members or members of the Communist Youth League, direct supervision of their work by state or Party officials, other than media managers, is rare. Difficult coverage decisions are usually left to management. During my time at CCTV, I saw only a couple of instances of interference. Once, an official from the State Administration of Radio, Film and Television rang to criticise the news for being too enthusiastic about NATO's entry into Kosovo at the end of the war against Yugoslavia. Kosovo was a touchy subject following NATO's bombing of the Chinese embassy in Belgrade in May 1999. That event triggered not only an outpouring of shock and anger amongst Chinese, but showed how the Party manages tension. With students threatening to march on the US embassy in Beijing, Party officials, wary of demonstrations just weeks ahead of the tenth anniversary of the Tiananmen incident, provided buses to keep the students off the streets. In the newsroom, we were waiting to see how much of the story we could put in the evening bulletin.

The embassy bombing, like 9/11, was one of those rare and catastrophic events that stun the public and are actually 'news' and not 'olds'. Such events are exceptions for news, which, as Tuchman (1978), Schlesinger (1979), Schudson (1991) et al. have shown, tends to a narrow range of familiar narratives in line with ideological and organisational parameters, routinisation, and newsroom culture. The pattern in Beijing tended towards this expectation, although the instability of the media environment lent some scope for experimentation. The shifting Party line primarily was a psychological barrier to reporting, although the consequences of breaching it were real. Self-censorship as a survival mechanism, not censorship, was the norm amongst my colleagues.

One manager spoke of the pressure, since ultimately senior staff like him took responsibility for what went to air:

> The hardest part is knowing that you are making a kind of borderline story, that has never been reported like this before. And you are trying to widen your scope of reporting. To be critical at some point but not obviously crossing the borderline, this is a hard decision to make.

For the most part managers supported reporters' efforts to be as hard-hitting as possible. Editorial meetings tended to function like editorial meetings the world over, with the focus on upcoming stories and the logistics of coverage. Sensitive issues were discussed. At times, stories were ruled off-limits for political, budgetary or logistical reasons. Each news shift also had an experienced senior editor to check stories for accuracy, and for possible breaches of reporting guidelines. The respect journalists and management had for one another enabled most contentious issues to be negotiated and resolved through compromise. For example, when the Party ordered media to vilify Falun Gong after the crackdown on the cult began in April 1999, management at one point faced stirrings of a newsroom revolt, fuelled by sheer boredom at the relentless coverage, and the lack of professional pride reporters could take in this kind of work. The story slipped quietly down the bulletin.

Dealing with the inadmissible was easier than dealing with the borderline since the guidelines on the former were more clear-cut. In terms of constraints on media, Tiananmen is still the absolute limit on reporting. The crackdown on journalists in the aftermath of 4 June 1989 has been exhaustively chronicled (Lull, 1995; Simmie and Nixon, 1989). While the younger generation of journalists was still in high school with few of them directly involved in Tiananmen, the memories of the older generation had not faded:

> I think after the incident everybody knows, you have to obey the Party, you have to obey the government being at CCTV, otherwise you just quit.

> Is that still the case today, or is it changing again?

> More or less the same. It's apparent, it's obvious that the opportunities are not ripe, the time is not ripe yet for us to voice our true opinions.

However, amongst others of the older generation, bitterness was also tinged with regret:

> During the late eighties, there was a rush, a kind of fever, a rush, a kind of craze for Western culture, for Western ideology and denying all that the communists have done in China. Democratisation overnight may not necessarily be a good thing for China. Maybe socialism with Chinese characteristics is a practical way, very practical way to change China step by step and for the huge benefit of the people.

Differences of opinion about Tiananmen were common in the newsroom. The tenth anniversary passed quietly, with little mention of the heady atmosphere that had prevailed in the Chinese capital ten years earlier, and at CCTV (Simmie and Nixon, 1989). My colleagues were aware of the limits to their work. At the same time, they were committed to accurate reporting and to presenting a side of China inaccessible to journalists from abroad, whose work is carefully monitored by the authorities. As one young reporter who was still in high school in 1989 noted:

> You are trying to correct some misunderstanding of this word communism and communist country, to portray it in a way that it is. There's a word 'demonise China'. But people like us living here don't feel it so much. I mean it's not a horrible place to live.

Newsroom Culture, Dissonant Sources, Conflicting Narratives

The employment and corporate issues, socialisation into the norms of the workplace, and routinisation of news production that frame professional practice in the West are well known (Schlesinger, 1979; Schudson, 1991). Similar enabling and constraining processes operate in China (He, 2000a; Pan, 2000). Television journalists worldwide would be familiar with CCTV's English newsroom. Constant deadline pressure drives round-the-clock conveyor-belt production of news. The channel is housed in the twenty plus storey CCTV building, about seven kilometres from Tiananmen Square on Beijing's main East-West thoroughfare. Home to several thousand editorial personnel, the environment at CCTV is fiercely competitive. At the time of writing, *Jiaodian Fangtan* (Focus), seen by some 300 million people nightly, was the jewel in CCTV's reporting crown. A brief investigative report influenced by US shows like ABC's 20/20 and CBS's 60 Minutes, *Jiaodian Fangtan* goes to air after *Xinwen Lianbo* (News Link), the prime time national nightly news on CCTV's flagship channel, CCTV-1 (Li, 2001; Zhao, 1999).

The English news team measured itself against these news programme. Even the use of English was seen to provide an edge, enabling reporters to push the envelope, knowing that as a niche program in China, the English news was unlikely to attract as much attention from censors as did CCTV's most watched programmes. But if the use of English emboldened reporters, while the Party line functioned as a background check to reporting, source material was as important as the intentions of newsmakers in shaping the story. Because of limited resources, the English news relied on *Xinwen Lianbo* for most of its domestic stories. Like broadcasters worldwide, it relied on the international news agencies for the bulk of its foreign news. But the differences in news values between CCTV's flagship bulletin and the agencies, in particular the emphasis on positive stories in the Chinese news and negative stories from the agencies, gave one a sense of watching two different programmes in the domestic and international segments.

Writers attempted to overcome this discontinuity by consistently applying what management called 'Chinese perspective,' telling the story from a Chinese point of view. Whereas Chinese perspective came built in to stories accessed from *Xinwen Lianbo*, it had to be added to foreign news. In contrast to the cult of objectivity in Western newsrooms, most of the English news journalists seemed to regard their position as Chinese as a key influence in the way they saw the world. If China wanted to make its voice globally available it would have to compete with other discursive formations in the field. Not surprisingly, management tended to reject the objectivist assumptions behind the claims made by Western news theory in the name of professionalism:

> Does reliance on agency video make the news end up looking like the same news we see on CNN?

> It's quite different. We have our Chinese perspective. We look at things from the angle of the Chinese viewer, not from the angle of the Western media. We rewrite the stories based on the original video and original scripts.

> Although we depend on the agencies for supplying us with international coverage, we find that their news values are sometimes different to ours. So we need our own reporters to look at stories from our own viewpoint.[3]

In making the news, writers clearly tried to carry out this injunction from management to rework agency video and scripts. But content analysis conducted over a two-month period in late 1999 of a representative sample of news, measuring source material against on-air narratives, suggested that agency material largely resisted re-framing (Jirik, 2001). Comparison of source material with on-air stories showed that eighty-four per cent of the foreign news was taken from APTN and RVN. Seventy-five per cent of the domestic and foreign policy news was taken from *Xinwen Lianbo*. As a result, the picture on the English news was contradictory, with the domestic and international segments characterised by different news values, despite the best efforts of journalists to reconcile contrasting narrative styles. The journalists themselves were the first to admit that reworking agency narrative was difficult:

> We try to add Chinese perspective with foreign news agency video. Everybody knows that. But since our working staff is young – I'm young, I only have four years of television experience, and the bulk of our staff is younger than me – there are times when this principle is not well carried out. So they just depend on what the AP or Reuters say.

Tsan-Kuo Chang and Yanru Chen argue that the framing of agency material is not a critical issue at CCTV so long as the story does not bear on Chinese interests (Chang and Chen, 2000). They are correct, and content analysis confirmed that despite the attempt to put a Chinese spin on international news stories, the English news tended towards systematic typification in the manner outlined by Galtung and Ruge (Chang and Chen, 2000; Galtung and Vincent, 1992). But analysis of the end product cannot reveal the degree of frustration news editors encountered in trying to deal with what they saw as limitations to agency video. Conversations in the newsroom bore out the frequent criticism of agency video that it privileges a particular set of for the most part developed countries, to the neglect of much of the world, except in terms of extreme reductionism in terms of conflict and disaster coverage (Boyd-Barrett, 1996; Paterson, 1996). News editors were critical of the structural configuration of agency coverage, but lacking political and financial resources were powerless to change it.

> How do you feel about using so much agency video?

> I don't think it is a good thing. I don't like it. But you have no choice. You have to use it. I'm not saying I don't like agency video. I think it's great. I think they make every effort to get excellent shots. I just want some news from other parts of the world.

Self-cover

One area where journalists did have a lot of control was in self-cover. When they felt a domestic story deserved attention beyond that given it by *Xinwen Lianbo*, or wanted to report a story not available from CCTV-1, they would do the story themselves. As part of the team's task to present an accurate image of China abroad, often these stories picked up on what were seen as misrepresentations in foreign media. As one reporter noted:

> I look through news studies and find issues which are controversial in the world, or in the foreign television news, like human rights, Tibet. I find that if there are misunderstandings by foreign media, I will probably go to investigate this subject. I will do a story just to clarify how this issue is biasly reported. I'll add in Chinese perspective.

The team produced dozens of reports on aspects of China simply not seen in foreign media. The highly professional and often critical coverage opened my eyes to the sophistication of the news team's handling of a desire to push the reporting envelope. At the same time, what I came to see as a significant limitation to Chinese perspective was also evident. A typical example of self-cover was *Tibet Religion*, which subsequently aired on CNN's *World Report*.[4] A human-interest story, it traced the fate of an elderly man, persecuted for his beliefs during the Cultural Revolution, but free now to pursue his faith. The story focused on the revival of the monastery, but contrasted this with the separation of life into spiritual and material spheres as the religion-centred worldview of modern Tibet encounters China's secular modernity. The government's mixed record in the region, including its attempt to wipe out religion during the Cultural Revolution, was acknowledged. However, the report ignored the questions of the ongoing colonisation of Tibet and sinification of the region, which today are intensifying (Shakya, 2002). The story was an excellent example of what the English news team saw as its forte. It was beautifully shot. It countered claims about Tibet common in reports from non-Chinese sources. The reporter was genuinely sympathetic to the elderly man for his suffering at the hands of the Chinese. Most importantly, it provided Chinese perspective, taking for granted China's claim to the region.

From a Tibetan or Western perspective, *Tibet Religion* may have appeared unbalanced, privileging a Chinese point of view. But from a Chinese perspective, Tibetan and Western stories about the region often appear unbalanced, neglecting China's point of view. Although China's long history of involvement in the region cannot be disputed, Tibetan attempts to assert sovereignty in the context of China's evolution from being the regional hegemon to a modern nation-state also cannot be ignored (Shakya, 2002; Wang, 2002a). Conversely, since the collapse of the Qing Dynasty in 1912, one must ask whether China's actions in Tibet, where it sees itself playing the role of the modern bringing civilisation to the natives, are any more egregious than were Western actions in the colonies of the Americas, Africa and Asia, including the sense of mission driving the colonisers to save the indigenous peoples from themselves. The Tibetan government in exile clearly opposes current developments, seeking genuine autonomy for the region within China. But in the context of the historical role of Western journalism in imperialism and colonisation, Western reports criticising Chinese actions in Tibet today appear sanctimonious at best. The English news, to its credit, suffered less from the posturing of a journalism all too adept at ignoring its own deficiencies while highlighting shortcomings elsewhere, than from selective memory.

The Problem of Perspective, the Future of News in China

The English news team had a difficult remit. Its role was to report accurately and in a timely fashion on events and issues considered relevant to China's interests and of interest to foreign audiences, a role it continues today for CCTV-9. Although I noted that Tiananmen marked the limit to reporting, another perhaps more important story was Taiwan. During my time in Beijing, the English news reported more often about the politically isolated island than any other single topic. But none of the coverage addressed Taiwanese attitudes to the mainland from a Taiwanese perspective because Beijing considers the island a renegade province, and therefore speaks on its behalf.

Although Chinese perspective was designed to counter what were seen as shortcomings in news about China from non-Chinese sources, on contentious domestic issues Chinese perspective amounted to repeating the Party and government line, ignoring the range of perspectives amongst the peoples of China, which by the government's own definition, include, for example, Tibetans and Taiwanese. To my mind, this was the chief limitation to the English news, its reluctance to discuss contentious issues from the full range of Chinese perspectives at stake. But to criticise the English news team in this manner is to apply to their work a standard that for too long Western journalists have refused to apply to their own work. If certain topics are off limits in China, in many respects the English news was no more blinkered than, for example, network news is in the United States, where coverage is often as selective and also ignores a range of topics. Balanced reporting on politically sensitive and emotionally charged issues such as Tibet or Taiwan is as unlikely in China as is a balanced discussion of, for example, 9/11 and consequent global developments on the US news. In both cases it would not happen without a massive shift in the political and cultural consensus, and a radical shift in the dynamics of power in which both media systems are embedded. Dissidence is no more visible in mainstream US media than it is in China. Why expect it of Chinese journalists, when mainstream Western journalism is characterised by an abiding subservience to power? The pattern in the West is for ideological consonance and the routines of news making to preclude serious investigation of shortcomings in the political, economic and cultural consensus. In China, ideological dissonance is the norm, making journalists all too aware of the range of problems facing the country. But they are compromised from reporting them by their function as Party and government mouthpieces.

China's reform has been uneven. On the one hand, living standards in coastal regions and major cities have improved dramatically. On the other hand, as the social stratification necessary to capitalist relations of production spreads, many people are being left behind, even as the economy continues to expand rapidly (Castells, 1998; Zhou (Zhao), 2000). The English news team was adept at the human-interest story, focusing on the plight of individuals and personal suffering. But it was unable to address policy issues driving reform, and responsible not only for improving the common lot, but also for widespread immiserisation. Historically, Chinese journalists have been social activists first, reporters second. But as China's middle class grows, it is unclear whether media, organically tied to this class through increasing dependence on the market, will speak for, or silence, the growing army of unemployed and poor being disenfranchised by 'progress' (De Burgh, 2000; Zhou (Zhao), 2000).

Media analysts and journalists are conflicted about the future trajectory of media reform in China. The market has liberated journalism to a degree from Party control, only to deliver it increasingly into the hands of commercial, including Party-commercial, interests. In broadcasting, the question of serving the public is emerging as a key issue. The shift to a market-driven system provides an alternative to Party control, and opens up space for entertainment and avenues for a limited public discourse on personal and socially contentious issues (Donald and Keane, 2002; Li, 2001). At the same time marketisation commodifies audiences, reducing them to consumers, while binding journalistic agency to market dynamics (Zhao, 1999; Zhao, 1998). In this context, news makers are increasingly asking themselves whether a commercialised media system is any better than a Party-driven news system in providing a news making environment independent of power in which journalists serve the public free of the constraints of both Party and market (Sun, 2001).

As Zhao Yuezhi (1998) points out, the Chinese broadcast system has always been closer to the European public service broadcasting model than to the commercial US network model. Given that for ideological and economic reasons the Party does not intend releasing control of major news media, the question facing CCTV's news divisions is less the choice between Party and market, than a question of how to develop greater autonomy from political supervision, without losing more autonomy to market regulation (Zhao, 1998). Key here is the further development of Party media relations in the context of either greater Party pluralisation and marketisation of the political economy, or increasing tension if the Party's internal development is unable to keep pace with economic reform. In a best-case scenario, and reminiscent of the French model, CCTV could emerge as a new media form, an advertiser-supported public service broadcaster addressing audiences as citizens and consumers, rather than bifurcating them into categories ill-served by under-funded or over-commercial television systems (Zhao, 1998). CCTV's position as China's monopoly broadcaster, the size of advertising revenues, and the Party's insistence on supervision, including supervision of the Party and government by media, while developing television as an information, education and entertainment medium, suggests this is not impossible. Given the continued importance of broadcast television for China's national development, the worst-case scenario would be collapse of the media system, a possibility only if the Party loses control of the reform process. Considering the increasing decentralisation of power associated with reform, even as the Party retains control of the centre, further regionalisation of media in China seems likely, alongside expansion and consolidation of the centralised broadcasting system.

Summary and Conclusion

China's size, its diversity, the scope of its myriad imaginings, historical inertia and the rapidity of change are a daunting challenge for news. The English news team may have been part of 'Party Publicity Inc.' But the Party line is best understood as the constant psychological pressure on journalists not to make certain kinds of mistakes, rather than a brief to act as a Party mouthpiece. Chinese perspective is no more an apology for power in China than are mainstream journalistic practices in much Western media. If nothing else, US coverage of 9/11 and developments since should warn us against facile comment on the limitations to Chinese news.

Finally, China's elite journalists share much with their foreign colleagues. I worked as a television news producer at Reuters for almost seven years. I felt as at home in the English newsroom as I did with RVN. The English news team was a dedicated group of professionals, hungry to make news and devoted to the trade. Nevertheless, while the English news remains an exemplar of what is possible in Chinese news today, far from won is the battle for news that serves the public without fear of censure from the Party. Decades of struggle by journalists in China, despite setbacks at every turn, have provided a legacy for future inspiration. In the wake of 9/11, the history of internal developments, more so than foreign models, is a journalist's best resource.

References

AFX News Limited (2002) 'China leads Asia in advertising industry in Q2', www.lexisnexis.com/universe.

Amnesty (2002) 'State Control of the Internet in China', Amnesty International Report, web.amnesty.org/web/content.nsf/pages/gbr.

Bodeen, C. (2002, July 15) 'Web Portals Sign China Content Pact', Associated Press.

Boyd-Barrett, O. (1996) '"Global"' News Agencies' in Boyd-Barrett, O. and T. Rantanen (eds) *The Globalisation of News*. London: Sage.

Castells, M. (1998) *End of Millennium* (2nd ed). Oxford: Blackwell.

Chan, J. M. (1995) 'Calling the tune without paying the piper: the reassertion of media controls in China', in Lo, C. K. and M. Brosseau (eds) *China Review*. Hong Kong: The Chinese University Press.

Chan, J. M. (2000) 'When Capitalist and Socialist Television Clash: The Impact of Hong Kong TV on Guangzhou Residents', in Lee, C.C. (ed) *Power, Money, and Media: Communication Patterns and Bureaucratic Control in Cultural China*. Evanston: Northwestern University Press.

Chang, T. K. and Y. Chen (2000) 'Constructing international spectacle on television: CCTV news and China's window on the world, 1992-1996', in Malek A. and A. P. Kavoori (eds) *The Global Dynamics of News: Studies in International News Coverage and News Agenda*. Connecticut: Ablex Publishing Corporation.

CNNIC (2002, July) 'Semiannual Survey Report on the Development of China's Internet', *China Internet Network Information Center*, www.cnnic.net.cn/develst/2002-7e/index.shtml.

Cohn, M. R. and G. Baker. (2001, July 21) 'China seeks to build the Great Firewall', *Toronto Star*.

De Burgh, H. (2000) 'Chinese Journalism and the Academy: the politics and pedagogy of the media', *Journalism Studies*, 1(4): 549-558.

Ding, Y. (2001, April) 'The Dragon and the Phoenix', *New Internationalist*, 333: 22-23.

Donald, S. H. and M. Keane (2002) 'Media in China: New Convergences, New Approaches', in Donald, S.H., M. Keane, and Y. Hong (eds) *Media in China: Consumption, Content and Crisis*. London: RoutledgeCurzon.

Donald, S.H., M. Keane and Y. Hong (eds) (2002) *Media in China: Consumption, Content and Crisis*, London: RoutledgeCurzon.

Forney, M. (2001, June 18) 'Killing the Messenger', *Time Asia* online edition, www.time.com/time/asia/news/magazine/0,9754,129945,00.html.

Galtung, J., and R.. Vincent (1992) 'The international news flows: reflections on a debate', Leicester: Centre for Mass Communications Research, University of Leicester.

Gao, Z. (2002) 'Advertising with Chinese Characteristics: The Development of Advertising in China, 1979-1999', in Jia, W., X. Lu, and D. R. Heisey (eds) *Chinese Communication Theory and Research: Reflections, New Frontiers, and New*

Directions. Westport, CT: Ablex Publishing.

Greenspan, R. (2002, April 22) 'China Pulls Ahead of Japan', *Jupitermedia Corporation*, http://cyberatlas.internet.com/big_picture/geographics/article /0,,59/11_1013841,00.html.

Grobe, K. (2002, December 8) 'Jiang's New Clothes', *Frankfurter Rundschau*, www.gvnews.net/demo/html/GlobalviewsAsia/alert4.html.

He, Z. (2000a) 'Chinese Communist Party Press in a Tug-of-War: A Political-Economy Analysis of the Shenzhen Special Zone Daily', in C.C. Lee (ed) *Power, Money, and Media: Communication Patterns and Bureaucratic Control in Cultural China*. Illinois: Northwestern University Press.

He, Z. (2000b) 'Working with a Dying Ideology: dissonance and its reduction in Chinese journalism', *Journalism Studies*, 1 (4): 599-616.

Huang, C. (2000) 'The Development of a Semi-Independent Press in Post-Mao China: An overview and a case study of Chengdu Business News', *Journalism Studies*, 1 (4): 649-664.

Hui, Y.M. (2001, October 31) 'Phoenix one wing short: Good coverage can mean bad news in the mainland', *South China Morning Post*.

Jacob, R. (2002, December 6) 'Star TV rises on a promising eastern horizon', *Financial Times* (London).

Jia, W. (2002) 'Introduction: The Significance of Chinese Communication Theory and Research in a Glocalizing World', in Jia, W., X. Lu and D. R. Heisey (eds) *Chinese Communication Theory and Research: Reflections, New Frontiers, and New Directions*. Westport, Connecticut: Ablex Publishing.

Jirik, J. (2001, August 5-8) 'What is the state of the Emperor's clothes? An investigation into the Chinese news as the mouthpiece of the Party and government', paper presented at the Association for Education in Journalism and Mass Communication, Washington, D.C.

Kahn, J. (2002, December 4) 'China Has World's Tightest Internet Censorship, Study Finds', *New York Times* online, www.nytimes.com/20 02/12/ 04/international/asia/04CHIN.html.

Kempner, M. (2001) 'AOL in pact with China to trade TV programs; "Miami Vice," other shows to run in Communist nation; deal to benefit viewers in three US cities', *Atlanta Journal and Constitution, Home Edition, Business*.

Landler, M. (2001, October 29) 'AOL Gains Cable Rights in China by Omitting News, Sex and Violence', *The New York Times*.

Lee, C.C. (2000a) 'Chinese Communication: Prisms, Trajectories, and Modes of Understanding', in Lee, C. C. (ed) *Power, Money, and Media: Communication Patterns and Bureaucratic Control in Cultural China*. Evanston: Northwestern University Press.

Lee, C.C. (ed) (2000b) *Power, Money, and Media: Communication Patterns and*

Bureaucratic Control in Cultural China. Evanston: Northwestern University Press.

Lee, C.C. (2001) 'Rethinking the Political Economy: Implications for media and democracy in Greater China', *Javnost - The Public*, 8 (4): 81-102.

Leung, L. (2002, July 1) 'Europe eyed for CCTV-9 broadcasts', *South China Morning Post, Business Post*.

Levander, M. (2001, June 25) 'A Great Leap Forward?: Legend's innovative partnership with AOL may signal the direction of China's Internet market', *Time Asia: International Edition*.

Li, X. (2001, August) 'Significant Changes in the Chinese Television Industry and Their Impact in the PRC: An Insider's Perspective', *The Brookings Institution, Center for Northeast Asian Policy Studies*, www.brook.edu/fp/cnaps/papers/li_01.htm.

Li, Y. (2002) 'How Chinese Television and New Media Presented the U.S. 9-11 Tragedy: A Comparative Study of SINA, CCTV, and PhoenixTV', *Television and New Media*, 3 (2): 223-229.

Lull, J. (1996) 'China turned on (revisited): television, reform and resistance', in A. Sreberny-Mohammadi, D. Winseck, J. McKenna and O. Boyd-Barrett (eds) *Media in Global Context*, London: Arnold.

Lynch, D. C. (2000) 'The Nature and Consequences of China's Unique Pattern of Telecommunications Development', in Lee, C. C. (ed) *Power, Money, and Media: Communication Patterns and Bureaucratic Control in Cultural China*. Evanston: Northwestern University Press.

Ma, E. K.W. (2000) 'Rethinking media studies: The case of China' in Curran J. and M. J. Park (eds) *De-Westernizing Media Studies*. London: Routledge.

McDonald, J. (2001a, October 23) 'AOL Time Warner Inks Landmark Deal', *Associated Press*.

McDonald, J. (2001b, August 15) 'China closes Marxist journal', *Associated Press*.

Mitchell, T. (2001) 'Staid papers nourish saucy little sisters', *Probe International*.

Mooney, P. (2001, November 12) 'Phoenix Rising', *Newsweek, Atlantic Edition*.

O'Neill, M. and L. Leung (2001, December 7) 'New conglomerate aims to compete with global giants', *South China Morning Post, Business Post*.

Pan, Z. (2000) 'Improvising Reform Activities: The Changing Reality of Journalistic Practice in China', in Lee, C.C. (ed) *Power, Money, and Media: Communication Patterns and Bureaucratic Control in Cultural China*. Illinois: Northwestern University Press.

Paterson, C. (1996) 'Global television news services', in Sreberny-Mohammadi, A., D. Winseck, J. McKenna and O. Boyd-Barrett (eds) *Media in Global Context*, London: Arnold.

Redl, Anke and Rowan Simons (2002) 'Chinese Media: One Channel, Two Systems', in Donald, S.H., Keane, M. and Y. Hong (eds) *Media in China: Consumption, Content and Crisis*. London: RoutledgeCurzon.

Schlesinger, P. (1979) *Putting Reality Together*. London: Constable.

Schudson, M. (1991) 'The Sociology of News Production Revisited', in Curran, J. and M. Gurevitch (eds) *Mass Media and Society*. London: Arnold.

Shakya, T. (2002) 'Blood in the Snows', *New Left Review*, 15 (2): 39-60.

Shen, J. J. (2002) 'Computer-Mediated Communication: Internet Development and New Challenges in China', in Jia, W., X. Lu and D. R. Heisey (eds) *Chinese Communication Theory and Research: Reflections, New Frontiers, and New Directions*. Connecticut: Ablex Publishing.

Simmie, S. and B. Nixon (1989) *Tiananmen Square*. Vancouver: Douglas and McIntyre.

Sun, X. (2001) *An Orchestra of Voices: Making the Argument for Greater Speech and Press Freedom in the People's Republic of China*. Connecticut: Praeger Publishers.

Straits Times (Singapore) (2002, March 31) 'China's media war goes on air', *The Straits Times*.

Tuchman, G. (1978) *Making News*. New York: Free Press.

Wang, L. (2002a) 'Reflections on Tibet', *New Left Review*, 14 (2): 79-111.

Wang, X. (2002b, November 15) 'Historic moment as capitalists embraced', *South China Morning Post*.

Wu, Guoguang (2000) 'One Head, Many Mouths: Diversifying Press Structures in Reform China', in Lee, C.C. (ed) *Power, Money, and Media: Communication Patterns and Bureaucratic Control in Cultural China*. Illinois: Northwestern University Press.

Zhao, B. (1999) 'Mouthpiece or Money-spinner? The Double life of Chinese Television in the Late 1990s', *International Journal of Cultural Studies*, 2(3): 291-305.

Zhao, Y. (1996) 'Toward a propaganda/commercial model of journalism in China? The case of the Beijing Youth News', *Gazette*, 58: 143-157.

Zhao, Y. (1998) *Media, Market, and Democracy in China: Between the Party Line and the Bottom Line*, Illinois: University of Illinois Press.

Zhao, Y. (2001) 'Herbert Schiller, the U.S. Media, and Democracy in China', *Television and New Media*, 2 (1): 51-55.

Zhou (Zhao), Y. (2000) 'Watchdogs on Party Leashes? Contexts and implications of investigative journalism in post-Deng China', *Journalism Studies*, 1 (2): 577-597.

Notes

1 I wish to thank Professors Chin-Chuan Lee and John Downing for their critical comments on an earlier draft of this chapter. The research component of this chapter was first presented as a paper at the Association for Education in Journalism and Mass Communication Conference, International Communication Division, Washington, D.C. Aug. 5-8, 2001. Editors note: The editors also thank Uldis Kruze of the University of San Francisco for commenting on a draft of this chapter.

2 For radio, see Zhao (1998) as a good starting point.

3 This quote is from Sheng Yilai, at the time of writing, Director of CCTV's Overseas Service Center, from an interview he gave TVNewsWeb.com on 23 August 1999.

4 At the time of writing, the English news team had provided all of CCTV's contribution to CNN World Report. CCTV-1 and the Xinwen Lianbo news team were not involved.

Chapter 8
Al-Jazeera Satellite Channel: Global Newscasting in Arabic
Naomi Sakr

The big story in the changing international news environment is the meteoric rise to global prominence of the Arabic news channel Al-Jazeera after the events of September 11. Al-Jazeera had unrivalled access to new political actors like al Qaeda and its modes of representing conflict in all its gory detail during the Iraq war challenged established Western news practices. Some analysts felt it to have a growing and radicalising importance in the Middle Eastern 'street', a position that probably underscored Western military attacks on the channel during both the Afghanistan and Iraq conflicts. Sakr provides detailed economic and organisational background to the formation of the channel in Qatar and the complex financial and editorial environment in which it operates. She argues that rather than mobilising Arab opinion, the channel simply filled a need for uncensored news in a region where state media remain dominant and to which the only previous alternatives were non-Arab media.

Never before has any Arab-owned media venture attracted as much Western attention as Al-Jazeera Satellite Channel, broadcaster of 24-hour news and current affairs from the tiny Gulf emirate of Qatar. Al-Jazeera was just five years old in late 2001 when it soared to international prominence after the September 11th suicide attacks that killed thousands of people in the United States. The channel's sudden fame stemmed from its facilities inside Afghanistan and access to videotape of Osama bin Laden, Saudi Arabian-born dissident, leader of the Al-Qa'ida network and – initially at least – prime target of the US bombing raids on Afghanistan that began in October 2001.

With the September 11 attacks having exposed a failure of Western intelligence about Al-Qa'ida and glaring gaps in Western understanding of opposition movements in the Middle East, media commentators and politicians from the East and the West seized on Al-Jazeera's programming as pertinent to the knowledge deficit. Broadly speaking, opinions of Al-Jazeera were split according to whether they regarded the station as part of 'the problem' (militant anti-Western extremism), or part of the solution (providing a pan-Arab space where people in the thick of regional controversies could debate issues that other heavily-censored Arabic newscasters would not allow even to be mentioned on air). Partisan assessments of the channel came thick and fast. Some (eg Ajami, 2001) saw its unusually outspoken coverage of a troubled region as deliberately fanning the flames of Arab radicalism and dissent. Others (eg Soueif, 2001) regarded it as a potentially benign influence in a region where conspiracy theories have traditionally flourished because credible information and public dialogue are lacking.

It is germane to the present study that the two alternative interpretations of Al-Jazeera cited above correspond in some measure to two divergent trends in the scholarly study of newsgathering and dissemination in general. On one side is a propaganda model of the media, in which news coverage is seen to have a mobilising function on behalf of special interests that dominate the state and/or private activity, whether in the West or elsewhere (Herman 1986; Herman and Chomsky 1988). On the other is the view that news output in any context is a complex and contingent outcome of practical organisational circumstances, specific legal, financial and technical considerations, access to sources and journalists' professional ethics (eg Schudson 1991, Williams 1993). Clearly these approaches are by no means mutually exclusive.

It is conceivable that analysis of specific practical factors in a given situation will reveal that certain groups do exploit news organisations to their own advantage. The current study, however, does not start from the assumption that this is so in Al-Jazeera's case. It avoids doing so because it aims to determine whether Al-Jazeera has conformed more consistently to a mobilisation model or to a model in which a range of factors at various organisational levels combine to produce news that does not regularly serve the same set of political or business interests. To this end it seems necessary to take account of the full range of possible influences and linkages identified in both approaches. The study therefore does consider whether particular political and business forces stand to gain from Al-Jazeera's editorial policy and news values. But it also examines operational aspects in their own right. These include the political and legal environment, the channel's ownership and sources of finance, staffing, news sources, audience ratings and competition. As noted by the author of a recent study of global communication, material resources that are crucial to the autonomy of media institutions should be taken to include not only human resources, from journalists to technical staff, but also access to major political and economic actors, audiences and institutions, as well as the time available in daily and weekly schedules for covering current affairs (Wilkin, 2001). It goes without saying that each of these aspects of any news operation deserves in-depth research. The aim in this chapter can only be to highlight key characteristics and dilemmas specific to Al-Jazeera and, from them, derive pointers as to the nature of its contribution as a non-western source of news.

Political and Legal Environment

Al-Jazeera Satellite Channel was established in Qatar in 1996, in a part of the world where, for decades, harsh censorship prevented free reporting on affairs of state. In his 1970s typology of the Arab press, republished in the 1980s, Rugh found what he styled a 'mobilisation' media system to be widespread and to have replaced a previously 'diverse' or 'loyalist' press in several Arab states (Rugh, 1987: 165). In this typology, mobilised news media were linked to political systems in which there were no political opposition activities for the news media to report on and criticism of government policies was not allowed. In fact, one inference to be drawn from Rugh's account was that even the supposedly unmobilised press, notably in Lebanon before the 1975-90 Lebanese civil war, still practised a form of mobilisation. This was true insofar as individual newspapers, in promoting a single viewpoint and surviving despite obvious financial losses, would be assumed by readers to be furthering the vested interests of some paymaster in a foreign state (Rugh, 1987: 92). Rugh's references to laws governing press ownership and censorship likewise revealed strong similarities between the so-called loyalist press and the mobilisation press. In none of the three media types would a single newspaper publish a diversity of views.

Comparisons of Arab press laws in the early to mid-1990s showed little had changed since Rugh conducted his research. All Gulf countries, for example, still imposed prison sentences for such vaguely-worded offences as 'criticising the ruler', 'disseminating false information', 'disturbing public order', or 'harming' national unity, public morality or relations with friendly states. The main difference from one country to the next was in whether the length of the prison sentence incurred for such offences was measured in months or years (Derradji, 1995: 168-192; 206-217; 317-340). All had information ministries running the broadcast media and enforcing press censorship through methods such as licensing of publications, registration of journalists and obligatory deposit of newspapers before (or, in one case, at the time of) distribution. These restrictions in Gulf countries echoed those prevailing across the Arab world from Egypt, Jordan and Syria in the east Mediterranean (ARTICLE 19, 1997a, 1997b, 1998a) to Tunisia in the west (ARTICLE 19, 1998b). Government ownership and control of terrestrial television stations meant that media practitioners in television were effectively government employees. As such their jobs would depend on observing codes of conduct built around a plethora of elaborate prohibitions – prohibitions on 'causing offence' to the head of state or other public figures or even expressing disdain for the ruling regime.[1] The practical outcome of these restrictions could be seen daily on television screens. The typical 'news' broadcast would lead with what one critique describes as a 'seemingly endless and substance-free' listing of the 'doings' of the head of state (Napoli and Amin, 1999: 72). Shots of hand-shaking and sitting on couches with a succession of visiting dignitaries would not be disturbed by anything as troublesome as a run-down on what was discussed. On the contrary, the only reference to trouble would be found in items of international news, consisting of soundless agency footage of floods, wars and earthquakes in conveniently far-away places. Commentary on such occurrences would be minimal to avoid the risk of unwittingly criticising a 'friendly state.'

For television news on so many terrestrial stations to follow this pattern so long after the supposedly mould-breaking advent of Arabic-language satellite channels in the early 1990s indicates the continuing impact of multiple layers of censorship. The description of a typical newscast, given above, draws on television in Egypt, the Arab world's most prolific broadcaster and, traditionally at least, a media trendsetter for the region. Professionals working in Egyptian television news noted entrenched resistance to any emulation of the style and content of news introduced into the region by CNN during the 1991 Gulf war. Evidence of resistance was plentiful. News stories were still being presented in the same order in the early 1990s as they were in the 1960s. Single items could still last ten minutes or more, while correspondents would persist with analysing or commenting instead of going 'straight to the point' (Weisenborn, 1992: 9). Egypt's early role in Arabic-language satellite broadcasting, undertaken by the state-owned Egyptian Radio and Television Union, meant that its staid approach to terrestrial newscasts was carried over to the satellite sector, at least until the creation of Nile News in 1998 (Sakr, 2001: 127). In comparison, the Saudi-owned, London-based Middle East Broadcasting Centre (MBC) appeared to represent a new departure in the sphere of Arabic-language news. Created in 1991, MBC stressed its vocation as a 'news-led' channel for its first six years. It set a local precedent by opening a news bureau in Jerusalem and, in 1993, became the first Arab television station ever to interview a US president (MBC, 1997). This did not mean, however, that MBC interpreted 'news' to mean investigative reporting on politics in the Gulf. It avoided material that might embarrass its backers within the Saudi ruling family, focused instead on international news (Ayish, 1997: 482) and cut costs in the late 1990s by decreasing the length and frequency of its news bulletins (Sakr, 1999: 98).

This brief outline of prevailing political and legal restrictions circumscribing the content and presentation of Arab-owned news media would not be complete without reference to other leading pan-Arab satellite channels. These included two Lebanese satellite stations launched in the same year as Al-Jazeera. Lebanese media legislation is unusual in the Arab world because it allows private ownership of radio and television stations. The 1994 Audiovisual Media Law, which went into effect in 1996, drastically pruned the profusion of small broadcasters that had sprung up during Lebanon's 1975-90 civil war and cleared the path for the country's two top television companies to expand terrestrially and by satellite. Importantly, they remained subject to formal and informal censorship of their news and current affairs reporting, by both the Lebanese and Syrian governments (Kassir, 2000; Sakr 1998). As for the two top Saudi Arabian digital broadcasters – both transmitting from outside Saudi Arabia so as to avoid the kingdom's media laws – one (Arab Radio and Television, ART) opted not to include a news channel in its digital bouquet. The other, Orbit, started off at the other extreme, signing a 10-year contract with the BBC in 1994 to provide an Arabic television news service. That contract survived for just two years. It was terminated prematurely when Orbit baulked at BBC news reports about Saudi dissidents in London and finally drew the line at an edition of the current affairs programme, *Panorama*, reporting on Saudi Arabia's human rights record. By virtue of its demise, the BBC's television news service in Arabic demonstrated with abundant clarity the incompatibility between BBC news values and the apparently all-encompassing controls on news output in the Arab world.

As it happened, however, those controls proved to be less all encompassing than most Arab governments assumed. A small chink had opened in Qatar following a change of government in June 1995, in which a new *emir*, Sheikh Hamad bin Khalifa Al-Thani, ousted his father in a palace coup. Sheikh Hamad, educated at Sandhurst Military Academy in the United Kingdom and the Gulf's youngest head of state at the time of his accession, took power armed with a modernising agenda for his very small and very rich emirate.[2] It was a political opening that was to attract favourable international attention to Qatar and highlight contrasts with neighbouring authoritarian regimes. Such contrasts in turn served to boost the emir's prestige at home and enhance his government's leverage in regional forums, such as the six-member Gulf Co-operation Council (comprising Bahrain, Kuwait, Oman, Qatar, Saudi Arabia, and the United Arab Emirates) (Dazi-Héni 2000).

An early step was to abolish the Ministry of Information. This move alone, approved by the Qatari cabinet in February 1996, instantly distinguished Qatar from all other Arab states. Rhetoric accompanying the ruler's decision stressed the need to do away with secrecy and 'feel the people's pulse'.[3] Later that year, the emirate achieved another first in the Arab world by agreeing to the 24-hour relay of BBC radio programmes in Arabic and English on FM from its capital city, Doha. A BBC World Service press release also announced that the BBC would train Qatari broadcasters. Thereafter, more precedents were set in other areas of political life. When municipal elections were held in 1999, women were allowed to vote and stand for public office, in stark contrast to norms of political participation in other Gulf States at that time. A committee was formed to draft a new constitution complete with provision for an elected parliament. It was in this environment of partial, top-down political liberalisation in the Arab world's smallest and richest country that Al-Jazeera Satellite Channel was created. Residents of Qatar could not receive the channel on satellite dishes, because a national ban on satellite dishes, imposed in 1993, remained in force. After the 1995 coup, however, it seems to have been preserved more out of social conservatism than political sensitivity.

Indeed, Qatar's own local radio and newspapers started to air public grievances (Hindley, 1999) and in 1999 broke a longstanding taboo by carrying criticism of the stipends paid to members of the Qatari ruling family (AP, 1999). Qassem el-Imadi, head of the Qatar Cablevision network, told an interviewer in 1999:

> Dishes are banned here; we are not ashamed of that …. Remember, Qatar is a conservative nation and having an open sky is an invasion for some people in the community. They do not want all the European channels … especially those that are abusing their powers (Forrester 1999: 22-3).

Instead of dishes, access to numerous foreign channels was obtainable via cable, for a subscription of around US$35 per month.

Ownership, Finance and Staff

In several respects, Al-Jazeera Satellite Channel started where the BBC Arabic television news service left off. Qatar's cable network gave viewers in the emirate access to the Orbit subscription channel that offered the BBC service. Sheikh Hamad and his entourage were consequently familiar with BBC-style news in Arabic and had already decided they wanted to launch something similar even before the BBC service went off the air.[4] Recruitment efforts were under way when the Orbit-BBC link was severed in April 1996, with the result that around 18 BBC editorial and technical staff made redundant by the collapse found jobs with Al-Jazeera in Doha (TBS, 2001).

Al-Jazeera started up in November 1996, financed by a five-year interest-free loan from the Qatar government. This funding formula, together with the choice of a name and logo that contained no reference to Qatar, was designed to distance the Qatari authorities from Al-Jazeera output. Despite some early talk of possible privatisation once the five years were up, the privatisation option was not pursued. Moreover, arrangements for repaying the loan were left open-ended. Questioned on this subject after the five-years had expired, the channel's general manager, Mohammed Jassem al-Ali, said the Qatari leadership believed it would recoup its investment in Al-Jazeera in the form of non-financial, 'intangible' benefits.[5]

Al-Jazeera thus officially became an independent broadcasting entity – a novelty in the region – being directly owned neither by shareholders nor a state. The publicised start-up money was not generous, especially for a channel devoted to the expensive business of gathering news. At 500 million Qatari riyals (US$137 million) it would have lasted MBC or MBC's Lebanese rivals barely two years, based on these station's annual budgets at the time (Sakr, 2001). Al-Jazeera's managers therefore had every interest in minimising costs and maximising income through advertising revenue and other means. As one member of staff commented, the first rule of careful spending was to avoid corruption.[6]

In practice, spending decisions were a mix of the careful and not so careful. On one hand expensive leases on analogue satellite transponders were gradually cancelled in favour of cheaper digital alternatives, even where these meant viewers would need to upgrade their receiving equipment. On the other hand, stringent criteria for hiring new personnel appear to have been applied in some cases but not in others. Occasional interruptions in cash flow reportedly impinged on salaries and payments for essentials such as mobile phones. Yet, with the total workforce up to 500 by early 2002, and twenty-seven offices in operation, including eight fully staffed bureaux, questions arose as to whether the start-up credit formally advanced by the Qatari government was being supplemented informally behind the scenes.

Either way, the task of establishing a steady stream of revenue from advertising was a major challenge for a broadcaster of uncensored television in the Arab world. In countries where the state continues to dominate the economy and privatisation generally means transferring state assets to members of the ruling elite, the placing of advertisements is liable to be determined more by considerations of political expediency than the targeting of audiences based on their preferences and purchasing power. Random qualitative responses such as faxed messages and phone-ins are relied on as a source of audience feedback by most Arab-owned satellite channels. Quantitative studies have generally to be commissioned ad hoc because systematic surveys of public opinion, whether for ratings or other purposes, meet resistance from the politically powerful who fear that results will be detrimental to their interests (Tessler, 1998: 79).

Given these constraints, Al-Jazeera could not rely on building up advertising income quickly, especially since its audience reach was also constrained during the first year of operations while it waited for a chance to move from Ku-band on Arabsat 2A to the more widely available C-band. The channel was assured a space on Arabsat by the fact that Qatar, with a 9.8 per cent stake in the Arab Satellite Communications Organisation, was the fourth biggest of the organisation's twenty-two shareholders. At the time of Al-Jazeera's launch, however, Arabsat's C-band capacity was already fully used and the newcomer had to wait for a vacant slot. The wait took its toll. The Pan-Arab Research Centre (PARC), a Dubai subsidiary of Gallup, recorded a meagre US$3.2 million worth of advertising income for Al-Jazeera in 1998, compared with levels of US$77 million and above for the top three pan-Arab satellite channels (PARC 2000). At this point Tihama, the Saudi company retained from the outset to bring in advertising for Al-Jazeera, withdrew, and the channel set up its own advertising agency, based in Doha and Dubai. But even with a spectacular 250 per cent increase in the following year, income from advertising was still reported at just US$8 million in 1999.

It took two more years for international companies to warm to Al-Jazeera as an advertising vehicle. In the aftermath of the September 2001 suicide attacks on the World Trade Centre and Pentagon, Al-Jazeera's worldwide audience was said to have reached 35 million, including around 150,000 in the United States (Wells, 2001). Yet this figure was not sufficient to counteract a negative response by some US companies to coverage of Osama bin Laden. Decisions by

General Electric and Pepsi Cola in late 2001 not to advertise with Al-Jazeera reportedly cost the channel US$4.5 million in that financial year.[7] The US$ 250,000 earned in royalties from a single videotape of Al-Qa'ida training camps in Afghanistan hardly compensated for the loss.

Alongside the sale of airtime, the station's managers sought to raise revenue from other sources. A dramatic increase in viewers after September 11 facilitated the sale of subscriptions for encrypted delivery in countries outside the Middle East. This was in addition to income earned from renting out studios, editing suites and satellite slots and selling exclusive filmed footage. The objective of capitalising on facilities guided decisions about where to locate bureaux, the aim being to focus on places unpopular with Western television crews. In Kabul, where Al-Jazeera and CNN both received authorisation from Afghanistan's ruling Taliban regime to open offices at the beginning of 2000, CNN later pulled out while Al-Jazeera stayed (Kamel, 2002).

This strategy, although amply vindicated in 2001 by lucrative sales of Al-Jazeera film from inside Afghanistan, carried its own risks, in that the presence of a bureau in a particular country would leave Al-Jazeera and its local staff vulnerable to penalties imposed by the government of that country, or to physical attack.[8] For example, Al-Jazeera's facilities in Baghdad enabled it to cover the Desert Fox raids by US and UK bombers on Iraq in December 1998. This provoked fury from the governments of Kuwait and Saudi Arabia, which interpreted such coverage as being aimed at mobilising popular sentiment in favour of Iraq. But Al-Jazeera's own reporter in Baghdad, himself an Iraqi, was reportedly detained by the Iraqi authorities in September 2001, accused of failing to pay a commission on advertising receipts to the eldest son of the Iraqi president Saddam Hussein (Iraq Press, 2001).

Similarly, Palestinian security forces stormed the Al-Jazeera office in Ramallah on the West Bank in March 2001 and ordered its closure. Most observers found this puzzling in light of the station's extensive coverage of the Palestinian struggle against Israel's continued military occupation of Palestinian land. The closure, which was lifted a few days later, appeared to have been prompted by an Al-Jazeera trailer for a documentary on the Lebanese civil war. The trailer contained footage of an activist holding a poster deemed insulting to the Palestinian Authority chairman, Yasser Arafat (*Middle East Times*, 2001). In November 1998, Al-Jazeera's office in Amman was closed by Jordan's Minister of Information in protest at its airing of a panel debate in which one of the guests opined that Jordan had been created for Israel's benefit and was plotting with Israel to deprive Syria of water resources (Sakr 2002: 122).

In 2001 Al-Jazeera was forced to pay damages amounting to US$16,000 in a lawsuit in Kuwait. The case was brought after one of the station's presenters mentioned an allegation of Kuwaiti atrocities committed against people suspected of collaborating with Iraq during the 1990 invasion. Had Al-Jazeera declined to pay up, its property in Kuwait City would have been seized

(*Washington Times*, 2001). Given the costs and risks attendant on establishing offices in Arab capitals, the decision to establish a presence in the Afghan cities of Kabul and Kandahar may not have appeared at the time to represent a break with precedent. In fact, the Kabul office proved extremely unsafe. On 13 November 2001, it was destroyed by a US bomb, leading to widespread suspicions that US forces had deliberately targeted Al-Jazeera in order to silence its reporting from Afghanistan. Journalists who probed the incident found evidence to support the suspicions (Wells, 2001), while a US State Department source revealed in private that sections of the US military had advocated bombing Al-Jazeera's headquarters in Doha.[9] The bombing occurred after Qatar's ruler, Sheikh Hamad, had visited Washington, where he was asked by his hosts to have Al-Jazeera 'toned down' (BBC, 2001).

Ultimately, for any broadcaster, there is a trade-off between the cost of doing what it takes to provide exclusive news coverage and the benefits of attracting audiences and maximising advertising revenue. In Al-Jazeera's case, decisions about newsgathering have regularly put the station's staff in the firing line – sometimes literally, as shown above. Arab nationals working in their own countries for an employer based elsewhere are often more vulnerable to local 'law enforcement' than expatriates who trust that diplomats will intervene on their behalf. It is a particular feature of Al-Jazeera that its staff originates from several different Arab states. Like the diversity of its revenue sources, or insecurity of its bureaux in potential war zones, Al-Jazeera's approach to recruitment and retention of staff may provide an indicator as to how it compares with other Arabic-language broadcasters in the 'mobilisation' stakes.

The man nominated to head the new channel was Sheikh Hamad bin Thamir Al-Thani, a young nephew of Qatar's head of state. He was barely ten years into his career when, as under-secretary at the Ministry of Information and Culture, he moved to Al-Jazeera in 1996. Given the seniority attached to age in Gulf cultures, it was widely assumed that the real power behind the channel lay with closer associates of the ruler, himself in his late forties when Al-Jazeera was launched. Most prominent among these were the outspoken foreign minister, Sheikh Hamad bin Jassem bin Jabour Al-Thani, and the ruler's wife, Sheikha Moza bint Nasser Al-Misnad. Meanwhile Al-Jazeera's Qatari managing director was drawn from outside the ruling family but shared with the chairman a background within Qatar's own media and information apparatus. Mohammed Jassem Al-Ali's previous 20-year career was mainly spent with Qatar's terrestrial television station, except for a few years spent establishing a cultural television channel backed by Sharjah in the United Arab Emirates.

In the editorial staff as a whole, however, as in many other Qatari-based enterprises, expatriates outnumbered Qataris. The first recruits included journalists from the BBC Arabic news service, some of whom had worked with public service broadcasters elsewhere in Europe before being hired by the BBC. Salah Negm, an Egyptian who was editor-in-chief at Al-Jazeera for its first five years, joined the BBC from Netherlands Radio, which axed its Arabic service in

1995. Two of Al-Jazeera's best-known political talk show presenters, Faisal Al-Qassim of Syria and Sami Haddad of Jordan, also honed their skills at the BBC. At Al-Jazeera they found new opportunities both in terms of the time available for programming and the scope for producing original material. Whereas the BBC's Arabic television news service went on air for only a few hours each day, Al-Jazeera built up gradually to 24-hour transmission. Whereas the BBC service relied heavily on the organisation's existing English-language newsgathering and production resources, staff at Al-Jazeera were able to make their own original material. Within the BBC, as in the Arabic service of France's Radio Monte Carlo, it was technically acceptable for presenters and translators to come predominantly from one country of origin – such as Egypt or Lebanon – because these stations' editorial policies were those of their European managers, not their Arabic-speaking personnel. Indeed, the extent to which Arab staff at the BBC felt sidelined in the coverage of Arab current affairs, and bypassed for promotion, led by the late 1990s to serious discontent (Mulholland, 1998).

At Al-Jazeera, in contrast, the regional knowledge of editorial staff from across the Arab world was brought to bear on programming choices that left few conflicts and controversies, from Morocco to Yemen, untouched. The channel's willingness to station two correspondents in Afghanistan in 2000 may be understood in light of its editors' familiarity with aspects of regional affairs that were consistently overlooked by Western media before September 2001. Few Western correspondents or politicians seem to have understood the 'Afghan Arab' phenomenon, involving the cross-border movements of Arab nationals who fought against Soviet forces in Afghanistan and believed themselves called upon to defend Muslims in Bosnia and Chechnya. As a leader of the Afghan Arabs, Osama bin Laden had a particularly large following among Saudi Arabia's alienated and unemployed youth.

News Values, News Sources and Competition

In the eyes of those working for Al-Jazeera, a balance of staff from a dozen different Arab states contributes towards editorial balance, in both topics and perspectives. The Arab world has been deeply split, within and between countries, since Iraq invaded Kuwait in 1990, Algeria descended into civil war in 1992 and the Palestinians signed the Oslo accords with Israel in 1993. Convulsive regional reactions to these three events and others like them are sufficient to demonstrate the lack of consensus within Arab society. They also point to disagreements likely to exist among Al-Jazeera's multinational staff. According to one insider, the staff is a unique mixture of the 'tribal with the urban, the Eastern with the Western, the leftist with the rightist, and the religious with the secular' (Fouda, 2001).

Like the management of BBC World or CNN, with which they see themselves competing, managers at Al-Jazeera identify 'balance' as the criterion by which they select news stories and seek out sources of information and comment. The managing director, Mohammed Jassem Al-Ali, stressed this repeatedly in interviews before and after September 11 2001. Asked about the station's contacts in Afghanistan he said: 'We have correspondents in the United States and we have correspondents in Kabul and Kandahar. We give equal coverage to both sides and that is our role. We present both sides' (*Jordan Times*, 2001). Indeed the aim of giving 'equal coverage' is arguably one of the features that have distinguished Al-Jazeera most effectively from other Arabic-language television channels. As a mission statement, it is displayed most prominently in the titles and formats chosen for the channel's political debates. The best known include *Al-Ittijah al-Muaakis* (The Opposite Direction) and *Akthar min Rai* (More than One Opinion). These programmes, like *Bila Hudud* (Without Bounds) or *Shahid ala al-Asr* (Witness to the Era), highlight an appreciation that viewpoints are exactly that: points of view.

Before Al-Jazeera arrived, stormy confrontations on screen were unheard of on Arab television because of government censorship. Thus the opportunity existed to provide something totally new. 'New' to Al-Jazeera's Qatari backers did not mean the glamorous female presenters and hilarious game shows of Lebanese television but the 'clashing perspectives' of real life political opponents, and programmes that would 'respect viewers' intelligence' by leaving them to make up their own minds.[10] As an approach to news and current affairs broadcasting, this was not only an innovation on Arab television but was also unfamiliar in a region where the voice of authority is rarely challenged openly, whether at school or university, within families or at work.

When dissent is eventually expressed, it tends to be extreme. In the aftermath of September 2001 and with the benefit of hindsight, a few commentators inside and outside Al-Jazeera homed in on the necessity of encouraging internal dialogue and free debate to pre-empt explosions of violent protest. Arguments to this effect found their way into pan-Arab newspapers, such as *Al-Hayat*. In December 2001 *Al-Hayat* published a column by Abdel-Hamid al-Ansari, dean of the College of Sharia and Law at the University of Qatar, suggesting that the notion of opposition in Arab countries had become associated with bloodshed. There was an urgent need, he said, to 'abandon the idea of hatred and enmity towards others merely because of differences of interests and intentions' and, instead, to 'educate our children in the ways of dialogue and respect for other opinions' (Ansari, 2001).

Like conflicting opinions in talkshows, conflicting news sources caused some confusion and suspicion among Arab viewers. Al-Jazeera was not the first Arab satellite channel to seek comment from Israelis; MBC had blazed a trail by opening a news bureau in Jerusalem in the early 1990s and Orbit had set a precedent in 1996 by interviewing Benyamin Netanyahu when he was Israel's prime minister. Nevertheless, Al-Jazeera's frequent recourse to Israeli journalists and commentators, especially during Israeli elections in 2000, gave rise to accusations by establishment figures in Egypt and elsewhere that the channel had a 'Zionist' bias and was backed by the CIA.

To discredit the channel for broadcasting Israeli voices, the pro-government *Egyptian Gazette* carried a cartoon depicting an Al-Jazeera correspondent pouring petrol onto Palestinians who were already on fire (Khan, 2001). In the same way the channel was accused of being pro-Iraqi when it broadcast from Baghdad, and when it screened tapes of Osama bin Laden it was dubbed 'Osama TV'. Explaining their editorial policy during the US bombing of Afghanistan, Al-Jazeera insiders repeatedly cited their past practice of reporting both sides of a conflict, whether the conflict was local, national, regional or global. Some also harked back to their experience with the BBC. Grappling with the editorial dilemmas arising from the so-called war on terror, one said: 'even after five years [of being with Al-Jazeera instead of the BBC], if we're in doubt in a certain situation, we convene and ask ourselves, if we were in London now, what would we do (Sullivan, 2001)?' Mohammed Jassem al-Ali, refuting the charge of propaganda, said:

> When we aired the tape of Osama bin Laden's spokesman Suleiman Abu Ghaith, directly after that we brought Edward Walker, former US Assistant Secretary of State for Near East Affairs for his comments, and after that a Muslim cleric to talk from an Islamic perspective ... to raise points such as that Islam doesn't allow you to kill innocent people, that Bin Laden will condemn American bombings but at the same time give orders to kill innocent Americans. To air the statements without any comments, without any opposing statements or viewpoints or analysis, that's when it's propaganda (TBS, 2001).

Despite concern in some quarters that broadcasts showing Al-Qa'ida leaders would increase their following among disaffected Arab youth, the same broadcasts also prompted wider debates in the Gulf about the root causes of disaffection, together with efforts to neutralise the militants' appeal. When Al-Qa'ida spokesman Suleiman Abu Ghaith was shown on Al-Jazeera threatening the ejection of Western troops from the Gulf and warning Muslims in the US and UK to avoid aeroplanes and tall buildings, Kuwaiti cabinet ministers reacted by stripping Abu Ghaith of his Kuwaiti nationality (EIU, 2001b: 15). At the same time, a large number of US officials took the opportunity to put their points across on Al-Jazeera. In mid-October 2001 these included the White House National Security Advisor, Condoleeza Rice, and the Defense Secretary, Donald Rumsfeld.

Media analysts based in Arab capitals observed that such appearances were doing both Arabs and Americans a favour, by forcing members of the US administration to engage with Arab opinion and mistrust, while simultaneously demonstrating to Arab viewers that American officials are capable of understanding Arab concerns. One memorable interview occurred in early November 2001, when Christopher Ross, a senior State Department official and former US ambassador to Syria, responded entirely in Arabic to questions such as why US President George W. Bush had described the so-called war on terror as a 'crusade'.

Optimism about US-Arab dialogue proved premature, however. US media organisations mobilised themselves on behalf of the war effort against Al-Qaeda (Gumbel, 2001) and US allegations mounted about bias and misrepresentation on Al-Jazeera's part. Critics of the Arab channel complained that it devoted much more time to civilian casualties in Afghanistan and anti-US or pro-bin Laden demonstrations around the world than to the suicide attacks in New York or excesses of the Taliban regime.

There were objections that Al-Jazeera showed images of old devastation in Afghanistan, allowing viewers to infer that destruction wrought during a decade of war had actually been caused by US bombing. It was likewise argued that Arab partisanship regarding the Israeli-Palestinian conflict had coloured Al-Jazeera's coverage, as reflected in its use of the Arabic word *shuhada* (martyrs) in reference to Palestinian fatalities, its description of Israeli forces as 'aggressors', and its live screening of clashes between Palestinian stone-throwers and Israeli soldiers in tanks.

What these criticisms ignored was the consistency between Al-Jazeera's editorial policy on the Israeli-Palestinian issue and that of other leading Arab satellite channels. A study of these channels, presented at a conference in Hamburg in March 2001, found that all devoted the bulk of their pan-Arab news coverage to the Palestinian uprising and that all used the term 'martyr' to refer to Palestinians killed by Israeli fire. The main difference identified by this study was a quantitative one, whereby stories from the Arab world accounted for 72 per cent of total news items on Al-Jazeera compared with levels of 43 per cent to 57 per cent for the other channels (Ayish, 2001). Western criticisms of a perceived lack of balance in Al-Jazeera's news reports also tended to overlook the long-standing imbalance in international coverage of the Israeli-Palestinian conflict, often brought about by Western journalists' tendency to neglect basic history and international law – a tendency exposed by textual analysis (Ackerman, 2001: 61-74; Lynch, 2002: 65-69).

At the same time, attacks on Al-Jazeera's reporting on Afghanistan seemed to ignore the virtual declaration by the US of an 'information war' against Al-Qaeda and the Taliban, apparently along the lines of previous media battles fought as part of the 1982 Falklands war (Harris, 1983), the 1991 Gulf war (eg Keeble, 1997) and the 1999 Kosovo conflict (Taylor, 1999). Sometimes media warfare is waged in the guise of blocking enemy propaganda. Walter Isaacson, chairman of CNN, wrote a memo to his staff urging them to be more balanced in reporting the effects of US air strikes on Afghanistan. Instead of focusing 'too much' on Afghan casualties or hardship, he asked them to show how the Taliban had harboured terrorists and were hiding themselves among civilian populations (Khan, 2001).

Amid such contested interpretations of 'balance', Al-Jazeera viewers familiar with Western media felt that Al-Jazeera's approach meant a degree of balance had been restored. As one Arab businessman put it: 'It is a delight to see a professional news service that reflects our biases, not yours, for a change'

(Zanoyan, 2001). In any event, the channel's output was not deemed extremist by official Western monitors. With Al-Jazeera beamed into six million British households via Sky Digital, the UK's Independent Television Commission (ITC) monitored Al-Jazeera's output for material that might incite racial or religious hatred. It judged that proscription would not be justified (*Telegraph*, 2001).

Nevertheless, disapproval of Al-Jazeera's news agenda, both in the United States and among Arab ruling elites, attracted a great deal of attention in late 2001, highlighting the absence of any other pan-Arab news and current affairs channel in Arabic that could compete with Al-Jazeera on its own terms, or take its place. Nominal competitors put themselves out of the running for one reason or another. Nile News, for example, was made available only in digital, concentrated on local Egyptian issues and was reluctant to emulate Al-Jazeera in broadcasting so many programmes live. Arab News Network (ANN), established in London by a relative of the Syrian president in 1997, made no serious attempt to match Al-Jazeera in terms of consistency and professionalism. MBC's plan to launch a dedicated news channel fell by the wayside in the late 1990s, scuppered by budgetary constraints and a recognition that Al-Jazeera's candid reporting was beyond the reach of a Saudi Arabian television channel.[11] Consequently, in seeking to formalise co-operation agreements with potential competitors, in the time-honoured tradition of Western news agencies (Read, 1992).

Al-Jazeera found itself dealing mainly with non-Arab allies. It signed an exclusive contract with CNN in 2001, before the September 11 attacks, whereby CNN and Al-Jazeera reporters would appear on each other channels. This relationship was strengthened three days after September 11, when CNN's senior international editor, Octavia Nasr, a Lebanese American, travelled to Doha to arrange the sharing of footage and access (Sullivan, 2001). A row occurred a few months into the relationship, when Al-Jazeera accused CNN of airing an Al-Jazeera interview with Osama bin Laden without permission.

The interview, conducted in October 2001, had been withheld by Al-Jazeera. Whereas CNN anchors alleged that it had been withheld because it incriminated Osama bin Laden as instigator of the September atrocities, sources on the other side of the dispute gave different explanations as to why the interview had not been aired. They said it would have reflected negatively on the Al-Jazeera reporter who made a poor job of the interview, would have cast Al-Jazeera in the role of mouthpiece for bin Laden and would have contravened an unwritten agreement sealed between Qatar's ruler and the US vice-president Dick Cheney when the latter visited Qatar the day before the bin Laden interview took place (VOA News, 2001; *Gulf Times*, 2002a; Al-Atraqchi 2002). Cheney had reportedly gained Sheikh Hamad's consent not to allow Al-Jazeera to become a vehicle for bin Laden propaganda.

As demonstrated by the CNN-Al-Jazeera dispute, almost any decision by Al-Jazeera to air or not to air sensitive material related to September 11 was doomed to be presented in terms of a battle for hearts and minds. On the US side at least, George Bush's post-September 11 dictum that 'you are either with us or against us' was adopted as a statement of policy towards media outlets serving Arab audiences. This was evident in the emergence of plans, backed by Senator Joe Biden, Democrat chairman of the Senate Foreign Relations Committee, to pump US$500 million into an Arabic-language satellite television station that would combat alleged anti-Americanism and counter the appearances of bin Laden and his supporters on Al-Jazeera (Campbell, 2001).

CNN also pursued its own agenda in this respect. Despite their practical co-operation in getting news and interviews out of inaccessible areas of Afghanistan, Al-Jazeera and CNN continued to compete via their respective Arabic-language websites. CNN opened its website in Arabic in January 2002, following a plan devised several months before September 11. Al-Jazeera's website, launched in January 2001 with a budget of US$50 million, was already well established in September 2001, when the number of visitors to all news websites soared. Aljazeera.net registered a reported 38 million visitors and 265 million page views during its first year in operation (*Gulf Times*, 2002b). Celebrating this achievement, its chairman announced that plans were under discussion for Al-Jazeera to branch into English, in both television programming and website content.

The aim of such English-language activities was not immediately clear. Al-Jazeera board members indicated that they had been inundated with requests for an English version of the website. However, the plans were announced at a time when Arab information ministers had decided collectively to mount a campaign to disseminate Arab views through Western media, including views about US foreign policy in the Middle East. The months after September 2001 also saw public relations advisers devising ways to enhance Saudi Arabia's image in the West, while Saudi-backed MBC contemplated the possibility of broadcasting some material in English. Al-Jazeera had only the fractious nature of its programmes to stop outside observers regarding its flirtation with English-language content as a similar public relations exercise. (Editors' note: Stuart Allan details the development of the Al-Jazeera English language website in Chapter 16.)

Impact and Prospects

As of 2002, it remained to be seen how far expanding its output would increase Al-Jazeera's audience. After five years in operation, the channel could claim 35 million regular viewers in the Arab world, in addition to 150,000 in the United States and thousands more elsewhere. Data collated by Canal France International (CFI) show that access to satellite television soared throughout the Arab world during the 1990s, with satellite penetration reaching particularly high levels of 73 per cent and 81 per cent of households in Saudi Arabia and Kuwait respectively by 2000/01 (Belchi 2002). Of the total Arab audience able to receive the three main television news channels, CNN, BBC

World and Al-Jazeera, surveys show that the preference for Al-Jazeera was unequivocal even before the suicide attacks on the United States. The channel reached nearly thirty-eight per cent of Saudi viewers and thirty-four per cent of Omani viewers in 2000 and thirty-one per cent of Kuwaiti viewers in 1999 (Belchi, 2002).

In Egypt, where the proportion of households with satellite access remained in single figures by mid-2001, anecdotal evidence suggests that it increased rapidly after September 11 as viewers turned to Al-Jazeera in place of the sanitised news and tame discussion available on their terrestrial channels. They did so even though Egypt's government-controlled broadcaster had introduced new programmes with apparently daring titles like 'Breakthrough', 'Without Censorship' and 'In-depth' in a bid to keep audiences loyal and deter them from switching to Al-Jazeera (Hammond, 2001). Evidence like this, of viewers' ability to distinguish between programmes that really are uncensored, as opposed to ones that merely claim to be, is believed to have triggered an acknowledgement on the part of camera-shy officials in the Arab world that public opinion counts. Whereas politicians would previously boycott Al-Jazeera in protest at its presenters' disregard for sensitive egos, the dramatic rise in the channel's audience since the late 1990s has reportedly led those same politicians to ask to be interviewed.[12] The increasing number and conciliatory nature of appearances by Syrian government spokesmen on Al-Jazeera seemed to testify to this trend (Ghadbian, 2001).

Al-Jazeera's board were anyway sufficiently confident of their company's growth potential to plan two new projects in 2002 besides the English-language ventures mentioned above. One of these was a channel dedicated to screening documentaries in Arabic, a genre hitherto conspicuously absent from television screens in the Arab world. Based on experiments with documentary-style programmes in Al-Jazeera's existing schedules and tested at film festivals sponsored by Al-Jazeera in London and Doha in 1999 and 2000, the documentary channel was to be a joint enterprise in which sixty per cent of output would consist of co-productions and the remainder would be produced in-house. Unlike the original Al-Jazeera channel, which was not preceded by a feasibility study, the documentary channel was assessed for feasibility and pronounced worthwhile in terms of prospective viewers and income. Comparable to the National Geographic and Discovery channels, it was not expected to involve a large increase in editorial staff or overheads.

The second project, in contrast, involving an Arabic business channel, represented a much bigger financial and editorial commitment. If pursued it was expected to establish a partnership between Al-Jazeera and CNBC. With these projects in hand, Al-Jazeera managers and staff professed themselves unconcerned about the possibility that they might eventually face serious competition on the home front. On the contrary, their message was that a true competitor would strengthen and even safeguard Al-Jazeera. It would do so, they said, by demonstrating that other Arab media organisations had finally accepted Al-Jazeera's mould-breaking appetite for uncensored news, conflicting opinions and 'hot spots' (Fouda, 2001).

Conclusion

This chapter examined everyday aspects of Al-Jazeera's news operation, from funding and staffing to decisions about content and delivery. In doing so it noted various forms of media mobilisation at work, not only with respect to the channel itself but also in the international media context within which it exists. No one denies that Al-Jazeera owes its existence to a mobilisation of resources by the ruler of Qatar. Paradoxically, its editorial freedom also represents a form of mobilisation, insofar as it is aimed at attracting international attention and prestige to Qatar's government, allowing it to 'punch above its weight' in pan-Arab forums. This fact, demonstrated in aspects of Al-Jazeera's management and seemingly elastic finances, shows the ambiguous nature of its autonomy. That is to say, it has relative editorial autonomy so long as it has the Qatari ruler's moral support. As one of the channel's presenters expressed it:

> The crucial card, which made, and still makes [Al-Jazeera] the center of attention – ie the unprecedented freedom – is but a grant from upstairs. This grant can simply be claimed back at any moment for whatever reason, and this is the fact that should not be driven aside by false conquests (Fouda, 2001).

Yet, as the chapter also showed, Al-Jazeera operates in a global environment where news broadcasters are frequently used to mobilise opinion on behalf of particular interest groups, be they Arab governments or those who seek to buttress military campaigns with information warfare. Ironically, when judged according to whether it sets out to manipulate public opinion, Al-Jazeera seems ill-equipped to achieve such a goal. Its heavy reliance on unscripted live broadcasts, its insistence on juxtaposing conflicting viewpoints, the diverse national backgrounds and political leanings of its editorial staff: all these features seem geared to injecting unpredictability into the messages conveyed by the channel's programmes. Where its editorial approach is most predictable, namely on the Israeli-Palestinian conflict, this approach reflects deepseated political judgements already shared by the vast majority of Arab viewers and – as studies show (Ayish, 2001) – by other Arab satellite channels.

In covering the carnage in that conflict from an Arab perspective, Al-Jazeera was blamed for radicalising Arab public opinion. A more sober assessment might point out instead that it was merely filling a gap in a market for uncensored news and views that has traditionally been dominated by non-Arab channels. People outside the Arab world remained dangerously unaware of the depth and strength of Arab public opinion on local and international affairs until that public opinion found an outlet through Al-Jazeera.

References

Ackerman, S. (2001) 'Al-Aqsa intifada and the US media', *Journal of Palestine Studies*, 2: 61-74.

Ajami, F. (2001, November 18) 'What the Muslim world is watching', *New York Times*.

Al-Atraqchi, F. (2002, February 5) 'CNN owes Al-Jazeera an apology', *Palestine Chronicle*.

Ansari, A.H. (2001, December 13) 'The Arabs are preoccupied with a worrying question: how do we improve and correct our image in the world?', *Al-Hayat*, translated in *Middle East Economic Survey*, XLV(1): C4.

Associated Press (1999, June 19) 'Qataris break taboo by criticizing funds for extended royal family', *Associated Press*.

ARTICLE 19 (1997a) *The Egyptian Predicament: Islamists, The State and Censorship*. London: ARTICLE 19.

ARTICLE 19 (1997b) *Blaming the Press: Jordan's Democratisation Process in Crisis*. London: ARTICLE 19

ARTICLE 19 (1998a) *Walls of Silence: Media and Censorship in Syria*. London: ARTICLE 19.

ARTICLE 19 (1998b), *Surveillance and Repression: Freedom of Expression in Tunisia*. London: ARTICLE 19.

Ayish, M. (1997) 'Arab television goes commercial', *Gazette*, 59: 473-493.

Ayish, M. (2001) 'American-style journalism and Arab world television: an exploratory study of news selection at six Arab world satellite television channels', *Transnational Broadcasting Studies*, http://www.tbsjournal.com.

Belchi, J. M. (2002) 'Evolution of TV viewing in the Middle East 1996-2000', paper presented to the conference on New Media and Change organised by the Konrad Adenauer Foundation in Amman, 27 February – 1 March.

BBC (2001, October 4) 'US urges curb on Arab TV channel', http://news.bbc.co.uk.

Campbell, D. (2001, November 23) 'US plans TV station to rival Al-Jazeera', *The Guardian*.

Dazi-Héni, F. (2000) 'Des processus électoraux engagés dans les monarchies du Golfe: le cas du Koweït et du Qatar', *Monde Arabe – Maghreb Machrek*, 168: 76-88.

Derradji, A. (1995) *Le droit de la presse et la liberté d'information et d'opinion dans les pays arabes* [Press law and freedom of information and opinion in Arab countries]. Paris: Publisud.

EIU (2001a) *Bahrain/Qatar Country Profile 2001.* London: Economist Intelligence Unit.

EIU (2001b) *Kuwait Country Report December 2001.* London: Economist Intelligence Unit.

Forrester, C. (1999) 'Gulf TV: situation normal, everything changing', *Gulf Marketing Review.* January: 22-23.

Fouda, Y. (2001) 'Al-Jazeera: Here we stand; we cannot do otherwise', *Transnational Broadcasting Studies,* http://www.tbsjournal.com.

Ghadbian, N. (2001) 'Contesting the state media monopoly: Syria on al-Jazira television', *Middle East Review of International Affairs,* http://meria.idc.ac.il.

Gulf Times (2002a, February 2) 'Al-Jazeera "to sue CNN"', *Gulf Times.*

Gulf Times (2002b, January 29) 'Al-Jazeera considering English programmes', *Gulf Times.*

Gumbel, A. (2001, September 28) 'Free speech has become second casualty of war', *Independent.*

Hammond, A. (2001, June 8) 'Egyptian TV fights Arab rivals with tepid glasnost', *Middle East Times.*

Harris, R. (1983) *Gotcha! The Media, the Government and the Falklands Crisis.* London: Faber & Faber.

Herman, E. (1986) 'Gatekeeper versus propaganda models: a critical American perspective', in Golding, P., G. Murdock and P. Schlesinger (eds) *Communicating Politics: Mass Communications and the Political Process.* New York: Holmes and Meier.

Herman, E. and N. Chomsky (1988) *Manufacturing Consent.* New York: Pantheon.

Hindley, A. (1999, March 12) 'Heading for the polls', *Middle East Economic Digest.*

Iraq Press (2001, September 23) 'Saddam's son sends local reporter to prison', *Iraq Press.*

Jordan Times (2001, October 5) 'Al-Jazeera TV dismisses US criticism', *Jordan Times.*

Kamel, A. (2002) 'Al-Jazeera: An Insider's View', *ISIM Newsletter,* 9: 20.

Kassir, S. (2000) 'Red lines and media blues', *Index on Censorship.*

Keeble, R. (1997) *Secret State, Silent Press.* Luton: John Libbey Media.

Khan, A. (2001, November 9) 'Al-Jazeera annoys everybody', *Middle East Times.*

Lynch, J. (2002) *Reporting the World: A Practical Checklist for the Ethical Reporting of Conflicts in the 21st Century, Produced by Journalists for Journalists.* Taplow, UK: Conflict & Peace Forums.

MBC (1997) *Background Information*. London: MBC Public Relations and Promotions Department.

Middle East Times (2000, March 31) 'Al-Jazeera says Arafat reopens its office', *Middle East Times*.

Mulholland, R. (1998), 'The Empire's last outpost?', *Arabies Trends*, May: 54-55.

Napoli, J. and H. Amin (1999) 'The good, the bad and the news: twenty years of the Egyptian media', *Cairo Papers in Social Science*, 21(4): 72-85.

Napoli, J., H. Amin and R. Boylan (1995) *Assessment of the Egyptian Print and Electronic Media*, report submitted to the United States Agency for International Development.

PARC (2000) *Advertising Receipts of Pan-Arab Satellite Channels 1998-9*. Dubai: Pan-Arab Research Centre.

Read, D. (1992) *The Power of News: The History of Reuters*. Oxford: Oxford University Press.

Rugh, W. (1987) *The Arab Press: News Media and Political Process in the Arab World*. New York: Syracuse University Press.

Sakr, N. (1998) 'Daring to talk', *The World Today*, 54(12): 121-123.

Sakr, N. (1999) 'Frontiers of Freedom: Diverse Responses to Satellite Television in the Middle East and North Africa', *Javnost/The Public*, 6 (1): 93-106.

Sakr, N. (2001) *Satellite Realms: Transnational Television, Globalisation and the Middle East*. London: I B Tauris.

Sakr, N. (2002) 'Jordan: the stop-go transition', in Price, M., B. Rozumilowicz and S. Verhulst, *Media Reform: Democratizing the Media, Democratizing the State*. London: Routledge.

Schudson, M. (1991) 'The sociology of news production revisited', in Curran. J. and M. Gurevitch (eds), *Mass Media and Society*. London: Edward Arnold.

Soueif, A. (2001, October 9) 'It provides the one window through which we can breathe', *Guardian*.

Sullivan, S. (2001) 'The courting of Al-Jazeera', *Transnational Broadcasting Studies*, http://www.tbsjournal.com.

Taylor, P. (1999) 'Propaganda and the web war', *The World Today*, 55 (6): 10-12.

TBS (2001), 'Interview with Mohammed Jasim Al-Ali', *Transnational Broadcasting Studies*, http:www.tbsjournal.com.

Tessler, M. (1998) 'The contribution of public opinion research to an understanding of the information revolution and its impact in North Africa and beyond', in Emirates Center for Strategic Studies and Research (ed), *The

Information Revolution and the Arab World: Its Impact on State and Society. Abu Dhabi: Emirates Center for Strategic Studies and Research.

The Telegraph (2001), 'Al-Jazeera TV faces ban for inciting hatred', http://www.portal.telegraph.co.uk/news/2001/11/05.

VOA News (2001, December 13) 'Al-Jazeera has unaired Bin Laden TV interview', *VOA News*.

Washington Times (2001, October 10) 'Al-Jazeera penalised by court in Kuwait', *Washington Times*.

Weisenborn, R. (1992) 'Cool media, the war, and then – CNN', in Weisenborn, R. (ed) *Media in the Midst of War*. Cairo: Adham Center Press.

Wells, M. (2001, November 19) 'How smart was this bomb?', *Guardian*.

Wilkin, P. (2001) *The Political Economy of Global Communication*. London: Pluto Press.

Williams, K. (1993) 'The light at the end of the tunnel: the mass media, public opinion and the Vietnam War', in Eldridge, J. (ed) *Getting the Message: News, Truth and Power*. London and New York: Routledge.

Zanoyan, V. (2001) 'Political and diplomatic challenges facing US-GCC relations in the aftermath of 11 September', *Middle East Economic Survey*, XLIV(50): D1-D6.

Notes

1 A list of 33 prohibitions contained in the Code of Ethics of the Egyptian Radio and Television Union is given in Napoli et al, 1995: 171-2.

2 Qatar's total population was estimated at 566,000 in March 1999, of whom only 160,000 were Qatari nationals and the rest expatriates from countries such as India and Pakistan (EIU 2001a: 47). Gross domestic product (GDP) per head of the population was US$23,544 in Qatar in 2000 (EIU 2001a: 52), putting it well ahead of the second and third richest Arab countries as measured in GDP per head, namely Kuwait and the United Arab Emirates.

3 This was the phrase used by the outgoing information minister in an interview with the pan-Arab daily *Al-Hayat* on 11 February 1996.

4 According to a former member of Al-Jazeera management in conversation with the author, Cairo, 16 September, 2000

5 Interview with the author, Amman, 1 March, 2002

6 Conversation with the author, Cairo, 19 September, 2000

7 Author's interview with Mohammed Jassem al-Ali, Managing Director of Al-Jazeera, Amman, 1 March 2002.

8 Editors note: Following the bombing by the US Air Force of Al-Jazeera's Kabul offices, their bureau chief was attacked as he tried to leave the city, according to some reports. In the Iraq war in April, 2003, an Al-Jazeera journalist was killed when US war planes attacked the Baghdad bureaux of Al-Jazeera and Abu Dhabi TV (CNN.COM, 8 April 2003) and international press organisations and Al-Jazeera continue to protest the detention (since 2001) of an Al-Jazeera cameraman in Guantanamo Bay, Cuba, by the US government (Associated Press, 15 October 2002).

9 Communication to the author, London, 6 December 2001

10 The phrases between quotation marks are repeatedly used by Mohammed Jassem al-Ali in press interviews.

11 Private communication to the author from an MBC source, 12 October 1999. The plan for an MBC news channel was actively revived in 2002.

12 According to Mohammed Jassem al-Ali, addressing a conference on New Media and Change in Amman, Jordan, on 28 February 2002.

Part III: Meanings

Chapter 9
Post-Political Journalism: Ethics and Aesthetics Among News Manufacturers
Andrew Calcutt

Many authors in this section of the book are concerned broadly with the relationships between media and morality. Calcutt's interest lies in the relationship between the ethical and aesthetic dimensions of the work of journalists and the way in which ethical aims and aesthetic interests often work at cross-purposes in the construction of news. Writing as a 'hackademic,' Calcutt explores how the overly-aestheticised images of the first Gulf War connected with a sense of ironic detachment and post-modern irony, summed up in the infamous line from Baudrillard that the 'Gulf War did not happen.' He then discusses the emergence of a journalism of attachment, and critiques the arguments about the 'spiritual calling' made by journalists such as Brayne, himself a contributor to this volume. Calcutt's detailed focus on the form and nature of news representation explores the tensions between the critical and the myth-making practices of journalism, the latter being currently in the ascendant. The need is therefore for a more critical practice by both journalists and academicians of journalism.

This chapter considers changes and continuities in the sense of moral worth exhibited by journalists in recent years and it explores the relationship between the ethical and aesthetic content of their work. It suggests that ethics and aesthetics are core components in today's journalism, and that the interdependence of these components is now to the detriment of a third aspect, namely politics.

The substitution of a diptych (ethics and aesthetics) for the long-established triptych of ethics, aesthetics and politics, is identified as a new trend which is characteristic of journalism at the turn of the 21st century. Yet among both journalists and commentators on journalism, this new trend has been projected backwards onto the previous history of journalism, to the point where it is now identified with journalism itself.

I begin the chapter with an account of various journalists' estimations of their profession's practice during the first Gulf War before I introduce academic evaluations of contemporary journalistic output. This trajectory mirrors my own career path as a journalist turned academic (a self-styled 'hackademic'). I go on to explore the relationship between the changing self-image of journalists and developments within the broader ideological context in which they have been operating. Finally, through a reading of Lule's influential commentary (2002) on the role of myth in the *New York Times'* response to the events of September 11, 2001, I review the increasing readiness to subordinate the political role of journalism to its cultural (ethical and aesthetic) function.

Rather than emphasise institutional pressures in the formation of news values, an approach which dates back to Galtung and Ruge (1965), my concern is with news manufacturers as both products of and participants in shifting societal values, a tradition at least as old as Raymond Williams' *Culture and Society* (1958). As my title suggests, I am mindful of Cohen and Young's seminal observation that news has to be made, not merely reported (1973). The notion of journalism as a unit composed of distinct and sometimes antithetical parts (ethics and aesthetics versus politics) is partly derived from Eagleton's (1998: 97) critical reading of Kant, in whose philosophy the 'ethico-aesthetic sphere (and its...) utopian community of subjects, united in the very deep structure of their being', stands in contrast to the 'instrumental pursuit of ends' in the domain of politics. For Eagleton, 'if culture thus sketches the ghostly outline of a non-dominative social order, it does so by mystifying and legitimating actual dominative social relations' (1998: 97). Similarly, I seek to show that, contrary to appearances, the cultural turn among both journalists and journalism scholars is tending to diminish the critical, hence political, role of journalism.

Mea Culpa

Looking back at the media's coverage of the first Gulf War from a distance of five years, the *Guardian*'s Maggie O'Kane lamented the lapse of moral duty on the part of news pool journalists who filed stories synonymous with the 'Coalition forces' order of the day. 'This is a tale' she reported, 'of how to tell lies and win wars, and how we, the media, were harnessed like beach donkeys and led through the sand to see what the British and US military wanted us to see in this nice clean war' (1995).

But O'Kane's admission was no scoop. With only one year's hindsight, renowned press reporter Robert Fisk had accused television of offering 'war without responsibility', leading up to the *denouement* of 'war without death' (1992). Even while 'Operation Desert Storm' was still raging, columnist Edward Pearce complained that the press corps had taken shelter in officialdom. He observed 'a press which can be worn by the executive like a dress handkerchief' (1991). Similarly, John Pilger berated his malleable peers for neglecting their duty of criticism:

> In the Gulf, television and newspaper people can be corralled and controlled. They report from Saudi Arabia as if they are themselves prisoners of war held in Colditz Castle. The difference between present-day journalists and Colditz POWs was that the latter understood very well their duty to escape (1991).

In one of the earliest academic studies of television coverage of the first Gulf War, Morrison noted that 'very few pictures of death and injury were broadcast' (1992: 93), confirming the journalistic assessment made previously by BBC foreign affairs editor John Simpson: 'As for the human casualties, tens of thousands of them, or the brutal effect the war had on millions of others...we didn't see so much of that' (1991).

This latter observation was made during a retrospective television series, *Our War*, broadcast in May 1991. If Simpson's reflective approach was widespread at that time, it would indicate that, only five months after the onset of Desert Storm, more journalists were becoming less sanguine about the sanitised view of war which they themselves helped propagate. This is in accordance with Philo's findings that 'there was a growing feeling amongst journalists that the media had been manipulated for crude political purposes' (1995: 154).

Journalists felt they had been had. Furthermore, in allowing themselves to be swept along by military and governmental PR, they also felt they had lost their integrity and even their identity as servants of the public sphere. By the end of the Gulf War, journalism seems to have been a profession ill-at-ease with itself, and determined to make amends. Thus the *British Journalism Review* recorded that 'Most British journalists who were involved with covering the Gulf War have since sworn that they will never again allow themselves to be manipulated as they were' (*British Journalism Review*, 1991).[1]

Aestheticism and Postmodernism

Did British journalists really become separated from their sense of moral responsibility during the first Gulf War and, if so, how did they allow this to happen? One explanation is that the ethics of journalism were overwhelmed by aestheticism: journalists saw the first Gulf War as kinetic art instead of mass killing, but subsequently awoke from their dream-like state and recovered their sense of right and wrong. Thus Philo notes that 'the Pentagon videos seemed to transfix journalists' and some journalists were torn between 'fascination with hi-tech weaponry' and 'the humanitarian ethos of broadcasting' (1995: 150). In their mind's eye this dilemma was temporarily resolved by the spin of 'surgical precision' bombing (1995: 150). Acceptance of such rhetoric eventually gave way to 'many doubts' (1995: 154), but during the initial period of aerial bombardment journalists were ready to present war as a 'Hollywood movie' (1955: 155).

Similarly, Gerbner, in a chapter entitled 'Persian Gulf War: the movie' described Desert Storm in terms which indicate the gross intrusion of aesthetic concerns into the theatre of war, that 'the power to create a crisis merges with the power to direct a movie about it' (1992: 244). It was plausible, therefore, to construct a narrative of first Gulf War coverage in which the narrative itself became a parable of the dangers of aestheticism. The moral of the story is that ethical aims and aesthetic interests are generally at odds in the manufacturing of news. Ethical and aesthetic content tend to be in inverse proportion, so that over-investment in aesthetics will necessarily lead to moral bankruptcy.

The parable was reprised in an edition of Channel 4's *Right to Reply* during the Mozambique floods of February/March 2000, when Richard Kirkham complained that 'the demand for good pictures' prompted journalists to behave unethically, by taking up space in helicopters which could have been used to rescue disaster victims. Facing down television news editors from the BBC and ITN, Kirkham concluded that 'if you don't have that dramatic image ... you don't cover it'. In the hierarchy of broadcasting news values, he was saying, moral sense comes second to aesthetic sensibility.

In respect of the first Gulf War, this narrative conveniently situated news coverage of the war within the (then) fashionable framework of postmodernism. This was a framework which included aestheticisation alongside ironic detachment and the 'waning of affect' (Jameson, 1991: 11), and revealed the absence of an 'appropriate source for an impassioned commitment' (Grossberg, 1988: 42). A post-modern social (dis)order, is in short, characterised by the domination of aesthetics over ethics.

The narrative seems to ring true. The year of Desert Storm, 1991, was also the year in which London hosted the UK's first conference on virtual reality. 'VR' swiftly entered media jargon, not as shorthand for a highly specific type of new technology but as a promiscuous metaphor for the atmosphere of not-quite-reality arising from the convergence of art, life, and in the case of the first Gulf War, death. The impression was confirmed by the fact that virtual reality originated in the flight simulation technology designed to train military pilots. The vague idea of 'virtuality' was also projected onto Baudrillard's journalistic essays on the first Gulf War ('The Gulf War Will Not Take Place', 'The Gulf War: Is it really taking place?', and 'The Gulf War Did Not Take Place', collected and published in book form in 1995), even though these meditations were really more critical and thought-provoking than this interpretation suggests.

While VR was London's latest fad, the hottest property in the United States was novelist Douglas Coupland whose *Generation X: tales of an accelerated culture* depicted a cohort of young people dominated by 'knee-jerk irony' (1991). The combination of aestheticism and irony seemed to be the ambience of the late1980s and early 1990s. These were also the boom years for Jeff Koons, the visual artist who combined kitsch sentiment and cool detachment in a knowingly enigmatic mix, and the Memphis Group of Italian designers ('Memphis' after a Bob Dylan song), who developed a playfully decorative and equally kitsch 'new international style' in deliberate contrast to the original 'international style' of modernist functionalism.

Various commentators complained of irony in the soul. Among those concerned about the spread of irony into parts of human activity where it really should not reach, were Ed Barrett (latterly of *Arena*, *Esquire* and now the website *Anorak*) and Toby Young, then editor of *The Modern Review*. Their polemic against 'the plague of postmodernism' began as a review of Coupland's *Generation X* before developing into a wide-ranging attack on 'the Quotation Generation' – those among the authors' peers who put quotation marks around every experience and who 'treat ironic detachment as the basis for an identity' (1992). Young and Barrett were attacking what they regarded as the dominant mood of the moment. Their message that 'being ironically detached is ultimately to be nowhere' (1992) was intended as a salutary warning against the siren call of the post-modern aesthetic as playful but fundamentally unproductive.

Detachment and the Demand for Re-attachment

Young and Barrett felt besieged by irony, but they were not as isolated as they may have thought. Indeed their apprehension about ironic detachment may be seen as presaging a broader demand for re-attachment. In the political sphere this demand has taken a wide variety of forms. In 1993 Prime Minister John Major called for Britain to go 'back to basics', although his plea for re-attachment to 'previously held values of decency' was soon undermined by the widely publicised infidelities of various Conservative ministers (and, latterly, by those of John Major himself). Tony Blair, elected as Labour leader following the death of John Smith in 1994, avoided such embarrassments but issued a similar message in his highly publicised espousal of Christian socialism. Meanwhile in the United States, during President Clinton's scandal-ridden second term, the writer and social critic Jedediah Purdy, who combined the trustworthiness of a home-educated farm boy from West Virginia with the sophistication of Harvard University, launched a *Waltons*-style clarion call for 'a kind of thought and action ... aimed at the preservation of what we love most in the world, and a stay against forgetting what that love requires' (Kirn, 1999).

Purdy attacked irony in terms which could easily have come from Barrett and Young: 'Irony is one of the prevalent personal styles ... the ironic individual is a bit like Seinfeld without a script: at ease in banter, rich in allusion, and almost debilitatingly self-aware' (1998). He then went on to advocate the rescue of irony and the re-formulation of 'trust and commitment'. His first book, *For Common Things: Irony, Trust and Commitment* (1999) was required reading in Washington, sounding a paean to ethical attachment that was as influential at the end of the 1990s as Coupland's detached *Generation X* was at the start of the decade.

The demand for re-connection has also found expression, and come to fruition, among journalists. International news reporters now seem confident – bullish, even – about their duty 'to give witness to the suffering' (Keane, 2000). This function, and the accompanying sense of purpose, enabled some journalists to see themselves as a new kind of moral entrepreneur. This was best personified in Michael Buerk's pathway from being *Visnews'* witness to the Ethiopian famine in 1984 to chair of BBC Radio Four's programme *The Moral Maze*, and Martin Bell's progress from veteran BBC war correspondent to 'anti-corruption' general election candidate (1997) and then white-suited independent MP for Tatton. Acknowledging Propp as the source of his terminology, Benthall observed that television journalists had joined pilots and medics in the ranks of 'magical agencies' and 'magical helpers' (1993: 208).

Nowhere is this sense of mission more keenly felt than among journalists themselves. When former BBC China correspondent Mark Brayne characterised journalism as 'a spiritual calling' (2000), he was really describing the partial transformation of the hack into a quasi-priestly figure. The same pattern of development is also discernible in the influential idea of a 'journalism of attachment,' summarised in the following terms by Bell: 'In place of the dispassionate practices of the past I now believe in what I call the journalism of attachment. By this I mean a journalism that cares as well as knows; that is aware of its responsibilities; and will not stand neutrally between good and evil' (1997: 8).

Bell's manifesto for journalism is indicative of a broader narrative of moral re-connection as told to journalists, by journalists. It reads broadly like this: In our original incarnation we were detached, dispassionate, supposedly objective but as this way of working ceased to be workable, so detachment became debilitatingly ironic. Finally we got sick of postmodernism's giddy games. We knew we had to get real. In order to escape from irony's ontological hell-hole we turned ourselves into witnesses to the incontrovertible reality of human suffering. Here at last we found life, not art. Furthermore, we made a new way of life for ourselves in the post-ironic, post-aestheticist, post-post-modern journalism of attachment.

Instead of the loss of ethics in the face of aesthetic bombardment, the second half of the parable is about prodigal aesthetes finding their moral selves again. Through attachment to other people's suffering, journalists have found a way to escape the cage of irony and re-enter the ethical fold.

It is an uplifting tale of transformation. But the speed at which the conversion from aesthetics to ethics has allegedly occurred is nothing short of miraculous. According to this legend, Britain's international news journalists rediscovered their ethical selves during the Kurdish crisis, which arose as both continuation and consequence of the 1991 war against Iraq. So sudden was the change in their orientation that Shaw congratulates them for making a highly moral response to the plight of the Kurds at a time when other parties were mired in either bureaucracy or ideology: 'The media's flexibility and responsiveness to the Kurd's sufferings stand in contrast to the immobility of the other institutions of civil society' (Shaw, 1996: 123).

Damascene Road?

Did Western journalists in the Middle East really go down their own private road to Damascus? Or is their ethical turn explicable without a Pauline moment of conversion. It is, but only if we recognise first Gulf War coverage and the journalism of attachment as not only opposites but also as two sides of the same coin. Rather than focusing exclusively on changes within international journalism and its ideological context, it is equally important to identify continuities in the mindset of journalists throughout the 1990s.

From the outset, news manufacturers were transfixed by the moral aspect of the war in the Persian Gulf, which they initially presented as a highly ethical enterprise. The depiction of Saddam Hussein as Hitler and the description of British and American troops as 'the Allies', indicate the moral status ascribed to Desert Storm. This may have been war as war-game but it was a war-game portrayed, and widely accepted, as 'correct and just' (Morrison, 1992: 93), a crusade as morally uplifting and ethically justified as it was aesthetically arresting. Far from being a late entrant into coverage of the first Gulf War, ethics were always a key component: no less important to gung-ho Gulf War journalism than to the journalism of attachment.

Not that those first Gulf War journalists ignored the aesthetic element, rather they sought to combine it with the ethical aspect, and in doing so they were staying within a recognised journalistic tradition. For centuries, journalists have known that their best chance of presenting war as 'correct and just' is to use artistry in their presentation. In war reporting, moralising and aestheticising have often gone together and coverage of the first Gulf War was no exception. Indeed the formulaic combination of ethics and aesthetics was highlighted by Philo in the observation that journalists 'could not resist such a "good story" and the chance to present a real war as a kind of Hollywood movie in which "our side" were the good guys' (1995: 155). Here the word 'good' is used first in an aesthetic sense and secondly as a sign of moral quality (the inverted commas show that this shorthand for moral worth is not shared by Philo himself).

If the 'aestheticist' first Gulf War journalist was never really unhinged from morality (however questionable), neither is the new, ethical journalist unattached from aesthetic considerations. With its emphasis on the personality and emotions of its subjects, the journalism of attachment requires a more personal and emotional form of reporting, a tendency which pulls the reporter further away from the stenographer, detective or social scientist, and closer to the working methods of the artist. Under the strap line 'journalism of attachment', the 'New Journalism' of the 1960s has finally made it from features to the front page. The connection between ethics and aesthetics has never been more integral to mainstream journalism, and, as Eagleton observes of the Kantian ethico-aesthetic, such 'culture' is based on 'the most intimate subjectivity' of citizens, to the exclusion of the public and political (1998: 97).

Just as the New Journalism of the 1960s was inspired by youth culture and its new aesthetic (Wolfe, 1968), so the born-again journalists of the 1990s seem to have been in tune with the ethical turn of prominent figures from pop music and youth culture. International charitable projects in which pop personalities have played central roles include Bob Geldof's *Live Aid* in the mid-1980s and Brian Eno's *Help* in 1995. Such is the vogue for ethical activity among pop stars that even Robbie Williams made a millennial visit to Mozambique.

There may also be a growing correspondence between the emotional tone of some journalists' reports and that of numerous song lyrics. Neither its title, 'Weeping for Africa's Misery', nor the opening paragraph of Jane Standley's report from the Congo would be out of place in a lyric sheet issued by pop performers such as P.J. Harvey or Radiohead: 'In the lobby of Kinshasa's Hotel Memling, I sat down and wept. It gets to you sometimes this way – this country – and indeed, this continent' (Standley, 2000a).

The trend connecting journalism with personal expression and expressive arts such as music was confirmed by the launch in September 2000 of a BBC Radio Four programme, *Reporter's Notes*, in which BBC foreign correspondents were invited to discuss pieces of music which either reflect or informed the contexts in which they wrote their reports. Meanwhile in academic circles also there has been increased recognition of journalism's relationship with affect (McGuigan, 1998: 98, 104. Dahlgren, 1995: 150) and the realm of aesthetics associated with it.

The interdependence of ethics and aesthetics was again confirmed in Kirkham's piece for *Right to Reply*, despite its author's complaint against their coupling, when Fiona Fox, then press officer for the charity Cafod, pointed to the existence of a whole of chain of ethical agents (journalists, aid agencies, donors), all with an aesthetically-trained eye: 'The reality that aid agencies are working in today, in this media world, is that we really, really need the images' (Fox, 2000).

After the Cold War

During and after the first Gulf War, journalism continued to combine ethics with aesthetics. As we have seen, this combination is as old as war journalism itself, but its significance, its weighting among the components which constitute war journalism, is subject to historically specific variation. Such variations may be derived from factors which are not primarily ethical or aesthetic. In the early 1990s, one such factor was the relative decline of traditional politics and the concomitant tendency to attach more significance to the search for moral certainties. This, in turn, tended to have the effect of making morality even more uncertain than before.

The combinations of ethics and aesthetics practised by journalists during the 1990s were articulated with a political context specific to the period after the fall of the Berlin Wall and the end of the Cold War. On the one hand, the fall of the Berlin Wall in 1989 confirmed the demise of the conflict between left and right which had been the crucible of social change for two centuries since the French Revolution. This was the context which Jacoby describes as 'the end of the end of ideology' (2000: 26).

On the face of it, the defusing of what had once been an explosive form of social conflict should have had a stabilising affect on Western societies. After all, the collapse of the Soviet Union meant that capitalism had triumphed over the fiction of actually existing socialism. But it also meant the end of an era in which US-SU bi-polarity, whether or not it was more apparent than real, had not only offered a kind of stability in international relations (Gaddis, 1990), but also provided politicians and intellectuals in the West with moral as well as political ground on which to stand. With the fall of the Berlin Wall and the end of the Cold War, this ground was pulled from under their feet, first by the demise of politics itself, and second by the uncoupling of morality from political necessities which were suddenly superfluous. No wonder many among the West's ruling elites felt insubstantial and incoherent (Furedi, 1994), and especially inclined to offset the open-ended character of the present by repeated reference to the past, the outcome of which is always a matter of interpretation yet never in doubt.

Thus the momentum behind the first Gulf War can be interpreted partly as an attempt to maintain the re-assuring certainties of the Cold War by re-enacting the moral absolutes of the Second World War ('evil' Saddam portrayed as Hitler, for example). This suggests that Western motivation for the first Gulf War (motivation initially shared by politicians, the military and journalists) may not have been so very different from the motives behind the journalism of attachment which arose subsequently. Both are driven by what Gay (1974), referring to the predicament of German culture in the Weimar period, has referred to as 'the hunger for wholeness'. In such circumstances, the search for morality is often the preferred remedy for inner emptiness. During the 1990s, this may have had the effect of turning what was ostensibly news reporting into a progress report on the journalist's quest for something to believe in (Hume, 1997).

In an essay on the consumption of international news by television viewers, Tester (1994:95), following Ignatieff, separates 'voyeurism' from 'conscience', gratification from moral duty. In approaching changes and continuities within the subjectivity of news producers, however, it is important to recognise the interaction between the two polarities: at a time when we feel undermined as ethical subjects, the re-discovery of conscience may itself be a source of aesthetically pleasing gratification.

In this reading of journalism's recent history, ironic detachment and the journalism of attachment are articulated moments. First Gulf War journalism and the journalism of attachment were successive responses with the same intent, to re-enact 'conscience' and re-affirm journalists as ethical subjects. Both were derived from the end of Cold War consciousness and the unhinging of the West from previous moral certainties as, also, was the mode of ironic detachment which they identified themselves against. This is a reading borne out by contemporaneous occurrences in the broader cultural sphere, such as Douglas Coupland's swift passage from 'knee-jerk irony' to the form of do-it-yourself spirituality articulated in his collection of short stories, *Life After God* (Coupland, 1992).

Anti-hierarchical

There is no denying, however, that after the first Gulf War increasing numbers of journalists did break ranks with the military and political classes. Reporters reacted against being corralled and controlled. As if acting on Pilger's instructions, they rejected sanitised wars and went in search of dirty ones. But if they were not against moralising war or aestheticising disaster, why put themselves out on a limb?

As we have seen, it is not that the journalism of attachment is against ethics or aesthetics, or combinations thereof, any more than its predecessors. What it seems to have reacted against are the chains of command through which ethical and aesthetic criteria have long been established and enforced; traditional hierarchies of politicians, generals, bishops or editors. This reaction is also part of a wider trend, to the point where even Hollywood depictions of the first Gulf War are now overtly anti-hierarchical. *Three Kings* (dir: Russell, 1999) is a case in point.

Hostility to hierarchy has even spread throughout the most-hated hierarchies (Frank and Weiland, 1997). The ubiquity of this sentiment indicates that the whole gamut of Cold War institutions, developed in an era of mass mobilisation and dependent on a high degree of centralisation, was out of step with the ethical emphasis and organisational requirements of the post-Cold War period, characterised by de-massification and de-centralisation. By the time of the Second Gulf War, which is being waged as I write, 'humanitarian' and 'flexibility' has loomed large even in the vocabulary of the US-UK armies. This is the anti-corporate context in which the figure of the maverick journalist has become something of a standard type, a symbol of the widespread reaction against anachronistic forms of organisation.

Morality and Mythology

While the combination of ethics and aesthetics is not new to journalism, what is new is the downgrading of the third element of the established triad, politics. 'Politics' is here taken to mean the politicising function of journalism: its role in facilitating the public sphere by re-posing apparently natural occurrences and revealing them to be anything but natural. If myth is depoliticised speech (Barthes, 1977: 154), since the eighteenth century part of the function of journalism has been to de-mythologise and politicise, not least by exposing vested interests and the social forces underlying them. Indeed the English radical journalist William Cobbett (1763-1835) devised his *Twopenny Trash* as a pared down version of his *Weekly Political Register*. This re-formatting was necessitated by the newly introduced tax on newspapers – a tax introduced largely because of the politicising influence of journalists and pamphleteers like Cobbett.

The political role of journalism did not necessarily tie the journalist to any particular political party, but was nevertheless tied to the historical development of political parties as the organisational expression of competing interests and social forces, and hence to the emergence of modern politics (Crick, 1964: 18). Journalists whose stories politicise/demythologise their subject matter have often made it their business to criticise the moralising, aestheticising and hence mythologising tendencies not only of politicians but also of their peers in print and broadcasting. These three aspects of journalism (ethics, aesthetics and politics) have up to now enjoyed a relationship both complementary, in that they have been interdependent; and contradictory, in that the third element has facilitated criticism and consciousness of the first two. In the modern era, journalism might therefore be said to have been 'reflexive' (Habermas, 1984), or self-monitoring.

The co-existence of these elements within a contradictory relationship is highlighted by the juxtaposition of two observations made by Marx. In a letter to Kugelmann, which makes specific reference to the biased coverage of the Paris Commune, Marx emphasised the media's capacity to mythologise:

> Up till now it has been thought that the growth of the Christian myths during the Roman Empire was possible only because printing was not yet invented. Precisely the contrary. The daily press and the telegraph, which in a moment spread inventions over the whole earth, fabricate more myths ... in one day than could have formerly been done in a century (Cohen and Young, 1973).

Yet Marx was himself a journalist, and, as editor of the suppressed *Neue Rheinische Zeitung*, he extolled the progressive role of the press:

> What makes the Press into the most powerful lever of culture and the intellectual education of the people is precisely that it transforms material battles into ideal battles, the battle of flesh and blood into that of the spirit and intellect, the battle of necessity, cupidity and empiricism into one of theory, understanding and form (Marx and Engels, 1956-68).

This passage is complex and requires careful interpretation. A superficial reading might suggest that Marx was recommending the translation of 'material struggles' into archetypes, and thereby advocating the mythologising role of the press. To the contrary, he was celebrating journalism in its critical, political function as the 'lever' through which human subjects can raise

181

themselves above the pre-modern dichotomy between material and myth and thereby acquire 'understanding'.

With the advent of the journalism of attachment, however, this critical role seems in danger of disappearing. The threat to the critical dimension of journalism is documented by Monteiro in her account of 'journalism of affection'; as she argues 'the problem with the argument of "fighting for a good cause".... is that it erodes one of the central *raisons d'être* of news media: the ability to question' (2002: 285-6).

Some might refute this by saying that the journalism of attachment provides a critique of dishonest governments and slow-witted bureaucracies: it cuts through the verbiage and the statistics and gets to what really matters, how people feel. But besides distancing itself from the machinery of politics, the journalism of attachment also seems alienated from the politicising standpoint of critical distance. Moreover, in trying to get close up to its subjects, it can actively obstruct long-shot journalism, the politicising journalism of unattached analysis. If it is more value-laden yet less critical in its social role, this may be because instead of providing the material for political debate by non-journalists in the public sphere, it tends to offer journalists the chance to empathise with their subjects, while also providing them with the opportunity to soliloquise or sermonise.

Proximity to events is not necessarily antithetical to critical analysis. But in this instance, given the decline not only of commitment to political parties but also to the political attitude itself, the more journalists are attached to their subject matter, the closer they come to the exclusively ethico-aesthetic. Accordingly, the journalism of attachment is often ready to retreat from investigation and comprehension of causes and effects towards description and affect. Indeed its preferred form of descriptive affect may even be the negation of comprehension. Thus Fergal Keane, reporting on the floods in Mozambique, described them by saying that '"Biblical" is genuinely justified' (Keane, 2000), while his BBC colleague Jane Standley spoke of suffering 'beyond human understanding' (Standley, 2000b). In each instance, the effect is to project events into a realm beyond analysis and explanation; a realm in which occurrences can only be captured descriptively, metaphorically; the realm of myth.

The device of dividing journalism into two separate camps – the critical and the myth-making – is an abstraction. In practice individual journalists have always found their own positions somewhere between these two abstract journalisms, and have frequently moved positions during the course of their career. But such manoeuvrability may be harder to accomplish in future, now that the mythological role of journalism is so much in the ascendant.

Today, many journalists feel that their mythologising is morally justified. Indeed, as we have seen, some of them have developed a morally uplifting, self-affirming narrative – a myth – of their conversion to this new type of journalism which focuses on the aesthetic framing of ethical concerns. Furthermore, commentators are more confident in suggesting that myth has always been the core activity of journalism. In so doing, they too are myth-making, in that the recent cultural turn in journalism is hereby naturalised and depoliticised. For example, Lule, in an authoritative review of the *New York Times* response to 9/11, concludes that the production and dissemination of myth has been the key role of journalism throughout its long, seamless history:

> The pages of the *New York Times* will surely be one record consulted. And on those pages, future scholars will find what present day scholars have found in the mythologies of the Ancient Greeks, Native Americans, African tribes and other cultures: People and societies of all times make sense of the world through the eternal stories of humankind. In our time, journalism has that mythological role and news is myth (2002: 288).

This is a simplistic reading of the contradictions that typically constitute journalism, achieved by the backwards-projection of priorities and limitations which have only recently emerged. The result is a seamless, continuous narrative, a myth of journalism as myth. Thus:

> News is deeply rooted in the tradition of storytelling. Even before the advent of writing, news was cast in dramatic stories told in tribal gatherings or town squares. Early journalists understood news as story with roots in drama, folktale and myth (2002: 277).

Indeed 'story' is an element in journalism. Yet, at least until recently, it tended not to be the primary element. This was the case not only in op-ed pages but in reporting, too. In 1972, when Harold Evans wrote *Newsman's English*, and even in its revised guise as *Essential English for Journalists, Editors and Writers* (2000), narrative took not second but third place to the intro, which 'distils the essence of the news', and 'the news lead', which 'has concentrated on results' (2000: 122). Only when 'news points' and 'results' – information arranged in order of significance – have been communicated to the reader, is the reporter advised to offer a chronological narrative.

Under Evans' analysis and direction, the action news story has neither the same form nor function as, say, Virgil's *Aeneid*. Historically, journalism *qua* journalism was by definition discontinuous with pre-existing literary or oral forms of communication, just as the social context which spawned it was distinct from preceding social formations. But such specificity is glossed over by Lule in his efforts to establish an ahistorical continuum. While briefly acknowledging Walter Lippmann's *Public Opinion* (1922) and Schudson's work in this area (1978), for Lule the 'informational' is a mere 'model', at odds 'with the very nature of news – as story' (2002: 277).

This is to gloss over the history of ideas since the Enlightenment, and the role of journalism within the dissemination of ideas and their application as both explanatory and contributory factors to social conflict and development. *Pace*

Lule, while myth has been significant throughout human history, it has not always enjoyed the same degree of significance, in journalism or any other sphere of human self-knowledge. In the nineteenth and twentieth centuries, for example, magical-mythical thinking declined in inverse proportion to the rise of the rational-scientific. Elias (1998), like other twentieth century sociologists, expected it to be confined to the realm of the unconscious.

In recent decades, however, the forward march of human understanding has been halted, and among the signs of this obstruction are the revival of magical-mythical thinking together with a growing insistence that the role of myth has been constant throughout human history, thereby occluding the historically specific character of what is really a very recent regression.

The response to 9/11 highlighted the lack of confidence in the West with regard to modern modes of explanation and intervention, with, in turn, a predictable resort to the descriptive, emotive, metaphorical realm of myth. Within this wider uncertainty, journalists and journalism professors are uncertain of the demythologising aspect of their own heritage, to the point where some seem to have forgotten it entirely.

References

Barthes, R. (1977) *Image, Music, Text*, translated by Stephen Heath. Glasgow: Fontana.

Baudrillard, J. (1995) *The Gulf War Did Not Take Place*, translated and introduced by Paul Patton. Sydney: Power Publications.

Bell, M. (1997) 'TV News: how far should we go?', *British Journalism Review*, 8(3): 8.

Benthall, J. (1993) *Disasters, Relief and the Media*. London: I.B. Tauris.

Brayne, M. (2000, September 3) interviewed on the first edition of *Reporter's Notes*, BBC Radio Four.

Cohen, S. and J. Young (1973) *The Manufacture of News: deviance, social problems and the mass media*. London: Constable.

Coupland, D. (1991) *Generation X: tales of an accelerated culture*. New York: St Martin's Press.

Coupland, D. (1992) *Life After God*. New York: Simon & Schuster.

Crick, B. (1964) *In Defence of Politics*. Harmondsworth: Penguin.

Dahlgren, P. (1995) *Television and the Public Sphere*. Thousand Oaks: Sage.

Eagleton, T. (1998) *The Ideology of the Aesthetic*. Oxford: Blackwell.

Elias, N. (1998) *On Civilisation, Power and Knowledge: selected writings*. Chicago: University of Chicago Press.

Evans, H. (2000) *Essential English for Journalists, Writers and Editors*. London: Pimlico.

Fisk, R. (1992, January 8) *Independent.*

Fox, F. (2000, March 4) 'Right to Reply', *Channel 4.*

Frank, T. and M. Weiland (eds) (1997) *Commodify Your Dissent: the business of culture in the new gilded age.* Chicago: W.W. Norton & Co.

Furedi, F. (1994) *The New Ideology of Imperialism: renewing the moral imperative.* London: Pluto.

Gaddis, J. (1990) *Russia, the Soviet Union and the United States: An Interpretive History.* New York: McGraw-Hill Publishing Co.

Galtung, J. and M. Ruge (1965) 'Structuring and Selecting News', in Cohen, S. and J. Young *The Manufacture of News: deviance, social problems and the mass media.* London: Constable.

Gay, P. (1974) *Weimar Culture: the outsider as insider.* London: Penguin.

Gerbner, G. (1992) 'Persian Gulf War: the movie', in Mowlana, H., G. Gerbnerand H. Schiller (eds) *Triumph of the image: The Media"s War In The Persian Gulf − a Global Perspective.* Boulder : Westview Press.

Grossberg, L. (1988) *It's a Sin: politics, post-modernity and the popular.* Sydney: Power

Habermas, J. (1984) *Theory of Communicative Action, Volume One.* London: Heinemann.

Hume, M. (1997) *Whose War Is It Anyway?: the dangers of the journalism of attachment.* London: Informinc.

Jameson, F. (1991) *Postmodernism, or, the cultural logic of late capitalism.* London: Verso.

Jacoby, R. (2000) *The End of Utopia: politics and culture in the age of apathy.* New York: Basic Books.

Kant, I. (1929) *Critique of Pure Reason.* Translated by Norman Kemp-Smith, Basingstoke: Macmillan.

Keane, F. (2000, March 3) interviewed on *World Today,* BBC World Service.

Kirn, W. (1999, September 20) *Optimist In A Jaded Age,* interview with Jedediah Purdy, *Time* magazine, 154 (12).

Kirkham, R. (2000, March 4) 'Right To Reply'. *Channel 4.*

Lippmann, W. (1922) *Public Opinion.* New York: Harcourt, Brace.

Lule, J. 'Myth and Terror on the Editorial Page: the *New York Times* responds to September 11, 2001', *Journalism and Mass Communication Quarterly,* special issue 'Mythology in Journalism', 79 (2).

McGuigan, J. (1998) 'What Price The Public Sphere?', in Thussu, D.K. (ed) *Electronic Empires: global media and local resistance.* London: Arnold.

Marx, K. and F. Engels (1956-68) *Harausgegeben vom Institut fur Marxismus-Leninismus beim ZK der SED*, Supplementary Volume 1.

Mearsheimer, J. (1990, August) 'Why We Will Soon Miss The Cold War', *The Atlantic Monthly*

Monteiro, C. (2002) 'Covering the Lost Empire: the Portugese media and East Timor', in *Journalism Studies*, special issue 'Journalism, Conflict and War', 3(2).

Morrison, D. (1992) *Television and the Gulf War*. London: John Libbey.

O'Kane, M. (1995, December 16) *Guardian*.

Pearce, E. (1991, February 18) *Guardian*.

Philo, G. (ed) (1995) *Glasgow Media Group Reader, Volume 2: Industry, Economy, War and Politics*. London: Routledge.

Pilger, J.(1991) 'Censorship by Omission', *Living Marxism..*

Purdy, J (1998) 'The Age of Irony',*The American Prospect*, 39, July-August.

Purdy, J. (1999) *For Common Things: Irony, Truest and Commitment*. New York: Knopf.

Schudson, M. (1978) *Discovering the News*. New York: Basic Books.

Shaw, M. (1996) *Civil Society and Media in Global Crises: representing distant violence*. London: Pinter.

Simpson, J. (1995) 'Our War', quoted in Philo, G. (ed) *Glasgow Media Group Reader, Volume 2: Industry, Economy, War and Politics*. London: Routledge.

Standley, J. (2000a, September 1) 'Weeping for Africa's Misery', *From Our Own Correspondent*, BBC Radio Four.

Standley, J. (2000b, March 4) *From Our Own Correspondent*, BBC Radio Four.

Tester, K. (1994) *Media Culture and Morality*. London: Routledge.

Wolfe, T. (1968) *The Kandy-Kolored Tangerine-Flake Streamline Baby*. London: Mayflower/Granada.

Williams, R. (1958) *Culture and Society*. London: Chatto & Windus.

Young, T. and E. Barrett (1992) 'Irony In The Soul: the plague of postmodernism', *The Modern Review*. 1(6).

Note

1   Editors note: A similar journalistic mea culpa from the US perspective can be found in Dennis, E., et al, (1991) *The Media at War: The Press and the Persian Gulf Conflict* New York: Gannett Foundation (now, the Freedom Forum).

Chapter 10
September 11, 2001:
Sociological Reflections
Keith Tester

While some commentators have been quick to proclaim the 'death of distance' produced by the contemporary globalised media environment, others have explored new forms of cultural and moral distancing that the media may themselves exacerbate. Tester, for whom the relationship of media to morality has been an on-going focus of work, is concerned with understanding the powerful impact of the events of September 11 on media audiences. To do this he picks up and reworks Boltanski's powerful exploration of the moral obligations of the news audience toward the suffering seen on their screens that connect the 'obligation to watch' with the 'obligation to act'. Tester argues that it was the impossibility of constructing a clear narrative to frame the events, indeed the failure of news organisations to provide ordinary coverage, that brought the audience close and moved them the most.

There are some television pictures which will never be forgotten by anyone who saw them broadcast live. For every generation these pictures will be different and what is remembered is likely to sit well with that generation's fears and anxieties. As such, American audiences of the 1960s have the shooting of Lee Harvey Oswald (1963) and the assassination of Robert Kennedy (1968) seared into their consciousness (two deaths which symbolised endings of the American Dream). Meanwhile, for those who lived through the Cold War, the opening of the Berlin Wall (1989) is likely to be etched in their memories. For today's generation the images from Lower Manhattan on September 11, 2001 will always be there. What is remembered is also likely to say something about the moral horizons of each generation, and the network of interdependencies in terms of which they went about their everyday lives: from the nation, to the continent, to the world itself.

International news has been an important mechanism of the extension of people's horizons so that they have now reached their this-worldly limit. In so far as international news can report human suffering wherever it may be perpetrated then, in principle, the action of men and women can be oriented towards human beings as such, rather than any particular social and cultural group. And this historically unique situation creates the distinctive moral problem with which this generation must learn to grapple; how to translate that *de facto* human solidarity into human solidarity *de jure*. This is the moral and political challenge of globalisation.

On September 11, 2001 it became clear that globalisation is indeed one of the most absolutely important processes shaping the present. The atrocity at the World Trade Centre was truly global in its impact and reach even though, like all events, it happened at a specific time and in a particular place. International news played an enormous part in giving the event its high global profile. To some extent, that comment is nothing more than a platitudinous truism. Of course international news was important. Without it few people outside of Manhattan and Staten Island (and relatively few people inside, for that matter) would have been able to be moved by the collapse of the twin towers because they would not have seen it. But thanks to international news many millions of us witnessed live the impact of the second aeroplane and the collapse of the second tower. And what we saw perhaps had an impact upon this generation greater than any news coverage before and, one can only hope, ever again.

Certainly, and writing from within mainland Britain, it is true to say that the coverage on September 11 had a far greater impact than any news from geographically closer places such as Belfast or Sarajevo, or from other distant places like Rwanda or Afghanistan. There was something about the coverage of the deliberate destruction of the World Trade Center that lent this event a moral enormity that other disasters, atrocities and mass sufferings rather seem to have lacked. The first question is what was so special about the coverage of this event? The second question is why did the international news coverage of the destruction of the World Trade Centre have such an enormous impact on media audiences (Tester, 2001)? These are the questions that this chapter seeks to answer.

These reflections should be read as *provisional* contributions to a sociology of international news on September 11. Many of these reflections are made without supporting evidence (although I believe that such evidence could be provided by an analysis of relevant media texts or by ethnographies of audiences) and therefore it is hoped either that this essay will be treated as a framework to be filled in by other researchers or as a point of departure for further and independent analyses.

Three Explanations

It is possible to point to three more or less obvious answers to the questions of what and why. First, it is undoubtedly the case that the coverage from Lower Manhattan was lent additional degrees of impact because it was inescapable. The destruction of the World Trade Center met with global saturation coverage in no small part because New York is one of the centres of international news institutions. The technologies and personnel of global news were already in place, and they could be mobilised with great speed and efficiency. In this way the coverage was truly 'as it happened' rather than, as with so much unplanned live broadcasting, news of the aftermath. This might explain why coverage on September 11 was felt by Western audiences to be so much more compelling than coverage from Rwanda during the genocide or from the Balkans during the war of the 1990s. In both of those cases the news was about the *results* of atrocity (the piles of corpses, the damaged survivors and so on), rather than of the *moment* of atrocity itself. In those latter cases the news had already happened.

Second, impact was exacerbated because of the extraordinary familiarity of New York. It is, in many ways, a truly global city in so far as its streets and sights have become the *mise en scène* of a massive number of the productions of the culture industries. That aesthetic familiarity is attenuated by immigration into the United States as well as tourism, two movements of people which mean that in principle anyone from almost anywhere might feel that they have some kind of stake in the city. New York is *the* city of the present, and perhaps it is also the city of our global future. To this extent it is no surprise that Richard Sennett's book *Flesh and Stone*, which attempts to map a history of Western civilisation against the spaces of cities, ends with a very fine essay on New York (Sennett, 1994). This point suggests a reason why the coverage of the destruction of the World Trade Center had a greater public impact, even in Britain, than news about bombings in Belfast or Birmingham. Although the latter two places are much closer geographically, they are much farther away symbolically, imaginatively and aesthetically.

Third, there can be no doubt that the coverage of the atrocity was compelling in a way that little other international news has been able to be because the terrorists were keenly aware of the symbiotic relationship of their plans with television. This is a relationship which is much deeper than that which is implied by the evident terrorist adoption of the old anarchist principle of propaganda by deed.

Scott Stossel has gone so far as to suggest that, 'television almost inevitably plays a complicit role in terrorist acts. It is the ideal delivery vehicle for the dramatic visual images terrorists create'. Stossel says that, 'it should be obvious that the priorities of television and those of terrorism are somewhat aligned'. On the one hand television relies on dramatic images to secure audiences, which in turn keep advertisers happy, whilst terrorism is dependent on visual images in order to achieve its central aim of the generation of fear far beyond the killing fields. Stossel explains that the essence of the tight relationship of terrorism with television is that: 'Each strives to make an ideological point through dramatic impact; each seeks to amplify this impact (and therefore its ideological point) by reaching the broadest possible audience' (Stossel 2001: 35).

Given that one of the main aims of terrorism is to make a dramatic point which transcends the immediate witnesses and instead terrifies everybody, there could have been no better city to attack than New York and, apart from the Empire State Building, no better building to attack than the World Trade Center (although even had the Empire State Building been destroyed, the pictures would not have been so dramatic because other buildings would have been in the way; long-focus shots would have been impossible). The coverage of the destruction resonated at the level of the symbolic and the aesthetic, and it was able to do this in no small part for institutional reasons.

In this way, September 11 was also a day on which it became clear that in the context of globalised interdependencies and communication, it is possible for the imaginative horizons of media audiences to stretch beyond the boundaries of physical time and space. What happened on September 11 was nothing less than an especially stark moment of the suppression of distance. It might even be possible to go so far as to propose that the destruction of the World Trade Center will come to be remembered in no small part as *the* moment when it became clear that physical distance has nothing whatsoever to do with moral (ir)relevance. Distance is, instead, cultural and symbolic and it can be lengthened or shortened by social factors.

It is indeed my contention that one of the things that happened on September 11 was precisely the suppression of physical and geographical distance. It was because of that suppression that the images of the destruction of the World Trade Center had such an impact on the day, and are likely to be etched into the memories of those who watched.

Commitment and Distance

Any treatment of these kinds of issues has to take into account the work of French sociologist Luc Boltanski. According to Boltanski the central problem which is raised by news in the present is one about the moral obligations which the non-suffering members of the television audience have towards the suffering others who are shown on the screen and in the report. He points out that in conventional moral discourse, the obligations of the non-sufferers (the fortunate) towards the sufferers (the unfortunate) are based on the ability of the latter to force themselves into the conscience and consciousness of the former by means of sheer overwhelming physical presence (that is to say, proximity). This is a thesis which Boltanski clearly derives from Hannah Arendt's account of the social question, where she argues that the French Revolution represented a pivotal moment in Western attitudes to poverty and suffering; during the Revolution, and for the very first time, suffering became identified as an inescapable political and moral problem which demanded to be solved because the suffering were able to force themselves into the consciousness of the non-suffering. According to Arendt the social question is at the heart of Marx's thought (Arendt, 1973). Boltanski's thesis means that the sufferers are faced with the political problem of how to make their lack of fortune proximate to the fortunate. In these terms, the distance between the two groups is overcome through a politics of presence, which the sufferers can themselves commence.

But the sufferers are unable to make *themselves* present when it comes to the context of television. Television means that, even though the fortunate can become aware of the suffering of the unfortunate, awareness is not due to the political power of the unfortunate. Rather it is entirely connected to the abilities of international news producers. Whereas in politics distance can be overcome through mobilisation, platforms and immediacy, with television it is overcome through mediation. Consequently the possibility of a sense of obligation on the part of the fortunate non-sufferers towards the unfortunate sufferers is entirely contingent and intensely mediated (Boltanski, 1999).

These are themes that can be applied to the issue of why coverage of the destruction of the World Trade Center had such a great impact on media audiences. Boltanski is dealing with exactly our problem, the ways in which physical and geographical distance can be suppressed such that audiences might feel a certain obligation towards what they see. In Boltanski's work, this obligation is essentially moral (it boils down to the question of ethics: what ought I to do?), and we too are concerned to unravel a certain obligation: the obligation to watch.

In the context of the media, Boltanski calls the audience by the name of the spectator, and he says that the spectator only feels a sense of obligation to the extent that she or he is the subject of a 'proposal of commitment' (1999:149). As Boltanski explains what that phrase means, the emphasis that his approach places on international news, and more specifically upon news producers, becomes very clear. He writes that a proposal of commitment is made by news producers to the spectator when, 'A different spectator, who recounts a story to him [i.e. to the spectator, to the member of the audience], and who may be a reporter, that is to say an eye-witness, or who may have gathered information supposed to have come from eye-witnesses (as in the case of press agency reports), conveys statements and images to a spectator' (Boltanski, 1999:149).

The proposal of commitment is accepted to the extent that the member of the audience, 'pass[es] on in turn what he has taken from these statements and images and the emotions they aroused in him.' The point Boltanski is making here is that the acceptance on the part of audiences of the proposal of commitment that is made by the news reporter or report, leads to the emergence of action, of politics, which the fortunate spectators who are not suffering carry out on behalf of the unfortunate sufferers. In this way, Boltanski implies, distance can be overcome; the members of audiences (the spectators), bring the reports and the representation close; they overcome distance, by turning them into principles and occasions of their own action in the world. But Boltanski knows that it is not at all inevitable that the proposal that is made by the reporter will be accepted. After all: 'The spectator can accept the proposal made to him, be indignant at the sight of children in tears being herded by armed soldiers; be moved by the efforts of this nurse whose hands are held out to someone who is starving'. Similarly, the spectator can be moved to tears by the interview with the woman who managed to get out of the collapsing tower but has lost all sight of her friends. But equally the spectator, 'can also reject the proposal or return it' (Boltanski 1999: 149).

According to Boltanski, the proposal of commitment might be refused or returned because the spectator (and once again, it should be noted that the 'spectator' is his term) is not the dull and passive recipient of whatever news is broadcast. Boltanski has learnt the lesson of media analysis that audiences need to be conceptualised as being possessed of critical capacities and critical reading abilities. And he contends that these abilities on the part of audiences means that any proposal of commitment that may be made is very likely to be challenged and questioned rather than accepted at face value: 'The critical spectator must then assume responsibility for unmasking the *manipulation* of which he thinks he is the target and endeavour to establish a different way of being concerned by what happens, by what the presenter passes on to him for him to pass on to someone else in turn'.

What this means is that even as the proposal of commitment holds out the possibility of a suppression of physical distance (thanks to the ability of news producers to create an immediacy of the suffering about which audiences feel obliged to act) the fact that audiences are not passive means that the proposal of commitment can be undermined. And with that undermining, a measure of distance reappears. As Boltanski makes plain, the proposal of commitment only works effectively when audiences *trust* what they are shown. However, the critical abilities and activities of audiences mean that *suspicion* is likely to arise as soon as any plea to be trusted is actually made by international news producers. Trust breeds uncertainty. If this line of argument is applied to the question of international news it is reasonable to agree with Boltanski that: 'The media situation, by not only distancing the spectator from the unfortunate but also from the person who presents the unfortunate's suffering to him…makes more exacting the necessary conditions of trust which … are broadly dependent upon an effect of presence.' But those conditions of trust do not exist, precisely because audiences are active and not passive. Their critical abilities mean that audiences are always likely to ask why and how they are being asked to trust (Boltanski, 1999: 150, 151).

Now, it is possible to extract threads from Boltanski, which hold out the promise of assisting in the task of understanding why the coverage of the events of September 11 had such an impact on media audiences. In Boltanski's terms, the compulsive watching of the coverage can be identified as an acceptance of the proposal of commitment, which was being made by the reporters and the news institutions. That proposal was accepted rather than refused or returned because there was a remarkable sense of immediacy about the coverage. This takes us back to the more or less obvious explanations that have already been discussed. The saturation coverage combined with the familiarity of the New York skyline meant that there was indeed an extraordinary 'effect of presence'. That effect was multiplied even more for international news audiences by the obvious confusion and panic which was reigning in the news rooms, where rumours became confused with fact (for example, at one point, BBC News 24 reported that a fifth hijacked plane was heading for Chicago). In all of these ways, there were intimations that this coverage was trustworthy, that no manipulation was being carried out (the news producers were themselves too obviously in a state of panic to be able to worry about manipulating their audiences) and, therefore, that the critical capacities and activities of audiences could be suspended precisely because there was neither room nor cause for suspicion.

However, if this line of thought is accepted then it also has to be accepted that the basis of the argument has shifted from that which Boltanski presumes. Boltanski seems to assume that the proposal of commitment is made by reports and representations, which are the definite and deliberate productions of news professionals and institutions. Boltanski assumes that the news is a finished product. But on September 11, the news was not at all finished in this way. Indeed, the logic of the preceding argument is that the coverage held out a proposal of commitment which media audiences accepted *precisely because it was wholly unfinished*. The logic of the argument is that the proposal of commitment worked on this particular occasion because the coverage was so interim, so unusual, so uncontrolled. It was the immediacy of the temporary which lent the coverage its enormous impact and which enabled it to suppress distance. Consequently, it can be concluded that coverage from the other killing fields of the world is less capable of suppressing distance for the simple reason that it is too professional and therefore too easily capable of causing audiences to speculate about their being manipulated.

News and Uncertainty

The unique nature of the coverage on September 11 has been discussed by Scott Stossel (2001). He makes the point that one of the implications of saturated news coverage, and especially of coverage in which all other broadcasting is suspended, is that, 'what you're watching is not news but the news-gathering process' (Stossel, 2001:37). This is exactly what happened on September 11, and it meant that initially at least the news could not be presented as a story possessed of a narrative but could only take the form of a repetition of the event itself. The destruction of the World Trade Center was visually overwhelming, and no small part of that enormity was due to the failure of the news to place it into any kind of narrative context. As Stossel comments, 'Television in the era of 24-hour-a-day coverage is news as a process. Print, even the daily paper, is almost always a better place to get information in its proper perspective; it is news as a set of fixed points in an understandable constellation' (2001:37). According to Stossel, if it is true to say that journalism is the first draft of history, then television coverage 'is the first rough draft of journalism' (Stossel 2001: 37).

Stossel's comments cast light both on why the continuous news coverage had such an impact and also on why newspaper sales on the morning of September 12 were so high. It leads to the suggestion that newspapers were bought and read so avidly (for a week or so after the attack many people complained of having become 'news junkies'), because they were capable of fixing the event in a system of meanings that made sense both as a narrative and as an event. The newspapers took the images of the destruction beyond a repetition of the fact and placed them into a narrative, which started to make some kind of sense. It can therefore be speculated that as the narrative became more and more coherent and all-encompassing, the need to consume news on the part of audiences proportionally declined (and instead boredom could begin to replace anxiety).

It was noticeable, and of course inevitable, that as the events of September 11 unravelled the balance between newsgathering and storytelling started to tilt in the favour of the latter. This happened as soon as narrative questions were posed about the search for the perpetrators, the progress of the rescue efforts, the psychological and economic impact of the attacks and so forth. At an empirical level it was fairly easy on September 11 to identify the moments when the shift from newsgathering to the telling of the story of the news started to happen. In the minutes and hours after the initial attack, it was noticeable that the coverage from New York tended to consist of little more than a repetition of the images of the smoking towers. As soon as additional images were provided they too were broadcast; the impact of the second aeroplane, the perpendicular collapse of the tower with the television antenna. These images were broadcast over and over again. That repetition can perhaps be interpreted in terms of an attempt to make the images speak for themselves. Initially, what were noticeably absent from the coverage were human beings. There were few reporters and few victims.

To this extent, the news coverage once again ran contrary to Boltanski's presumptions. He assumes that the coverage of suffering will focus on humans either as witnesses or sufferers, but at first on September 11 each and every member of audiences was a witness on a basis of parity and common incredulity with the news professionals, and the sufferers were noticeably absent. It was as the day progressed that humans became increasingly visible. The news anchors slowly started to recover their professional equanimity, reporters started to tell the story of what was going on in Lower Manhattan and the first survivors and eyewitnesses were interviewed. The news institutions moved from what Stossel calls 'continuous-coverage mode' to story-telling mode. With that transition the proposal of commitment was made to audiences and yet, with that proposal, audiences were increasingly able to treat this story as similar to any other. They could become suspicious about their manipulation.

As soon as narrative questions started to become dominant, the proposal of commitment, which was made by the news coverage, started to fit in once again with the conventional framework of news production and audience readings as highlighted by Boltanski. And as soon as that happened, the suppression of distance was itself subjected to a certain suppression, as audiences once again started to become able to carry out their habitual practices of critical suspicion. As the framework of story-telling narrative was imposed on September 11, and as the framework was imposed all the more successfully over the next few days, then the audiences could begin to practice what Boltanski calls the *principles of uncertainty*. The result of this was the re-establishment of distance.

According to Boltanski, it is possible to identify four principles of uncertainty from within the general attitude of suspicion that audiences adopt as soon as a proposal of commitment is directed towards them. The first principle, which Boltanski identifies, is what he calls the 'conflict of beliefs' and it involves the problems which are thrown up by the fact that the world does not only contain one suffering group, but many. This multiplicity of suffering leads to questions being asked as to whether this particular incident counts as suffering at all. In the wake of the destruction of the World Trade Center, this principle was reflected in the numerous ethically vacuous but smug letters to newspapers, which claimed that *only* so many thousands of people had died and that the event was not really terribly significant in quantitative terms. Here, suspicion prevails as to whether there really are victims in this particular story, or enough victims to make this story newsworthy (Boltanski 1999: 154-159).

Second, Boltanski talks about the principle of 'the avoidance of reference'. Within this principle it is accepted that there really are victims and perpetrators, but uncertainty surrounds which group fills which category: 'The uncertainty bears on the ability of different candidates to occupy the available places.' Boltanski goes on in a way which makes the uncertainties very clear: 'This or that person suffers; someone shows it, someone sees it; he is a victim; but then this or that other person might be responsible; this or that person gives his support; but it could be otherwise; one could give miserable representations of the persecutor also' (Boltanski, 1999: 159). This principle of uncertainty is reflected in the argument which emerged that the people in the World Trade Center were Americans and/or workers for global capitalism and therefore actually the bearers of a greater and more original guilt than their murderers.

The third principle of uncertainty is somewhat opaquely labelled by Boltanski 'the opacity of desire'. It takes the form of 'the unmasking of a hidden motive to fire a desire in television viewers to see suffering on the screen' (Boltanski, 1999: 170). The argument is that behind all representations of suffering there is some interest on the part of producers and presumably audiences to see others suffer. That interest consists in a form of pleasure. Clearly, this is a principle of uncertainty which can be traced back to Freudian analyses and, if such an approach is accepted, ultimately to a desire for power and omnipotence on the part of news producers and (albeit to a lesser extent) audiences alike.

According to this approach, audiences would take pleasure in the suffering of others because it gives them power; audiences have the power to alleviate the suffering or ignore it. The suffering other is put at the mercy of the audience that thus becomes omnipotent; the audience has an interest in the suffering. Boltanski makes it very clear that this principle of uncertainty tends to be practised and validated by only a very small sector of audiences – certain intellectuals. When he discusses this principle of uncertainty Boltanski gives it short-shrift and criticises it for its reductionism (everything can be reduced to hidden desires). For anyone who thinks outside of Freudian categories it is hard to provide any examples of how this principle of uncertainty casts light on coverage of September 11 or, for that matter, anything else. This principle is a fine example of cleverness getting in the way of intelligence.

Finally, Boltanski identifies the principle of 'the vanity of intentions to act'. Here, uncertainty is generated because it is possible to query the motivations of the world-be actors. As Boltanski points out, if a member of the audiences (and to recall, Boltanski would call that person a 'spectator'), believes that in the face of what she or he has seen she or he is called upon to engage in action, 'he must reasonably believe that his words are effective, that is to say, that they are capable of acting on reality and transforming it'.

The principle of uncertainty consists in the exposure of the pretension of this belief and the narcissism of its corollary: 'Now this belief itself presupposes a clear distinction between the real world in which action is deployed and the world of representation which provides the information needed about reality to guide action' (Boltanski, 1999: 173). One way in which this principle was played out in the days after September 11 was in the suspicion which welcomed many of Tony Blair's statements that Britain was standing 'shoulder to shoulder with America.' For many commentators, behind this particular intention to act was the vanity of post-imperialist hubris.

The irony is that these four principles of uncertainty are all predicated upon the ability of audiences to be certain about what they are seeing or hearing. It is only possible to generate uncertainty if one is certain that one is being manipulated. From this it follows that when a news broadcast, or any other television programme, advertises its trustworthiness most loudly (that is, when it is based on foundations which are in principle certain), then the uncertainty that it generates will be exacerbated. Where news coverage is provisional, as it was for a while on September 11, then the critical practices of audiences and therefore the principles of uncertainty are suspended. And then distance is suppressed and human solidarity does for a moment become a reality *de facto*.

Conclusion

Another social critic who has worried about the moral significance of news broadcasts is Michael Ignatieff. He has argued that in the context of the evident failure of conventional news broadcasts to inspire audiences to engage in moral action on behalf of the unfortunate sufferers whom they see, perhaps the *genre* of news should be replaced with documentaries. Read through the prism of Boltanski, Ignatieff's argument is that if television journalists worked on documentaries instead of news then they would be far more able to make a proposal of commitment which audiences would find it difficult to reject (Ignatieff, 1998: 32).

These largely provisional reflections on the ability of international news to suppress distance and to intimate a certain proximity on September 11, point in exactly the opposite direction to Ignatieff's proposition. I conclude that if news institutions followed Ignatieff's suggestion then the only result would be the increasing suspicion of audiences and their ever-greater distanciation from the suffering of others. Admittedly, the multiplication of documentaries could be interpreted as an educational measure in that it would enable audiences to hone their critical practices to a very high degree of excellence, but that would only make the principles of uncertainty even more inescapable than they presently are, and Ignatieff does not want documentaries to be educational in that particular way. More documentaries would almost certainly mean more indifference.

By contrast, the line of thought which is pursued in this paper points to the conclusion that on September 11, it was in that temporary moment when international news was failing to, and incapable of constructing a narrative about what was happening that the distance between audiences and sufferers was at its shortest, that the proposal of commitment was greatest, when images were broadcast that audiences will never forget. The moral moment was strongest when storytelling collapsed in the face of the weight of news-gathering. It was when the news institutions failed to make the expected kind of proposal of commitment that audiences were most committed.

Consequently instead of documentaries or for that matter conventional finished news broadcasts, the answer to the problem of how to make the non-sufferers come close to the suffering is the broadcasting of the news-gathering process. If audiences are uncertain about the proposal that is being made to them, and indeed if they are uncertain about whether *any* proposal is being made to them, then the principles of uncertainty cannot be brought into play quite so readily. Audiences will have to work out what all of this means for themselves, they will have to talk about it with each other and thus the story will be the basis of the constitution not just of a moral engagement but also a human-centred politics and justice in the globalised world.

But the institutions of international news are not going to let that happen, are they?

References

Arendt, H. (1973) *On Revolution*. Harmondsworth: Penguin.

Boltanski, L. (1999) *Distant Suffering. Morality, Media and Politics*. Translated by Graham Burchill. Cambridge: Cambridge University Press.

Ignatieff, M. (1998) *The Warrior's Honor. Ethnic War and the Modern Conscience.* London: Chatto & Windus.

Sennett, R. (1994) *Flesh and Stone. The Body and the City in Western Civilisation.* London: Faber & Faber.

Stossel, S. (2001, October 22) 'Terror TV', *The American Prospect.*

Tester, K. (2001) *Compassion, Morality and the Media.* Buckingham: Open University Press.

Chapter 11
The Mass Production of Ignorance: News Content and Audience Understanding
Greg Philo

There is surprisingly little research work that focuses on audiences' consumption of and understanding about international news, yet important corporate decisions are made on assumptions about levels of audience interest and need. Philo's chapter synthesises research findings that speak to this set of issues. Not only do programme commissioners appear to know what the audience wants, but when programmes are produced about the developing world, a dramatic narrative often overwhelms any explanation of events. Using an innovative research process of connecting news professionals with focus groups, his team was able to help the news producers better understand how audiences process information about international events and what kinds of information would be helpful in engendering a different kind of response, whereby the British news audience felt more interested in and even implicated with the international stories they were watching.

This chapter examines key issues in the relationship between television news content and the manner in which audiences respond to it. In past research this relationship has been analysed from various theoretical perspectives. Some have seen news content as essentially ideological and as having the power to limit and structure audience belief (Glasgow Media Group, 1976, 1980, Philo; 1990, Herman and Chomsky, 1988). Others have seen the news as a constant recurrence of routinised journalistic practice (Rock, 1973; Enzensberger, 1974). Still others have seen news content as primarily directed by commercial criteria, based on assumptions about what audiences 'really' want to watch (Stone, 2000). There is also a strong current in contemporary research which suggests that media are engaged in the mass production of social ignorance. This is well expressed in the title of Danny Schechter's *The More You Watch the Less You Know* (1998).

There are other ways in which in which the relationship between news content and audiences have been theorised (for an account see Philo and Miller, 2000). I will concentrate here on the above perspectives as I think elements of each of these can add very importantly to a developed understanding of this issue. In making this case I will draw upon three major studies which were undertaken by the Media Group at Glasgow University. They all focused on news content and public understanding of the developing world. The first was a study of television coverage of the Rwandan refugee crisis of 1994. This was undertaken together with the Overseas Development Institute and the role of the Media Group was to analyse the major themes in news content relating to the crisis. We worked jointly with Lindsey Hilsum (now the diplomatic correspondent of Channel 4 News) who at the time was working in Rwanda as a journalist. She contributed to the report by writing about the production processes which influenced editorial content (Philo et al, 1999). The second study was of news coverage of the subsequent war in Zaire. The study was undertaken jointly with the Save the Children Fund and its purpose was to analyse the range of explanations in news coverage which was being made available to viewers (Beattie et al, 1999). There was a good deal of concern at this time amongst NGOs and government departments that public understanding of crises in Africa and in other parts of the developing world was severely limited and that one reason for this might be the nature of television coverage.

Our third study in the area was undertaken for the Department for International Development (Glasgow Media Group, 2000). This study focused on television reporting of the whole of the developing world and examined which countries, issues and types of events were covered. We also selected a number of case studies for detailed analysis. These were examples of the more frequent categories of TV news coverage of events, including for example conflict/war/terrorism and disasters such as earthquakes. The method employed in these content studies was a version of thematic analysis and consisted of a detailed examination of the language and visuals of news reports. The purpose is to examine how key themes emerge in TV news reporting and how they are used to structure and develop stories. In practice the news text is broken down into separate references (phrases or sentences) which relate to the range of themes which are covered in the story. A numerical account of these is also given, which allows some judgements to be made about the dominance of specific themes. For the DFID study, explanatory and contextualising references were identified in order to assess how much the content might assist audiences in understanding development issues. For the same reason we also examined other types of television format such as cookery and travel programmes and other documentary output. This work on content was accompanied by an extensive audience study which was conducted using focus groups.

We interviewed a total of twenty-six groups, selected on criteria of age, income, ethnic background and gender (totalling 165 people). The purpose of the interviews was to identify patterns of understanding and belief about the developing world and to trace the origin of these in, for example, media accounts or from other sources such as schooling or peer groups. We also wished to examine how media products might work to compel audience attention, to entertain and create lasting images as well as how they might produce more negative responses from viewers.

The DFID study was undertaken in close contact with senior production staff from the BBC, ITN, Channel 4, Sky and Discovery Television. As a result of these links with broadcasters, there was a further pilot study in which senior journalists worked directly with a focus group. In this extension of the study, the journalists took part in the group discussion to investigate issues of audience interest and comprehension and how these might be influenced by changes in the structure and content of news reporting.

There are three key issues emerging from these studies which I will outline here:

1. That the decision made by broadcasters (on commercial criteria) about what viewers would desire to watch have in the long run produced very negative responses in TV audiences towards the developing world.

2. That audiences are misinformed about the developing world because of the low level of explanations and context which is given in television reporting and because some explanations which are present are partial and informed by what might be termed 'post-colonial beliefs'.

3. That a change in the quality of explanation which is given can radically alter both attitudes to the developing world and the level of audience interest in the subject.

Production Decisions and Assumptions about Audiences

There is a widespread belief in British broadcasting that audiences are not interested in factual programming on the developing world. This is the conclusion of a study of the beliefs and attitudes of broadcasters by the Third World and Environment Broadcasting Trust (3WE). This study was commissioned by DFID to run parallel to our work and an extensive sample of 38 senior broadcasters, commissioning editors and programme makers were interviewed. The responses in these interviews highlighted the issue of audience demand and the assumptions which were made about this within broadcasting. As George Alagiah, a senior BBC journalist, notes:

Programme editors are driven by audience interest, but this can lead to a fixation with home, leisure and consumer items instead of the broader agenda (3WE, 2000: 160).

His words find an echo in the comments of George Carey of the production company Menton Barraclough Carey:

> I try and guess what the audience wants. Most people switch on to be entertained not to get a message. Instinctively I feel domestic stories will be more interesting than foreign ones (3WE, 2000: 159).

The point is spelt out more forcefully by Steve Hewlett, Director of Programmes at Carlton Television:

> I know from past experience that programmes about the developing world don't bring in the audiences. They're not about us, and they're not usually about things we can do anything about (3WE, 2000: 159).

Commercial criteria are now a key consideration for programme makers and this comes down in part to providing what they assume the audiences will want to watch. As Charles Tremayne, controller of factual programmes at Granada TV puts it:

> We're past the days of giving audiences what they should have – now it's all about what they want (3WE, 2000: 159).

But the assumptions made are not necessarily well informed about why audiences watch and what conditions their level of interest. As Alex Holmes, editor of the programme *Modern Times* at the BBC admits:

> Audience interest is very important, second only to a good story, but we don't know exactly what people want. I imagine what they want. It's blissfully unscientific on *Modern Times* (3WE, 2000: 159)!

One consequence of these assumptions on audience interest has apparently been the drastic reduction of factual programming about the developing world. A report by Jennie Stone for 3WE concluded that the total output of factual programmes on developing countries by the four terrestrial channels dropped by fifty per cent in the ten years after 1989 (Stone, 2000:4). Our own study showed that when the developing world is featured on the news a high proportion of the coverage related to war, conflict, terrorism and disasters. This is especially so for the main television channels with over a third of coverage on BBC and ITN devoted to such issues. Much of the remaining coverage is given over either to sport or to visits by westerners to developing countries. For example, in our sample the Bahamas were in the news because Mick Jagger and Gerry Hall had visited and some countries were featured simply because Richard Branson's balloon had floated over them (Glasgow Media Group, 2000: 20-21).

Programmes such as BBC2's Newsnight and Channel 4 News had a wider coverage of issues such as trade and politics but it was clear that the focus for mainstream TV news was more likely to be on dramatic and negative images of the developing world. The 3WE study for example found that although coverage had declined overall, the reporting of disasters had actually increased by five per cent (Stone, 2000: 15). When disasters are covered, journalists select news angles and visual images which they assume will compel audience attention, e.g. news of an earthquake will feature scenes of destruction, chaos, visuals of collapsed buildings, frantic rescue efforts and appeals for help. These become the basic themes of earthquake/disaster coverage. For example, we analysed news of the Colombian earthquake in January 1999 and showed how it featured these elements. But there was very little said on the country itself or of what distinguished this crisis, or about what it meant to the society other than it being simply a horrific occurrence. There was nothing said on the impact of the earthquake on Columbia's coffee-growing region or the long term economic repercussions on unemployment and investment. Coffee was being planted as an alternative to cocaine so there were potentially also very great consequences in terms of the development of the drug trade.

As we noted, the focus of television on pictures and extraordinary visual moments to illustrate the crisis had led to a neglect of context and explanation. But if Columbia was to be seen and understood as anything more than a disaster area, then it is important that its people be shown as having a history, politics, economy and everyday life which both pre and post-date the visual images of an earthquake (Glasgow Media Group, 2000: 60). This does not mean that journalists should avoid reporting the terrible human consequences of such an event. The problem arises when these are the only themes in the coverage and they become routinised and occur each time there is a similar disaster. Then, for the viewer there is in practice little to distinguish one such crisis from another in the developing world other than the name of the country. Such stories and those of conflict and violence are visually striking and in fact constitute a high proportion of the coverage. So it is not surprising that viewers perceive the developing world to be not much more than a series of catastrophes.

Another key problem with such coverage is the very limited nature of explanations which are given (if at all) of events such as political conflict and war. In our study of TV news coverage of the Rwandan refugee crisis of 1994, we found a very large number of references (122 in our sample) which stressed the scale of the flight and the huge number of people involved but gave no account of why any of these events were occurring. We hear of 'the exodus of a nation,' 'Rwanda on the verge of catastrophe,' 'there is a flow of people … some hundred thousand people have fled … at the rate of 4000 an hour,' 'you can see only a portion of this mass of humanity at any one time … a million desolate people' (BBC1 , 1994). We found only twenty-seven references which gave any explanation of what was occurring. Many of these were very limited and sometimes incorrect as in the suggestion that the refugees had 'fled the killing in Rwanda' (BBC2 Newsnight, 1994). This is unclear in the sense that the Hutu refugees actually contained the militias who had perpetrated the genocide in Rwanda. They were not therefore fleeing from the genocide but from the consequences of it, in the sense that they were seeking to avoid retribution (Philo et al, 1999: 215).

In a subsequent study, we analysed media coverage of the events of 1996 in which the refugee camps on the borders of Rwanda were dissolved by the Rwandan army and the Hutu militias fled to the interior of Zaire leading eventually to a full scale war in that country. This news coverage contained many more references to the genocide in Rwanda and its link to the refugee exodus. By November 1996 it was quite frequently stated on the news that Hutu militias had perpetrated massacres upon the Tutsi population. But an explanation at this level is still very limited. To state simply that Hutus have massacred Tutsis does not move far beyond explaining the events as a 'tribal conflict' between what may be assumed by the audience to be 'primitive' peoples of Africa. As we showed, Africa was referred to on the news as a place of 'tribal conflict,' 'tribal enemies,' 'ethnic war,' 'insanity,' 'chaos' and 'anarchy,' inhabited by 'wild men.' Against these descriptions are put explanations of why the West is concerned about military intervention in the region. For example: '*Reporter*: There remained extreme caution about being sucked into the region's blood-thirsty politics' (BBC1, 1996).

On ITN the people of Africa were compared to the topography of the landscape which they inhabited. The volcanoes were described as being 'far more predictable than the people they watch over' (ITN,1996). One difficulty with accounts such as these is that Africa tends to be seen as a country rather than as a continent with many different cultures which have complex political and economic histories. As Lindsey Hilsum has shown in her account of the genocide, Rwanda was a highly organised and disciplined society. She describes the hierarchies and the social structure of the country:

> A group of households comprised a cellule; every cellule has a spokesman who reported to the conseiller who was in charge of the next administrative unit up the ladder, the secteur ... and so on to the highest reaches of the government ... Unlike most African capitals, Kigali remained small and largely immune to urban drift; Rwanda had pass laws stricter than those of South Africa (Hilsum, 1995: 165-166).

As she noted the Swiss government had given more money to Rwanda than to any other country in Africa, because they saw a society that was as disciplined as their own and in which there was very little corruption. It was exactly because Rwanda was so highly organised that the Hutu military regime was able to put into effect such an appalling genocide in such a short time. As she writes:

> The same efficiency – the discipline and order so admired by the foreign aid workers – meant that when the orders came on 7 April for the killing to begin they were usually obeyed (Hilsum, 1995: 170).

As she commented to us in an interview, many journalists found it difficult to understand this because of their own preconceptions about Africa:

> Most journalists couldn't believe that Africans could be so organised – they couldn't recognise the genocide for what it was ... Rwanda was

more similar to Nazi Germany in that there was a group with an extremist, racist ideology. They defined other groups as the enemy because of the historical relationships between the ethnic groups, in the way that there were reasons for the Jews being chosen. Politicians manipulate relations between the different ethic groups and turn them into ideology. In Rwanda to stay in power, they exterminated the other group (Interview, 1998, April 24).

But in the absence of more complex social and political explanations, it is possible to fall back on images of 'tribal passions'. The BBC for example showed shots of Africans dancing in grass skirts at a border post, and described them as 'the wild men of the murderous interahamwe militia' (BBC1, 1996). They were not in fact Rwandans at all but were apparently Zairian border guards who had dressed in this way in order to insult the Rwandan army. It was a very misleading image of the conflict but it was very widely used both in this country and abroad. We found, not surprisingly, that the assumptions made by many journalists tended to be held within the general public. In a pilot for the DFID research I asked a focus group what image came into their minds when they heard the word 'tribe'. They replied that it would be people with grass skirts and spears standing in front of huts. At the end of that group meeting I explained to them something of the history of Rwanda and commented that the Hutu military regime in 1994 had killed all opposition groups including moderate Hutus, Belgium nationals and UN soldiers, as well as the Tutsi population. In Butare, a city in the south of the city which was known for its tolerance and liberalism, the Hutu students and lecturers at the University were killed because they were assumed to be in opposition to the Hutu government. One woman in the focus group commented 'Oh you don't think of them as having universities' (St Albans Group, 1998).

Audience Responses

A key finding of our research was that the images which audience groups recalled of the developing world were overwhelmingly negative (including famine, poverty, refugees, war and conflict). The source of these images was given routinely as the media (press and television) as in this comment from a woman in a focus group in London:

> Well every time you turn on the TV or pick up a paper, there's another [war] starting or there is more poverty or destruction. It is all too much (retired group, London, cited in Glasgow Media Group, 2000: 137).

It was also clear that children's attitudes had been influenced very strongly. In this example, teenagers discuss travel programmes about India. They believed it would not be worth having them:

1st: Not on India.

2nd: No one goes there so why do they want to?

3rd: It is not a popular tourist attraction because in India they have always got problems.

2nd: It would be a holiday nightmare if someone went to India. The houses are full of bugs.

Moderator: So it doesn't sound appealing to go there?

2nd: The swimming pools are full of cockroaches and stuff.

3rd: There is always terrorists over there anyway.

(15 year olds, London, Glasgow Media Group, 2000: 138).

A small number of people had experienced living and working in the developing world or in occupations which gave them a different perspective. As one woman from Glasgow commented:

I do some voluntary work for Oxfam so I hear a lot about things from there. I mean, you wouldn't believe half of what is going on, really positive things, I mean that you wouldn't hear about anywhere else. I watch the news sometimes and think, oh yeah, here we go again, why don't you tell us about the people who are trying to change things and the huge advances that are being made (Low income focus group, Glasgow, Glasgow Media Group, 2000: 137).

In the sample as a whole, ten per cent claimed an active interest in development issues while twenty-five per cent said they had no interest at all. Amongst the remaining people there were varying levels of interest and concern for what were seen as the problems of the developing world (Glasgow Media Group, 2000: 3). A second key finding of our research was that most of the people in our sample had a very low level of understanding about events in the developing world and there was widespread confusion over what was happening there and why. The extraordinary mixture of ideas in popular understanding of the developing world is conveyed in this exchange between fifteen year olds in London who are discussing the issue of third world debt:

Moderator: Does anybody know anything about or has seen anything on TV about the debt campaign?

1st: The what?

2nd: Yes.

Moderator: Removal of third world debt.

1st: No.

3rd: Is it 50p a month and you can help them?

2nd: We pay them and they don't pay us back.

4th: You get to help a child and all that stuff.

5th: Pay 50p a child.

2nd: Do they owe us?

6th: They owe us twice the amount.

2nd: We will never get it back.

1st: They haven't even got an economy.

(15 year old, London, Glasgow Media Group, 2000: 139).

For the great majority of the people in our sample the workings of the world economy were simply a mystery. Organisations such as the IMF and the World Bank were recognised as names that were frequently mentioned but we found that there was very little knowledge about what these institutions were or how they operated. These are typical exchanges:

Moderator: Do terms like the World Bank mean anything to you?

1st: Yes, but not very much.

Moderator: International Monetary Fund?

1st: Yes, IMF. They always say the same sentences but there is never much explanation about who controls them or whatever else and how they operate as a body… They talk about them as though everyone knows what they are.

(Middle class group, London).

1st: I have heard the initials IMF but I couldn't tell you what it is or what it does.

2nd: It is to do with money, something to do with trade and economics or something.

(Ethnic minority, Afro Caribbean, London).

1st: The IMF is something to do with currency, isn't it? It lets you get money in another country easily. I don't know any more than that.

(Retired group, London, Glasgow Media Group, 2000: 140).

People in the groups readily admitted that they simply did not understand the news and thought that the external world was not being properly explained to them. As one group member expressed it:

I have a constant sense of not being properly informed about background to issues and things like that. (Middle class, London, Glasgow Media Group, 2000: 139).

In other groups it was commented that television presumes an understanding which may not exist. One person spoke of his experience in watching news about East Timor:

> Sometimes with the East Timor thing, it is assumed you know exactly what is happening ... but I don't know what is happening (Low income group, Bath, Glasgow Media Group, 2000: 139).

Some of the groups also identified a key issue in the organisation of television journalism, which might be termed the 'half way through problem'. This is when journalists covering a long-running story tend to assume that their audience has watched the full sequence of reports, and so they do not need to repeat background issues mentioned in earlier reports. But in practice audiences come into stories at different points in the sequence. If they have missed the explanation that may have gone out two days before, they will have difficulty following the next series of reports. As this group member comments, the critical issue for him was to catch a story when it is 'young':

> It is whether or not you catch a story young, like the first time it has been on or whatever, then you will follow it through. If you hear about it and you haven't seen it on the television you tend to not know much about it (Low income, Bath, Glasgow Media Group, 2000: 141).

There is now some recognition of these problems by professional broadcasters and a desire to find new ways of structuring news and other programmes so that viewers may be better informed. The 3WE research project recorded these comments from Ian Stuttard a documentary producer at the BBC:

> The whole angle is wrong. We look at the results of things most of the time instead of the causes. Wars rather than the arms trade is an example of this so we're conditioned to think of the developing world in a distorted way because we don't look behind the scenes. It's a challenge because viewers are less politically aware (this isn't helped by television!), and because 'causes' are not always very visual. How do you film money-laundering and arms deals? But it can be done! (3WE, 2000: 162).

'How' it could be done was the subject of the next phase of our work.

Audience Understanding and Interest

This is an account of a pilot study in which senior BBC news personnel took part in focus group discussions. The purpose was to investigate how changes in the structure and content of programming might affect audience comprehension and levels of interest. In the event, Vin Ray, the world news editor, and David Shukman, a world news correspondent, both took part. The method used for the focus groups had three elements. First, the group was given a series of still photographs which had been taken off screen from an actual news story. The story was chosen in conjunction with the BBC and they also provided the video material which was used for the taking of the still pictures. These were chosen to represent the main elements of the story and this selection was done in collaboration with a BBC news journalist. In the research exercise, the focus group members are asked to look at the photographs and then to imagine that they are journalists and to write their own news story using only the pictures as a stimulus. The story is then read out by the group and there is a brief discussion about the sources of information which they have used and their level of knowledge of the area. In the second part of the session the actual news item from which the photographs were taken was shown to the group. This was then followed by a moderated discussion which focussed on six specific points:

1   What was the knowledge base which was used for the story which was written by the group members?

2   What was their level of comprehension of the issues involved in the story?

3   How much was added to their understanding of the story by the viewing of the actual news item?

4   What would need to be added to their knowledge to produce a better understanding of the issues involved?

5   How does the manner in which the content of the story is shaped or presented affect levels of interest?

6   How might such interest by affected by changes in presentation and content?

Using this method we conducted two groups in Glasgow and then a third in Bath in the south of England, at which the BBC journalists were present. At this meeting the journalists joined the group midway through the discussion and the whole of the meeting was filmed by the BBC. In all, there were twenty people in the groups (two of six, one of eight people). They were 'naturally occurring', in that their members normally worked together. The first Glasgow group were janitors, the second office staff, while the Bath group were postal workers.

The news story which was used for the groups featured the continuing conflict in Angola. It was presented by David Shukman and had originally been broadcast over two nights on the BBC news (2000, 3 an 4 May). The first part of the story dealt with the human effects of the conflict and the tragedies caused by land mines. Shukman reported that a million people were trapped in one part of Angola and could not escape because the roads were mined. There were images of children in hospital who had suffered appalling injuries. The report ends with the story of three sisters who had all lost limbs because of land mines:

> This family of refugees has had to learn how to cope. First, this sister lost a leg to a mine, looking for water. A few months later, a second sister suffered the same fate. Then a third sister lost both her legs searching for food. They're surviving but they're scared.

One sister is interviewed as she holds her baby:

> I think so often about being disabled – and of course the war keeps going on and so we feel maybe we don't want to live anymore (BBC 1, 2000, 3 May).

The second report looked at the ongoing war and at some of the reasons why it continued. There is a brief history of the conflict given and Shukman notes that it began as a cold war struggle between east and west. The report then showed mounds of weapons to illustrate claims made by the Angolan government that they were winning the war against UNITA. Shukman comments that the war has its own momentum: 'It is a conflict without an obvious end, there is no attempt either at a peace process. The suspicion is that there are people on both sides actually keeping the war going, for money.'

As he goes on to comment, Angola has immense natural riches. The rebels of UNITA control the diamonds, while the government controls huge reserves of oil. He notes that America buys more oil from Angola than from Kuwait. The report then shows people in churches and a bishop praying for peace and an end to the corruption which is fuelling the war. Shukman then comments that: 'Much of Angola's wealth goes on weapons but some goes on extravagance like this new presidential palace which is hardly ever used and huge sums simply vanish into private hands.'

The Angolan Defence Minister is then interviewed and he admits that senior figures are stealing, but nobody tries to stop them:

> Minister: Imagine you are an investigator who accused some hot shot minister of pinching the money, you'd just be banged up in prison ...
> Lots of Angola's money is just flowing outside to bank accounts in Europe and Switzerland – it's a dreadful situation.

This corruption is then contrasted with the fate of the refugees from the war. A woman from a refugee camp is interviewed talking about the fate of her own children. A spokesman from the United Nations is then interviewed and Shukman notes that 'the UN accuses the Angolan government of wasting its money.' His final comment summarises the central theme of the report: 'Once this country profited from peace, now a few profit from war and there are many who suffer the consequences' (BBC1, 2100, 4 May 2000).

Group Exercises and Results

The still photographs given to the groups were taken from each of the elements of the above news reports. They showed mounds of weapons, children, land mines, a mine clearance operation, casualties in hospital, an oil rig, diamonds, the bishop, people praying, a palace, refugee camps, the government minister and a UN spokesman. In practice the groups discussed the pictures and then wrote a short news account. This normally draws its information from a variety of sources including their own experience but more usually they draw information from a range of new stories which they have seen. For example, in a story written by one of the Glasgow groups there are references to child soldiers which are drawn from news stories about other African conflicts. That said, their story is in many respects very close to the original news:

> Today in Angola due to the conflict, children as young as eight are being armed with varieties of guns and weapons. Arms were retrieved by the government from the rebels. The reason for the conflict was due to the unfair distribution of the country's wealth. The bishop has come out to condemn this behaviour and had made a passionate plea to the Angolan to stop this unnecessary killing. He held a service for the locals praying for a peaceful conclusion to the feud. Local soldiers can be seen trying to unearth deadly mines, the very same mines that Princess Diana condemned and worked hard to put a stop to (Glasgow Group one, 2000, 28 August).

In another group one member goes beyond the actual content of the programme to discuss the arms trade and comments that this is a relationship which is often missing from television reports:

> When you look at the (pictures on) the table you think this is an internal dispute...It doesn't get mentioned that people are selling guns out there (Bath group, 2000, 21 September).

This person also mentions that the 'white man wants the goodies' and therefore raises the possibilities of international links to the conflict (and one other concurred in this). But overall, the members of the groups tended to see the problem as a specifically African issue as these exchanges from the Bath group indicate:

Male Group Member 1: They can't look after themselves ...

Moderator: You see a lot which you see as being tragedy and fighting?

Male Group Member 1: We can't do a lot can we?

Moderator: But you don't actually see it as relating to you at all?

Male Group Member 2: What can we do? Send money but that is as far as it goes really?Moderator: Is it too strong to say that they are not very good at governing themselves?

(They all nod)

Moderator: Would most people agree with that or not?

(General agreement)

(Bath Group).

In the second phase of the exercise, the groups watched the actual news programmes from which the photographs had been taken. The reports engaged them to the extent that they felt strong sympathy for the victims. A small number thought that the British government should intervene and most supported a ban on land mines. But there was a general feeling in these groups and indeed in those which we interviewed in earlier research that the situation in such countries was hopeless and had very little to do with people in Britain. The only possible response for the individual was to give money to charities. The explanations that existed in the news bulletins which these groups were shown did little to challenge such established views on Africa. They tended to fit in with popular assumptions about it as being corrupt and misgoverned.

The great majority of people in the groups knew very little about specific conflicts and as with our earlier research people commented that the different wars and countries tended to shade one into another. Given this general lack of knowledge it is very easy for a news programme to actually increase confusion. For example several people in these groups misunderstood the reference in the news bulletins to the conflict in Angola as having originated in a cold war struggle. They assumed that this meant that the struggle was still going on and as one put it 'the Americans are buying the oil, the Russians have taken the stones' (Glasgow group one). There was a sense amongst some in the groups that 'big power' involvement might be to blame. As one put it 'the Americans are making money … and maybe feeding it' (the conflict) (Glasgow group two, 2000, 6 September). But overall the groups saw the problem as an "African" issue. It had nothing to do with them or their own everyday lives. It was suggested that the problems of Africa related to peculiarly African factors such as the low level of education in the population as a whole. This is made clear in the following exchange:

Moderator: What about the mass of the people …?

Male 1: They can't do anything about it.

Male 2: They can't read or write so …

Moderator: Would it make a difference if they could read or write?

Male 1: They would be more educated. If you can't read or write you can't really go to a government and say …

Male 2: Obviously as a nation we are more educated and we wouldn't let that sort of thing happen.

(Bath group)

The important point here is that no-one in the groups related the continuing problems of Angola to their own actions and there was little or no sense of the world system of socio-economic relationships which sustain such conflicts. The news report by David Shukman had pointed in some ways to these wider relationships, for example in the comments on America purchasing Angolan oil and the movement of funds to Europe and Switzerland. But these brief references were not developed or their significance explained. They did not therefore greatly affect the understanding of the groups.

In the final part of the discussion, the moderator pursued a series of questions which were intended to explore the social and economic relationships which underpinned the continuing conflict and the inability of the mass of the population in Angola to end it. These questions related to the following themes: 1. the role of education, 2. the use and supply of weapons, 3. the resourcing of the conflict and 4. trade and financial links to the industrial countries. On the first of these issues, as we have seen, education was understood by some as a key difference between Africa and Britain in the sense that it affected the political choices that would be made by their populations. To explore this, the moderator pointed out to the groups that in his own professional work he had encountered many African people who were well educated, religious and very principled but who were not allowed to be part of the political process in their own societies. So would education, by itself, make any difference to naked military force? The group members saw the point, as in this exchange:

> Moderator: I just wondered if you went up to (the corrupt rulers) and said "I am well educated and I want you to stop stealing the money", what would they do.
>
> Male: Probably shoot you.
>
> (Bath group)

There were similar ideas about the nature of power and control expressed in the other groups:

> Moderator: If the mass of the population very clearly don't want it to happen …
>
> Female 1: They don't have any control over it do they? All these women and children, what control do they have? It is not as though they can pick up a phone or …
>
> Moderator: So who does have control?
>
> Female 1: The men.
>
> Female 2: The people making the money. (Glasgow group two).

And in this exchange from the first Glasgow group:

> Moderator: Why can't (the population) actually resolve it?
>
> Female: They have got no power over it.
>
> Male 1: They haven't got any say in the matter; do you know what I mean?
>
> Moderator: So who has got the say then?
>
> Male 1: Your government again and the rebels.

Moderator: Why would the government and the rebels have more say than the people?

Male 1: They are the ones with the arms, the guns ...

Male 2: And the money.

(Glasgow group one)

These points had been made in the news item by David Shukman and the groups readily understood them. The discussion then moved on to consider the external relationships which made possible this absolute control of the population. A central issue here was the supply of arms. The moderator pointed out that Angola had no armament industries, so the question was raised as to where the arms came from. Some identified Eastern Europe as a major supplier of arms but all understood that the weapons and mines must be coming from outside:

Moderator: You said that it all carries on because the rebels and the government have got arms and they have got guns and they have got money. Is that anything to do with us?

Male: Yes, Where are they getting the guns, is it an outside source?

Moderator: But that is not in the programme is it, Angola hasn't got a gun industry and doesn't make tanks that is one point isn't it? Where are all these arms coming from?

Male 2: Russia, Communist countries.

(Glasgow Group one)

The moderator then raised the issue of how the guns and mines were paid for and the groups all understood that the money came from the sale of diamond and oil to the industrial countries. The groups were then asked what happened to the additional profits and the moderator pointed out that money had been moved to banks in Europe, including Britain.

Information about international links to such conflicts is available in the public media, but it tends to exist in diverse fragments which are scattered across a variety of sources. In October 2000, the *London Evening Standard* reported allegations on the laundering of funds in the city of London under the headline 'City Banks Helped Nigerian Dictator to Launder £4 Billion' (2000, October 20). In December 2000, the *Guardian* reported on a crack down on 'blood diamonds,' citing recommendations from the UN that African leaders who traded gems for arms should be punished. The UN report also pointed to Switzerland as a transit point for almost half of the rough diamonds entering Britain. It showed how Switzerland was then listed as 'country of origin' and their true source was lost (2000, December 20). In January 2001, the *Guardian* ran the headline 'Oil Firms Accused over Angola Bribes.' It reported allegations that 'international oil companies had been complicit in the looting of Angola's assets by the countries ruling elite' (2001, January 17). The allegations were made at the Parliamentary Select Committee on international development.

Although such information can be identified in the media, the crucial point is that it is not routinely referenced in television news accounts and when it does appear in the media it is in diverse and fragmented form. It is as if all the different pieces of the jigsaw puzzle which are needed to explain Angola appear one at a time and in different places. It is not therefore surprising that there is little effect on public consciousness. In the focus groups for this study very few people had any understanding of such links and relationships when they were first shown the news items. The group discussion changed this. The news items by David Shukman could now be seen as offering an image of Angola as being run for the profit of what were effectively two groups of bandits – one was the guerrillas who controlled the diamonds and the other the corrupt government who controlled the oil.

It was also possible to see why the conflict continued. As long as the Angolan economy was based on simple extraction processes (oil and diamonds) then the mass of the population were not involved. All that was required was for a military group (guerrillas or army) to ensure that the process continued. The industrial countries purchased the product, laundered the money and supplied arms. Of course, it is true that the African government was corrupt, but any society based on such relationships can generate an elite which will take advantage for itself. A key difference from a country such as Britain is that it has an integrated industrial and commercial economy. The mass of the population in Britain have over time been able to demand representation, civil rights and political change, because they have been able to withdraw their labour and thus influence the economy. This is as true of the Chartists and striking miners demanding the vote from the 1830s as it of lorry drivers demanding cheap fuel in November 2000. This option is simply not available to the mass of the Angolan population, or indeed to that of other countries in a similar position, such as Sierra Leone. These points were made in the focus group by the moderator. It seems clear that without this additional information most of the people in the groups would not have understood the international links which effectively promoted and prolonged the conflict. This is partly because of their own preconceptions about Africa and also because the references in the news items to external relationships were partial and undeveloped.

For these group members, the discussion of the international links came as a revelation. There was real surprise and some shock. This was for two principal reasons. The first was that their perception of Africa changed. Instead of the chaos and civil conflict being seen as a specifically 'African' (or 'Third World') phenomenon, it could now be understood as the product of a series of economic and social relationships. This is important because it can also be understood that such relationships may be changed. In contrast, a belief that Africans are innately incapable of running their own countries suggests that nothing can be done. Secondly, and most crucially, the group members could see that the relationships which sustained the conflict involved them directly, at the most simple level in their own purchasing decisions. The moderator made this clear and asked them if they had ever thought that when they bought an object such as a diamond, it might be linked to such conflicts:

> Moderator: Do you ever think of yourself, that each time you drive your car or each time you wear a diamond that the diamond is paying for the landmine and the car is paying for the ...?
>
> Female 1: And that is causing ...
>
> Female 2: I have never thought of that.
>
> Female 3: I don't think of that.
>
> Female 1: Oh no.
>
> Female 3: You never look at yourself.
>
> Moderator: Have you ever seen anything on TV to make a link like that, that this diamond finances this landmine?
>
> Female 1: No.
>
> Female 3: No, because they don't, they don't actually do a chain (of thought) so you know.
>
> (Glasgow Group two)

It was apparent that such knowledge would have affected the purchasing decisions of many people in the groups if they had been informed of the link between the war and the sale of diamonds. This was not true of everyone and three people in the Bath group dissented saying that it would not affect them if they were getting the product cheaper:

> Moderator: If you knew that you were getting a diamond half price because it was from the guerrillas ...
>
> Male 1: If it wasn't you it would be someone else, wouldn't it?
>
> Moderator: It would just be you or someone else so you wouldn't bother?
>
> Male 1: Yes.
>
> Moderator: Anybody here would worry if what they were buying is paying for landmines?
>
> Female: I would.
>
> Male 2: Yes.
>
> Male 3: Maybe landmines I would.
>
> (Bath Group)

For most of the people in the groups the effect of making the link between their own conduct and events in Africa was both shock and a sense of revelation as if they had been given 'secret knowledge' that 'opened their eyes'.

> Male 1: It certainly opened my eyes …
>
> Moderator: Did you understand it better this time because of the discussion?
>
> Male 1: Better this time because of the discussion.
>
> Male 2: Yes.
>
> Male 3: Without a doubt.
>
> Male 1: All of our views have been changed some what already because of this.
>
> (Bath Group)

The Glasgow groups spoke of the knowledge as a revelation and the effect it would have on the population as a whole:

> Female: It would open a lot of peoples' eyes, I think, if they heard that like people are buying so many litres of oil or petrol or whatever and it is contributing to the landmines and killings and it would open a lot of peoples eyes and make you think a wee bit more as to what is happening (Glasgow Group one).

They also made clear the difference between seeing the problem as "African" and relating it to other factors:

> Moderator: What was the difference between watching (the news) and then what we discussed? What were the new things?
>
> Female 1: The revelation that wealth is being used perhaps to fund a more comfortable lifestyle for us westerners.
>
> Female 2: And that we are helping to contribute to it.
>
> Female 1: That is definitely what I picked up once we started discussing it. After watching the programme I wouldn't think of that. I would still isolate it as their problem.
>
> Female 3: It is their problem.
>
> Female 1: But it was not until after we started discussing that you actually think there is more involved than just the people of Angola. There are other countries involved. There are other individuals involved.
>
> (Glasgow Group two)

They are also clear about the effect of the information about international relationships on the process of their own understanding. They distinguished between seeing a jumble of confusing news images and making clear conceptual links:

> Female 1: When I looked at all these photographs you could look at them as all separate photographs ... They could all have a separate story. It is not until you see not even the first film but the second one as well and then the discussion that you can actually put it together and say now I know what it is all about. I have got a better idea of what caused it and who is involved ... It certainly makes a lot more sense in my head now. From looking at the photos at first it was just nothing much. Now I have got more of an idea and it makes more sense to me.

> Female 2: As far back as I can remember watching news there has always been something about Africa or whatever in the news. Now you understand why it had been going on for so long there is so much wealth involved and so many other people involved that you just don't know.

> Moderator: It is not hard to understand, is it?

> Female 1: No it is not.

> Female 2: Once you make the obvious link.

> (Glasgow Group two)

There was a sense of surprise in the groups at this 'new' way of understanding, and in all of them it was strongly suggested that such a way of explaining the Angola conflict would not be allowed on television. The groups were convinced that it would be censored by the government. This was not a theme which was introduced by the moderator but was raised spontaneously in all of the groups, as in the following exchanges:

> Male 1: The government wouldn't allow you to come out with things like that. It would be cut out wouldn't it?

> Moderator: Saying what?

> Male 1: Going into so many details. Don't buy diamond rings and don't buy so much petrol and ... If that was in a programme it would be cut out wouldn't it? ...

> Moderator: Do you think the government just wouldn't allow that sort of thing to be said?

> Male 1: I don't think so.

> Male 2: There is too much money involved.

> (Glasgow Group one)

And in the second Glasgow group:

> Female 1: I think people would find it shocking.

Female 2: Yes.

Female 1: Why not put that message across? Because the government doesn't want us to feel that way?

Female 2: That is why they don't tell you.

Female 3: Is there a hidden agenda?

(Glasgow Group two)

And in the Bath group:

Male 1: I just feel that maybe more news should be made on that America are involved.

Male 2: If they said that Great Britain is part of this there would be mayhem.

Male 3: They would all be asking questions ...

Male 2: Politicians wouldn't say it in the first place because they would be worried they would get kicked out.

Male 4: They probably wouldn't allow the programme to go ahead anyway.

(Bath Group)

They were convinced that journalists were censored. At the group in Bath the two journalists from the BBC were actually present and at this point they were invited to join the discussion. The first question to them followed on directly from the comments on censorship:

Male 1: Can I just ask you then, are you influenced by the hierarchy to say what you have to say?

David Shukman: Not at all.

The journalist then goes on to argue that the only kind of censorship is over the pictures which can be shown and this is on the grounds that they may cause offence or be too shocking:

David Shukman: We take the view that some people would be offended or shocked too much by some images. For example, there was a young lad who lost his lower legs in the hospital at twelve years old and the doctor was describing how outrageous it was that new mines were being laid and making it all worse. He offered to take us into the surgery with that young boy to see the next stage of the amputation going on. I said we can't do that and we can't show that. That is a kind of censorship. We . . . try and work out what viewers might really object to and be really offended by and what they can handle. That is the only type of censorship (Bath Group).

The point is confirmed by Vin Ray:

> We get more complaints about the use of pictures than any other thing. When you are out in the field and you see what is really happening, you want people to see it in all its gruesome glory, to understand what it's like, the problem is that people turn off. (Bath group).

The obvious question which follows is, if there is no censorship other than on grounds of 'taste' then why is the role of the industrial countries and their powerful interests not highlighted in the story? Later in the discussion, David Shukman made an interesting statement in relation to British oil companies and government policy. He is asked again by a group member about what he can say:

> Male 1: Can you say anything you like on the TV about the government and what is going on? Going back to this, could you say these are blood diamonds and this is what is happening and it is the government's fault and end it?
>
> David Shukman: If it was the government's fault and I have proof then I could say it. It is all indirectly the government's fault. You could say the British oil companies are buying Angolan oil and it is ending up in the forecourts here and that money goes to the Angolan government that BP pays and …
>
> Male 1: What kind of knock-on effect do you think would come with our government?
>
> David Shukman: I don't know. If enough people were interested in the fact that BP was getting oil from Angola and the money was vanishing into the Angolan government's pockets and ended up buying weapons or whatever, conceivably people would not want to buy BP oil … You could certainly make a link and there would be no censorship on that.

He then comments that they had intended to do an interview with the oil company in Angola, but it was cancelled:

> David Shukman: As it happens we were hoping to do an interview with BP in Angola and they cancelled at the last minute. My first thought was that they didn't want to talk about it but I can't prove that. You never know exactly why someone has cancelled. There might have been a bit more on that angle if that interview had happened … There is no censorship in the sense that you think about it. Every BBC journalist has their own rules of impartiality and fairness as far as you can, therefore if you are going to accuse BP you would probably want to invite BP to respond to the accusations you were going to make in the report in order to be fair (Bath group).

But the logic of this position is that if the oil companies refuse to appear then any accusations would disappear. This definition of the need to be balanced could actually produce a major imbalance in the explanations which are given. It also begs the question of who had the right (and the power) to insist on 'balance.' There was apparently no problem with accusing the African government of corruption and no need to balance these accusations with an interview defending their record. This does not mean that the accusations were not true. They may very well have been, just as the accusations against oil companies and against banks in the city of London may also be true. But it is clear that some interests are very much more likely to demand 'balance' and to create problems for investigative journalism than others.

Another area of the group discussion which most interested the journalists was the possible changes which could be made to the structure of news items. How could core issues and explanations be conveyed more clearly to audiences? The feeling in the group was that they should be highlighted in the bulletin and the actions of people in Britain and their consequences abroad should be emphasised:

> David Shukman: We have been talking about making things clearer. It seems to me from listening to your discussion before, one of the things you all picked up on was the point that you might be driving a car with Angolan oil in the tank or you might wear a diamond ring with an Angolan diamond that was paying for a landmine. If we had said that at the start of the news report, would it make you sit up a bit more and listen?

> Male 1: When you do this piece and whatever you have got to do in Angola, if you had put that across first, you think it might have made people look up, yeah. I do.

> Male 2: Inadvertently the government is paying for it as well.

> Male 1: That is where western corruption comes in and I think it would open up a lot of eyes ...

> Male 3: I think you have got to just shock people. If you want to do a story it has got to start off gory with arms and legs or silence or (saying) you've caused this or ...

> Male 1: Like you said you would get thousands of letters but it wouldn't stop the person from watching the news the next evening.

> (Bath group)

Two points which emerged most clearly were expressed as 'you need somehow to relate this to us' and the need 'to come in at the end and explain what is happening' (Bath group).

A final and important result, which was apparent in all of the groups, was a greatly increased level of interest in the subject matter once the conflict was understood as resulting from a system of relationships in which the group members themselves were in some way involved. This change in the level of interest was noted by the journalists. David Shukman refers to it in his own account of his experiences with the focus group which he wrote later for the the *Independent*.

> Attitudes were shifting. Viewing my reports had kindled interest in Angola but it had taken talk of the possible connections with Britain to raise real concern ... The discussion had come alive. These were people who could follow the arguments and did not want to be short changed or patronised. Muttering about being kept to a tight duration in my packages cut no ice. For this group, foreign news, not always the favourite of news rooms, was becoming stimulating (Shukman, 2000).

Conclusions

There are a number of key issues which emerge from our research. The first is that TV audiences have in general very little understanding of events in the developing world or of major international institutions or relationships. This is in part the result of TV coverage which tends to focus on dramatic, violent and tragic images while giving very little context or explanation to the events which are being portrayed. The development of television organised around crude notions of audience ratings is likely to make this situation worse. The irony is that in seeking to grab the attention of audiences, programme makers are actually fostering very negative attitudes towards the developing world and other international issues and in the long run will reduce audience interest. We also found that in the absence of other explanations on the news, audiences (and some journalists) will 'fill in the gaps' with what are effectively post-colonial beliefs about Africa and the innate faults of Africans.

Our new research with BBC journalists showed that the explanation of the core relationships which link the industrial countries to the conflicts of the developing world can produce a distinct change in the understanding and attitudes of audience groups. The crucial point is that the conflict in Angola was located in a world system of commercial and political relationships in which the group members themselves played a part. The importance of this is that it was the understanding of the core relationships which made a difference and meant that audience members could link different elements of the news story to produce a coherent explanation. For some years now, within broadcasting, there have been arguments about the need to better inform and explain in news programmes. These have resulted in demands for longer bulletins, in-depth interviews and more detailed accounts. Such changes can indeed play a part but we should remember that audiences can get lost in detail and longer interviews with prevaricating politicians may simply add to the confusion. The important point for the journalist is the need to summarise the key relationships that explain the events which they are reporting, to say why these matter and how they relate to the audience. These relationships then need to be referred to *routinely* in news accounts as it cannot be assumed that audiences will have heard and understood them the first time or indeed that they carefully watch each bulletin.

A key result of our work was that the audience groups showed an increase in their level of interest when they did understand the economic and political links which underpinned the continuing war. The reports by David Shukman had been extremely powerful and had produced a very strong emotional response towards the victims of the conflict. But this was accompanied by feelings that the situation was hopeless and essentially an 'African' problem. It was the change in this perception that produced the increased interest. Finally, if we look at world news as a whole it does seem clear that many of the problems which viewers experience result from the actions and practices of the broadcasters themselves. If they are not to be held responsible for the mass production of ignorance then it is they who will need to redress the balance between the current priorities of reporting and the need to properly inform their audience.

References

Beattie, L., D. Miller, E. Miller and G. Philo (1999) 'The Media and Africa: images of disaster and rebellion', in Philo, G. (ed) *Message Received* London: Routledge.

Enzensberger, H. (1974) *The Consciousness Industry*. New York: Seabury.

Herman, E. and N. Chomsky (1988) *Manufacturing Consent*. New York: Pantheon.

Hilsum, L. (1995) 'Where is Kigali?', in *Granta*. Penguin: London.

Glasgow Media Group (2000) *Viewing the World: News Content and Audience Studies*. London: DFID.

Glasgow Media Group (1976) *Bad News*. London: Routledge.

Glasgow Media Group (1980) *More Bad News*. London: Routledge.

Philo, G. and D. Miller (2000) *Market Killing*. London: Longman.

Philo, G., L. Hilsum, L. Beattie and R. Holliman (1999) 'The Media and the Rwanda Crisis: Effects on Audiences and Public Policy', in Philo, G. (ed) *Message Received*. London: Routledge.

Philo, G. (1990) *Seeing and Believing*. London: Routledge.

Rock, P. (1973) 'News as Eternal Recurrence', in Cohen, S. and J. Young (eds) *The Manufacture of News*, Constable: London.

Schechter, D. (1998) *The More You Watch the Less You Know*. New York: Seven Stories Press.

Shukman, D. (2000, 7 November) 'Watching Them, Watching Me', *The Independent*.

Stone, J. (2000) *Losing Perspective: Global Affairs on British Terrestrial Television 1989 – 1999*. London: Third World and Environment Broadcasting Project.

Third World and Environment Broadcasting Trust (3WE) (2000), *Viewing the World: Production Study*. London: DFID.

Chapter 12
Cosmopolitanism, Culture and Televised Social Suffering
Nick Stevenson

Stevenson, like Tester, is also concerned with the moral relationship between the cultural consumption of news images and the political expression of cosmopolitan citzenship. Focusing mainly on news images of Africa and exploring his own responses to such images, Stevenson develops a dialogue with Tester and others. He suggests the need to delineate a more complex set of emotional reactions beyond indifference to account for the lack of audience response. He also returns to the news construction of 'others' and the sense of ethnic exclusivity and Western superiority that are built into news representations. He proposes the 'critical politics of the image' that analyzes news framing, audience response and wider political concerns together, but still refuses any guarantees.

The development of a cosmopolitan politics is dependent upon an active civil society that has been able to deconstruct oppositions between the national and the international and public and private. In such a view civil society acts not only as the realm of voluntary organisations, legal rights and elections but also encompasses the realm of symbolic communication. The media of mass communication in modern societies is an important resource in the construction of diverse civil societies which foster public narratives, symbols and identities, providing the ground for a number of imagined communities (Alexander and Jacobs, 1998).

The construction of cosmopolitan civil societies depends upon an intersubjective framework of human rights, political activism, and common symbols and markers which might be stretched to include common rituals and media events and raise questions of solidarity and identity across a number of divides (Sreberny, 1998). Such a view of civil society would take us beyond the usual distinctions between information and entertainment, and quality and commercial broadcasting, to encompass the normative and cultural horizons of everyday life. Within such contexts an inclusive cultural citizenship or public sphere not only enhances shared attempts to critique official politics, but also involves symbolic attempts to deconstruct boundaries between 'insiders' and 'outsiders' through a variety of mediated cultural forms (Stevenson, 1999). Civil society in this analysis becomes 'the process by which individuals construct together with others the social meanings through which they interpret reality – including the reality of moral obligation itself' (Wolfe, 1989:208). Such an emphasis takes us beyond overly pessimistic constructions of a global civil society, which are primarily concerned with rationality, or the capacities of an exclusively defined global elite (Garnham, 1992, Sparks, 1998).

Yet given some of the harsh realities of the world post September 11 we might be pressed to ask what space is actually left for cosmopolitan initiatives? Within President Bush's binary logic of 'you are either with us, or against us', what chances are there for more ambivalent forms of identification? In a world increasingly dominated by nationalist rhetoric, tightening immigration controls, fundamentalist violence and a gathering global hegemony around the need to fight terror surely cosmopolitanism is nothing more than a pipe dream? My answer to these questions is both 'yes' and 'no'. Yes, the prospects for a genuinely cosmopolitan global public sphere are currently distant from dominant constructions of media politics, but no, there remain plenty of openings and opportunities, as we shall see, to work within the ideological cracks of the present.

Here I aim to link questions of cosmopolitan citizenship to the construction and production of mediated perspectives. In other words, the flourishing of cosmopolitan political perspectives is actually dependent upon a range of semiotic material that is most likely to come through the news. First, I want to look briefly at some of the arguments in respect of cosmopolitan citizenship. Here I shall argue that while these are important developments, the arguments as they currently stand need to develop a more concertedly 'cultural' understanding of cosmopolitanism.

From here I want to look at two ways (there are of course many more) in which cosmopolitanism can be hindered and limited by certain cultural dispositions and practices on the part of journalists and audiences. As Lawrence Grossberg (1992: 64) has commented, 'no democratic political struggle can be effectively organised without the power of the popular.' At this point I link questions related to ethnocentrism and indifference. My aim then is not to dismiss cosmopolitan concerns but to locate them more precisely within contemporary media and political cultures. The argumentative strategy that I pursue here is that while the prospects for a cosmopolitan civil dialogue is difficult within an atmosphere of fear and paranoia, other global changes have brought such prospects onto the agenda.

Cosmopolitan Citizenship

Since the fall of the Berlin wall the cosmopolitan view has sought to dispense with specifically national responses. This has largely been due to the argument that processes of globalisation have significantly undermined national forms of citizenship. According to Richard Falk (2000a), globalisation has minimised political differences within states by converting elections into trivial rituals, while simultaneously weakening the internal bonds of community and consideration. Issues such as growing ecological awareness, the impact of global poverty, feminism, the participation of racial and ethnic minorities are not readily integrated into a concern for the declining fortunes of territorial states. Following Beck (1998), Held (1995) and Linklater (1998) is the view that without a politically robust cosmopolitan culture, global civil society and cosmopolitan institutions, we will remain a world at the mercy of the interests of nation states and economic markets.

Democracy has to become a trans-national form of governance by breaking with the cultural hegemony of the state. A cosmopolitan political community would be based upon overlapping or multiple citizenships connecting the populace into local, national, regional and global forms of governance. The cosmopolitan polity, guided by the principle of autonomy, would seek to achieve new levels of interconnectedness to correspond with an increasingly global world. These dimensions remain vital, surpassing older divisions in the democratic tradition between direct and representative democracy by seeking to maximise the principle of autonomy across a range of different levels. Within this framework, therefore, the argument for a cosmopolitan democracy is guided by the argument that problems such as HIV, ecological questions and poverty are increasingly globally shared problems.

We are witnessing growing calls for the democratic ideal to detach itself from national boundaries. This is in response to a number of related developments. For David Held (1995), this is both because specifically national democracies have been undermined by more global flows, and because for local forms of accountability to survive and be revived the democratic ideal must find expression at the trans-national level. The task of securing democracy in an increasingly interconnected age must allow for the development of a cosmopolitan democratic law. In this respect, Held has identified the United Nations as an institution that could play a key role in the transformation of governance from a world system built upon the competing ambitions of nation states to one with a deeper orientation to cosmopolitan forms of democracy. The UN Charter provides a forum where states are in certain respects equal, offering the beginnings of a break with a world order whereby specifically national interests are paramount. However, as Held is well aware, the United Nations is in need of considerable reform before it is able to generate its own political resources, and act as an autonomous decision making centre.

Similarly Habermas (1997) and Honneth (1997) locate ideas of cosmopolitan democracy in Kant's (1970) desire to replace the law of nations with a genuinely morally binding international law. Kant believed that the spread of commerce and the principles of republicanism could help foster cosmopolitan sentiments. As world-citizens, individuals would act to cancel the egoistic ambitions of individual states. Kant's vision of a peaceful cosmopolitan order based upon the obligation by states to settle their differences through the court of law has gained a new legitimacy in a post cold war world. For Habermas (1997), while this vision retains a contemporary purchase it has to be brought up to date by acknowledging a number of social transformations including the globalisation of the public sphere and the declining power of states, while also recognising that it is individuals and citizens and not collectivities who need to become sovereign.

Cosmopolitanism then requires the implementation of legal mechanisms that act in the interests of global citizens rather than states. This would build upon the UN charter model of governance creating a society of world citizens who were able to challenge their own governments. Like Held, Habermas recognises that the weak link in these arguments is that the UN currently both recognises nation states as sovereign as well as being open to challenge. This contradiction is further magnified if we recognise that globalisation processes have both increased the social and economic divisions across the planet, while introducing the idea of a global community based upon shared risks. The prospect of a global cosmopolitan democracy takes on the role of a 'necessary utopia' leading us out of the ambiguities of the present into a new world whereby international relations become progressively moralised through the rights of individuals rather than states.

However the project for cosmopolitan governance is not without its own internal sympathetic critics. The most pronounced of which has been the voice of Richard Falk (1995, 1999, 2000a, 2000b). Falk has argued that rather than being concerned with institution building as an end in itself, arguments for a cosmopolitan polity need to become focused on the recovery of democratic sensibilities. It is an active citizenry committed to substantive cosmopolitan viewpoints that remains the key agency of change. Cosmopolitanism therefore is actually dependent upon the development of a global civil society that is in itself dependent upon pressure and struggle from below. A democratic identity will have to forge itself in opposition to consumerist inclinations, fundamentalism, neo-liberalism and outright cynicism. The recovery of a substantive ethical agenda in a world driven by consumerism, nationalist sentiment and market calculations is more than a matter of building new levels of governance.

The key principle here is that multi-level cosmopolitan governance would offer new opportunities for dialogue across a number of levels. Revitalised local and trans-national political structures would seek to provide the institutional basis for conversation that would dissolve older divisions between citizens and aliens.

In the absence of an Archimedean standpoint that transcends differences of culture, time and place such dialogues would provide the basis for a new world society. As Linklater (1998) argues, a cosmopolitan position would need to bring the 'other' into an extended dialogue. A genuinely cosmopolitan dialogue would need to avoid the negative representations of 'alien' cultures, while deconstructing the assumption that 'national' or 'local' conversations have the right to override the interests of 'insiders' over that of 'outsiders'. In these terms cosmopolitan moral progress can be accounted for when 'they' become 'us'.

As I have already indicated cosmopolitanism's detractors could simply argue that in a post September 11 world such lofty ideals have little purchase on current geo-political realities. Susan Buck-Morss (2002) has recently argued that the terrorist attack on New York has been used by the global media and powerful states to legitimate intellectual repression, racist stereotypes and exclusionary loyalties in the 'war against terror'. It is on these grounds we must assess the 'possibility' of cosmopolitan politics. Yet as Buck-Morss herself points out, cosmopolitan questions remain the only questions capable of challenging the new global hegemony. The selectivity of Western double standards in respect of human rights, and the current Bush administration's intransigence on questions as far reaching as global warming and a permanent human rights court can be criticised within cosmopolitan terms. Such a view would resist the idea that the United States (or any other nation for that matter) can simply act in the name of global humanity.

Cosmopolitanism requires a form of double thinking. Firstly, genuinely cosmopolitan dialogue would need to argue against the rights of states to act in the interests of everyone. Cosmopolitanism requires a multi-vocal dialogue empowering the rights of 'minorities' both within and outside the nation-state. Secondly, attempts to reach agreement and consensus actively disallow the disproportionate use of force or wealth to secure dominant interests. As this brief sketch should indicate, cosmopolitan positions have substance. The problem is not that cosmopolitanism has been displaced by an entrenched right wing hegemony that emphasises the role of the security state over and above democratic currents. Rather the challenge is for human rights groups with cosmopolitan sympathies to speak up for 'minorities' and refugees in a way that interrupts the dominant assumptions of existing news agendas.

However if cosmopolitanism aims to de-centre purely national viewpoints by bringing in the 'other' then we need to ask what sorts of relations and imaginative horizons do our news cultures ordinarily foster with distant others? If the possibility of cosmopolitan politics depends upon shared senses of community and identity then we need to understand these dimensions in relation to the narratives that are routinely provided by news and media cultures.

Representations of the 'Other', Racism and Media Politics

Recently many of the debates connected with post-colonialism have pointed to the ideological necessity of 'decolonising' the global or at least Western imagination (Pieterse and Parekh, 1995). This means critically reworking the West's cultural conception of itself in respect of its historical relation with colonialism and empire, and the continued relations of force between North and South. Such a project entails deconstructing lingering forms of colonial nostalgia, breaking with Eurocentrism and rethinking existing relations through more culturally complex frameworks. The legacy of colonialism continues to inform contemporary images of 'non Western' cultures as well as the West's own collective self-identity.

In traditional colonial imagery, Africa was seen as a world of nature rather than of culture. The most popular image of the African male was of a primitive savage or warrior who needed to be civilised and cultured by the West. The African's lack of technical know-how and ignoble customs represented a homogenous people incapable of self-government or civilised behaviour. These cultural images and representations evident within Western literature and the newspapers of the colonial administration served to justify the continued dominance of European nations and to maintain a sharp distinction between civilised and uncivilised. It was an imperative of imperialist ideologies to repress any hint of similarity between the peoples of the North and South and thereby conceal the political and economic links that existed between them.

Much of the research in this area has been built upon the directions opened out by Said (1978) who demonstrated how discourses, values and patterns of knowledge served to construct the facts about 'other' cultures. Said uncovers the ways in which Western forms of power and knowledge combine in order to divide the globe between the Occident and the Orient. The former is the site of human values and rationality, while the latter is seen as irrational, dangerous and exotic. Similar to what was described above, Orientalism reduced the complex interrelations between East and West to simple binary oppositions.

The power of the West in relations with the East and the South was to be able to name the sites of cultural difference, while maintaining colonial inequalities. The discursive construction of difference served to mask ideological relations and to repress more ambivalent cultural connections. Said has sparked a number of works all pertaining to be more sensitive to the cultural construction of 'other' cultures (Turner, 1994). However, according to Pieterse (1992), what is currently lacking in the literature is a detailed examination of the ways such assumptions are being rearticulated in the context of contemporary image cultures.

These dimensions have been discussed by too few contemporary perspectives. Notably if we explore the cultural flow of imagery between the North and South it is overwhelmingly one way. That is while representations of the 'Third

World' remain important in terms of global intersubjective relations this should not obscure the fact that the vast amount of cultural representations and perspectives are moving in the opposite direction. Hence while the West uses the South as a dumping group for out-of-date cultural products, the West receives images of the South that continue to be discursively shaped by well worn stereotypes. For instance, studies of the ideological construction of Africa in the British press and global media generally by Brooks (1995) and Sorenson (1991) point towards a remarkable consistency in this area. Both Brooks and Sorenson argue that the media tends to 'naturalise' African conflicts by inadequately contextualising the reported events in the appropriate political and historical context. Ideologically this reproduces a tendency to neglect the historical location of Africa within colonial and neo-colonial social relations.

Africa, in this reading, is represented as intrinsically violent and anti-democratic while constituted through tribal rule and excessive use of force. Further, the continent's economic underdevelopment is explained through anti-modern forms of superstition and cultural backwardness. Overall this promotes a view of the 'Third World' as passive beneficiary of Western generosity as well as being intrinsically dangerous and insecure. Sorensen and Brookes speculate that these ideologies serve a dual purpose in that ethnocentric discourses promote satisfying feelings of Western superiority and that the otherwise troubling fact of 'Third World' poverty can be explained with reference to their own cultural lack. The perpetuation of Western superiority, from this perspective, provides a forceful means of legitimating existing geo-political relations of dominance.

More recently I found in my own study of the 1994 Rwandan genocide the reproduction of similar ideological strategies (Stevenson, 1999). The overwhelming focus of the television coverage on Rwanda was not on the genocide itself, but on the mass exodus of refugees to nearby Zaire. Rwanda did not translate into an international news event worthy of global television's focus until the RPF had defeated the government army in July 1994, thereby halting the genocide. This led to one million people, mostly Bahutus, fleeing to Zaire where 50,000 of them died of disease, hunger and lack of water. The first the outside world knew of the genocide was when thousands of dead bodies floated over the Tanzanian border into Lake Victoria. Until that point the government had effectively managed to confuse the international media by representing the genocide as a form of tribal violence or civil war, which they could not control, and by making sure that the media were denied access to the areas where genocide had taken place. Seemingly, both the African and Western media largely accepted the view that the government had very little control over events and that the killing was a mostly 'tribal' affair. The reports of a tribal or civil war spiraling out of control lead initially to a reduction of United Nations troops and eventually to their withdrawal.

The French government in particular was actively involved in the supply of arms, military training, the provision of troops to assist the army and the extension of credit facilities, all of which aided the government in the build-up to the genocide. According to Gerard Prunier (1995), it was largely due to France's guilt over its complicity with the genocidal government and for 'internal' political reasons that they launched 'Operation Turquoise', which set up a 'humanitarian' zone within Rwanda. Despite the claims made by the French government, the intervention failed to stop the genocide, and did little to address the needs of a devastated nation. How then, we might ask, given the complicity of the Western media and international agencies with the extremist Rwandan government, did the media represent the genocide and the subsequent refugee crisis?

Most of the television news coverage of the genocide represented the refugee crisis through a discourse of 'suffering humanity'. This discourse almost completely ignored the context of the genocide and either referred to the in-coming refugees as escaping from a tribal conflict or more often a civil war. This is a familiar trope in media representations of Africa in that the historical relations between Bahutu and Batutsi become naturalised in exclusive ethnic categories. Many of the refugees were leaving Rwanda not so much to receive 'generous' Western help, as they were to escape the invading RPF army, and possibly regroup for a counter attack. The refugees themselves were either coded as helpless and passive victims requiring generous Western assistance, or as an irrational aggressive tribal people who actually cared very little for one another. This confusion about the nature of the refugees is evident in the remarks of BBC journalist George Kigali: 'Three months of strife and genocide has put paid to any sense of community. Those who might have dug graves looked around for anything useful in this land of exile. 30/40/50 dead I haven't the heart to count and it doesn't really matter - the fact is that these were innocent civilians and this was meant to be a place of refuge' (BBC News, 1994, July 18).

The innocent and yet guilty refugees are not placed inside any political/social historical context, so what we are being presented with are the essential attributes of a suffering people. The breakdown of basic civility amongst the refugees was often contrasted with the simple humanity of the French soldiers, the Aid workers or even the journalists, all of whom are of Western origin. This, it would seem, is the basic mark of Western civility and cultural distinction. Black Africans are violent or helpless, needy or dangerous, desperate or vicious in stark contrast to the selfless, 'giving' nature of the Europeans. The maintenance of binary categories of representation is important in the sustenance of social distance between the audience and the Rwandans. The genocide was 'managed' through the maintenance of stable social and psychic boundaries between a civilised 'us' and a helpless and uncivilised 'them'.

These configurations are evident in more contemporary media debates concerning the war in Afghanistan after the events of September 11. Again the regimes of representation that have come to the fore oscillate between the 'innocence' of the refugees and the 'barbarism' of bin Laden and the Taliban.

The displacement of 'aggression' onto the 'other' enables the West to maintain an image of themselves as pure and unsullied by associations with violence (Kovel, 1995). Notions of inner superiority are maintained by splitting away parts, which would seemingly threaten this self-identity.

Despite the fact that the United States has bombed Afghanistan it is able to maintain a judicious and fair minded self-image due to its generosity (the dropping of food parcels) and lack of violence (most of which goes unreported or is contested) when compared to the inhumanity of those they are fighting. My argument here is, whatever our own political convictions in respect of African politics or September 11, the discourses and representations that entrap the 'other' cancel the necessity of democratic dialogue. If cosmopolitan politics actually requires the development of a discursive space for the 'other' such practices are poorly served by an international media that regularly circulates racist assumptions about the West's inherent superiority. In this respect, we could argue that the binary assumptions constructed by media discourses actually mimic the ethnic politics involved in calls to genocide and assumptions evident in the so called clash of civilisations (Huntington, 1998).

Both ethnic exclusiveness and notions of Western superiority are built upon the idea that identity is tied to territory. Here identity ceases to be constructed through dialogic interaction and takes on the mark of destiny. As Paul Gilroy (2000) has pointed out, the images and practices of national/ethnic exclusivity embodies a form of 'camp thinking'. Gilroy (2000) writes:

> Any unsettling traces of hybridity must be excised from the tidy, bleached out zones of impossibly pure culture. The safety of sameness can then be recovered by either of two options that have regularly appeared at the meltdown point of this dismal logic: separation and slaughter.

Moral Indifference and Compassion

A different way of exploring these questions is to ask what effects the televisualisation of suffering has upon our shared moral landscape. We might argue that practices of time/space compression make it increasingly difficult to ignore the plight of the 'other'. Irrespective of the way in which the 'other' becomes culturally coded, we could argue that at least they have become more visible. The daily screening of images of suffering on our television sets means that it has become increasingly difficult to shrug off our responsibilities towards others in a shared world (Adam, 1998). Through televised appeals on behalf of peoples we will never meet we become aware that a donation 'right now' could have an immediate impact upon the well being of distanciated others across the planet's surface. Television and new media technologies arguably make cosmopolitan compassion and moral solidarity more possible. This is especially the case when such concerns become connected to the emergence of a cosmopolitan civil society, which includes the global spread of human rights, charitable agencies such as Oxfam, and the globalisation of communication networks. The globalisation of culture means that while we might seek to turn away from the suffering of the other, we cannot claim that we did not know.

However there are a growing number of more sceptical voices in this respect. Keith Tester (1995: 475) argues that television cannot actually create moral solidarity, but it can provide a cultural resource for those who have a predisposition towards 'moral leaps of the imagination'. The images and perspectives of the media do not have any automatic moral consequences. The representation of murder, war and suffering on television has no necessary connection to the development of cosmopolitan solidarity. In this respect, Zygmunt Bauman (1993) offers the notion of *telecity* to explain some of these aspects. Telecity, Bauman argues, is where objects and subjects appear only as forms of pleasure and amusement. The television screen may allow us to go travelling without leaving home, but its integration into privatised leisure patterns means that our experience of the alterity of the 'other' becomes blunted. The space opened up by telecity is one based upon individual pleasure – one that allows the subject to wander through a variety of media texts without any strings attached.

Tester (1995) continues that a world that is awash with images helps to foster a blasé attitude amongst the audience, whereby they repeatedly fail to be shocked by the pictures of horror and distress that are the daily diet of the television news. Television images are too fast and fleeting to leave any lasting moral trace of their presence. The box presents the moral issues and problems of living in an interconnected world as crumbs that can be easily swept off the collective table. The television screen in this regard can be seen as a 'door' which we stand behind, rather than a 'bridge' directly connecting the viewer to the sufferings of others. In this the screen is not really a 'window on the world', but can literally be seen as both a barrier between the viewer and those whose lives are represented. If the media are a 'door' rather than a 'bridge' we can then keep it shut in order to maintain our social and moral distance from the sufferings of others (Tester 1999).

Indeed in this scenario the act of giving is largely a means of maintaining rather than closing social distance. Tester (2001), along with Devereux (1996), argues that global news, telethons and documentaries are more often concerned with the cleansing of suffering and the sanitisation of the "other." Again we could argue that the dropping of humanitarian supplies on Afghanistan (in obviously inadequate amounts) and the fact that television shields us from the misery of those seeking to flee the bombing acts to sanitise rather than inform us of social suffering.

If we take the mediated charity event *Red Nose Day* that appears on British screens biannually it may illuminate our understanding. *Red Nose Day* seeks to co-ordinate different fund raising activities during the day with the emphasis placed upon showing concern for others while having fun. In the evening these activities are supplemented by a five to six hour-long television programme that runs continuously through the night. The programme is presented by well-known celebrities (giving their time for free) who present 'serious footage' from people 'in need', which are then supplemented by guest appearances, comedy sketches and interviews from participants involved in charitable activities. On one level, *Red Nose Day* is a mediated example of cosmopolitan solidarity enjoyed by 'freedom's children' (Beck, 2000). Indeed when I asked my students to view the event as part of a media course their reactions were mainly positive.

In 2000 *Red Nose Day* dedicated a third of its resources to helping the genocide victims of Rwanda. Many of my students reported how the clips of film (interspersed by celebrity appearances) from Rwanda had made them aware of the sufferings of others. The plight of the peoples from Rwanda was confirmed by comedian Lenny Henry who kept reminding the audience 'we are all brothers'. Undoubtedly the information provided by *Red Nose Day* taps into a latent cosmopolitan sensibility. Yet the students also reported other feelings further away from the surface. There were concerns that the shocking images could be used to guilt trip the audience, and further that such help that 'the needy' received may be short term. There was then a concern about the moral distance between the givers and receivers of the money that is donated. However what the students did not comment upon was the lack of depth, voice and complexity available within many of the images. To treat a person or a community justly we would need to take seriously their commitments, concerns and ethical complexity. A cosmopolitan human rights culture that failed to do this could not expect to sustain relations of solidarity.

Typically the plight of the Rwandans was represented as a homogeneous people united by suffering. Within the images and representations *Red Nose Day* made available they were given little opportunity to speak for themselves or be connected to a recognisable political or social context. Further, many of the students (and me included) found it difficult to distinguish the reports from Rwanda and other stories of suffering from different African locations also presented on *Red Nose Day*. While such criticism would need to take into account the limitations inherent within the genre of the telethon many of the facets of *Red Nose Day* seem consistent with the observations made by Tester. Such events could be characterised as 'carnivals of charity' whereby giving takes place outside of lasting relations of solidarity (Bauman, 1998).

While these perspectives pose difficult questions for cosmopolitan concerns they are in need of further discussion. Morley (2000) has argued that whereas privileged consumers can progressively de-link themselves from a national territory the same can not be said of the planet's poor. It is the ability of the planet's relatively privileged to withdraw into the pleasures and comforts of their own living rooms away from their obligations towards those that are suffering, which is troubling. In this reading, the planet's privileged can afford to look the other way. Similar questions have also been raised in connection with the spread of so called 'compassion fatigue' where the world's privileged, despite being awash with images of poverty and deprivation, are accused of retreating behind the walls of closed communities and the pleasures of consumer culture. The problem with these perspectives however is their unrelenting pessimism as regards the political possibilities of cosmopolitanism.

The political question is often not that of 'indifference' but of knowing how to translate concern into activity. For example, that I 'do' little to help the refugees in Afghanistan may have less to do with my indifference than of simple despair or of not knowing how best to help. Of course we could also point to the fact that many political groups and social movements are currently campaigning on an agenda of ethical globalisation. The decline of territoriality as the foundation for political activity has promoted a number of concerns that seek to interrupt mainstream news agendas with different discourses and perspectives.

In this context, Stanley Cohen (2001) has argued that the normalisation of suffering ordinarily involves processes of denial. Cohen's study points to the need to form an understanding of the ways in which social ideologies and unconscious feelings operate less through outright frauds or powerful codes and more through our common ability to hide from what we half know or fear. What is troubling is that we know only too well about much of the social suffering that takes place in the world, and that we find such 'realities' difficult to face. Hence the problem with accounts like Tester's is that they bracket off a number of complex emotional reactions to televised war, famine, and atrocity under the sign of indifference. Here how we might point to the ways in which social suffering is represented actually protects the audience from painful feelings by fostering a form of psychological deadness (Ogden, 1989). The blunting of the 'other' does not foster 'indifference', but can be more accurately related to an attempt to deal with an unconscious anxiety that partially recognises that the rights and needs of others are being violated. Here we might summarise that the audience is complicit with ethnocentric media cultures as they 'know' only too well what is being obscured from view.

These concerns link into some of the post-colonial viewpoints discussed in the previous section. Cosmopolitan concerns inevitably involve a politics of representation that needs to move beyond an argument of combating negative stereotypes with more positive images. The construction of more 'multivalent and multidimensional' images and responses inevitably depends upon dispensing with a view of the 'other' as either 'evil' or 'innocent' (West, 1993). Further, we need to recognise that even if we could deconstruct ethnocentric media cultures it may not be met by a more concerned cosmopolitan politics on the part of the television audience.

Conclusion

In conclusion, this short essay has argued that the prospects for cosmopolitan citizenship are both hindered and fostered by current media forms and cultures. While mediated time/space compression can often give us the sense that we live in 'one world' there are many other cultural features that bend our sensibilities in different directions. Modern news cultures ordinarily foster forms of ethnic exclusivity, Western superiority and indifference. While the dominance of these perspectives can easily become overstated they remain real enough for those who seek to foster cosmopolitan questions to exhibit concern if not out-right pessimism.

Yet we also saw how much more attention needs to be paid to the affective sensibilities of modern audiences in the ways in which their structures of feeling contribute towards their mental maps. While we need to be able to point towards the dominant discourses and codes which represent others within the global village we should also be open to the complex traces and effects such images and perspectives are likely to leave within their wake. In other words, while a cosmopolitan sensibility is generally hindered by ideas such as national cohesiveness, Western superiority, ethnic exclusivity and psychological blankness, these features are constantly being disrupted by other more submerged narratives, affects and concerns.

References

Adam, B.(1998) 'Re-vision: The Centrality of Time for an Ecological Social Science Perspective', in Lash, S. et al. (eds), *Risk, Environment and Modernity*. London: Sage.

Alexander, J.C. and R.N. Jacobs (1998) 'Mass communication, ritual and civil society', in Liebes, T. and J. Curran, *Media, Ritual and Identity*. London: Routledge.

Bauman, Z.(1993) *Post-Modern Ethics*. Oxford: Blackwell.

Bauman, Z.(1998) *Work, Consumerism and the New Poor*. Buckingham: Open University Press.

Beck, U. (1998) *Democracy Without Enemies*. Cambridge: Polity Press.

Beck, U. (2000) *What Is Globalisation?*. Cambridge: Polity Press.

Brooks, H. J.(1995) 'Suit, Tie and Touch of Juju – The Ideological construction of Africa: Critical Discourse Analysis of News on Africa', *Discourse and Society* 6(4): 461-494.

Buck-Morss, S.(2002) 'A Global Public Sphere?', *Situation Analysis*, 1: 10-19.

Cohen, S.(2001) *States of Denial: Knowing about Atrocities and Suffering*. Cambridge: Polity Press.

Devereux, E.(1996) 'Good causes, God's poor and telethon television', *Media, Culture and Society* 18: 47-68.

Falk, R.(1995) 'The World Order between Inter-State Law and the Law of Humanity: The Role of Civil Society Instituions', in Archibugi, D. and D. Held (eds), *Cosmopolitan Democracy*. Cambridge: Polity Press.

Falk, R.(1999) *Predatory Globalisation; A Critique*. Cambridge: Polity Press.

Falk, R.(2000a) 'The decline of citizenship in an era of globalisation', *Citizenship Studies*, 4(1): 5-17.

Falk, R.(2000b) *Human Rights Horizons; The Pursuit of Justice in a Globalising World*. London, Routledge.

Garnham, N.(1992) 'The media and the public sphere', in Calhoun, C.(ed), *Habermas and the Public Sphere*. Cambridge, Massachusetts: Massachusetts Institute of Technology.

Huntington, S.P. (1998) *The Clash of Civilisations and the Remaking of World Order*. London: Touchstone Books.

Gilroy, P.(2000) *Between Camps; Race, Identity and Nationalism at the End of the Colour Line*. London: Penguin.

Grossberg, L. (1992) 'Is there a fan in the house?: The affective sensibility of fandom', in Lewis, L. *Adoring Audience*. London: Routledge.

Habermas, J.(1997) 'Kant's Idea of Perpetual Peace, with the Benefit of Two Hundred Years Hindsight', Bohmann and M. Lutz-Bachmann J. (eds), *Perpetual Peace: Essays on Kant's Cosmopolitan Ideal*. Cambridge: MIT Press.

Held D.(1995) *Democracy and the Global Order: From the Modern State to Cosmopolitan Governance*. Cambridge: Polity Press.

Honneth, A.(1997) 'Is Universalism a Moral Trap? The Presuppostitions of a Politics of Human Rights', in Bohmann, J. and M. Lutz-Bachmann (eds), *Perpetual Peace: Essays on Kant's Cosmopolitan Ideal*. Cambridge: MIT Press..

Kant, I.(1970) 'Perpetual Peace. A Philosophical Sketch', in Reiss, H (ed), *Kant Political Writings*. Cambridge: Cambridge University Press.

Kovel, J. (1995) 'On Racism and Psychoanalysis', in Elliott, A. and S. Frosch (eds), *Psychoanalysis in Contexts*. London: Routledge.

Linklater, A.(1998) *The Transformation of Political Community*. Cambridge: Polity Press.

Morley, D.(2000) *Home Territories: Media, Mobility and Identity*. London: Routledge.

Ogden, T. (1989) *The Primitive Edge of Experience*. London: Jason Aranson Inc.

Pieterse, J.N.(1992) *White on Black; Images of Africa and Blacks in Western Popular Culture*. New Haven: Yale University Press.

Pieterse, J.N. and B. Parekh (1995) 'Shifting imaginaries: decolonisation, internal decolonisation, postcoloniality', in Pieterse and Parekh (eds), *The Decolonisation of the Imagination; Culture, Knowledge and Power*. London: Zed Books.

Punier, G.(1995) *The Rwandan Crisis 1959-1994; History of a Genocide*. London: Hurst and Company.

Said, E.(1978) *Orientalism*. London: Routledge and Kegan Paul.

Sorensen, J.(1991) 'Mass Media and Discourse on Famine in the Horn of Africa', *Discourse and Society*, 2(2): 223-242.

Sparks, C.(1998) 'Is there a global public sphere?', in Thussu, D.K. (ed), *Electronic Empires; Global Media and Local Resistance*. London: Arnold.

Sreberny, A. (1998) 'Feminist internationalism: Imagining and building global civil society', in Thussu, D.K. (ed), *Electronic Empires; Global Media and Local Resistance*. London: Arnold.

Stevenson, N.(1999) *The Transformation of the Media: globalisation, morality and ethics*. New York: Longman.

Tester, K.(1995) 'Moral solidarity and the technological reproduction of images', *Media, Culture and Society*, 17: 469-482.

Tester, K.(1997) *Moral Culture*. London: Sage.

Tester, K.(1999) 'The Moral Consequentiality of Television', *European Journal of Social Theory*, 2(4): 469-483.

Tester, K. (2001) *Compassion, Morality and the Media*. Buckingham: Open University Press.

Turner, B.S.(1994) *Orientalism, Postmodernism and Globalism*. London: Routledge.

West, C.(1993) 'The New Cultural Politics of Difference', in During, S. (ed), *The Cultural Studies Reader*. London: Routledge.

Wolfe, A.(1989) *Whose Keeper? Social Science and Moral Obligation*. Berkeley: University of California Press.

Part IV: Innovations

Chapter 13
Slaying the Media Beast: The MediaChannel as an Act of Personal Responsibility and Political Mission
Danny Schechter

'Media activists' have long argued that the problems with corporate domination of information and culture cannot be solved exclusively through pressure on these institutions – crucial though this is. Many dedicate themselves instead to making their own media, and the Internet overflows with examples. MediaChannel demonstrates the confluence of both approaches. Leading US media critic Danny Schechter once produced international news for US network television, and has since created television programme series focusing on human rights which aired around the world: South Africa Now *and* Rights and Wrongs. *Here, Schechter describes how and why he created MediaChannel – now a leading global media criticism website focusing on journalism. Apart from the limited critical academic literature, which gains little public exposure, MediaChannel is one of just a few media outlets with a large readership dedicated to holding corporate journalism accountable for their reporting.*

There are laws to protect the freedom of the press's speech, but none that are worth anything to protect the people from the press.

Mark Twain, 1873

In media-saturated countries worldwide, we live in an age of media politics governed not just by politicians but by what is, in effect, an unelected 'media-ocracy'. The term points to the mutually dependent relationship that exists between major media and politics, a nexus of power in which political leaders use media exposure to shape opinions and drive policy while media outlets use politicians to confer legitimation on their own power, while offering what *Time* magazine has called 'electotainment'. By providing access to people in power, media becomes a platform for power. Media coverage validates what we call democracy; the political system in turn validates media.

Media have become the fulcrum of political life throughout the West and a driver of economic life as well. Commercials excite demand. Television celebrities become commodities. Marketing strategies sell products. And programs focused on financial markets sell ideology. The ups and downs of share prices get more attention from journalists than rates of unemployment or indices of social misery. Young people spend more time in the living room watching television than in the classroom. Many scholars believe that television has become their principal teacher. Some critics call it a 'plug-in drug' (Winn, 1985).

The New York Media Heartland: Where Consumption Trumps Citizenship

For me, this media world is a physical part of my environment, surrounding me in the neighborhood in which my work is based, in the middle of New York City, which proudly calls itself the media capital of the world. From where I sit, literally, it is clear that market forces are the driving forces. Times Square, where my company Globalvision is located, was once known for shows, sleaze and sex. For nearly a century, it has been the 'Great White Way' with its bright lights and titillating attractions. But much of that has been transformed as overt sleaze gave way to a more corporatised surreality with big media companies at its heart.

Just outside the window from our Times Square office, investment banker Morgan Stanley's giant billboard pulsates around the clock, and like the city that never sleeps, it electronically chronicles every important trade, deal and currency fluctuation in the world. It is a scorecard of the world's winners and losers, offering Dow Jones news, Reuter's financial information and Bloomberg bulletins. Stare at it for more than a few minutes, and it is dizzying. Its function is to impress, not to inform, and to project financial power and media brands. Its presence underscores how the world has changed, ticking off the winners and losers of globalisation in digits on a moving screen. There are no human faces, no sense of the social and economic consequences behind a blinking parade of endless deals and developments.

Then, as you look around from one building to another, the glue attaching big media to big business becomes apparent. Just a block away, down the street, Rupert Murdoch commands his Orwellian News Corp and rightist Fox News Channel. Down the street, Viacom, home of MTV, VH-1, Nickelodeon and now CBS, once considered the 'Tiffany Network', stares across the Square at the tower of the German conglomerate Bertelsmann and the studio of ABC's Good Morning America. The new Reuters Tower went up diagonally opposite the new Disney building, next door to the World Wrestling Federation studio, and in clear view of NASDAQ's showplace. NASDAQ is the technology stock exchange but it is a virtual operation with no trading floor, just banks of computers; this location was added to 'brand' the company and to make it appear to be a real exchange. To do that the company built a TV studio in front of a bank of high tech TV monitors so that reporters could use it as the backdrop or set for their stand-ups, making it appear that NASDAQ is a real place.

Scholars who write tomes about media concentration need only distribute a map of this ten-block area to illustrate what it physically looks like. Here, also, tourists and those who have come to hustle them can get their news fix in the form of a headline hit parade from three different sources but all with the same stories. They can stand in the street and become mesmerised by ABC's multi-coloured 'bulletin board', the original *New York Times* 'zipper' now run by Dow Jones or on the giant NBC Panasonic TV screen a few yards to the right. There it is, the hour by hour digest of what these companies think we should know, all compressed into a few words and punchy phrases. For a few seconds, you feel part of a larger world, its chaos and its celebrities, but actually the media distances us from the real world

Taken together, this media mecca is not about educating citizens about the world, but informing us of media's dominant place in it. It is an obscene display of the iconography of media presence and impact. The real message of this media environment is that consumption, not citizenship, is what matters. The physical proximity of financial trading rooms and World Wrestling Federation restaurants, ads for news companies next to slogans about 'Being Bullish' is quite blatantly a commercial for how ever-expanding media *octopi* serve certain economic interests. It is not surprising that there are now at least five channels focused on business and market watches but there is none focused on labour.

The global economy relies on the marketing reach of globalised media, with many of its finely tuned components closely interconnected. When technology stocks collapsed in the fall of 2000, other parts of the economy went into a tailspin. Media companies began to lay off hundreds and thousands of employees to placate a nervous Wall Street that views cost-cutting as a sign of smart management and on the road to reviving the stock price. By mid June 2001, it was announced that as many as 100,000 jobs have been lost in the media sector. Has this had any effect on the quality of what they are producing and selling?

The Unthinkable: Empty Billboards

As I write, in the winter of 2003, the unthinkable has come to Times Square. Billboards that once demanded two-million-dollar-a-year rentals go begging. They have become advertisements for themselves and the reality of economic decline, just white blotches like some conceptual art piece.

A knowing anthropologist from another planet or culture studying these signs and symbols as hieroglyphics would understand a great deal about forces shaping modern America. For starters, they would see the centrality of media in stoking our global commercial culture. It is only by analysing the coverage on a daily basis that one spots the patterns and formulae that offer cultural insights. Our hypothetical 'outside expert' might recognise that what often looks like information for the masses is really there to serve the upper classes in the sense that the needs of ordinary people are focused on far less in the media than the conflicts and achievements of the people at the top of the pecking order, in the highest circles of economic, political or celebrity 'power'. Our imagined onlooker would also be able to note the visibility and endless promotion of media 'brands' that are far more alike than they are distinctive.

They would also recognise the effects of the ideology the media have fostered, even if many on the left and the right do not fully appreciate its full impact in depoliticising public awareness, or the primacy of challenging its power. The right has made influencing media a priority, opting to take it over rather than just criticise it. Many on the left do not deal with media much at all, as if exposure represents a form of contamination. How many among us say proudly 'I don't watch TV' as a gesture of personal protest? Yet such a unilateral cultural withdrawal often cuts progressives off from understanding the ideas and information that shape the consciousness of many, especially younger, people. As a result, a gap grows between media users and media critics. It is also sadly true that philanthropists of the right like the Scaife Foundation and many others put media at the top of their funding agendas while more liberal philanthropists, who are often better endowed, (ie richer) leave media funding for last, if it is on the list at all.

Media Degrades Democracy

Media in the United States operate under the constitutional sanction of the First Amendment, because a free press was viewed by the founding fathers as critical to informing the public. However, contemporary media often misinform, degrading democracy rather than enhancing it. They promote their own interests, and the business system of which they are a part, over culture and the public interest. Some media companies become billion dollar businesses with disproportionate, often monopoly, power thanks to mergers and acquisitions. This has led to unprecedented consolidation and concentration of ownership in fewer and fewer hands. It has spawned a web of strategic alliances of collaboration between nominal competitors who clone each other's programming concepts.

As commercial media expand, infiltrating into every corner of life, public service media imitate their formula for survival by joining in the dumbing-down of content while compromising their own mandates and public interest purpose. In some instances, public media become more conservative than their commercial counterparts because they become establishment-centred bureaucracies rather than gutsy watchdogs of the abuse of power. Bottom-line pressures impact on every side while the hyper-competitiveness for ratings and branding leads to the splintering of the audience into smaller and smaller demographically fragmented niches. At the same time, deeper economic system failures limit advertising revenues for commercial media as well as state subsidies for public ones.

As a result, media outlets we depend on to report on a world in crisis are themselves in crisis. Entertainment values have not only corroded news presentation but have led to a genre of 'reality programming' driven by sensationalism, while pandering to the lowest common denominator. These trends make media manipulation easier as television becomes a weapon of both mass distraction and misinformation. Broadcasters are forced to cut back on international coverage and tend to abandon more costly in-depth or investigative news projects and programs.

A Critical Stance

I have been watching, experiencing and writing about all of this as a media maker cum media critic who is convinced that the media's role in world conflicts and crises is central to understanding them. Marshall McLuhan observed how oddly media surround us yet remain invisible to us, even as they narrow issues and limit information. Yet their power and role is mostly ignored in public debate. Media rarely call attention to their own role. And yet, the media's impact in all of our crises are at once total and at the same time, elusive. As someone who has worked as a print journalist, radio newscaster, local TV reporter, talk show presenter and producer with CNN and ABC News, I came to realise that the media need to be understood more deeply, to be dissected, in order to be challenged.

As the news biz fuses with show biz in the United States, ideological biases are now built into the very structure of media presentation, as hard edge formula driven discussion programs become 'shout shows' that increasingly resemble wrestling matches. (Wrestling, a form of violent entertainment often staged to simulate a sporting event, is the most popular programme format on US cable television). Heat, not light, drives formats that thrive on offering a clash of extremes with polished sound bite specialists hurling often simplistic arguments, not information, at each other. No participant in this theatrical spectacle really listens to the other. There isn't time.

This point was driven home by former US government official Ned Walker, now head of the Middle East Institute, who noted his own experience in trying to explain the underlying context of the Israeli-Palestinian crisis:

> We deal with media quite differently than anybody else in the world does. It is a whole different culture. Our system is not geared towards thoughtful debate. If I go on Canadian television I can have half an hour of discussion in which I can speak in sentences, and actually paragraphs, and talk about the issue. But if I talk at Fox News [a

national television network] I've got three catch phrases that I can get out there, if I'm lucky. That's the fundamental difference between our folks and the Canadians, the British and many European countries. (Hishmeh, 2003).

When You Enter the Media World, It Enters You

I've spent half a lifetime chasing stories about problems all around the world, running up impressive frequent flyer tallies along the way. As a writer and a TV producer, I tried to use all types of media outlets to reach audiences with news and information that was not readily available. In that work, I tried to fuse the concerns in my head with the passions of my heart. I was fortunate to be on the front lines of many stories of international interest. Sometimes that work took me to faraway places. In many instances, I found myself with unique access to newsmakers and breaking stories. I soon recognised that a deeper problem was much closer to home. It was the problem of how to get real news of the world into a media system that was increasingly shutting it out. As reporting and producing such stories quickly became easier, disseminating them became more difficult. Thanks to new technologies, a new means of digital production became affordable, but the means of unsanitised and uncensored distribution was not.

I came to see that one major source of 'my' problems and our political culture was right next door. And, as a media maker and critic, I was part of it. The media world I had joined surrounded me physically, psychologically and metaphorically. For years it was a world I identified with, living and working within, first as an 'underground' alternative journalist, then as an employee at big media outlets and later in an independent media company. All along I remained a compulsive media consumer, reader and viewer. I made media and it often felt like I 'ate' media, consuming endless amounts of it. This intellectual diet nourished my curiosity and fed my need to know. But like many people aware of how news is collected or even 'manufactured', to borrow the analysis put forth by Chomsky and Herman in their classic analysis *Manufacturing Consent* (1988), that diet became less filling as I became more conscious of its limits and more critical of its unspoken agendas.

I began spending less and less time producing for media and more time writing about insidious media trends of all kinds. Not surprisingly I soon found my own life and work impacted by them. It is often true that when you enter any profession, its values and outlook enter you. This is certainly true of the media world. As you take on its assumptions, logic and culture, you begin to reflect its worldviews.

I began to shift my own career from a producer of programming *for* this media system into more and more of an analyst *of* this media system. I became an outsider turned insider who was, decades later, back on the outside. I had joined the media to spotlight the problems of the world and realised that I was unintentionally contributing to one of them. I made the media more of a subject for personal scrutiny and an arena for activism. My first book, *The More*

You Watch, the Less You Know (1998), chronicled my experiences and offered a from-the-trenches view of a TV system which give viewers the illusion of choice inside a texture of sameness, a smorgasbord of formularised programming and predictable formats.

At first I fancied myself a defector and network refugee turned radical critic. I soon discovered that the library of media-critical books is voluminous. The shelves of journalism books are filled with the recollections of media mandarins with stories of this or that company's betrayal of journalistic tradition. Many express views in their memoirs that they conceal in their work.

I was especially surprised that on the day my book came out, Walter Cronkite, once the 'great god of American News', and a TV anchorman who always struck me as the paragon of the establishment, gave a speech at a convention of Radio and Television News Directors Association that was a direct attack on corporate media that made me sound quite moderate! It was clear then that just publishing jeremiads against the media was not enough. The industry was getting worse despite all the slings and arrows fired its way, from Hollywood films like *Network* to Broadway plays and critical essays. Words alone would not slay this beast, if it could be slain at all. Action of some kind and organising was what was needed.

Hundreds of organisations and thousands of individuals are engaged with these issues. Some are online. But they don't necessarily know about each other, or how to connect, or how to best use the Internet to promote their work. Until now, there has been no one place to turn, no easy-to-access credible source of diverse perspectives that brings together media news, criticism, education, arts, and proposals for enhanced citizen involvement. There has been no way for groups promoting socially responsible media practices to interact globally.

Challenging the Media Order

That's part of the reason why my colleagues and I set out to respond to this crisis with an online network and website called the MediaChannel (www.mediachannel.org). It grew out of a debate that has been raging for many years within a growing international community of independent media makers, editors, producers, academics and activists who are fighting for a more democratic and socially responsible public service-oriented media. We/they believe that challenging our increasingly monopolised media system is essential to promoting change in the world.

Increasingly, media concerns are rising to the level of a global social issue as opposition movements and activists realise that media attention for their concerns is crucial. At the same, time it is clear to many that the media system itself often stands in the way of change and is no longer, if ever was, a neutral force mediating between challengers and defenders for the status quo.

Enter the MediaChannel

I opted for fighting fire with fire, by creating a MediaChannel to monitor all the other channels, to focus on covering media just as it covers and miscovers so many aspects of news and pop culture. Envisioning such a channel is far easier than launching one. At first I wanted to produce it for television, but it quickly became clear that a media channel on cable television would be unaffordable, and even if it wasn't impossible to create, getting on the air at all would be hardly assured, even if you had the money. (Launching a cable channel these days costs in the neighbourhood of $100 million.) Carriage would also be a long shot given how few companies control access to cable TV, and how closed it is, for the most part, to controversial content. No media corporation would likely carry it.

If television was out, what was in? Access to radio was also shrinking. That left, happily, the Internet, where the cost of entry is far lower but where many other problems present themselves. Creating a web site is easy but the type of site I envisioned would have to be more ambitious. We needed one that would allow us to network with groups worldwide who work on media issues. We opted to create a supersite or what is known in the 'internet space' as a portal that can offer diverse content from many sources.

Since our idea was contrarian to the core, our methodology had to be as well. At the outside, we decided to go dot.org, not dot.com, to make MediaChannel a public interest not-for-profit site as opposed to a commercial enterprise. Then, in 1999, we were considered foolish for even thinking that way because it seemed as if every kid out of business school was being showered by Wall Street with fifty-million dollar initial public offerings (IPO) for every imaginable Internet scheme. Many of these later crashed and burned because business cycles could not and would not be abolished by false projections and phoney business plans.

We opted for a web site structure that could aggregate input from affiliated organisations, as well as feature original content, including the columns featured in this collection. MediaChannel.org was what we ended up with. It soon became a hybrid: a newspaper, magazine, interactive chat room, resource center and network all in one. We decided to offer a blend of media news, opinion, personal accounts, research studies, activist reports, arts coverage and debates about the nature of the media system and how it might be changed. Resources include thematic special reports, action toolkits, forums for discussion, an indexed directory of hundreds of affiliated groups and a search engine constituting the single largest online media-issues database. We concerned ourselves with the political, cultural and social impacts of the media, large and small. MediaChannel exists to provide information and diverse perspectives and inspire debate, collaboration, action and citizen engagement.

We affiliated with the already well-established One World online network in Britain (www.oneworld.net) that focuses on environment, development and human rights so that we didn't have to reinvent the wheel technologically and could keep our costs down. One World provided us with its software templates so that we could quickly get up and running. It also provided us with a global distribution platform. In turn, we based our servers in England, immediately making it an international project. We soon discovered on our own what has worked so well for so many larger media companies: the economic benefits of being synergistic.

It should be noted that our web 'architecture' is built around a proprietary database driven 'cold fusion' system in contrast to the open source technology adopted by many other alternative websites like indymedia.org, which offer up a more user friendly system where every reader can be a reporter, usually without any editing or adherence to journalistic codes. The newer systems permit more spontaneity, its advocates say, and more interactivity.

Our systems are clunkier but when one writes about media and for media, one has to try to ensure accuracy and perhaps that restrains more anarchistic interventions. In that respect, our site was forced to be more conservative in look and feel but not necessarily in content. The other aspect of all this is that we had to be conscious of the technology available to the user. Not every computer, especially in the developing world, can receive the latest state-of-the-art graphics and multimedia that may look good but take a long time to load. What's cool in New York may not be accessible in Bangladesh.

Going Global

For us, the Internet offered the type of distribution platform that independent producers yearn for: relatively free and unfettered transmission worldwide. For Globalvision, this was a way of realising our goal of globalising content and reaching audiences in other continents.

We had always considered the media issue, like so many issues, as an international one. But before the Internet came along, there were few ways small companies could report on it in those terms in a timely fashion. We were hardly the only media company to recognise in our interdependent globalised world that the idea of 'foreign news' was obsolete. CNN very early in its existence banned the word 'foreign' and replaced it with 'international'. The new world order demanded such an international approach.

As we began to move into the web, new global media companies were already there and consolidating in the global marketplace put in place by globalisation. Their self-styled 'New Economy' was built on three pillars: global trade, global capital markets, and global communications. All three are interconnected although, to many activists battling this trend, the critical focus falls only on global trade agreements and occasionally on companies like Nike or Shell Oil. It seemed as if the activist movements were unaware of the crucial role played by global media conglomerates in promoting the ideology of globalisation, and advancing the interests behind it. Magazines like *Forbes* were not shy about calling themselves a 'capitalist tool' but others were less explicit about their function and priorities, hiding behind clever slogans and populist advertising. For example, for many years, MTV claimed to be leading the youth revolution, although cultural commentators like writer Tom Frank of a small but influential magazine called *The Baffler* (www.thebaffler.com) and others have explained how MTV's corporate marketing co-opts and perverts radical impulses among youth.

As the media globalises, exposing and critiquing the media system in global terms is essential. If a global movement is to be built to challenge its impact, as in 'globalisation from below' taking on 'globalisation from above', (or in journalist Jeremy Brecher's words, the global village resisting global pillage), we need to hear from and learn about the experience of others in countries that are usually outside the US media discourse.

Of course many other countries still offer more diversity in their media outlets than the US outlets do, in part because of well funded public service broadcasters like the BBC who still promote a culture of quality programming and have the budgets to sustain it. We in the United States must learn a thing or two from the best practices and examples of broadcasters and journalists elsewhere. Coverage of global media trends can help fertilise activism in the United States as well. It is always an uphill battle to get people to fight for better media if they have never experienced it – or realised what better media is or could be. The MediaChannel.org set out to share this type of global media information, and connect journalists and activists worldwide.

MediaChannel: How We Created the Site

New projects require investment of funds and energy. They are expensive to launch and operate, although the costs of doing business on the web are lower than in traditional old media. For obvious reasons, not-for-profit ventures are rarely attractive to investors. Where would the money come from?

Without a funding base of readers to appeal to, which radical publications like the *Nation* or *Monthly Review* have, we had to put our hopes and our fate in the hands of foundations. We were well aware of how easy it is for those of us who want to be independent to quickly become dependent on their largesse. Going this route is hardly assured-or sustaining over time. Fortunately, perhaps because of our 14-year track record as recipients of foundation grants ('beggers in suits', we called ourselves) we were able to unlock generous support to get up and going from the Rockefeller Foundation, Open Society Institute, Arca, Reebok Human Rights Foundation, Puffin Foundation, and most recently the Ford Foundation. Behind each of those commitments were months of proposal writing, follow-up calls, meetings, and more meetings.

You never know how much work goes into raising money until you try it. Of course if you are well endowed to begin with and can invest in fundraising and development staff, generating support can become easier and more routine. When you don't, it's much harder. The sad truth is, 'those that have, tend to get'. You quickly learn that fundraising itself is a business. Working at it takes time – time taken away from other priorities. I am a journalist who wants to be writing and producing, not soliciting. And yet, in projects such as the MediaChannel, everyone becomes a de facto part of the fundraising effort.

Most news organisations separate all business and editorial functions. They pride themselves on the 'wall' separating the two functions. When that wall is breached, editorial compromises invariably follow. So in principle, one would prefer not to mix the two. Yet, small companies cannot often afford the infrastructure that permits a complete separation. I soon had to put my 'funding hat' on.

The good news is that we were successful in the first round of foundation grant seeking and, contradictions be damned, let us praise the great robber barons of an earlier time for their craftiness and generosity! That old monopolist and protagonist of the workers, John D. Rockefeller might be twisting six feet under if he were to learn how his fortune is being dispensed. The bad news is that no one foundation ever gives you what you really need. That forces you to reach out to many different sources to get enough in the bank to fund a budget, hire staff and pay the bills. Also, alas, you usually can count on support for only one year at a time. It is easy to see how the need to keep the money pump going then twists priorities and the allocation of staff time and resources.

I know I am not the only one with this complaint. An old buddy of mine, now a member of Congress, tells me that every day he is forced to spend hours fundraising. 'Dialing for dollars,' he calls it. We all know about how obsessive money raising distorts our political system. Well, here in the wonderful world of Indy media, we have similar problems.

The foundations know this too – which is why they have increasingly taken on the trappings of venture capital funds. Maybe it's the market logic of our times seeping into every crevice of public life, but most now insist their grantees become more business like. Also, many funding organisations willing to give you money don't really want to have you knocking on their doors again and again. So they insist they you come up with real business plans to avoid over-dependence on their support. They quiz you with questions that quickly come to resemble the Spanish inquisition, about how you are going to start capitalising your own venture. Suddenly, noble proposals and sometimes fuzzy or politically oriented ideas (ie. 'We want to raise consciousness' and promote revolution) are being evaluated through the hard lens of monetisation.

Their message is this: If you want to stay in business, you have to be business like and operate in a way that can sustain the business. Decentralised affinity-grouplike structures do not impress them. Process is more important than product as is common in parts of the NGO world.

The MediaChannel Strategy

Globalvision was already a business, and was run like one. If we weren't, we couldn't have survived over fifteen years while producing programmes not considered commercially viable. My own experiences in the movements of the sixties convinced me that only this type of structure could sustain a media venture like ours over so many years. We have shaped the MediaChannel as a public-private partnership, or in the words of Jonathan Peizer, the thoughtful technology chief of the Open Society Institute, a dot.corg, an .org.com fusion between our mission oriented non-profit work and business strategy.

Luckily, we found progressive investors for our new media company in Europe where there is more openness to projects critical of US dominated media culture. Those investors brought in, first as an advisor, and then as the chairman of our board, James R. Rosenfield, the former president of CBS. Soon Walter Cronkite was invited to join us as an advisor along with other respected media personas. The investors recognised that aggregating content and affiliates could help legitimise the company's commercial plans for a new global news syndication service and provide a base for further potential collaborations. They put their money where their convictions were. They wanted to do well financially, and they also wanted to provide a good service. The investors introduced more business like approaches, which we hope will lead to a better chance for survival.

Should You Take Corporate Money?

After considerable debate, we decided to try to reach out for corporate underwriters based on the understanding once attributed to the American bank robber Willy Sutton. When asked why he robbed banks, Sutton simply said, 'That's where the money is.' The corporate world is where the money is today and we decided to see if we could attract someone in the corporate world without compromising our mission. We were very mindful of the risks and dangers of moving in this direction. All one has to do is look at American public broadcasting to see how a reliance on corporate underwriters seemed partially responsible for keeping PBS so bland and tepid. At the same time we realised that there are companies who profess social responsibility in their mission who might be supportive. We were of course insistent on ensuring our editorial independence.

As a result of our outreach, one leading transnational corporation is already on board and others are in discussions with us. Many have public relations departments led by former journalists who are supportive of our critique and want to help. We realised that many companies want to reach the opinion leaders in the audience we are developing. In addition, we are working on a number of revenue producing modules of services that we intend to introduce.

This is all part of trying to generate a multiplicity of revenue streams. The MediaChannel sought to appeal to a variety of audiences and our hope was to attract support from a variety of sources. Are there potential contradictions and a minefield of possible conflicts with this approach? You bet. But what's the alternative? Where will the money for independent media come from? Ultimately, our supporters have to bank on our integrity.

The Mandate and Method to Building a Network of Affiliates

We then tested our idea by inviting media-related organisations to join as affiliates. Affiliates have no obligations but permit us to offer their content on the MediaChannel site. This is done via technology so that readers and users can, with a simple click of a mouse, visit the affiliate site and become familiar with what they do and have to say.

We started with 50 affiliated groups. By June 2001, we topped 700 affiliates, making MediaChannel the largest online media issues network in the world. (*Monthly Review* is an affiliate, along with *The Nation*, *Mother Jones*, *In These Times* and many other progressive organisations and their counterparts in other countries.) By December 2002, we were up to 1,034 affiliates.

Some of these affiliates simply saw us as another distribution platform for their web sites; others participated more actively. The public soon responded, with an average of 3.5 million hits a month. A survey we sent out received an eighteen per cent response and results showed that we are reaching a diverse audience, with half outside the United States. We confirmed that a substantial number work for media companies, study or teach the subject.

At the same time a large portion of the readers who come back day after day and week after week – we redo the whole page weekly on Wednesdays but update news and features during the week – are a cross section of web users of all ages and backgrounds who hear about us in the press or through links on other sites. The site is growing. More affiliates join weekly. It is working. With marketing and more outreach we hope to build an even bigger network and audience.

Why are they coming? We would like to think because MediaChannel positioned itself with a broad multi-pronged mandate offering a wide menu of content and services including news, information and opinion about the cultural, political and social impact of global media, including print, broadcast, film, video, music, the Web, and independent media.

Our goal is to engage and inspire citizen involvement by providing a professionally designed and accessible online forum for debate and discussion of the key issues regarding the media, as well as posting action alerts for events sponsored by affiliated sites. We sought to foster an online community that encourages individual engagement in media issues on a global scale.

To encourage visits, we offer a wide range of resources:

- A JOURNALISTS' TOOLKIT: created for journalism classes or school newspaper projects, also provides online writing and research tips valuable for any student.

- GLOBAL NEWS INDEX: links to hundreds of local newspapers worldwide, organised by region and country.

- AFFILIATE DIRECTORY: the index to MediaChannel's global network of organisations and publications.

- BOOK CORNER: find books for journalism, media studies, communication or cultural studies curricula, with excerpts, reviews and quick links to buy (purchases support MediaChannel).

The MediaChannel Mission

The MediaChannel has focused its mission around four key challenges: the challenge to understand what is happening in the media today, how those changes are impacting our politics and inspiring resistance, the role and impact of media and new forms of independent media activism, and finally the relationship of the 'media question' and media activism in a larger political context. What is all of this independent media energy, on line and off, contributing to oppositional politics in an age of globalisation?

There are four principal issues or questions that the MediaChannel explores:

1   What is happening within the media today? What are the 'economic pressures' driving media decision-makers? What are the results of growing concentration of ownership?

2   What is the nature of the media debate? Who is fighting whom over what? How does the public relate to media issues? And which group or groups are contesting these issues? How does this play out in society? What forms of activism are emerging?

3   What is the alternative media today and what impact do they have? Do the alternative media- NGOs, websites, independent radio, etc – provide a real alternative to mainstream media? What opportunities are there for them, and what obstacles? What role does the Internet play?

4   How do developments in the new media activism relate to a larger political context? What does an alternative media culture have to contribute to radical politics today?

There is no one set of politically correct answers to these questions. Instead, there is a struggle for independent media to remain vital while sustaining themselves financially, for new forms of media to grow and old forms to be renewed and for new generations to develop communication skills and forge new platforms of expression. All of this is playing itself out in exciting ways in countries on every continent, confronting different types of obstacles ranging from traditional government censorship to new high-tech surveillance and filtering; from terror and repression aimed at courageous journalists to corporate pressures and self-censorship imposed in subtle and not-so-subtle ways.

These are the issues that the MediaChannel seeks to explore on a daily and weekly basis. They are also the subjects for debate in our interactive forum and web logs and what I write about in a weekly column drawn from my own research, experience, reporting assignments and interactions with media insiders at conferences or media events. They are longer than most newspaper columns and tend to be topical with an analytical bite.

Defining MediaChannel's Issues

If you turn on a television set, radio or, in many instances, open a newspaper in the United States you can find problems to which MediaChannel and its affiliates propose solutions. These include media mergers; the 'dumbing down' of news; the global expansion of media cartels promoting the same formats and formulas worldwide; the media landscape changed by emerging technologies, like digital delivery and the Web. What are the implications for journalism? For democracy? Where can we find real news about what's happening in and to the media globally? How can we encourage media consumers to sharpen critical skills, discuss and debate news coverage and promote media accountability and reform? How can we connect those concerned about improving and renewing the media with one another, across borders, so they can work together more effectively?

There are fewer than ten transnational conglomerates dominating Western broadcasting systems, with only twenty major companies effectively running the majority of our newspapers, magazines, Web portals, film studios, radio stations and book publishers. With market values firmly in command in Western media, influencing changes in the developing world, we are witnessing the commercialisation of public space, which is a crisis for independent journalism, the denigration of public service ideas and the weakening of our political culture.

While these issues are most acutely felt in the United States, the 'American media model' is now influencing broadcasters and news companies worldwide. Across the globe, public service broadcasting is being cut back and diverse media sources are at risk. The media system has gone from being seen as the salvation of democracy to a global problem that threatens democracy. In many countries, the media arena has become a stage for contest, conflict and debate. How can we inform the public at large about what's happening in the media world and why they should care about it? Where can we even talk about these issues since the media itself rarely puts itself under the scrutiny it reserves for others?

MediaChannel has sought to become a response to the homogenising pressures of globalisation in which giant transnational corporations spread their tentacles from above, prompting a desire for more networking and resistance from below. The global Internet technology makes possible an instant form of interaction across borders and boundaries. And while it has not yet penetrated into every village in the developing world, it has been widely adopted by media organisations in virtually every country. It is the fastest growing technology in the history of the world, with its own set of problems and limits. And just as it is used by the dominant corporate world to market its dreams and products, it is also being used by organisers of every ideological stripe to build new structures for communication and resistance.

My Role and the Column

As I mentioned earlier, one of my contributions to the MediaChannel is a daily column, writing a weblog under a media *nom d'guerre*, 'The News Dissector.' In some ways, that is how I have chosen to brand myself as a wannabe media personality, affixing that catchy nickname to raise my recognition factor when I was an on-air newscaster on a Boston radio station for a decade. It is also part of who I am. Unlike many more sober traditional progressives who write in more mainstream academic or journalistic styles, I have always opted to inject more personality, punch and subjectivity into my work. I guess that's what I learned back in the insurgent sixties from my one-time political running mate Abbie Hoffman, who realised that in a culture dominated by personalities, it didn't hurt to become one, especially if you want a megaphone. His Marx was Groucho; his Lennon was John.

I know this approach may be dismissed as an ego trip by some, or somehow regarded as being less than 'serious', because folks on the left, by training, often have academic orientations where 'objectivity' is more highly prized to more stylised and subjective writing. I have always found, here in the United States, that by personalising feelings and analysis, one can be more effective. Humourlessness was part of how the old left isolated and marginalised itself. I think one can write in a personal way without being regarded as a simplistic 'diarist' or pedantic diatribist. I deliberately try to write a column that ranges from examining single issues in depth and reporting on events for and about the media.

I am a big believer in 'participatory journalism', a journalism of involvement. In my case, my status as a media veteran, having 'been there and done that' as a reporter, news director and producer in commercial media qualifies me, I hope, to comment knowledgeably and credibly on media developments. Reporting on personal confrontations with media moguls and conversations with media makers, in my view, enhances that credibility and makes the writing livelier.

The MediaChannel has permitted me to fuse personal values with a political mission, to use my skills as a journalist to try to improve journalism. Sure it is an uphill struggle but it is one worth attempting, and my hope is that some of the spirit of our work will rub off, to illuminate what's wrong and inspire what's right.

References:

Brecher, J., T. Costello and B. Smith (2000) *Globalisation from Below*. Boston: South End Press.

Chomsky, N. and E. Herman (1988) *Manufacturing Consent*. New York: Pantheon.

Hishmeh, G. (2003, January 24) 'Warheads and the media', Arabic Media Internet Network, http://www.amin.org/eng/george_hishmeh/2003/jan24.html.

Schechter, D. (2000) *Mediaocracy*. Germany: Inovatio Books.

Schechter, D., J. Brown and R. McChesney (1998) *The More You Watch, The Less You Know*. New York: Seven Stories Press.

Chapter 14
Reporting the World: The Ethical Challenge to International News
Jake Lynch

In Chapter Nine, Calcutt discussed 'journalism of attachment', born largely of (BBC correspondent turned MP) Martin Bell's refusal to treat the horrors of the violent break-up of Yugoslavia with the 'distance' proscribed by Anglo-US reporting traditions. These were born a century ago, as Michael Schudson reminds us in his book, The Sociology of News *(2003), to simplify the editorial process and to rid journalism of analysis which could alienate the increasingly valued mass audience. Like Mark Brayne, writing in the next chapter, Lynch leverages his experience as a journalist with major media outlets to rally professional colleagues toward a new journalism — one which confronts the journalist's own role in international conflict and prescribes specific, novel, strategies to use the power of the pen to ethical ends when reporting conflict. Some of the strategies, like the contextualisation of international developments, are hardly new, but as Philo powerfully demonstrates in Chapter 11, for many journalists they remain innovative.*

In an age of galloping commercialisation, many journalists are concerned about standards and ethics and whether readers and audiences are being equipped to make sense of our interdependent world. Since September 11, 2001, they have felt a renewed sense of urgency and vindication. Newspapers and broadcasters alike are accused of retreating from 'serious news' — what award-winning film-maker Damien Lewis called 'real coverage that is meaningful and that works'.

In response to this, and with funding from the UK Department for International Development, I started a project called 'Reporting the World'. The main job of Reporting the World is to bring journalists together and create an opportunity for them to discuss and define minimum standards for themselves, and practical ways to apply the best of their traditions and values in a modern setting. In the process, it is intended to enable us to be much more specific about what is meaningful and what works; about what we are trying to defend against a rising tide of news-lite, news-you-can-use, celebrity gossip and the 'animal du jour'.

Secondly, it addresses the new issues of media ethics. Traditionally, ethics simply meant straight dealing – accuracy; fairness in representing people's views; not taking bribes and so on. The Cable News Network's (CNN) influence effectively made it, as former United Nations Secretary General Boutros Boutros-Ghali famously said, 'the sixth permanent member of the Security Council (Strobel, 1998)'.

Plenty of writers since then have dismissed the unsettling thought that news organisations, however mighty, have the power to procure responses from policy makers as they see fit. While some research suggests there is little substance to a CNN effect, it has not proven difficult to examine particular instances where policy changes have been attributed to the impact of headline reports, and establish that a shift was already well underway, or being planned, by the time the reports appeared. But this does not altogether explain modern conditions at the news face, as encountered by senior editors, reporters and producers who have covered the big international conflicts of the last few years. The Reporting the World project has marshalled this wealth of collective experience in a series of debates which have pointed out the need to revise some of journalists' cardinal working assumptions.

Ethics of Conviction or Ethics of Responsibility?

Bob Jobbins, then head of news at the BBC World Service, was one who joined our discussions. At our first seminar, about coverage of the Arab-Israeli conflict, he said: 'Conflict resolution is something on which I report, not something in which I engage. A side-effect of my reporting may be that it makes conflict resolution harder or easier, but that's a judgment that is made after our reporting.'

This fits fine with traditional concepts of ethics. Jobbins, like many journalists, dedicated his career to uncovering the truth, reporting the facts 'without fear or favor'; to presenting the world, as Walter Cronkite used to say to American TV audiences every night, 'the way it is'. It's a journalist's version of what Max Weber, one of the founding fathers of social science, called an ethic of conviction.

Reporting the World picks up on the growing perception among journalists themselves that, whatever we think of claims and counter-claims about the CNN effect, something else is required – a workable ethic of responsibility. It's based on the post-modern understanding that discursive practices, like news, play a part in the social construction of reality. How? The jobs of commissioning, editing, producing and reporting involve choices; choices of which facts to include and which to leave out, how to juxtapose images and what contextual material to provide. These choices combine, over time, into discernible patterns, which exert a cumulative influence over the course of subsequent events.

Conflict Analysis

The third strand of Reporting the World is to introduce news professionals to the insights of Conflict Analysis, or Peace Research, and to development perspectives on world affairs.

Pioneered as a fieldwork method and academic subject over the last forty years, Peace Research is a quintessential discourse of the post-modern condition. Crucially, knowing about the dynamics of conflict enables journalists to predict and trace, in advance, the likely impact of particular patterns of coverage. We inhabit a media-savvy world, in which many people besides journalists are familiar with this game of consequences. Our environment, the very space in which we live and breathe, has become saturated with information. News is there when we pick up emails, receive text messages on the mobile phone, wait in airport departure lounges or simply walk along the street.

It means there is a widespread and profound understanding of how news works. Actors in news stories, from corporate spin doctors, through apparently unsophisticated militias in poor countries, to members of the public, turn out to be media-savvy. They know how to provide facts for journalists to report.

Think of Ali Ahmeti, leader of the National Liberation Army (NLA), the armed ethnic Albanian group in Macedonia which burst on the scene, apparently out of nowhere, early in 2001, with what members characterised as a struggle for greater minority rights. Mr. Ahmeti was asked on BBC television, in July of that year, what he and his group had gained by taking up the gun. 'The whole of Europe now knows about our situation,' he replied.

Think of contestants on reality TV game shows, re-inventing themselves as outrageous, larger-than-life 'personalities', saleable to the popular press with their colourful 'private' lives. The practical implications of operating in these conditions – trying, as journalists do, to report the facts – form a key part of our discussion.

The Feedback Loop

The effect is perhaps most familiar when dealing with 'official sources'. In the age of spin, every government policy, for instance, comes with a built-in media strategy. Calculations about the way it is likely to be reported can affect not just the presentation of the policy but the policy itself.

And this is just the most sophisticated and highly-organised version. Large numbers of people prove capable, once the media spotlight is upon them, of being their own spin-doctors. From international conflicts, through

Westminster and Washington politics to showbiz sex romps, there is no way for journalists to know that what they are seeing or hearing would be happening in the same way – if at all – if no one ever thought journalists would cover it.

A crucial question – how can any of these people know what to do, in order to be reported in a way they imagine will bring them fame, fortune or political gain? Only from the expertise or instinct accrued through long experience as consumers in a world saturated with information. (Politicians, notoriously, don't watch TV; they hire people to watch it for them). It means that when reporters report the facts today, they augment the collective understanding of how they and other reporters are likely to respond when presented with similar facts tomorrow.

The NLA, on closer inspection, turned out to be intimately connected with the Kosovo Liberation Army (KLA), in many cases the same people. How could they have gleaned the impression that a small-armed group could command the world's attention, and get journalists to present them as David against Goliath with the prospect of international intervention to follow? The answer, to anyone who remembers coverage of the Kosovo conflict, is obvious.

Entrants to game shows like *Big Brother* or *Castaway* have been reared, remember, on a diet of salacious tabloid 'sexposes' and celebrity lifestyle features. They have seen for themselves how it is possible to parlay one eye-catching episode into repeat exposure, and become 'famous for being famous'. Remember Liz Hurley in *that* dress.

None of this means the facts are inauthentic or not worth reporting. There is no useful distinction between those facts, which arrive 'already mediated' – perhaps, as I argue here, in the service of a media strategy –and 'real' or 'spontaneous' ones. We are not necessarily being cynical or synthetic when we create or present the facts in ways we have picked up from reading, listening or viewing.

The point is, an ever-expanding range of our behaviour and experiences – including our experiences of ourselves – are constructed by narratives we internalise. News is one of the most powerful and important narratives, and its role in constructing events effectively closes the circle of cause and effect between journalists and their sources, which is where the old ethics of conviction gives way to a new ethics of responsibility.

I call this the Feedback Loop, a way of describing the role of news as one among many influences on the complex processes at work in world events. Isolating media strategy – consciously or instinctively pursued – as a measurable factor in those events can be like trying to retrieve a single colour from a tin of mixed paints. But its presence, no matter how diluted, remains visible as part of the blend. The writing is on the wall – every journalist bears, at any time, an unknowable proportion of the responsibility for what happens next.

'Why?'

Throughout Reporting the World we have presented a critique of existing coverage, examined through the prism of the Feedback Loop, to mount an argument for judgments to be formed, not just after but also *before* and *during* the reporting of conflicts, about the likely consequences or 'side-effects' for the prospects of peaceful resolution. Take, for instance, the tendency in so much coverage to confine its attention to direct violence in a narrowly defined conflict arena.

The classic blow-by-blow account is a symptom of reporting in which 'why' questions remain unilluminated. Others would be the attribution of violence in the Middle East or Balkans to 'ancient hatreds' or, in Africa, to 'tribal anarchy'. These are sure signs of an incomplete understanding. Reporters' main job is to tell readers and audiences the who, what, where, when, why and how of what is going on, but a good deal of coverage after September 11, for example – especially, but not only, in the United States – lived down to James W. Carey's complaint that 'the question "why?" is the dark continent of American journalism' (Carey, 1986).

The suicide hijackings which shook the world's media and political capitals caught much of the US media in what Michael Wolff, writing in *New York Magazine*, called a state of 'notionlessness' (Wolff, 2001). The lack of a solid foundation of consistent world affairs coverage had left journalists, readers and audiences to 'identify the villain as some pure spasm of all-powerful, apocalyptic irrationality.'

It is the policy-maker's lament that so many policies have to be made as remedies to problems that crop up, unbidden, in their in-trays. This is what British Prime Minister Harold Macmillan called 'events, dear boy, events'. In the Feedback Loop, as any policy is being formulated, a calculation is underway as to whether and how policy can be credibly presented to the public, via news reports, as a likely solution. This calculation – and, therefore, the policy - depends, in part, on how the problem has been diagnosed in news reports.

Diagnose violence as *autistic* – mad, bad, irrational – and you can more easily accept further violence as the remedy. This is the habitual Washington designation of what drives its enemies – 'motiveless malignity', as Gore Vidal put it in his book reflecting on the hijackings, *The Last Empire* (Vidal, 2001).

The alternative is to diagnose it as part of a strategy – in this case, to dislodge the US-sponsored order in the Middle East, starting with the House of Saud and certainly including the State of Israel. Such a strategy is problematical, and the means with which it is pursued highly dysfunctional; but it does represent an essentially intelligible response to unresolved issues of structural and cultural violence, across a broad conflict formation.

These issues would include the differential effects of the global oil economy, which have seen average Saudi incomes plummet by two-thirds in the years since the 1991 Gulf War and millions impoverished and unemployed across the Islamic world. They would take in political stagnation and repression in Arab states as well as the dispossession of the Palestinians, and they would even extend to the pervasive power of western commercialised popular culture to collapse and displace indigenous culturally constructed norms. Place all this in the context of a thousand-year history of colonialism and subjugation. Examine it like that, and a multi-faceted response, based on fostering political and economic development, to create space for cultural adjustment, comes to seem more realistic.

In the Feedback Loop, these choices in diagnosing the causes of violence condition judgments about the likely reception for policies proposed as remedies. So, EU Commissioner Chris Patten, in an interview with the London *Guardian*, in February 2002, rejected 'targeted bombs' in favor of 'targeted development assistance' (Freeland, 2002).

Linkage

Hairline cracks in the post-September 11 transatlantic alliance began to appear two months after the cataclysm when George W. Bush and Tony Blair held a joint news conference at the White House. A lasting solution to terrorism would require the Arab-Israeli conflict to be resolved, the Prime Minister argued. No, the President said, it wouldn't – nor would there be, by implication, any progress on the rest of Blair's ambitious agenda for global development, first sketched out in his Labour Party conference speech weeks earlier.

In practical terms, for reporters and their editors, linkage of these issues would mean regular coverage of the structural violence of life under occupation – what US Secretary of State Colin Powell, in a speech in November 2001, called the 'indignities' facing Palestinians on a daily basis – as contributing to the conditions for direct violence and the context in which the strategy behind the suicide hijackings came to seem feasible.

This question of how violence is explained, and how the explanation is *constructed* by the choices journalists make while covering and contextualising conflicts, is one of the prime issues of responsibility in international news. This is at the head of a four-point ethical checklist, which we developed out of our discussions about covering particular conflicts, with journalists drawn from all the main newsrooms in London. We break down the first question as follows:

- How does the explanation arise from the way violence is reported?

- Is a report confined to a classic 'blow-by-blow' account of direct violence?

- Or does it also show the impact of structural and cultural violence on the lives of the people involved?

- Does it illuminate the intelligible – if dysfunctional – processes which may be creating the conditions for violence?

- What are we led or left to infer about what should, or is likely to, happen next?

Shape of the Conflict

The second of the four checklist points is about the way a conflict is *shaped* by its presentation in the news:

- Is the conflict framed as a 'tug-of-war' – a zero-sum game of two parties contesting a single goal, so whatever one side wins, the other side loses?

or

- As a 'cat's-cradle' – a pattern of many interdependent parties, with needs and interests which may overlap, or provide scope for integrated solutions?

Journalists and analysts who came to the Reporting the World seminar on coverage of Iraq complained that the story had become 'calcified', as the *Guardian*'s Maggie O'Kane put it. Another, Faleh Abdul Jabbar, an exiled Iraqi author and scholar, elaborated: 'Since the Gulf War there has been an oversimplified conception of the whole conflict, goodies on this side, baddies on that side. The media coverage was caged into this oversimplified framework, the war ended – the cage did not.'

The critical mass of coverage by UK and US media has always framed this conflict as *bipolar* – official London and Washington on one hand, a demonised Saddam on the other. This can be conceived as a question of geometry. Two points can only be joined by one shape – a straight line. So any movement – any change – must take place along this one axis, like a giant geopolitical tug-of-war.

The point is, the way the conflict is shaped, or framed, by news reports affects what we think of as the relevant questions. A front cover of *Newsweek*, in October 2002, was dominated by the heads of Presidents George W. Bush and Saddam Hussein, arranged so as to face each other, against a black background. "Who will win?", the magazine demanded.

This was at the point where the American and British governments were stepping up their efforts to convince their respective publics that Iraq, if left to develop weapons of mass destruction, would pose a direct, authentic threat to the United States and the United Kingdom themselves.

At a keynote speech to trades unionists in mid-September 2002, Blair had given a warning that this threat, if unattended, would some day 'engulf us'. And Bush, addressing supporters at an election rally in New Hampshire in early October, said the threat to America was 'grave and growing' and that Saddam had to be prevented from inflicting 'massive and sudden horror.'

US Defense Secretary Donald Rumsfeld, it was reported, was commissioning intelligence reports from the Pentagon to second-guess the CIA assessments and find evidence of a link between Iraq and the attacks of September 11.

Regional Security

There has never been any suggestion – even from the unnamed 'intelligence sources' which are the usual conduit for officially inspired scare stories – that Iraq possesses, or is about to acquire, long-range ballistic missiles of the kind necessary to project warheads to north-western Europe or the American continent.

One infamous example of these scare stories was about a 'drone aircraft', adapted from its original crop-spraying function, and capable of infecting a whole city with deadly anthrax spores. The plane, an M-18 Dromeda, turned out to have a range of between 250 and 300 miles, which would indicate a need to stop for refuelling several times over en route from Iraq to Britain.

Hence, public opinion has proved fairly impervious to suggestions that Britons or Americans should be scared of Saddam Hussein. After all, they were all brought up on the theory of nuclear deterrence, which has already been put to the test in the Iraqi case, and proved effective.

Think back to 1991. CNN earned its reputation as a de facto member of the UN Security Council by its omnipresence in that year's Gulf War. From being the 'Chicken Noodle Network', suddenly Ted Turner's cameras were everywhere, and one of the places they were was Geneva, for a meeting between US Secretary of State James Baker and Iraq's Deputy Prime Minister Tariq Aziz.

Were there to be any use of unconventional weapons against, for example, American troop concentrations, Baker averred, and 'the consequences will be incalculable.' In case the point was missed, he repeated the phrase – interpreted at the time as a warning that Washington would not stop short of a nuclear response. We know – because the United Nations Special Commission (UNSCOM) inspectors subsequently told us – that Iraq did indeed have germ weapons at its disposal, but it was successfully deterred from using them.

For all these reasons, the case for action on Iraq has often, in the years since 'Operation Desert Storm,' rested instead on the notion of 'regional security'. There are countries that, recent history suggests, do have genuine reasons to fear a potential military threat from Baghdad – namely Iran; Saudi Arabia and the Gulf Cooperation Council states, including Kuwait.

Israel, of course, can also rely on a nuclear deterrent. Another regular on our screens back in 1991 was Binyamin Netanyahu, then defence minister in the government of Yitzhak Shamir. For one of the Scuds falling on Tel Aviv to be tipped with something more sinister than high explosive was a scenario often put to him by interviewers. He would jut that famous jaw and promise, stonily, that in such an eventuality, 'Israel will know how to defend itself.' This was a formulation of deterrent strategy, which was well understood across the region and a response unlikely to cause any qualms to an administration led by Ariel Sharon.

What is striking is how seldom any of these countries' perspectives crops up in news coverage by British or American media. Take just one – Saudi Arabia.

Hardly anyone from Saudi Arabia is ever asked, 'What is your assessment of the Iraqi threat and how would you deal with it?'

Throughout 2002, war drums were beating ever more insistently. Around the middle of the year, there was a sudden quickening of the rhythm, as the trail to senior Taliban and Al-Qa'ida leaders in Afghanistan apparently went cold; the US economy remained hung over from the bubble years of booming stock markets, and crucial mid-term elections loomed. As official Washington began to turn up the volume on Iraq, Tony Blair returned to Britain from his summer break to clamorous demands to clarify his own position.

Clarification duly came in his constituency party offices, in Sedgefield, on September 4. Over the six weeks leading up to this point, an Internet search engine which scans all major UK newspapers reveals that the words, Bush, Iraq and Saddam occurred together in no fewer than 1,413 items.

Of those, 292 included 'Saudi' as well, or just over one in five of the total. Seventy-eight gave at least Saudi Arabia's response to US sabre-rattling, most accounted for by the official statement, on 7 August, from Foreign Minister Prince Saud al Faisal, that the Kingdom would not permit the use of military bases on its territory in support of any invasion.

But only a handful – seven – of these reports elaborated any further. Indeed, the most ambitious attempt to cover the Saudi perspective during this period was not in newspapers at all but on radio – Andrew North's interview with the Prince for *The World at One* on BBC Radio and the BBC news website. Here, finally, was a chance to hear an authoritative Saudi appraisal of the Iraqi threat – a serious one, borne out by the Minister's own experience of a Scud missile landing on his Riyadh home in 1991 – and the Kingdom's view of how best to deal with it.

The return of weapons inspectors, he said, was 'the most important thing' Instead of going to war, 'there [was] a chance for diplomacy to work ... at the Arab summit [in Beirut earlier in 2002] we received a solemn promise from the Iraqis that they will work towards the implementation of Security Council resolutions, and they've promised never to threaten the territorial integrity of Saudi Arabia.' Moreover, they were 'following this up' by talking to the UN.

Exclude countries that might genuinely have something at stake in any Iraqi military 'threat', and plans to deal with it, and you end up with Bush vs. Saddam. The natural question, as when you switch on to watch a sports game on television, with two teams facing each other – who will win? It comes, of course, with another question built in – who will lose?

Faced with only these two alternatives – victory or defeat – each side is likely to step up its efforts for victory, since defeat is unthinkable. The key framing decisions behind the *Newsweek* cover, along with so much coverage in US and UK media are, in other words, a contribution to a way of thinking about the conflict which is inherently escalatory.

Include other parties, and other issues in the frame, and these questions begin to make less sense. (Imagine a third team in a football match, with its own goal and its own ball.) Instead we might ask ourselves: 'How can we improve security for all these countries and their peoples?'

A Development Perspective

Throughout our discussions with journalists, we have picked up and commended to journalists the post-modern insight that shared security is necessary for development, and development for shared security. It's an understanding championed by the Toda Institute, under director Majid Tehranian, which has established a Commission on Cooperation and Security for West Asia, gathering together civil society representatives from several states of the region, plus the five permanent members of the UN Security Council.

This sets out to consider the relative security needs of countries throughout the Gulf region as a multilateral question. Whatever the nature of the governments in their respective countries, basic strategic and geographical factors will always lead Iraq, Iran and the Gulf Cooperation Council states around Saudi Arabia, to assess their security first and foremost relative to one another, albeit within a wider regional framework.

It offers a clue as to what made the former Baghdad regime so bellicose – is it simply because Saddam Hussein is mad and/or bad – if he is? Or is it also rooted in perfectly intelligible – in a sense, *reasonable* – security concerns, faced with revolutionary Iran on one hand, nuclear-armed Israel on another and Gulf states armed to the teeth with western military hardware on a third?

The Commission's launch paper includes a contribution from Shahram Chubin, of the Geneva Centre for Security Policy (Chubin, 1999). He believes Iraq is driven partly by historical fear of its larger neighbour, Iran and partly by Saddam Hussein's ambitions to lead the Arab world in confrontation with the Israelis.

The lessons for Baghdad of the last decade, Dr Chubin suggests, include 'first, that only nuclear weapons will deter a future humiliation like the one suffered in 1991, and, second, that nuclear weapons may be the only way to deter an Israeli attack.'

Experts with the Commission have called for the Middle East to be established as a 'weapons-of-mass-destruction-free-zone', an ideal to which all states in the region have committed in principle at some time or other, and one which is set out in Article Fourteen of UN Resolution 687, the ceasefire terms of the 1991 Gulf War.

Crucially, the scope to think in these terms requires regional security to be conceived in multilateral terms. Not so much a tug-of-war but a cat's-cradle, held in tension by many different strands pulling in different directions at once.

It is the job of such a Commission to bring many perspectives around a table and hold open discussions; the ethical approach to this story is for journalists to bring many perspectives to the metaphorical table of news reports, op-ed pages and studios, to open up discussion in society at large and to dislodge the 'calcified' structure of the way it has been reported up to now.

Peace Initiatives

The third of the Reporting the World checklist points is the visibility or otherwise, in news reports, of peace initiatives:

Is there any news of efforts or ideas to resolve the conflict?

- Is there anything in the report about peace plans, or any image of a solution?

- Must these aspects of a story wait until leaders cut a 'deal'?

- Do reports of any deal equip us to assess whether it is likely to tackle the causes of violence?

- Do we see any news of anyone else working to resolve or transform the conflict?

Back in 1996, before the Good Friday Agreement in Northern Ireland, a process of talks began at Stormont Castle. But, by then, the peace effort had already come perilously close to failure. There was an agonising wait while the biggest political party in the province, the Ulster Unionists, publicly squabbled over whether they should join in.

Their MPs at Westminster were, it was reported, evenly divided over the issue. A 'casting vote' might eventually lie with their leader, the 'Sphinx' of Northern Ireland politics, the inscrutable James Molyneaux.

Then a Belfast newspaper, the *Newsletter*, the daily read of choice for many Protestants, published the results of an opinion poll. The first question was the standard one – if a General Election were held tomorrow, which way would you vote? Then, to anyone who answered, 'Ulster Unionist', a second question – do you want to see your party enter the talks at Stormont? The answer – an overwhelming 86 per cent yes. The UUP did subsequently enter the talks process and their supporters voted decisively in favor of the Agreement when it was eventually put to twin referenda on either side of the Irish border. Some London newspapers had the good grace to suggest, in editorials, that they had misjudged the mood of Northern Ireland's Unionist majority, misled by posturing on the part of its leaders. But the critical mass of news coverage still inhabits realist orthodoxy.

News is, in one important sense, about change. We pick up today's newspaper to see what's changed since yesterday; or tune in to 24-hour rolling news to track developments over the last hour. Realism is the view that change is only brought about by states, governments or (other) men with guns. It is still the working assumption on which the majority of news is based.

But this often means the first stirrings of significant change are missed. Years of quiet peace work in Northern Ireland had prepared its people for the compromises necessary to 'jump together' to create a new reality – the principle of the Good Friday Agreement. But it took place below the radar of many reporters, biased in favor of official sources and accustomed to seeing the public as either victims or vox pops – people to whom things are done, not people doing things for themselves.

Israel and the Palestinians

As long ago as March, 2001, the first Reporting the World seminar heard from two grassroots peace activists in the Arab-Israeli conflict. The theme was 'Are we getting the story?', tackling head-on the question of where change was likely to come from and whether readers and audiences were being properly informed about it.

One of them, Gila Svirsky of the Coalition of Women for a Just Peace, spoke about the work of her group in carrying out what amounted to a non-violent intensification of the conflict – bringing home to ordinary Israelis the effects of their government's policies on the daily reality facing Palestinians in the occupied territories.

These ranged from demonstrations in Jerusalem, with banners draped down the walls of the Old City bearing the slogan 'peace' in Arabic, Hebrew and English; to direct actions to bring food and water to blockaded Palestinian villages and even a sit-down outside the Defence Ministry in Tel Aviv to mimic the effects of a 'closure' such as those being enforced by the Israeli Defence Force in the West Bank and Gaza Strip.

News of this ongoing programme of actions is efficiently circulated to journalists, and it seems clear that these are facts created, at least partly, in order to be reported. But – as with government policy announcements – still worthy of being covered, with due critical scrutiny, on their merits.

Their campaign was based on a peace plan, an image of a solution to the conflict, drawn up by elements of the coalition from both Jewish and Muslim communities. The essential elements are an end to the occupation; the establishment of two states, divided by the pre-1967 Israeli border and the recognition of Jerusalem as the shared capital of both states.

By about the middle of 2002, nearly two years after the second Intifada began, these proposals were just beginning to be taken seriously by journalists, and to appear in news reports. Stories included the highly public refusal of fifty-three reservists from the Israeli Defence Force to serve in the occupied territories; the peace plan unveiled by Prince Abdullah of Saudi Arabia, offering full Arab recognition of Israel in exchange for withdrawal from all the land occupied since 1967, and the formation of new peace groupings such as 'Green Line'.

But grassroots actions were, long before this, very visibly the first stirrings of change, and the emergence of a post-Oslo peace process. 'Post-Oslo' because it is based on fixing the fatal flaw that undermined and eventually destroyed the Oslo Accords – which interim steps towards final status were left to be negotiated between two asymmetrical entities, an Israeli state and a Palestinian Authority. This left essentially intact the structural violence, the inequalities, daily depredations and indignities facing Palestinians under occupation and settlement, and, with them, the conditions in which direct violence was likely to continue.

Interventions

There is a clue here to the handling of the fourth checklist point, the question of intervention:

What is 'our' role in this story?

- Is the message that 'these people will not be OK until our (benign) intervention, now in prospect?'

or

- Does the report suggest that 'they would be OK, but for our record of (malign) intervention'?

- Is there anything about interventions already underway, albeit perhaps undeclared?

- Is there any examination of the influence of previous or prospective interventions on people's behaviour?

- Does it equip us to assess whether more, or less intervention might represent a solution, or to discriminate between different kinds?

The Israeli-Palestinian Accords in Oslo in 1993 were an intervention, presented and almost universally reported as a peace process. But an understanding of the dynamics at work, based on Conflict Analysis, would have led to important caveats being entered from the start.

In some ways, journalists covering conflicts have an increasingly difficult job. Life in a media-savvy world means the parties concerned are intensely aware of the possible consequences of the way they are reported, and prepared to argue the toss about it – with the editor, or even the proprietor if necessary. Seldom are interpretations more keenly contested than when peace plans are being discussed.

For many reporters, an ethic of responsibility, forming judgments about the consequences of their reporting before and as they do it, is an unwelcome extra 'burden.' But this is precisely where it can be useful to have a reliable set of first principles against which to reach assessments, not on the say-so of any one party but derived, instead, from a well-established body of knowledge and research – Conflict Analysis – which belongs to none of them.

This can help to address a key question: will an intervention – whether or not it is presented as a 'peace plan' – do any good? Another, equally important question is about the effect any intervention, or even the prospect of one, has already had.

This entails telling it not just 'the way it is' but also 'the way it came to be.' Did the NLA's military campaign in Macedonia represent the spontaneous upwelling of 'ethnic hatred?' Or was it contingent on the ambiguities of the previous intervention in Kosovo, where the West took sides in a civil war, then presented itself as capable of holding the ring as a neutral arbiter?

To the extent that there was 'ethnic hatred' among the state's Albanian population, how was it constructed, by whom and for what end? What part did calculation or instinct, about the way the conflict would be presented to Western news audiences, play in this sequence of events?

The Reporting the World ethical checklist represents an honest and coherent response to the practical dilemmas posed by such developments in today's media-savvy world. It offers clear and specific criteria for assessing the 'seriousness' of news and its credentials as 'real coverage that is meaningful and that works.' It is intended to fortify reporters, producers and editors alike in overcoming self-censorship and the constraints of consensus and inertia, in favor of thinking through important stories for themselves.

But it will also need to be picked up by readers, listeners and viewers to demand a better deal from their news services. The checklist we propose represents an asset to anyone seeking to define – the better to defend – the kind of news we need in this interdependent world.

References

Carey, J. (1986) 'Why and How? The Dark Continent of American Journalism', in Manoff, R. K. and M. Shudson (eds), *Reading the News*. New York: Pantheon Books.

Chubin, S. (1999) 'Eliminating Weapons of Mass Destruction in the Persian Gulf', *Peace and Policy*, 4(1-2).

Freeland, J. (2002, February 9) 'Breaking the Silence', *Guardian*.

Schudson, M. (2003) *The Sociology of News*. New York, London: W.W. Norton & Company, Inc.

Strobel, W.P. (1998) *Late-Breaking Foreign Policy*. Washington DC: United States Institute of Peace.

Vidal, G. (2001) *The Last Empire: essays 1992-2000*. New York: Doubleday.

Wolff, M. (2001, October 15) 'This Media Life. World Beat', *New York Magazine*.

Chapter 15
Emotions, Trauma and Good Journalism
Mark Brayne

In this chapter, another London journalist describes the rapid development of a new and vital area of journalism research and practice: the reporting of trauma and the trauma of reporting. Though forever part and parcel of journalism, it is through the work of Brayne, Feinstein (2002) and Roger Simpson and Frank Ochberg of the University of Washington-based Dart Center, that the reporting of violence, and its impact on journalists and news subjects alike, has become a recognised and accepted topic of analysis within the media and the academy. Whether the 'emotional literacy' Brayne calls for in journalism will turn out to be another nail in the coffin of the dominant Anglo/US paradigm of 'objective' reporting, or a turn-of-the-century fad of limited practical value to reporters, news sources, and audiences, is an unfolding story.

Journalists have traditionally been trained well in skills essential to their job. These include how to write a good introduction; how to construct tight and compelling sentences; how to set a story in context and provide background; how to edit sound or compile pictures; how to get the best out of an interview or a press conference; how to make a story come alive with quotes and colourful detail; how to stay dispassionate and fair.

However, that traditional journalistic culture imparts little training or awareness about the deeper complexities of the profession. Nor does it prepare reporters for how they might respond emotionally to the stories they observe. It does not explain the deeper drivers of the human behaviour they are observing and seeking to report. Nor does traditional journalism prepare its practitioners for how, in any story, there are different, competing and often equally valid perspectives – not just one truth which the journalist is tasked to uncover.

At the start of a new century, it is time for a shift in journalistic awareness, and for the development of a media culture, which acknowledges without shame or confusion the central importance of emotions and trauma in the work we do. This matters because journalists themselves matter, arguably more than ever before. People build their understanding of the world through the information they receive: that which comes through individual experience (as a child constructs an internal image of the world through its relationship with its mother), and especially in this electronic age, importantly also through the information which reaches them through the media.

Journalists who construct that information compile not only the first draft of history; they reflect back to the world an understanding of itself. They tell the story of the planet, which helps or hinders each individual to understand his or her place, role and potential in how this world is changing. Distorted journalism reflects back to the world a distorted self-image, and blocks the powers of growth, change and healing that lie in individuals and society as in nature itself.

Unlike the arts or literature, physics or even political science, journalism so far seems largely untouched by the debate of the latter twentieth century about what has been called post-modernism and the recognition that merely by observing an event, one becomes part of it and affects how it unfolds, a concept well-known to anthropologists as the 'participant observer'. Journalists still like to believe, and are explicitly trained in this thinking, that they report objective facts dispassionately. They are not, on the whole, taught self-insight or humility.

In this task of culture change, there are many useful lessons in psychotherapy, a field of human exploration and wisdom that remains largely misunderstood and all too often cruelly misrepresented by journalists. As a start, imagine nations, or indeed the whole planet, as one living organism, like an individual personality. Individuals have their repressed emotions, their childhood traumas and experiences that direct how they respond as adults, often in ways that are no longer appropriate or productive.

A psychotherapist seeks with the client to explore those hidden impulses, to unpack why they suddenly get angry or are unable to nurture loving relationships or hold down a job. It is a journey into that person's own very personal truth, facilitated by reflecting back to that client a deeper and wider understanding of who he or she is, connecting behaviours and enabling the individual to take responsibility for his or her own actions. Good psychotherapy is an empowering experience, casting light into dark corners and untangling feelings, experiences and memories.

Good journalism might now learn to do the same thing, to open avenues of understanding rather than reinforce blame and patterns of victimhood. It is a journalist's job, or should be, as it is a therapist's, to listen to people's stories. It is their shared job to take that experience into themselves, to package it with understanding, and to reflect back to those they serve, whether client or audience, an authentic, accurate and respectful picture of their experience, in context – in other words, to construct meaning.

When journalism reinforces – because it sells newspapers and brings in viewers or listeners – the inability of individuals, or ethnic groups, or of a whole nation, to take responsibility for how they experience objective difficulty, then the vicious circle of destructive conflict is merely tightened further.

Like good psychotherapists, journalists are trained to tease out a story and (re-) tell it accurately. Many have a profound passion to do that well. Michael Buerk, former foreign correspondent and presenter for many years of the BBC's main evening television news programme, put it this way in a research interview: 'One wants to be there, to witness on other people's behalf the great events of the day – be they political, good or more often rather gloomy things. That's the drive' (Bowes, 2001).

That implies an awesome responsibility. In the flood of emotional response to traumatic events, journalists can get the story very wrong. There were, for example, no piles of bodies being burned on Tiananmen Square the day after the protests there were put down in 1989. Or take panicky reports from outside the Macedonian parliament in the spring of 2001, as crowds threatened to storm the building. 'Macedonia on the brink of civil war' screamed the headlines. Macedonia was not on the brink of such conflict. But the fear was understandable. What those reporters in Macedonia were unconsciously experiencing was perhaps a kind of traumatic flashback , to scenes in Sarajevo nine years before when a different state, Bosnia, was indeed on the threshold of terrible war.

Without training in emotional awareness, journalists can be spectacularly off-target. I was off target myself several times in my own career. I admit, although I tried not to show it in my reporting, I badly wanted the students to prevail in Beijing in 1989. Perhaps that was why I allowed myself to believe and report one wild rumour at the height of the demonstrations that led to the crackdown, that Deng Xiaoping had resigned. When Ceausescu fell in Romania in 1989, I recall writing a *From Our Own Correspondent* (FOOC) piece for the BBC from Bucharest predicting for Romania, in the warm, euphoric afterglow of the Revolution, a future of ethnic harmony and economic prosperity. That rosy prediction had more to do with euphoria-driven wishful thinking than it had to do with Romanian reality.

With a basic training in self-awareness, however, journalists – rather like psychotherapists – might learn to use their own experience of emotion during coverage of a story to understand the emotions of that story and its participants themselves. The jargon for this essential tool in any successful psychotherapeutic encounter is *counter-transference*, where the listener (or reporter) finds him or herself experiencing what the client – or story – cannot yet consciously articulate.

A journalist without self-awareness risks assuming that what he or she is observing is the objective and external truth, of which he or she is purely the witness. A journalist with understanding that whatever he or she observes is inevitably contaminated – coloured – to a greater or lesser degree by his or her own experience and assumptions is much more likely to get the story right; to do better justice to the essence and meaning of the story. In short, is more likely to be a better journalist and a more humble one, not a quality normally closely associated with this profession.

It is a tool that needs using with care, but one whose value is underlined for example by listener feedback to BBC reporters writing for *From Our Own Correspondent*. By themselves relating, personally, to the story they are reporting, and by using themselves as instruments to explain and understand that story, these correspondents convey a more accurate and accurately *felt* picture of a country or an event than any straight, dispassionate news report can do.

One of my own most effective pieces of reporting from the field was a FOOC about childcare and child rearing in China, linked to the birth of my own daughter in 1987 in Hong Kong. The Chinese at that time had no disposable nappies, so we flew back to Beijing, to the amazement of customs and our own BBC staff, with boxes upon boxes of such supplies. It was a perfect peg on which to hang an account of how the Chinese both deal with their babies' normal bodily functions, and of the psychological conditioning which young Chinese receive, and which explains much of their society's emphasis on the collective at the expense of the individual.

This is not an argument for journalists inserting their own emotional responses into every story they do. But reporters should always remember that their listener's or reader's or viewer's prime relationship is not with the story itself, but with the writer – who serves as a conduit, or channel, to the experience of that story. If the reporter cannot *emotionally* engage the listener, reader or viewer, the storytelling will fail. One BBC correspondent famously had to be taken off coverage of the school murders in the Scottish town of Dunblane because her reports – dry and dispassionate although largely correct – did not resonate with the viewers.

There *is* no story until it has been told – and heard. News is a relationship between reporter and reader. That is why, like psychotherapists, journalists must learn to work on themselves to deepen – or heighten – their own conscious awareness, so that they may serve better to understand and convey, as it were through a prism, the *felt* and *experienced* truth(s) of a story with minimum distortion.

As part of this new approach, journalists also need to understand how their reporting can misrepresent the world we live in – by focusing so heavily on the violent dimension of human experience. In BBC training courses about trauma, emotions and good journalism, I ask my students what percentage of their work relates at some level to trauma – either its actual experience (crashes, accidents, crime, violent conflict and so on), or the aftermath of trauma or the preparation for it (especially in terms of international politics). The answer is usually around 75 per cent.

Daniel Goleman, an American author of a hugely influential book about emotional intelligence, has explained in biological terms this fascination with violence. In order to survive in the evolutionary battle, human beings like all living creatures have had to be alert to danger. Benign events (call them good news if you like) are no threat – but violence (bad news) might be. In his paper 'Reinventing the News', Goleman argues that 'the largest single category of stories in the news are of threats and tragedies near and far – a formula that, paradoxically, is soothing to the savage brain, which finds relief in the fact that it happened there, not here' (1996 : 5).

Once reassured that there is no immediate personal risk, he continues, the ancient part of the brain that rules emotional life turns away. The news headlines move on to the next crisis. Ethnic war in Bosnia gives way to ethnic slaughter in Rwanda, followed by nuclear weapons in North Korea, which is followed by tyranny in Haiti, which is overtaken by the refugee flood from Cuba…

This is an argument for a broader news agenda, which more accurately reflects the reality of the world in which we live, including much more reporting of non-violent and perhaps less dramatic change, as well as the violence. It is also an argument for journalists to understand and report the roots of violent behaviour, and how pain that is (in the jargon of psychotherapy) not 'owned', is acted out and visited upon the Other.

That is evident in the behaviour of whole social and national groups as well as of individuals – evident in how Germans in the 1930s, for example, could be persuaded to blame Jews for all their ills; in how Hutus could be persuaded to kill Tutsis in the hundreds of thousands in Rwanda in 1994; in how Serbs could be persuaded to see themselves as victims of history and their neighbours and feel justified in the serial massacres of Muslims and Croats.

An understanding of pain and trauma is central to any journalistic understanding of how nations can be held in thrall by charismatic but emotionally dysfunctional political individuals such as Stalin, or Mao, or Hitler, or Ceausescu, or Idi Amin, or Sadaam Hussein, or Robert Mugabe, or Milosevic – the list is a long one. Without exception, all these men (and they are usually men) had profoundly disturbed and often both physically and emotionally violent childhoods. Their normal human capacity for empathy with another was disrupted early in their development, to the extent they became incapable of appreciating the pain of other human beings.

Curiously, but from a psychotherapist's vantage point not surprisingly, many of these men were said to be quite charming in private company and loving towards their immediate family. All of which are character traits of particular kinds of personality disorders as described in the Anglo-Saxon world's principal handbook of mental health, the *DSM-IV* (American Psychiatric Association, 1994).

Psychotic disorders, for example, can include grandiosity and delusion, giving an individual an inflated sense of worth, power, knowledge and identity.

A leader – whether political or military or religious – with a narcissistic personality disorder might share that grandiosity, mixed with inflation, arrogance and a need for admiration. They can be, according to *DSM-IV*, quite charismatic, but most importantly, such individuals have a marked lack of empathy for other human beings and their feelings or needs.

All of this expresses in traits and behaviour the other principle understanding missing from traditional journalist training and culture, the impact of trauma and traumatic stress. In Western and Anglo-Saxon cultures especially, journalists have been brought up to believe that they are not – or should not be – affected by the stories they cover. Professional distance has been assumed to be sufficient defence against any personal emotional wounding. Soldiers, policemen, rescue workers and many other related professionals used to believe the same thing. But journalists are in fact possibly the last front-line trauma-responders to recognise that this is not true, and that as soft-skinned individuals programmed by evolution, like all other living creatures, to respond to trauma, they *will* be moved, disturbed and even changed by what they witness.

Traumatic experience gets in, as it were, under the radar. The term 'trauma' comes from the Greek, meaning a wounding or a piercing. When it involves helplessness, fear or terror, particularly when associated with violent death or threat to life, trauma overwhelms the normal abilities of the psyche and the body to defend and protect itself. Trauma sets off dramatic rushes of hormones and adrenaline – all part of what is known as the body's 'Fight, Flight or Freeze' response. That leaves powerful traces in the very depths of the brain and body, well below levels of normal consciousness. If not addressed or processed, past traumatic experience can retain a debilitating hold on a person's ability to feel physically and emotionally safe in the present.

Until very recently, there was almost no research on how trauma relates to journalism. The very first piece of serious investigation anywhere in the world into traumatic stress among front-line correspondents, camera people and producers was published only in 2002. The Canadian psychiatrist Anthony Feinstein (2002: 1570-1575) surveyed 140 front-line correspondents and producers from main Western news organisations, with an average career length of some fourteen years. He found, not surprisingly, that about one in four had at some point in those careers experienced clinically definable symptoms of Post-Traumatic Stress Disorder, about the same level of PTSD as experienced by military veterans of conflicts such as the Falklands or the first Gulf War.

In some ways, journalists may well be more prone to developing PTSD than those rescue workers or police whose job it is to climb in and help people. Human beings are, it seems, programmed by evolution to want and need to help each other. Journalists, by contrast, are specifically tasked with not helping, and by both needing and learning to stay distant, they are setting up unconscious emotional conflicts, which can be profoundly damaging. If they work for some publications, their position is even worse, tasked as some journalists are to emphasise the personal trauma they are reporting in order to increase their newspapers' sales or television station's ratings. Add to that the soup of adrenaline in which the journalist is already bathed, with deadlines and the intense pressure to perform, and it perhaps becomes clear why journalists, for the sake of their long-term emotional well being, need to take trauma seriously.

Let us consider some personal examples. Jason Bridges, a freelance photojournalist, has spoken of how he witnessed a journalist in Africa paying a young girl to sit and pose for pictures holding a baby (Bowes, 2001). The photographer took a film pod from his pocket, which had some dead flies in it, and placed them on her face to enhance the dramatic effect. Bridges himself has embellished photographs. He and other photojournalists paid someone they found in a Turkish earthquake whom they called PV – 'professional victim' – five dollars to climb on top of rubble and look harrowed.

Another powerful example comes from Africa. One correspondent covering a famine there recalled being confronted by a child who was clearly dying. If he chose to, he could help that child. What should he do? Get help or film? He chose to film, arguing that 'once I start stopping, to help, I know I will never be able to stop stopping' (Brayne, 2000). This colleague has on the whole appeared to cope quite well with the effects of trauma, and would certainly deny that he has experienced symptoms of PTSD. But he is troubled by guilt at the knowledge that one of his own non-British colleagues in that same conflict *did* help that child whom he had filmed.

At the BBC, journalists in the Polish language service were disturbed in 2002 by an event in which a factory manager in Poland had been beaten up, and almost killed, by angry workers. This had all taken place in front of a group of journalists, none of who intervened, all of who kept filming and recording. Polish public opinion was incensed, and asked how could reporters be so callous and quite simply inhuman as not to want to help?[1]

But where does one draw the line? Some correspondents I know say quite explicitly that, whenever they can, without risk to themselves or the job they have to do, they will step in to save a life. Michael Nicholson of ITN (Independent Television News in the UK) famously smuggled a Bosnian orphan child out of Sarajevo because he felt so disturbed by what he was witnessing. There are other journalists for whom that would be beyond the boundary of acceptable behaviour for a reporter, however understandable the personal anguish.

PTSD is a useful concept in this process of building media awareness around the therapist's daily bread of emotion and personal pain. Because PTSD has been scientifically and intellectually proven, journalists do listen now when they are warned that PTSD is something they too might experience. More and more journalists are 'coming out' with personal stories of at times intense personal pain, suffered with guilt and confusion over many years as a result of their reporting careers.

I have heard more and more such stories as British journalists have engaged in this new debate around trauma and their personal experience. A producer who had witnessed appalling atrocities in the Bosnian war of the early 1990s, and who had at one point personally been held hostage at gunpoint by Croatian militia, spent years fighting the terrifying panic attacks, using alcohol to self-medicate. Another producer seemed to have coped well with extended experience in Sarajevo in 1992. But nearly 10 years later, raw pictures coming in from New York of the attack on the World Trade Center, and of people leaping to their death to escape the flames, stripped the cover off her personal emotional defences and triggered an attack of PTSD lasting several weeks.

At the BBC's Monitoring Service, one journalist who had merely reported at second hand the misery of his home town Sarajevo developed such bad PTSD that he had to take several months off work. Journalists do not need to experience trauma in person to be vulnerable to the experience of profound distress. And there is the distressing story of a British correspondent working in Israel. A young Palestinian came up to him holding the head of his dead friend in his hand. 'Film this,' said the Palestinian boy. 'This is what's happening to us, the world needs to know.' The footage was not shown, but the correspondent was so shaken that on returning home he had what he later realised was an emotional breakdown.

Trauma can ruin lives. More British army veterans from the Falklands have now died at their own hands than the numbers of those killed in action against the enemy, and even if PTSD is not the sole explanation, its contribution to that grim statistic is one reason why the British military are already some years ahead of journalism in setting up robust systems of training and emotional aftercare for those sent to experience trauma in the line of duty.

Employers and managers can do much to mitigate – or compound – the individual impact of reporting and experiencing trauma. After the Afghan military campaign of 2002, some BBC journalists spoke of how they had been distressed less by the dead bodies and the killings they had seen in their line of duty, but more by how they felt they had been handled by at times insensitive programme editors in London. When journalists are on a big story, especially where trauma and death are involved, their senses are heightened and their emotional defences in effect much reduced, an expression of their own physiological 'fight or flight' response to what they have witnessed. For outsiders, insensitive to that distress, to come in at such times with inappropriate criticism or harsh handling can literally retraumatise.

In fairness, much has changed and is changing more. There is a growing understanding within media organisations that it will be good business practice, including with an eye on possible litigation in the future, for them to train and support their staff around issues of trauma. That is new. Ten years ago, when journalists covered Tiananmen Square or the Romanian Revolution, there was nothing at all in the way of preparing a reporter for working in nasty places. One just built up experience, and hoped to survive. What shocked the

BBC into action was the death of radio reporter John Schofield in Croatia in 1995, killed by Croatian soldiers who mistook his team for Serbian fighters. The BBC rapidly laid down that anyone being sent to a 'hostile environment' had to have appropriate training beforehand and be properly supported in the field. For Reuters and AP TV News, it was the loss of two of their most experienced war reporters in Sierra Leone in 2000, which had a similarly sobering effect on their approach to training.

Most 'hostile environment' training courses now include a brief introduction to PTSD. But one hour or so is not enough. In a journalist's *core* training and culture, there is as yet insufficient preparation for the psychologically damaging cocktail of givens around the job of a reporter. Quite apart from any war reporting, there is the horrendous pressure of deadlines; the lack of control over what is about to happen next; the dramatic ebb and flow of addictive adrenaline as another report is delivered, just in time, heard, read or seen by millions, and then forgotten. Burn-out is a core professional risk.

The British culture of the stiff upper lip also needs to change. The bar is a very good place to wind down from a stressful assignment, but if alcohol becomes the main medication for troubled emotions that can be very damaging.

The war in Iraq unleashed in 2003 is certain to bring significant culture change across the news world, as employers, reporters and their teams experience first hand the pain, loss and confusion of covering the most significant violent politically-driven war since Vietnam, with its high toll of journalist casualties.

An organisation which is now making a particular contribution to the changing of this culture is the US-based Dart Center for Journalism and Trauma (www.dartcenter.org). The Center takes its name and core funding from a family which invented, of all things, the disposable polystyrene coffee cup. Launched in the mid-1990s, the US Dart Center began with the task of improving the journalistic coverage of home-grown violence and trauma in the United States: things like the bombing of the federal building in Oklahoma, the Columbine school killings, rape cases and local crime, and of course the September 11, 2001 attacks on New York and Washington. Dart set up a centre at Ground Zero in New York after the destruction of the Twin Towers to work with journalists and their organisations. On the other side of the Atlantic, a new Dart Centre Europe has been bringing media representatives, counsellors and trauma specialists together to consider how best to support journalists in their experience of trauma, and is collecting powerful personal stories on its new website, www.darteurope.org.

Journalists need a language and a space to express the emotional and feeling dimension to their work. They need support while on the job, as do their line managers and editors back on base. Journalists need support when they come off assignment, whether that was a one-off to report a car crash in the local community, or whether they are returning from years abroad as a correspondent and making the difficult transition back to ordinary life.

The prize will not only be the well-being of those who report the world back to itself. The even bigger gain will be journalists who are more self-aware and also more humble, and aware therefore of the deeper complexities of why and how events come about. The result will be a journalism, which – at last – more accurately and authentically tells the story of the planet.

References

American Psychiatric Association (1994) *DSM-IV, Diagnostic and Statistical Manual of Mental Disorder, 4th ed.* Washington, DC: American Psychiatric Association.

Bowes, S. (2001) *The British media: an evaluation of the spiritual effect of reporting on death through tragedy and disaster.* MA thesis, Theology and Religious Studies, Southampton University.

Brayne, M. (2000) *The Personal Experience of the Foreign Correspondent.* MA thesis, de Montfort University.

Feinstein, A. (2002) *American Journal of Psychiatry*, 159: 1570-1575.

Goleman, D. (1998) *The Contemplative Mind; Reinventing the News.* Williamsburg: The Centre for Contemplative Mind.in Society.

Note

1 Personal communication of Polish language section staff with the author, August 2002.

Chapter 16
Conflicting Truths: Online News and the War in Iraq
Stuart Allan

For many internet commentators, the US-led attack on Iraq represented the 'coming of age' of the internet as a news medium. Regularly singled out for attention was the role of high-speed, broadband internet access, not least its capacity to enable news sites to offer users live video and audio reports, multimedia slideshows, animated graphics, interactive maps, and so forth. The rapid rise in the number of users availing themselves of the technology – over 70 million people in the US at the time – meant that providers could further enhance existing types of digital reportage accordingly (Kirkpatrick, 2003). Moreover, other commentators pointed to the ways in which online news was consolidating its position as a primary news source. Of significance here, for example, was the extent to which users, especially office workers unable to watch television in the workplace, were relying on the internet for up-to-the-minute news of breaking developments. Research conducted during the first six days of the war by the Pew Internet & American Life Project (2003) indicated that 56 per cent of online users in the US had turned to news sites for reports about the conflict. 'More than half the people who are online are getting their news online – that's never happened before,' Lee Rainie, the project's director, maintained. 'It's another milestone moment for online news' (cited in Weaver, 2003).

Of particular interest for the purposes of this chapter, however, is the use of the internet by people who were looking for a wider array of reportorial perspectives about the realities of the conflict than was available from mainstream media in their own country. While the focus will be primarily on US and British users turning to international news sites, it seems reasonable to suggest that relatively similar kinds of imperatives may have been shaping online news consumption elsewhere. In one country after the next around the world, television was likely to be the principal source of news about the conflict for the majority of its citizens. It is also likely that where internet access is widely available, there was a marked increase in the size of the online audience. 'Viewers first turn to television in part because TV's strength is the delivery of a narrative story line. That's what people are looking for when an event like this first begins to unfold,' argued Kinsey Wilson, Vice President and Editor-in-Chief of USAToday.com. 'Eventually, though, television starts to loop back on itself and repeats the narrative over and over again' (cited in Outing, 2003). It is at this point, as he suggests, that a key advantage of online news comes to the fore. 'The best sites can move quickly to develop a story in multiple directions, add depth and detail, and give readers their own pathways to explore.' It is this latter consideration – that is, the ways in which the internet affords the user with the opportunity to engage with news and perspectives from afar – that concerns us here.

Searching for News

So-called 'Operation Iraqi Freedom' began on 19 March 2003 as the US-led military forces initiated air strikes on leadership 'targets of opportunity' in Baghdad. From the moment news of the first attacks broke, internet traffic to online news services surged dramatically. More people than ever, according to companies monitoring internet traffic such as Hitwise, Nielsen Net Ratings, and the like, were surfing the internet for news and information.

In Britain, that day saw the level of traffic to the *Guardian* newspaper's website soar by nearly 30 per cent to around 4.5 million impressions. According to Hitwise research, the *Guardian*'s site was the leading online newspaper service with a 7.26 per cent share of the market, followed by FT.com (5.17 per cent), the *Sun* (3.05 per cent), *The Times* (2.86 per cent), the *Telegraph* (2.24 per cent) and the *Independent* (1.51 per cent). Of the non-print sites, the British Broadcasting Corporation's standalone news site was ranked highest with a 4.69 per cent share. Evidently traffic to this BBC site was up by 30 to 40 per cent for the day, a level of demand which appeared to have caused the service to repeatedly 'crash' in the early hours (see Timms, 2003). Over the course of the days to follow, people going online during office hours appeared to be largely responsible for the surge in traffic to news sites. Many were seeking out alternative news sources, as well as wanting particular types of perspectives about the factors underpinning the conflict. 'These figures show the desire of British surfers to get a real range of informed opinion on the war,' argued Tom Ewing, a Nielsen Net Ratings analyst. 'This shows where the internet comes into its own when fast-moving news stories are involved' (cited by *BBC Online*, 15 April 2003).

In the US, Yahoo.com reported that in the first hour following President George W. Bush's announcement that the conflict had started, traffic levels to its site were three times higher. The volume of traffic to its news section jumped 600 per cent the next day (Thursday 20 March) and again the day after. The sites associated with different television networks proved particularly popular. On the Thursday, CNN.com evidently secured the highest figures for all news sites with 9 million visitors; followed by MSNBC with 6.8 million (about half of the visitors for both sites were accessing them from their workplaces). Other news sites witnessing a significant rise in demand that day included Foxnews.com (77 per cent increase), Washingtonpost.com (29 per cent increase) and USAToday.com (17 per cent). 'Without a doubt,' stated Daniel E. Hess of ComScore, 'people are glued to their Web browsers for virtually minute-by-minute updates of the war as it unfolds' (cited in Walker 2003; see also Richtel, 2003). Evidently ComScore's measurement of traffic patterns for that Thursday suggested that worldwide traffic to major news sites was 70 per cent higher than the daily average over the previous four weeks. Several news sites responded to the sudden influx of demand by temporarily removing advertising from their home pages so as to improve download times. All in all, most news sites in the US were able to bear the strain of sharp 'spikes' in activity, showing little by way of the 'performance degradation' that was all too typical for the same sites on September 11, 2001 (see Allan 2002).

During the early hours of the September 11 atrocities, most of the major news sites in the US – such as CNN.com, MSNBC.com, ABCNews.com, CBS.com and FoxNews.com – were so besieged by user demand that they became largely inaccessible. Criticisms levelled by some commentators were sharp and to the point. 'At a time when information-starved Americans needed it as never before,' Mike Wendland (2001) of the *Detroit Free Press* declared, 'the Internet failed miserably in the hours immediately following yesterday's terrorist attacks.' Even as the day wore on and the main sites stabilised, however, it was striking to note that just as people living around the world looked to US sites for breaking developments, far greater numbers of people in the US turned to foreign or international sites than was typical prior to the tragedy. For those users who wanted to draw upon news sources where different types of perspectives were being heard, international sites became a necessary alternative. Evidently the BBC's news site received the greatest share of 'hits' from US users looking abroad. These hits numbered into the millions, a level of demand engendering constant transmission problems. Streamlining the site's contents helped, but it remained a struggle for staff to maintain a presence online.

Also in London, the *Guardian*'s online site proved to be particularly popular with US users. Ian Mayes (2001a, 2001b), the daily's ombudsperson, later reported that letters sent to the editor almost doubled in the immediate aftermath of the crisis, with well over 600 arriving on both September 13 and 14. The majority of these letters arrived by e-mail, offering prompt responses to the coverage. According to Mayes, a large number of them (but apparently still a minority) were highly critical of some of the views being expressed. 'The email response,' Mayes (2001a) pointed out, 'has provided a graphic reminder that writers in the *Guardian* no longer address only a generally sympathetic domestic constituency.' This wider audience, it seems, is less likely to share the newspaper's centre-left political orientation than its regular British readership.

Some readers expressed their objections to particular articles using strong language, especially where they felt that they were intrusive, insensitive or anti-American (a few, Mayes noted, went so far as to threaten a given journalist with torture and mutilation). In contrast, readers writing to make appreciative remarks typically stated that it was the breadth of coverage that attracted them to the *Guardian* site. For many of them, the space devoted to diverse viewpoints was of particular importance.

Especially pertinent here was the inclusion of voices from the Muslim world, a distinctive feature of the news coverage when it is compared with that available via the mainstream media in other countries. To support this observation, Mayes (2001b) offered several quotations from letters written by US readers to the site:

> 'I am an American who fears, more than any terrorist, the apparently fierce determination among many Americans to remain ignorant about what lay behind this tragedy . . .' (reader from Massachusetts).

> 'You have somehow escaped the biases of the American press . . .' (reader from Hawaii).

> 'You help me sift through the smoke and soot fanned by America's media, their shrill jingoism, and [help me] to preserve my sanity' (reader from New York).

> 'Most of the US media tends to be rather shallow . . . word of mouth has a fair number of people who work for the film studios here perusing your site' (reader from Los Angeles).

> 'I live in a very small town in Kentucky, surrounded by radical fundamentalism. There is absolutely no one here to talk with about such modern ideas and interpretations' (reader from Kentucky).

Evidently Mayes examined a sufficient number of similar emails to deem these responses reasonably representative. He estimated that there are more than half a million regular readers of the *Guardian* site in the US alone, a number believed to have been significantly enhanced there – as well as in other countries – by the dramatic increase in demand for news and analysis after September 11. It is in relation to this growing international readership that he quotes the newspaper's editor, Alan Rusbridger, as stating: 'Many Arabs and Muslims are astonished at what they read. I love that thought.' Moreover, Rusbridger commented, 'I suppose that once you are aware of this international dimension you can't help but think a little more internationally and be a little less anglocentric' (cited in Mayes, 2001b; see also Allan, 2003).

Alternative Perspectives

In the months preceding the US-led invasion of Iraq, ever greater numbers of US users were turning to the *Guardian*'s online edition for news and information. Speaking in February, Jon Dennis, deputy news editor of the site, stated: 'We have noticed an upsurge in traffic from America, primarily because we are receiving more emails from US visitors thanking us for reporting on worldwide news in a way that is unavailable in the US media' (cited in Croad, 2003). Once again, of particular interest to US users, according to Dennis, was the 'breadth of opinion' available on the *Guardian*'s site. 'As a journalist,' he commented, 'I find it quite strange that there's not more criticism of the Bush administration in the American media.' In his view, it is 'as though the whole US is in shock [from September 11, 2001]. It's hard for [the news media] to be dispassionate about it. It seems as though they're not thinking as clearly as they should be' (cited in Kahney, 2003; see also Zelizer and Allan, 2002). Consequently, he suggested, it is not surprising that so many people in the US are turning to sites like that of the *Guardian*, given its ongoing commitment to reporting 'across the political spectrum rather than from just one perspective.' Both pro- and anti-war positions are presented, he added, with readers encouraged to debate the issues via the site's talk boards, as well as through various interactive features, such as live interviews with experts.

The differences between mainstream US and European news coverage of the build-up to war – not least with regard to the competing, and frequently contradictory, official justifications in circulation – were stark. The contrast was readily acknowledged by some US journalists, who offered critical insights. 'Given how timid most US news organisations have been in challenging the White House position on Iraq,' observed Deborah Branscom of *Newsweek*, 'I'm not surprised if Americans are turning to foreign news services for a perspective on the conflict that goes beyond freedom fries' (cited in Kahney, 2003). For *New York Times* columnist Paul Krugman, there were two possible explanations for what he termed the 'great trans-Atlantic media divide', as follows:

> One is that European media have a pervasive anti-American bias that leads them to distort the news, even in countries like the UK where the leaders of both major parties are pro-Bush and support an attack on Iraq. The other is that some US media outlets – operating in an environment in which anyone who questions the administration's foreign policy is accused of being unpatriotic – have taken it as their assignment to sell the war, not to present a mix of information that might call the justification for war into question (Krugman, 2003).

It was Krugman's contention that these differences were particularly pronounced with regard to television news, especially where CNN and Fox News (and their associated websites) are concerned. In his view, the cable newscasts appeared to be 'reporting about a different planet than the one covered by foreign media.' Here he provided a telling example, referring to the previous Saturday's (15 February) anti-war rallies:

> What would someone watching cable news have seen? On Saturday, news anchors on Fox described the demonstrators in New York as 'the usual protesters' or 'serial protesters'. CNN wasn't quite so dismissive,

but on Sunday morning the headline on the network's web site read 'Antiwar rallies delight Iraq' and the accompanying picture showed marchers in Baghdad, not London or New York (Krugman, 2003).

Contrasting this kind of news coverage with that offered in other countries, Krugman expressed his lack of surprise that many viewers seem somewhat confused about the factors underpinning the impending conflict. 'For months,' he wrote, 'both major US cable news networks have acted as if the decision to invade Iraq has already been made, and have in effect seen it as their job to prepare the American public for the coming war.'

For those members of the public concerned enough about the impending crisis to look beyond the confines of the US-centric reporting on offer, international news sources became a vital resource. Evidence garnered from some internet track monitoring companies suggests that in the days leading up to President George W. Bush's formal declaration of war, there was a dramatic increase in the numbers of US users turning to British and other international news sites. 'The new war in Iraq has made world news sources far more important,' online writer Stephen Gilliard argued. 'While not all news sources are reliable, there is such a gap between the way Americans see the world and the way other people do that it is invaluable to use these resources' (cited in Kahney, 2003). This point about the reliability of online news is a significant one. For users seeking to gain a sense of public opinion about the impending conflict from elsewhere in the world, the news and information provided by some international sites had to be evaluated with caution. The danger of extrapolating from opinions expressed on a news site in order to characterise the viewpoints of its readers always needs to be avoided, of course, but particularly so in those societies where state censorship is imposed as a matter of course. In the case of countries where public access to the internet is minimal, if not non-existent, issues around source accuracy and accountability required careful consideration. Nevertheless, while it was sometimes difficult for readers to judge whether any given source was sufficiently trustworthy, the sheer diversity of the perspectives available online enabled people to supplement their understanding of alternative, even opposing views.

'In the Internet age,' US journalist Elizabeth Putnam (2003) pointed out at the time, 'overseas newspapers are a few keystrokes away, making them more available and attractive to people who want to understand why there seems to be so much anti-American sentiment around the world.' Nowhere were these sorts of tensions more apparent than with regard to news sites in the Arab world. A considerable number of English-language newspapers with an Arab perspective are available online. Titles include Lebanon's *Daily Star* (www.dailystar.com.lb), a privately owned newspaper, as well as the government owned *Arab News* (www.arabnews.com) in Saudi Arabia, and *The Jordan Times* (www.jordantimes.com). There is also the *Bahrain Tribune* (www.bahraintribune.com/home.asp), *Kuwait Times* (www.kuwaittimes.net), *Syria Times* (www.teshreen.com/syriatimes), *Yemen Times* (www.yementimes.com) and Al-

Ahram (www.ahram.org.eg/weekly/) in Egypt. In addition to newspaper-based sites, a range of other types of news outlets are available in English that provide alternative perspectives. Examples included Arab.net (www.arab.net) of Saudi Arabia, the Kuwait News Agency (www.kuna.net.kw/Main.htm), as well as the Arabia.com (www.arabia.com) portal of the United Arab Emirates. KurdMedia (www.kurdmedia.com) acts as a news portal for Kurdish news. In neighbouring Iran, which is not an Arab country, there is the *Tehran Times* (www.tehrantimes.com), as well as the Islamic Republic News Agency (www.irna.com), which offers a focus on the Shi'a areas of Basra. From the vantage point of most US and UK users, however, no site in the region would attract more intense interest during the Iraq war than Al-Jazeera (www.aljazeera.net).

Al-Jazeera on the Web

Often described as the 'CNN of the Arab World', Al-Jazeera (which means 'an island' in Arabic) is arguably the region's most influential news organisation. Launched in the Qatari capital, Doha, in 1996, the 24-hour satellite television network attracts an audience currently estimated to be about 35 million regular viewers, making it the most widely watched Arab news channel. Available free of charge throughout much of the Arab world, it is typically a pay-television channel in Europe and North America. Although backed financially by the government of Qatar, Al-Jazeera's journalists consistently maintain that their editorial freedom is not compromised as a result. That said, the network's status as an independent voice in the Arab world, encapsulated in its slogan 'The opinion and the other opinion,' is frequently called into question by its many critics. For some, the network's commitment to providing news coverage from an Arab perspective means that it is ideologically compromised, and as such biased against the US and Israel. Other critics, in contrast, have denounced Al-Jazeera for being a Zionist tool, while still others insist that it is little more than a front for the Central Intelligence Agency (CIA). In any case, above dispute is the fact that its news coverage has recurrently placed a considerable strain on Qatar's relations with other countries in the region, including Bahrain, Jordan and Saudi Arabia where the network's offices have been closed on different occasions.

No stranger to controversy, Al-Jazeera came to prominence across the global mediascape in the aftermath of the dreadful events of September 11, 2001, due to its decision to broadcast taped messages attributed to Osama bin Laden. News organisations around the world paid considerable sums to air edited excerpts, much to the consternation of US officials – not least National Security Advisor Condoleezza Rice, for example, who demanded of television network executives that they 'exercise judgment' (ie, censorship) in re-broadcasting the messages. Interestingly, most of the considerable traffic to the network's site (www.aljazeera.net) at the time was from the US, despite the fact that its content was entirely in Arabic. During the subsequent 'war on terror' in Afghanistan, attention was once again directed at Al-Jazeera's role in making available reports of the conflict that challenged the preferred definitions of reality set down by military officials. For this reason alone, further controversy erupted in November 2001 when a US 'smart' bomb destroyed the network's Kabul offices. Intense speculation ensued that the offices had been deliberately destroyed. For example, Nik Gowing, a presenter on BBC World, stated afterwards that Al-Jazeera's only crime was 'bearing witness' to events that the US officials would prefer it did not see. In demanding that the Pentagon be called to account, he pointed out that when the presence of journalists is 'inconvenient' they risk becoming 'legitimate targets' in the eyes of the military – a charge promptly denied, as one would expect, by a Pentagon spokesperson (see Wells, 2001).

Following the start of 'Operation Iraqi Freedom', subscriber numbers surged dramatically in response to the intense demand for alternative insights into the conflict. The number of subscribers to the channel in Europe, it was claimed at the time, effectively doubled once the war was underway. The depth of its reporting was recurrently singled out for praise – or condemnation – depending on conflicting perceptions of the relative legitimacy of the war. In addition to reporting from Central Command in Qatar, four of Al-Jazeera's reporters were 'embedded' with the US and British military forces. In the main, however, the network ensured that most of its journalists roamed more freely. Together they covered the breadth of Iraq, including areas where western journalists did not venture. The Al-Jazeera television crews remained in Baghdad throughout the conflict, as well as in other major battlegrounds such as Basra, Mosul and in Kurdish-controlled northern Iraq. Not surprisingly, a very different kind of coverage ensued. Tarik Kafala (2003), a BBC News Online reporter, identified a case in point. 'When western journalists outside Basra were speculating about an uprising on the basis of coalition briefings,' he observed, 'al-Jazeera's correspondent inside the city was reporting first hand that "the streets are very calm and there are no indications of violence or riots".' This type of disjuncture between the network's reporting and that of its western rivals attracted considerable comment. US Secretary of State Colin Powell, for example, criticised the coverage, contending that it 'magnifies the minor successes of the [Iraqi] regime and tends to portray our efforts in a negative light' (cited in Delio, 2003). For others, however, it was the very extent to which Al-Jazeera's reporting called into question the more 'sanitised' representations of the conflict that made its presence so important – both on their television screens and, increasingly, on their personal computers (see Gubash, 2003).

Prior to the launch of Al-Jazeera's website, Arabic speakers were typically most interested in CNN.com (www.arabic.cnn.com) when looking for news online. Since the September 11 attacks, however, the page views for the Arabic-language site operated by Al-Jazeera reportedly grew from about 700,000 a day to 3 million, with more than 40 per cent of visitors logging-on from the US (Ostrom 2003). Indeed, at the outbreak of hostilities in Iraq, aljazeera.net was widely recognised as receiving the most 'hits' of any Arabic site in the world.

Of critical significance here was its commitment to pushing back the boundaries of western definitions of 'objective' journalism so as to help give voice to contrary definitions of the world. In the case of the conflict in Iraq, this meant those of the Iraqi people themselves – victims, in the eyes of the network, both of Saddam Hussein's regime and the invasion of US and UK forces to destroy it. By including in its reports what were frequently horrific images of civilian casualties, Al-Jazeera re-inflected western notions of 'balanced' reporting. It was precisely these images, in the view of Faisal Bodi, a senior editor for aljazeera.net, that made Al-Jazeera 'the most sought-after news resource in the world'. In his words:

> I do not mean to brag – people are turning to us simply because the western media coverage has been so poor. For although Doha is just a 15-minute drive from central command, the view of events from here could not be more different. Of all the major global networks, Al-Jazeera has been alone in proceeding from the premise that this war should be viewed as an illegal enterprise. It has broadcast the horror of the bombing campaign, the blown-out brains, the blood-spattered pavements, the screaming infants and the corpses. Its team of on-the-ground, unembedded correspondents has provided a corrective to the official line that the campaign is, barring occasional resistance, going to plan (Bodi, 2003).

At no time was this difference in news values cast in sharper relief than on 23 March, the night Al-Jazeera broadcast footage of US casualties, as well as Iraqi television's interviews with five US prisoners of war. Al-Jazeera's decision to air the interviews was promptly denounced by US Defense Secretary, Donald Rumsfeld, who alleged that it was a violation of the Geneva Convention protecting prisoners of war. In reply, the network's London bureau chief, Yosri Fouda, argued that western news reports were being constrained to the extent that they failed to provide accurate coverage. Regarding the Geneva Convention, he insisted that a double standard was being invoked. 'We and other broadcasters were not criticised for showing pictures of Iraqi dead and captured,' he stated, 'or those famous pictures from Guantanamo Bay' (cited in Kafala, 2003).

The more heated the ensuing furore became, of course, the more news headlines it generated around the world. The very images deemed by western news organisations to be too disturbing to screen were being actively sought out by vast numbers of people via online news sites. According to figures compiled by popular search engines, such as Google, Lycos and AltaVista, the term 'Al-Jazeera' was quickly becoming one of the most searched-for-topics on the web. Figures for the week in question indicated that the term 'Al-Jazeera' (and variant spellings) was the term that showed the greatest increase on Google, while Lycos reported that it was the top search term, with three times more searches than 'sex' (a perennial favourite with web surfers). For Karl Gregory of AltaVista, the popularity of Al-Jazeera's online sites was clear evidence of 'people branching out beyond their normal sources of news' (*BBC News Online*, 1 April 2003). The decision taken at Al-Jazeera to broadcast the images, as well as to display them online, was justified by its spokesperson, Jihad Ballout, as being consistent with its journalistic ethos of reporting the war as it was being fought on the ground. In his words: 'We didn't make the pictures – the pictures are there. It's a facet of the war. Our duty is to show the war from all angles' (cited in Whitaker, 2003). In the opinion of others, however, the network had become a mouthpiece for Iraqi propaganda. Citing the images, some military officials began ignoring questions from Al-Jazeera's reporters at briefings. At the same time, two of the network's financial reporters were evicted from the floor of the New York Stock Exchange, their press credentials having been revoked (NASDAQ would follow suit, citing 'Al-Jazeera's recent conduct during the war' as the reason), It was in cyberspace, however, that the backlash registered most decisively as various pro-war individuals and groups made clear their intent to make Al-Jazeera a target of retaliation.

News sites of all descriptions are always vulnerable to attack from hackers – typically involving little more than webpage defacements and graffiti – but those directed at Al-Jazeera's sites were remarkably vicious. The 'electronic onslaught', as aptly characterised by one internet commentator, began on March 25, the same day the English-language site, www.english.aljazeera.net, was launched. Two days later, hackers 'crashed' both sites, effectively forcing them offline by a 'denial of service' or DOS attack. This type of attack aims to close down a targeted site by overwhelming the associated server with so much meaningless data that it can no longer handle legitimate traffic. Few sites have sufficient resources, such as the necessary bandwidth, to withstand millions of simultaneous page impressions. Such was certainly the case with both Al-Jazeera sites. The English-language site was disabled virtually from the outset, while its Arabic-language counterpart struggled – with only limited success – to hold up against the storm. Efforts to restore the sites, which reportedly included re-aligning them with servers in France, encountered fierce resistance by repeated hack attacks. 'We come up for five or ten minutes,' stated Salah Al Seddiqi, IT manager at Al-Jazeera, 'and then the attacks bring us down again' (cited in Roberts, 2003).

Later the same day, even though security protocols had been reinforced for the sites, matters went from bad to worse. Evidently, a pro-war hacker was able to access the servers at Network Solutions Inc., a domain name registration service based in Mountain View, California that operates a database linking addresses (in this case, www.aljazeera.net) with the identification numbers of the servers responsible for maintaining its web pages. This meant that Al-Jazeera's domain was effectively 'hijacked' by the hacker, such that users were pointed to an altogether different site instead. Specifically, traffic was redirected to a pro-war webpage featuring a US flag, together with the messages 'Let Freedom Ring' and 'God bless our troops', signed by a self-proclaimed 'Patriot'. It was quickly determined that this latter site belonged to an internet provider based in Salt Lake City, Utah, albeit without their knowledge. Hackers calling themselves the 'Freedom Cyber Force Militia' had claimed responsibility for the attack, but in any case the registration information provided to establish the webpage proved to be fictitious. Hours later, traffic intended for the Al-Jazeera site was redirected again, this time presenting users with a webpage bearing the message 'taken over by Saimoon Bhuiyan.' Further attacks continued apace, one of which apparently succeeded in diverting users to a pornography site.

Meanwhile, as Al-Jazeera's technicians scrambled to reinstate the correct addresses for the sites, pressures of a different sort were brought to bear. As a result of the hacker attacks, DataPipe, a US-based hosting company, announced that it was terminating its services to the Qatar-based company that supported Al-Jazeera's sites. In the absence of a detailed explanation for the decision from DataPipe, some commentators speculated that it must have received complaints by other clients concerned that the hacking targeted at Al-Jazeera was harming their sites as well. Others argued that 'war sensitivities' were surely involved, once again pointing to the decision to air the controversial images of US soldiers and its alleged pro-Iraqi stance. Al-Jazeera's difficulties were further compounded when Akamai Technologies, brought in to help deal with the increased traffic to the sites and to provide protection against hacking attempts, abruptly cancelled its contract. Akamai, based in the US with clients such as ABC.com, MSNBC.com and Yahoo.com, refused to elaborate on the reasons behind its decision. 'It has nothing to do with technical issues,' Joanne Tucker, the managing editor of Al-Jazeera's English-language site, argued. 'It's non-stop political pressure on these companies not to deal with us' (cited in St John, 2003a; see also Granneman, 2003; Gray, 2003; Roberts, 2003). Commenting on the repeated hacking, she added: 'It's a narrow, pro-censorship attempt to silence a news site.'

Precisely who was behind the pro-war hacking attacks against Al-Jazeera has yet to become clear. Its communications manager, Jihad Ali Ballout, when asked for his opinion about where they originated, responded: 'I wish I knew. There are rumours that the attacks originated in the US but at this moment in time we cannot verify that. But it is worrying and an indication perhaps [that] in certain quarters there is a fear of freedom of expression and freedom of the press' (cited in Timms 2003). His colleague, Faisal Bodi (2003), a senior editor at aljazeera.net, was blunt in his reply: 'few here doubt the provenance of the attack is the Pentagon.' Meanwhile in the US, a representative of the Federal Bureau of Investigation (FBI) stated that the agency was investigating the hacking incidents. Technically such forms of hacking are a crime, but legal prosecutions are rare, leaving little room for optimism at Al-Jazeera. Indeed, some online commentators argued that the attacks on the sites represented the future of political protest, the virtual equivalent of burning books containing heretical viewpoints. By this logic, a site providing news or information which calls into question the legitimacy of a military campaign may be perceived, in turn, as constituting a threat to the war effort. Pro-war hacking thus becomes an insidious form of censorship. In this instance, however, it required a substantial technical and economic investment, one certainly well beyond the means of most individuals with an axe to grind.

Summing up the crisis engendered by the hacking attacks, Hafez Mirazi, the network's Washington bureau chief, commented: 'This is very typical of what Al-Jazeera has been through in the Arab world and in many authoritarian regimes. It's just sad that the US and US institutions didn't deal with us any differently than the Iraqi regime did' (cited in Carlson, 2003). Meanwhile, Al-Jazeera's sites have now stabilised to the point that they are now operationally sound. Those associated with the development of the English-language site are actively planning ways to enhance its provision, and seem remarkably upbeat about its prospects. 'We don't want this to be an Arab world site,' declared Joanne Tucker, the site's managing editor. 'At the same time, we're not a US site. It sounds idealistic and silly, but we want it to be a global citizen's home page' (cited in St John, 2003b).

Responsible Reporting?

'The Battle of Iraq,' an ebullient President George W. Bush declared to the world, 'is one victory in a war on terror that began on September the 11th, 2001, and still goes on.' Speaking before cheering officers and sailors aboard the aircraft carrier USS Abraham Lincoln, he stated: 'The liberation of Iraq is a crucial advance in the campaign against terror,' before adding that 'we will continue to hunt down the enemy before he can strike' (cited in the *Guardian* 1 May 2003).

This discursive alignment of the tragic events of September 11 with the war in Iraq was very much in keeping with official definitions of the crisis, definitions which sought to secure popular support for pre-emptive military action. Findings from a number of different polls carried out in the US in the weeks prior to the onset of 'Operation Iraqi Freedom' suggested that a large segment of the public remained seriously misinformed about the key issues at stake. Abi Berman, writing in *Editor and Publisher*, provided this overview of the polling results:

> In a Jan. 7 Knight Ridder/Princeton Research poll, 44 per cent of respondents said they thought 'most' or 'some' of the Sept. 11, 2001, hijackers were Iraqi citizens. Only 17 per cent of those polled offered the correct answer: none. [...] In the same sample, 41 per cent said that Iraq already possessed nuclear weapons, which not even the Bush administration claimed. Despite being far off base in crucial areas, 66 per cent of respondents claimed to have a 'good understanding' of the arguments for and against going to war with Iraq. [...] Then a Pew Research Center/Council on Foreign Relations survey released Feb. 20 found that nearly two-thirds of those polled believed that UN weapons inspectors had 'found proof that Iraq is trying to hide weapons of mass destruction.' Neither Hans Blix nor Mohamed ElBaradei ever said they

found proof of this. The same survey found that 57 per cent of those polled believed Saddam Hussein helped terrorists involved with the 9/11 attacks [...] A March 7-9 New York Times/CBS News Poll showed that 45 per cent of interviewees agreed that 'Saddam Hussein was personally involved in the Sept. 11 terrorist attacks,' and a March 14-15 CNN/*USA Today*/Gallup poll found this apparently mistaken notion holding firm at 51 per cent (Berman, 2003).

Several of these polls were conducted, as Berman acknowledges, after members of the Bush administration had abandoned explicit references to the assertion that Saddam Hussein had provided assistance to the terrorists involved in the September 11 attacks. Still, the alleged connection continued to form an implicit presupposition in a wide array of official pronouncements in addition to Bush's victory speech cited above. To the extent that it was reproduced as an unspoken, seemingly 'commonsensical' assumption in news reports, then, certain journalists became complicit – intentionally or not – in upholding a rationale for the conflict without an adequate basis in fact.

It is precisely this type of acquiescence on the part of some journalists where the dictates of official sources are concerned that throws into such sharp relief the limitations of much mainstream reporting. 'We are seeing this increased need for alternative news sources,' argued Catriona Stuart of the Independent Media Center (IMC) in New York, 'because many more people are feeling generally disillusioned with our government, our corporate leadership and the mainstream media which favors these interests.' Her colleague, Jeanne Strole, added: 'More and more Americans are waking up to the fact that the US corporate-mainstream media has been bought and paid for' (cited in Upadhyay, 2003). There can be little doubt, in my view, that there is a corresponding link between public distrust of mainstream media and the increased popularity of international news sites, although further investigation is required. Online journalism, at its best, brings to bear alternative perspectives, context and ideological diversity to its reporting, providing users with the means to hear voices from around the globe. News accounts that are overly reliant upon official truth-claims are likely to be revealed as such when compared and contrasted with reports from elsewhere available online, posing acute difficulties for those engaged in information management. 'After all,' as *Guardian* journalist Owen Gibson (2003) observes, 'when you can see opposing views at the click of a mouse, controlling the nation's perception of a conflict becomes a lot more difficult.'

References

Allan, S. (2002) 'Reweaving the Internet: Online News of September 11,' in B. Zelizer and S. Allan (eds) *Journalism After September 11*. London and New York: Routledge.

Allan, S. (2003) 'Mediating Citizenship: Online Journalism and the Public Sphere,' *Development*, 46 (1).

Berman, A. (2003) 'Polls Suggest Media Failure in Pre-War Coverage,' *Editor & Publisher*, 26 March.

Bodi, F. (2003) 'Al-Jazeera Tells the Truth About War,' *Guardian*, 28 March.

Carlson, P. (2003) 'In the Line of Fire,' *Washington Post*, 3 April.

Croad, E. (2003) 'US Public Turns to Europe for News,' Journalism.co.uk, 21 February.

Delio, M. (2003) 'US Tries Email to Charm Iraqis,' *Wired News*, 13 February.

Gibson, O. (2003) 'Spin Caught in a Web Trap,' *Guardian*, 17 February.

Granneman, S. (2003) 'Al-Jazeera, the First Amendment, and Security Professionals,' SecurityFocus.com, 22 April.

Gray, P. (2003) 'Al-Jazeera Suffers DoS Attack,' News.ZDNet.co.uk, 27 March.

Gubash, C. (2003) 'New Arab TV Channels Show Clout,' MSNBC.com, March 31.

Kafala, T. (2003) 'Al-Jazeera: News Channel in the News,' *BBC News Online*, 29 March.

Kahney, L. (2003) 'Media Watchdogs Caught Napping,' *Wired News*, 17 March.

Kirkpatrick, D.D. (2003) 'War is Test of High-Speed Web,' *New York Times*, 24 March.

Krugman, P. (2003) 'Behind the Great Divide,' *New York Times*, 18 February.

Mayes, I. (2001a) 'News Travels,' *Guardian*, September 22.

Mayes, I. (2001b) 'Worlds Apart,' *Guardian*, October 13.

Ostrom, M.A. (2003) 'Net Plays Big Role in War News, Commentary,' *Mercury News*, 28 February.

Outing, S. (2003) 'Stop the Presses!,' *Editor & Publisher*, 26 March.

Pew Internet & American Life Project (2003) 'The Internet and the Iraq war,' Project Report, 1 April.

Putnam, E. (2003) 'Foreign News Sites a Hit as War Looms,' *Wausau Daily Herald*, 9 February.

Richtel, M. (2003) 'Visits to Web Sites Surge as War Begins, and Most Are Up to Task,' *New York Times*, 23 March.

Roberts, P. (2003) 'Al-Jazeera Hobbled by DDOS Attack,' Infoworld.com, 26 March.

St John, W. (2003a) 'Akamai Cancels a Contract for Arabic Network's Site,' *New York Times*, 4 April.

St John, W. (2003b) 'The Texas Connection at Al Jazeera,' *New York Times*, 6 April.

Timms, D. (2003) 'News Websites See Traffic Soar,' *Guardian*, 20 March.

Upadhyay, A. (2003) 'US Media: Telling It Like It Isn't, *Asia Times*, 7 March.

Walker, L. (2003) 'Web Use Spikes On News of War,' *Washington Post*, 22 March.

Weaver, J. (2003) 'Iraq War a 'Milestone' for Web News,' MSNBC.com, 1 April.

Wells, M. (2001) 'How Smart was this Bomb?,' *Guardian*, 19 November.

Wendland, M. (2001) 'Overloaded Internet Fails Info-starved Americans,' Poynter.Org. 11 September.

Whitaker, B. (2003) 'Al-Jazeera Cause Outcry with Broadcast of Battle Causalities,' *Guardian*, 24 March.

Zelizer, B. and Allan, S. (eds) (2002) *Journalism After September 11*. London and New York: Routledge.

Contributors

STUART ALLAN is based at the School of Cultural and Media Studies, University of the West of England. His teaching and research focus on journalism, cultural theory, research methods and media history. He is currently researching online news as well as investigating media representations of science and risk. His books include *Media, Risk and Science* (2002), *Journalism After September 11* (2002), *Environmental Risks and the Media* (2000), and *News Culture* (1999).

NIGEL BAKER is the director of content for Associated Press Television News, the world's largest TV news agency by revenue and market share, according to the company's own marketing data. He has been the agency's senior editorial figure since 1995 – a year after it was originally launched by its parent company, the Associated Press, as APTV. He was recruited in 1994 to help set up APTV, having previously held senior editorial positions with the rival Reuters Television and with British TV news companies Independent Television News (ITN) and Sky News.

OLIVER BOYD-BARRETT is a professor at the Department of Communication, California State Polytechnic University in Pomona, California. He has published widely on issues relating to international communication, news agencies, and educational communication. His publications include *The International News Agencies* (Constable, 1980), *Le Trafic Des Nouvelles* (1981) *Contra-Flow in Global News* (1992), and *The Globalization of News* (1998). He is currently working on media coverage of the 'war on terrorism'.

MARK BRAYNE is the European News and Current Affairs Editor at BBC World Service where he is directing a new project to introduce training and support for journalists and their teams involved in reporting trauma which ranges from war and civil conflict to murder trials and rail crashes. During the Cold War, he was a foreign correspondent for Reuters and the BBC, with postings in Moscow, Berlin, Vienna and Beijing. In 1992 he trained as a transpersonal psychotherapist. He now runs a private psychotherapy practice and lectures and writes on issues of emotional literacy and journalism. He and his wife Sue run Dart Center Europe for Journalism & Trauma.

ANDREW CALCUTT teaches in Cultural and Innovation Studies at the University of East London. He is a journalist turned academic, and has written and researched cyber cultures, creative industries, youth and other aspects of contemporary popular culture. He is currently investigating the changing relationships between politics, business and culture.

JOHN JIRIK is a doctoral student in the Department of Radio-Television-Film at the University of Texas at Austin. Prior to arriving in Texas, Jirik worked as a consultant to the English news at China Central Television, Beijing, and as a television news producer and Bureau Chief for Reuters, based in Moscow, Hong Kong and Singapore. His research focuses on international news agencies and Chinese Media.

JAKE LYNCH is the co-director of Reporting the World, a London-based project that brings journalists together to debate issues of representation and responsibility in international news. He was the (London) Independent correspondent in Sydney in 1998-99 and spent the Kosovo crisis based at NATO headquarters in Brussels for the 24-hour channel, Sky News. He is the author of Conflict and Peace Forum papers, 'What Are Journalists For?' (1999) and 'Using Conflict Analysis in Reporting' (2000). He teaches an MA module in Peace-Building Media, Theory and Practice at the University of Sydney.

CHRIS PATERSON teaches in the Department of Media Studies at the University of San Francisco. He has written extensively on international journalism, news agencies and mass communication in Africa. He previously taught at the Centre for Mass Communication Research in Leicester, England, and has been a television journalist and video producer. His areas of interest include international journalism, television news and media in Africa.

GREG PHILO is professor in the Department of Sociology and Anthropology, University of Glasgow, and the research director of the Glasgow University Media Unit. He has researched media and cultural reception, media presentations of industrial disputes and trade unionism, the Falklands War and Northern Ireland. Current research includes research projects on political advertising, images of health and illness (including mental illness), migration and 'race' as well as risk and food scares. His recent books include *Seeing and Believing* (1990), *Media and Mental Distress* (1996), *Message Received* (1999), and *Market Killing* (2000).

TERHI RANTANEN is the director of the MSc Programme in Global Media and Communications at the London School of Economics and Political Science. Most of her research has been on news agencies, which provide case studies for the study of globalization and the introduction of new communications technologies, published in *The Globalization of News* (with Oliver Boyd-Barrett, 1998). Her latest book, *The Global and the National: Media and Communications in Post-Communist Russia*, was published in 2002.

NAOMI SAKR lectures on the political economy of communication and communication policy and development at the University of Westminster. She is the author of *Satellite Realms: Transnational Television, Globalization and the Middle East* (2003). She also writes on issues of media development and governance in the Middle East and North Africa for academic journals and various international organizations, including the London-based NGO Article XIX, and the Human Development Report Office of the United Nations Development Program.

DANNY SCHECHTER is a former network television producer and more recently an independent filmmaker and media expert and activist. He is the author of *Media Wars: News At A Time of Terror* (2002), *The More You Watch, The Less You Know* (1999) and *News Dissector: Passions, Pieces and Polemics* (2001). He is the executive editor of MediaChannel.org, the co-founder and executive producer of Globalvision, and the recipient of the Society of Professional Journalists' 2001 Award for Excellence in Documentary Journalism.

PRASUN SONWALKAR teaches at the School of Cultural Studies at the University of the West of England in Bristol. As a journalist he covered South Asia extensively over two decades, mainly for The Times of India; has been closely associated with programming for Doordarshan, and STAR TV, and was the news editor of Zee News channel. He has recently published in Media, Culture & Society, Gazette, Modern Asian Studies and Contemporary South Asia.

ANNABELLE SREBERNY is visiting Professor in Media and Film Studies at the School of Oriental and African Studies, London (SOAS), building up a programme that focuses on the Global South. She directed the Centre for Mass Communication Research at the University of Leicester between 1992-9. Most of her research lies at the intersection of globalisation, democratisation and gender, with an increasingly strong focus on the cultural geography of diaspora. Her books include *Small Media Big Revolution* (1985), *Globalization, Communication and Transnational Civil Society* (1996); *Media in a Global Context* (1997), and *Gender, Politics and Communication* (2000). She is currently writing a volume on global communication for Polity Press.

NICK STEVENSON is Professor in the School of Sociology at the University of Nottingham. His books include *The Transformation of the Media* (1999), *Globalization, Morality and Ethics* (1999), and *Making Sense of Men's Life Style Magazines* (2001). Currently he is working on a study of the celebrity David Bowie.

KEITH TESTER is Professor of Cultural Sociology at the University of Portsmouth. He has written widely on the sociology of moral life, and his books include *Moral Culture* (1997), *Compassion, Morality and the Media* (2001) and *Conversations with Zygmunt Bauman* (2001). He is currently writing a book for Palgrave on Zygmunt Bauman.

DAYA KISHAN THUSSU leads the MA in Transnational Communications and the Global Media at Goldsmiths College, University of London. He was a former editor of Gemini News Service, a London-based international news agency. His books include *Contra-Flow in Global News* (with Oliver Boyd-Barrett, 1992),

Electronic Empires (1998), and *International Communication – Continuity and Change* (2000).

CHRIS WESTCOTT was the head of New Media, BBC World Service, managing new media activities in forty-three languages. He has a PhD in chemistry from Oxford University and before joining the BBC he was a nuclear research scientist. In Spring 2003, he left the World Service to become the director of BBC Monitoring in Caversham Park.

H. DENIS WU teaches at the Manship School of Mass Communication, Louisiana State University. His main areas of research are political communication, mass communication theory and international communication. He has professional experience in magazine editing, survey research, and advertising in Taiwan. He has published in the Journal of Communication and Gazette.